Through
The Wheat

Through The Wheat

The U.S. Marines in World War I

Brig. Gen. Edwin H. Simmons, USMC (Ret.) and
Col. Joseph H. Alexander, USMC (Ret.)

NAVAL INSTITUTE PRESS
Annapolis, Maryland

Naval Institute Press
291 Wood Road
Annapolis, MD 21402

First Naval Institute Press paperback edition published in 2011.
ISBN 978-1-59114-831-9

The Library of Congress has catalogued the hardcover edition as follows:
Simmons, Edwin H., 1921–2007.
  Through the wheat : the U.S. Marines in World War I / Edwin H. Simmons
and Joseph H. Alexander.
    p. cm.
 Includes bibliographical references and index.
  ISBN 978-1-59114-791-6 (alk. paper)
  1. United States. Marine Corps–History—World War, 1914–1918. 2. World
War, 1914–1918—Regimental histories—United States. I. Alexander, Joseph
H., 1938– II. Title. III. Title: U.S. Marines in World War I. IV. Title: United
States Marines in World War I.
  D570.348.A1S56 2008
  940.4'5973—dc22

                                                    2008012911

*Cover: Tom Lovell's painting of Marines and German soldiers engaged in
hand-to-hand combat reflects the fury of the three-week battle for the square
mile of shattered trees and huge boulders that was the Belleau Wood hunting
preserve. (Marine Corps Art Collection)*

FOR FRANCES BLISS SIMMONS

Contents

Maps

Foreword

by Col. Allan R. Millett, USMCR (Ret.)

Marines buried Brig. Gen. Edwin Howard Simmons, U.S. Marine Corps (Ret.), at Arlington National Cemetery on July 25, 2007. He had died at home in Alexandria, Virginia, after a long illness.

Those of us who were there, from two former Commandants to the general's oldest grandson, agreed that Edwin Howard Simmons would have been pleased with the military pageantry. We all then had a chance to visit before the formation was dismissed. A considerable number of the mourners were General Simmons' intellectual heirs as historians of the U.S. Marine Corps. I am one of them, and I had plenty of good company, among them Col. Joseph Alexander, USMC (Ret.), the coauthor of this book. The general had not liked loose ends—"incomplete staff work," he would say. His history of the Marines in World War I fell into the category of unfinished business, and the general, health failing, persuaded Colonel Alexander to finish and edit the book he had in draft. This is it, and no one has a better literary headstone. Sound in research, richly written, the book is vintage Ed Simmons.

Throughout more than fifty-four years in his two Marine Corps careers as a combat leader in three wars and as the director of the History and Museums Division, Edwin Howard Simmons retained an abiding passion for the Marines of World War I. He knew many of the veterans of Belleau Wood, Soissons, Blanc Mont, and the Meuse-Argonne as World War II and Korean War senior officers and retirees. Clifton Cates, Lem Shepherd, Wilbert "Big Foot" Brown, Graves Erskine, Merwin Silverthorn, and Jerry Thomas were his friends and tutors, just as he was ours for World War II and Korea.

General Simmons' love of World War I stories predated his love of the Marine Corps. Born August 25, 1921, the general grew up in Billingsport, New Jersey, a small Delaware River town that had sent its young men off to war since the Revolution. By his own admission, he found the soldiers' tales of those years irresistible—no *Johnny Got His Gun*, no *Three Soldiers*, no *All Quiet on the Western Front* for him. He advanced through the wheat field west of Belleau Wood with John W. Thomason Jr. and learned about the price of glory from Laurence Stallings. "Do you want to live forever?" Edwin Howard Simmons knew that GySgt. Dan Daly spoke a truth all Marines faced, and he knew death was far better than a life without meaning. Being a Marine solved that problem.

General Simmons learned about combat and irony in the World War II Fleet Marine Force. The war took him to Guam and Okinawa and combat. The irony found him before battle. A Lehigh University graduate (1942) in journalism, he had been assigned to an engineer unit because someone thought Lehigh produced only engineers. In that capacity he served dutifully and with valor, but as soon as possible he sought reassignment as an infantry officer.

The Korean War confirmed his place in the postwar Marine Corps as an officer of exceptional ability. As the weapons company commander, operations officer, and executive officer of the 3d Battalion, 1st Marines, Maj. Ed Simmons served with distinction in the Inchon-Seoul campaign, the defense of Hagaru-ri, and the Walkout from the Changjin (Chosin) Reservoir. One of the last majors rotated home after the 1950 campaign, the general saw more combat in the 1st Marine Division's battles in February–April 1951, when the U.S. Eighth Army blunted the Fourth and Fifth Offensives of the Chinese People's Volunteers Force. For directing his battalion's defense against a nighttime North Korean tank-infantry attack in Seoul in September 1950, Major Simmons received a Silver Star for gallantry. Unlike most recipients, the general could explain how the army chief of staff, Gen. Douglas MacArthur, had invented the Silver Star in 1932 to transform the silver stars on the World War I campaign medal (the equivalent of the British "mentioned in dispatches") into a distinctive combat award. MacArthur also resurrected a Revolutionary War honor—the Purple Heart—to replace the "wound stripes" on one's uniform coat sleeve. General Simmons earned a Purple Heart in Korea but made light of his wounds. For the rest of his life he wrote about the Korean War with verve and authority. He appeared as a "talking head" on almost every documentary film made about the war and did the same for the Vietnam War. In one sense, he became the John Thomason (especially when paired with Marine artist Charles Waterhouse) of the Korean War.

Admittedly battle worn, Major Simmons welcomed an assignment as the Marine Officer Instructor in the Naval Reserve Officer Training Corps unit of The Ohio State University. During his Columbus years, 1952–55, Edwin Simmons earned a master's degree in journalism, which he prized. His taste in professors ran to eccentric storytellers like Walt Siefert, not technologists and communications theorists who had trouble with real words. Thereafter the general's varied skills and professional reputation brought him a series of demanding, rewarding assignments, the most notable of those as an infantry regimental commander,

Force G-3, and assistant division commander, 1st Marine Division, in two Vietnam tours. Vietnam was not his favorite war, and he deplored its corrosive effect on Marines' morale and operational standards. Returning to Washington after his second Vietnam tour (1970–71), Brigadier General Simmons was rewarded with a billet that would match his combat experience and leadership skills with his love of history. A staff reorganization at Headquarters Marine Corps created an independent History and Museums Division, with the promise of offices and a museum at the Washington Navy Yard. The director would have access to the Commandant and would have sufficient funding to build a professional staff that would rival the historical divisions of the other armed forces. Edwin Simmons wanted the job and got it as a retired brigadier general, recalled to active duty. In retrospect, it is unthinkable that anyone else would become director.

The Ohio State University connection brought General Simmons and me together in 1971, while he was still on active duty and I the commanding officer of Company L, 3d Battalion, 25th Marines. He had come to Columbus at the invitation of the late Maj. Gen. Walter Churchill, USMCR, a businessman-philanthropist from Toledo who had sponsored a statewide youth athletic event. My Marines had been "volunteered" to administer the event, which meant we lost an entire weekend of training, and I was not happy. I soon learned that General Simmons had a keen sense of humor and a courtly manner that fit his regal handsomeness. A prude he was not, an officer and gentleman he certainly was, and we got along from the start. Perhaps the general saw something of himself in me, at least a love of military history.

From that chance encounter thirty-six years ago, my life as a Marine Reserve officer and academic military historian intersected often with the Simmons Era (will there ever be another?) of Marine Corps history, 1971–96. For several years in the 1970s I did research for my book *Semper Fidelis: The History of the United States Marine Corps* (The Free Press, 1981) in his proximity at the new Historical Center at the Washington Navy Yard, "the House that Edwin Simmons Built."

General Simmons and I had already worked together outside the Marine Corps to change the American Military Institute, a moribund, Washington-centered Olde Boys Club of armed forces official historians. The general created the Society of Military History, now a respected professional society that brought together public, academic, uniformed, and independent historians—and, yes, even journalists. The birth of the SMH involved many midwives: Dick Kohn, Tim Nenninger, Robin Higham, Frank Cooling, Reg Schrader, and me. There was, however, only one father, Edwin Simmons. At that same time the general also created the Marine Corps Historical Foundation (now the Marine Corps Heritage Foundation) to raise money to support H&MD projects like research scholarships, internships, awards, museum acquisitions, and conferences that could not be paid for with appropriated funds. He played leadership roles in the Company of Military Historians, the Council on America's Military Past, and the Washington Military History Roundtable.

Marine Corps history for Marines remained General Simmons' mission as he defined it, but he recognized that the American public and other services need constant education on Marine Corps operations. The parallel interventions and crises in Lebanon and Grenada, 1982–83, revealed the weakness of H&MD's field capability and the Fleet Marine Force's lack of interest in filling its contingency billets for historians in crisis deployments. The division had a reserve component, Mobilization Training Unit DC-4, but its talented historians, artists, photographers, and museum specialists were not deployable for reasons of age, civilian occupation, lack of FMF experience, and specialization. General Simmons persuaded me to take over MTU DC-4 and begin its transition to a field history unit. We recruited new, field-capable members, preferably veteran line officers, and even managed to get special commissions for two former Marines. Our best recruit was Maj. Ronald R. Spector, USMCR, already a distinguished academic historian, who had served in the field in Vietnam as a Marine sergeant and Yale PhD. Our fighting historians made their bones in the Gulf War and thereafter.

Through all those years and shared interests, General Simmons and I remained fascinated by the birth of the modern Marine Corps in World War I. I too fixed bayonets with Thomason, read Stallings, and enjoyed the lesser-known works of Boyd, *Through the Wheat*, and March, *Company K*. I learned more about the Marines in France while writing *Semper Fidelis*, and, later, *In Many a Strife: General Gerald C. Thomas and the U.S. Marine Corps* (Naval Institute Press, 1993), a book the general cajoled me into writing. That book is my memorial to his good judgment.

In the 1980s I walked the legendary battlefields of Belleau Wood, Soissons, and the Meuse-Argonne, which feature so prominently in this book. I felt ghosts, so I'm sure the general did too during his tour of the same hallowed grounds. I actually was more shocked on the field of Soissons, terrain so barren of cover in the Age of the Howitzer and Machine Gun that it makes Pickett's Charge look reasonable by comparison. Yet I never rivaled the general's absorption in that war. He even had a German Maschinengewehr 08/15 outside his office, a forbidding Maxim machine gun perhaps meant to remind Marine visitors of his abiding interest in their common World War I heritage.

A book on the Marines in World War I always had an honored place among General Simmons' writing projects. For all his official duties (including chair, Marine Corps Uniform Board) and leadership of professional and veterans associations, the general wrote and wrote more. He appreciated his predecessors as historians of the Marine Corps—McClellan, Metcalf, and Heinl—but he liked his own *The United States Marine Corps, 1775–1975* (first edition, Viking Press, 1975) best. So do many others, since it has been continuously in print longer than any other Marine Corps history, having gone through four editions and three different publishers. It is now a Naval Institute Press book and a standard part of the Commandant's "Reading List." Bob Moskin, one of the general's best friends and author of *The U.S. Marine Corps Story* (McGraw-Hill, 1977, and the 3d revised edition, Little, Brown, 1992), and I offer alternative histories, but the general still holds the field for conciseness, insight, and style.

In 1998 General Simmons teamed with Bob Moskin as coeditors and lead essayists to produce their definitive, beautifully illustrated tribute to the Corps, *The Marines* (Hugh Lauter Levin Associates). Edwin Simmons also wrote two short histories of the Marines in Vietnam and several extensive essays, including a biography of Gen. Robert H. Barrow, for *Commandants of the Marine Corps* (Naval Institute Press, 2004), for which Millett and Jack Shulimson were essayists and coeditors. When the Marine Corps launched a series of book-pamphlets to commemorate the fiftieth anniversary of the Korean War, General Simmons wrote the official histories of the Inchon landing and Changjin Reservoir campaign. To assign these books to someone else would have been unthinkable.

The general knew the limitations of history as truth, so he turned to fiction, in *Dog Company Six* (Naval Institute Press, 2000), to honor the real Marines he knew on the March Out, November–December 1950. These Marines actually swore and discussed sex; the company commander was a reservist from Columbus, Ohio, with an Ohio State degree. I suspect George Bayard (of Dog Company Six) was a composite of the 3d Battalion, 1st Marines, company commanders: Joseph R. "Bull" Fisher, Carl L. Sitter, and Clarence E. "Skipper" Corley, all highly decorated regular officers of long and distinguished careers. Captain Bayard is more like the reserve captain played by Richard Carlson in the movie *Retreat Hell!*

As the general's health started to fail around the fiftieth anniversary of the Korean War, he worried about whether he would ever finish his World War I book. He had written parts of it over almost twenty years, but more urgent projects had always intruded. I was part of the problem, sending him draft chapters and articles as I became more mired in my own research on the Korean War. In his last letter to me (April 2006) before his death, General Simmons apologized that he had not yet read a draft chapter on the Inchon-Seoul campaign. His energy and attentiveness were rapidly waning, as all of us had observed with sorrow. Many of his closest friends—Bob Sherrod, Jim Lawrence, Brooke Nihart, Bud Shaw, and Ben Frank —were already dead or dying. His wife Frances, four children, five grandchildren, and various small dogs provided company and immediate affection, but his frustration with his incapacity showed. With all these struggles, he still looked ahead, past his own death. "I am not able in my present state to do any significant writing." He had, however, already persuaded Joe Alexander to finish the World War I book. The general had made one more inspired decision.

Over the past twenty years Joseph H. Alexander, a two-tour Vietnam veteran and career assault amphibian officer who had commanded a company in combat and a battalion poised for combat, has emerged as one of the most prolific and stylish writers of Marine Corps history. Joe served the Marine Corps for twenty-nine years, eleven in the Fleet Marine Force. Born in North Carolina, Joe graduated in 1960 from the University of North Carolina at Chapel Hill, where he majored in history and Naval ROTC (scholarship, Marine option). He earned two MA degrees (history and international relations) from civilian universities and became a distinguished graduate of the Naval War College. His ability to think straight and write fast took him to assignments of high responsibility: military secretary for Commandant P. X. Kelley, chief of staff of the 3d Marine Division, and director, Marine Corps Development Center. As a field-grade officer, Joe showed a rare talent for writing journal articles on Marine Corps history and contemporary defense issues. General Simmons encouraged Joe's mastery of the article form and study of military history. Given his demanding duties, Joe did not take on book projects until his retirement in 1988.

Colonel Alexander hit the literary beach running, and the books came in waves, including a half-dozen commemorative histories on the fiftieth anniversaries of Marine battles in World War II and Korea, beginning with *Across the Reef: The Marine Assault of Tarawa* (History and Museums Division, 1993) and extending through *Battle of the Barricades: U.S. Marines in the Recapture of Seoul* (History and Museums Division, 2000). His books include *Sea Soldiers in the Cold War* (Naval Institute Press, 1994) in collaboration with Lt. Col. Merrill L. Bartlett, USMC (Ret.); *Utmost Savagery* (Naval Institute Press, 1995), the definitive book on Tarawa, extending his earlier research; *Storm Landings: Epic Amphibious Battles in the Central Pacific* (Naval Institute Press, 1997); and, with Don Horan and Norman Stahl, *A Fellowship of Valor: The Battle History of the U.S. Marines* (HarperCollins, 1997) and *Edson's Raiders: The 1st Marine Raider Battalion in World War II* (Naval Institute Press, 2000). He has contributed to many edited works, including chapters in Simmons and Moskin, *The Marines,* and *Commandants of the Marine Corps.* He wrote the script (with Norman Stahl) for *A Fellowship of Valor,* a TV miniseries produced by Lou Reda. The same team produced *Fire and Ice,* a four-hour history of the Korean War that earned an Emmy nomination in 1999. Colonel Alexander applied all his skills as the principal historical writer for the exhibits at the National Museum of the Marine Corps, Quantico, Virginia.

I am delighted that Joe's writing and editing have preserved the tone and focus General Simmons sought for this book. Always a realist, the general knew that Joe Alexander wrote prose that sounded most like his own. The general wanted his history populated with real, individual Marines, facing fear with skill, honor, and a deep sense of comradeship. Joe Alexander has been true to his trust.

As long as there is a Marine Corps, Brig. Gen. Edwin Howard Simmons will be part of that future through his books and those that many of us, his protégés and legatees, wrote on the Marine Corps he helped us know. We are better Marines or historians for his leadership and counseling. So fix bayonets! Come join Edwin Howard Simmons at the assault position for his reunion with of those "Devil Dogs" of 1918. This book is his fitting memorial.

Col. Allan R. Millett, U.S. Marine Corps Reserve (Ret.);
Gen. Raymond E. Mason Jr., Professor Emeritus, The Ohio State University;
Stephen Ambrose, Professor of History and Director, Eisenhower Center for
American Studies, University of New Orleans
November 2007

Preface and Acknowledgments

Six days after the spectacular Inchon landing in the first season of the Korean War, the 1st Marine Division battled toward Seoul with two regiments abreast, the 5th Marines north of the Han River, the 1st Marines along the south bank.

Col. Lewis B. "Chesty" Puller's 1st Marines' headed for the industrial city of Yongdung-po, directly across the Han from the capital. One of Puller's field-grade officers was twenty-nine-year-old Maj. Edwin H. Simmons, commanding Weapons Company, 3d Battalion, 1st Marines.

The Kalchon Canal marked the western outskirts of Yongdung-po and served as the defensive line for elements of the North Korean People's Army. The defenders massed several Maxim heavy machine guns, similar to those used by the Germans in World War I, to protect the likeliest crossing point, a water gate near the center of the Kalchon. The Maxims took a toll of advancing Marines.

Major Simmons' battalion commander ordered him to suppress the fire. Simmons, a combat veteran of World War II, had few options. His 81-mm mortars lacked ammunition, and the steep banks of the Kalchon ruled out use of his direct-fire 106-mm recoilless rifles. With no hesitation and a slightly ironic grin, Simmons deployed his Browning M1917A1 water-cooled .30-caliber heavy machine guns. Years earlier, well before he became a Marine officer, Simmons had learned how the Germans and later the U.S. Marines' 6th Machine Gun Battalion had massed their heavy automatic weapons in World War I battles to smother enemy defenses and deliver midrange overhead fire for the advancing infantry. He positioned his gun crews near the crest of the west bank "with their barrels just clearing the top of the dike." A fierce duel ensued—"heavies against heavies"—at a range of fifty yards. Simmons' well-trained gunners prevailed, clearing the far bank and allowing the rifle companies to cross into the burning city.

The violent firefight produced an unexpected dividend. Several hundred yards north of the water gate, Simmons noticed a rifle company (commanded by the future twenty-seventh Commandant, Capt. Robert H. Barrow) approach a separate crossing left undefended by the distracted enemy. Barrow's subsequent penetration would cause the North Koreans to abandon Yongdung-po and retreat into Seoul. "They were beautifully deployed," Simmons recalled. "As they came through the dry rice paddy I thought of the Marines coming through the wheat fields at Belleau Wood in 1918."

These two vignettes from a firefight that occurred half a world away and thirty-two years after the battle of Belleau Wood reflect Ed Simmons' lifelong interest in the Marines' experiences in World War I, an interest that yielded both tactical and literary applications for the three-war veteran who would become the director emeritus of Marine Corps History.

In a 2005 interview with Richard Latture for *Naval History* magazine, Simmons talked about growing up during the 1920s and 1930s in Billingsport, New Jersey, site of a Revolutionary fort on the Delaware River, just south of Philadelphia. The social center of this small town, he said, was the American Legion Post, of which his father was a member. "As a very small boy Eddie Simmons was a fly on the wall, listening to the stories these veterans, now in early middle age, had to tell. There were magical names such as Chateau-Thierry, Soissons, St. Mihiel, and Meuse-Argonne. A few of the members seemed to receive special respect when they spoke of fighting in a place called Belleau Wood."

During his college years at Lehigh (1938–42) General Simmons befriended the housekeeper of his fraternity, a former German infantry NCO (noncommissioned officer) who had served in the 3d Guards Division on both the eastern and western fronts. Among many insights into German infantry tactics in World War I, the veteran described the employment of heavy machine guns, a lesson Simmons well remembered.

Decades later General Simmons would walk the hallowed ground of Belleau Wood and the other Marine battlefields in northern France with his son, Clarke, a memorable experience for both men.

Inspired and informed by his contact with so many surviving veterans of that war, General Simmons began writing his ultimate book of American military history, a narrative account of the Marines in World War I. Over the years he broadened the scope to include not just the heralded 4th Marine Brigade but also those men performing rear-echelon logistics duty in French ports; the pioneering Marine aviation units flying combat missions in France and the Azores; and the thousands of other Leathernecks who served on board warships of the fleet around the world, fought insurgents in the islands of the Caribbean, or trained other Marines for combat at the newly acquired bases at Paris (as it was then known) Island and Quantico.

After fifteen years of stop-and-go work on the project, General Simmons realized that his health was making its completion problematical. In early 2004 he invited me to his home in Alexandria, Virginia. Sitting in his beautiful garden, on grounds formerly part of George Washington's estate at Mount Vernon, he asked for my assistance in completing the book. I was deeply honored, and I have done my best, but readers should know that Edwin Howard Simmons was the architect and master builder of this project; I was an apprentice carpenter pecking away with a light hammer and finishing nails.

On General Simmons' behalf, I would like to acknowledge those whose assistance contributed significantly to the publication of this work.

Charles G. Grow, assistant director of the National Museum of the Marine Corps and a former Marine combat artist, crafted the ten battlefield maps. Steve Hill of the Historical Division, Marine Corps University, provided the four "vicinity maps."

Superb assistance by other members of the Historical Division included that of former director Col. Dick Camp, USMC (Ret.); chief historian Charles D. Melson; reference historians Dan Crawford, Robert Aquilina, and Annette D. Amerman; historian Charles R. Smith; photo archivist Lena Kaljot; and former head librarian Evelyn Englander. J. Michael Miller, director of the Marine Corps Archives at Quantico, and his assistant, Dr. James Ginter, were repeatedly helpful. At the National Museum, Joan Thomas, combat art curator, and Beth Crumley, researcher and assistant ordnance curator, provided helpful and timely support.

Other associates who provided assistance included combat artist Col. Donna Neary, USMCR (Ret.); Col. Gary Solis, USMC (Ret.); Col. W. Hays Parks, USMC (Ret.); Mr. Robert K. Krick; Lt. Col. Merrill L. Bartlett, USMC (Ret.); Col. Jon T. Hoffman, USMCR (Ret.); Mr. Henry E. Colton, nephew of the late Lt. Johnny Overton, USMC, killed at Soissons; Col. Walter Ford, USMC (Ret.), editor of *Leatherneck* magazine; Col. Charles Westcott, USMC (Ret.); and Maj. Rick Spooner, USMC (Ret.), World War II veteran and longtime owner of the Globe and Laurel Restaurant, Triangle, Virginia, within whose decorative walls the battles of World War I were taught and refought by several generations of Marines.

At the Naval Institute Press, I render appreciative salutes to press director Rick Russell, acquisitions editor Lt. Cdr. Thomas Cutler, USN (Ret.), assistant editor Elizabeth Bauman, publicist Judy Heise, editorial manager Susan Corrado, production editor Marla Traweek, and copy editor Pelham G. Boyer. Elsewhere within the Naval Institute, special thanks to Richard G. Latture, editor in chief of *Naval History* magazine; Fred Schultz, senior editor of *Proceedings*; and senior designer Jen Mabe.

Gen. Carl E. Mundy Jr., USMC (Ret.), the thirtieth Commandant of the Marine Corps, provided steady encouragement to both General Simmons and myself throughout the book's completion. In his eulogy for General Simmons at the funeral service in the Fort Myers Chapel, General Mundy described him as "a warrior historian," recalling that "Ed liked to say that in early life, he wanted to be either a soldier, a teacher, or a historian—and the Marine Corps enabled him to be all three."

General Simmons had many other close colleagues with whom he often discussed his work in progress. They were legion, but among them were fellow historians Mr. J. Robert Moskin, Dr. Timothy K. Nenninger, Dr. Edward M. Coffman, and several close associates who preceded him in death, including Col. F. Brooke Nihart, USMC (Ret.), Mr. Benis M. Frank, and Brig. Gen. James Lawrence, USMC (Ret.).

Finally, I especially appreciated the support and patience of General Simmons' family: his widow Frances, daughters Bliss Simmons Robinson and Courtney Simmons Elwood, and sons Clarke and Edwin Jr. Clarke Simmons, the family's main point of contact for the book project, was particularly helpful.

Semper Fidelis

Joseph H. Alexander
Asheville, North Carolina
January 2008

Prologue

Eight thousand U.S. Marines of the 2d Division crouched in a ragged line of hastily dug rifle pits north of the Paris–Metz highway, enduring increasingly accurate German artillery fire and keenly aware that—on this day and in this place—their division represented the last organized barrier between the advancing enemy and the French capital, less than sixty-five kilometers away.[1]

The Marines found their role in this highly dynamic situation ironic. The troops of the yet untested American Expeditionary Forces (AEF) had spent nearly a year being trained in static trench warfare by French and British veterans of the defensive systems that had gridlocked the western front since 1914. Then, unexpectedly, in March 1918, German general Erich Ludendorff breached the Allied trench defenses in a series of brilliant offensives, ending the long tactical stalemate and threatening the Allies with wholesale defeat. Once again the Hun was on the loose in France. And once again dispirited French troops and frantic refugees clogged the roads leading west toward Paris. The Marines and soldiers of the AEF until recently had expected their first major battles to be fought between the trenches. Now they were hurrying blindly eastward, toward the sound of German guns, through a nightmarish montage of disorganized stragglers, rampant rumors, and conflicting orders.

It was Monday, June 3, 1918, and a very hot day in northern France. The day before Capt. John Blanchfield, commanding the 55th Company, had taken over his share of the line to be held by the 2d Battalion, 5th Marines. He anchored his left flank on Les Mares Farm. His right flank met the road that led north from the village of Champillon to Bussiares. On his right he tied in with Capt. Lloyd Williams' 51st Company, but on the left there was a gap of about 450 meters before the 43d Company, 2d Battalion, picked up the line at the edge of Bois de Veuilly, one of the small forests dotting the rural countryside.

Lt. Col. Frederic "Fritz" Wise had formed the 2d Battalion, 5th Marines, in the Philadelphia Navy Yard shortly after war was declared in April 1917. It had

ne in the first troop convoy to head for France. It had cooled its heels
a year in training and jobs behind the lines, a year in which the 5th and
ents were combined to form the 4th Brigade of Marines for service with
the 2d U.S. Division. In March 1918 the division, a composite of Marines and army
regulars, began advanced training and moderate combat in the old trenches near
the 1916 battlefield of Verdun. Now the division had been hurried west toward
Chateau-Thierry to stop the Germans who had broken through the French and
English at Chemin des Dames and were now headed for Paris. On this date Gen.
John J. Pershing, commanding the AEF, telegraphed an urgent, confidential message to the army chief of staff, Gen. Peyton C. March: "Consider the military situation very grave."

French farms, strong points with their stone walls and structures dating back
to the Middle Ages, had been fought over many times in the past. Such was Les
Mares, with its walls already loopholed perhaps in the Franco-Prussian War. The
Hun had come this way before. In the helter-skelter movement of the 2d Division
to find and blunt the German advance, the infantry had arrived well ahead of its
supporting heavy machine-gun elements. In his exposed forward position, Captain
Blanchfield cursed the absence of the sturdy, 70-pound Hotchkiss weapons and
paid careful attention to positioning his few Chauchat automatic rifles to cover the
likeliest enemy avenues of approach. There were no trenches. His Marines scraped
shallow depressions that they were beginning to call "foxholes" in the chalky soil.

Wheat fields of knee- to hip-high ripening grain, dotted with blood-red poppies, stretched to the front and to the left of the farmhouse. An exhausted French
poilu falling back through Blanchfield's position told him that the *Boche* were just
to the front of him on the reverse slope of Hill 165.

During the night the Germans had given them a dusting of shell fire. When
morning came, Blanchfield sent forward his second in command, 1st Lt. Lemuel C.
Shepherd, with about fourteen Marines. Shepherd took with him his little French
dog, Kiki. He was to outpost a knoll in the wheat field about 275 meters in front
of the line. From there Shepherd could see the church spires in the village with
the beguiling name of Lucy-le-Bocage. Beyond Lucy was brooding Belleau Wood,
which the Marines would come to know well.

Lem Shepherd, a twenty-two-year-old Virginian from a strongly Confederate
family in Norfolk, had been on active duty since his commissioning in May 1917
after graduation from the Virginia Military Institute. By the standards of the day,
his year's service qualified him as an "old-timer."

Blanchfield had ordered Shepherd to hold his position as long as he could and
then to fall back. The shelling increased. The Germans had set up a base of fire with
machine guns in the edge of the woods that faced the outpost. At about 5 PM the
German barrage thickened and the Germans came forward, scouts out in front,

followed by tactical units moving swiftly, purposefully, in a very open formation. Shepherd's handful of Marines had never seen a German assault in daylight, and for a split second they paused to appraise the formations. Then, estimating the closing range, they adjusted the folding-leaf rear sights on their Springfield 1903 rifles ("Our sights were set for three hundred yards," said Shepherd) and began tumbling German soldiers into the wheat. German machine guns raked the outpost. As Shepherd leaned against a lone tree directing the fire of his men, a machine-gun bullet tore at the collar of his tunic, cutting into his throat frightfully close to his jugular vein. In a 1980s interview Shepherd said, "My first thought was, 'My God, a bullet's gone through my gullet!' I was gulping air—funny what you do—I spit in my hand to see if I was spitting blood but I wasn't, so I felt relieved. A bullet . . . just missed my jugular vein. Another quarter of an inch and I'd be dead." Shaken but stubborn, he stayed in the fight.

Almost simultaneously the Germans engaged the rest of Blanchfield's line, building up a strong attack against the farmhouse. Blanchfield's Marines peppered the oncoming enemy ranks in the wheat fields with Chauchat automatic weapons and well-aimed rifle fire from their Springfields—a weapon the Marines had come to love with an affection befitting a corps of aspiring sharpshooters. A nearly contemporary account said, "The Marines had no machine guns to aid them, but their rifle fire was exceptionally fine, each man aiming coolly and deliberately, and not a German got closer than a hundred yards of the line." After two waves had been consumed by rifle fire, the third wave of Germans fell back and began to work around the left flank of the 55th Company, trying to come into the rear of the farmhouse. Blanchfield moved a section from his right-flank platoon over to the left to strengthen his dangling flank.

To Blanchfield's right and left, the 43d and 51st companies of Wise's 2d Battalion opened up with long-range rifle fire. Salvos of 75-mm shells fired by the army's supporting 12th Field Artillery came crashing down in the wheat. The Germans wavered, halted, and then resolutely came on again, three more times, but they could not break through the wall of fire. The fight for Les Mares Farm lasted just an hour. It was as close to Paris as the Germans would get.

CHAPTER ONE

"The War to End All Wars"

S eventeen months before the Marines' first engagement with German troops at Les Mares Farm, the American people first sensed that the United States was being drawn inexorably into the European bloodbath.[1]

On a wintry night late in January 1917, a telephone call interrupted a small dinner party at 2008 R Street, NW, the Washington home of Brig. Gen. John A. Lejeune, USMC. The guest of honor, Secretary of the Navy Josephus Daniels Sr., was called to the phone. He returned to the dinner table deep in thought and repeated the gist of the message: The German ambassador, the very elegant and correct Count Johann von Bernsdorff, had delivered a note to the State Department advising that on February 1 Germany was going to resume unrestricted submarine warfare in the war zone. The gentlemen left the ladies to go to the upstairs sitting room to smoke and talk. Daniels blew clouds of judicious smoke from his after-dinner cigar and pontificated that a nation at times in its life must choose between war and the loss of self-respect. Rolling his cigar between his fingers, he mused, "This is one of those situations. I prefer war to national dishonor."

Daniels' host that evening, John Lejeune, the assistant to the commandant of the Marine Corps, was his favorite Marine general. Lejeune had come to the job at the beginning of 1915, serving first as a colonel, but now, in 1917, he wore the new stars of a brigadier general on his shoulder straps. Daniels thought far more of Lejeune than he did of George Barnett, the Marine Corps' Major General Commandant.

The Road to War

Woodrow Wilson had been reelected president in November 1916, largely on the slogan, "He Kept Us Out of War." On January 22, 1917, he went before the Congress with his "Peace Without Victory" speech. "Only a tranquil Europe can be a stable Europe," he said. "There must be, not a balance of power, but a community of power; not organized rivalries but an organized, common peace. . . . [I]t must be a peace without victory."

Germany's resumption of unrestricted submarine warfare came scarcely a week later, a virtual slap in the face to the president and a jolt to the nation. On February 3 the State Department returned Ambassador Bernsdorff's passport, signifying the break in diplomatic relations with Germany.

The British, playing their own wily game, had known for two weeks that the Germans were going to renew unrestricted U-boat operations in the waters around Britain and France. British naval intelligence had made an unusual wireless intercept on January 17. Cryptographers in Whitehall discerned that it was written in a German diplomatic code. A numeral group yielded a signature well known to them: Arthur Zimmermann, the German foreign secretary. Other words gradually emerged: "Most Secret," "Mexico," "Japan." The message was addressed to Bernsdorff in Washington.

The first part of the message informed him that unrestricted submarine warfare would be resumed on February 1. The second part of the message was to be delivered "by a safe route" to the German minister in Mexico, Heinrich von Eckhardt by name. The message expressed the hope that despite the resumption of unrestricted submarine warfare, the United States would remain neutral. If not, Von Eckhardt was to offer the Mexican government a proposal: "Make war together, make peace together, generous financial support, and an understanding on our part that Mexico is to reconquer the lost territory in Texas, New Mexico, and Arizona."[2]

For reasons of their own the British kept this amazing information to themselves. Not until February 23 did they give a copy of the deciphered "Zimmermann Telegram" to the American ambassador in London. Three days later, Wilson appeared before a joint session of Congress to ask for arms to protect American ships and people "in their legitimate and peaceful pursuits on the seas." Even as Wilson spoke, news tickers brought in word that the Cunard liner *Laconia* had been torpedoed without warning, with the loss of two American lives.

By March 1 the story of the Zimmermann Telegram was in the newspapers. Mexican president Venustiano Carranza stubbornly refused American demands that the German overtures be repudiated. Pershing's punitive expedition into northern Mexico had just recently been withdrawn. Hard feelings persisted on both sides of the border.

Barnett and Lejeune and the handful of Marine·officers at their minuscule headquarters in the Walker Johnson Building at 1734 New York Avenue in northwest Washington wondered if another expedition into Mexico, perhaps a landing such as that at Veracruz in 1914, was in the offing. Such war planning as was done was performed by Lejeune and Barnett's three aides, all captains: Thomas

Holcomb, Earl H. "Pete" Ellis, and Ralph S. Keyser—names to remember. In addition to Lejeune and his three aides, General Barnett had an adjutant and inspector (Charles H. Lauchheimer), a paymaster general (George C. Richards), and a quartermaster general (Charles L. McCawley). Each of the three senior staff specialists had recently been promoted to brigadier general in the same 1916 legislation that had benefited John Lejeune. The clerical load at headquarters fell on twenty or so enlisted Marines.

Wilson's second inauguration, bristling with security, was held on Monday, March 5. The day was cold, clear, and windy. The president's address, delivered from the steps of the Capitol, had a grim tone. The sparse crowd was unresponsive. Wilson's campaign promises of keeping America out of the war and negotiating peace in Europe now seemed naïve. Within a few days German U-boats sank eight American ships.

American merchant ships, hurriedly armed with deck guns and navy crews, proved no match for U-boats. Sinkings of American shipping continued. Wilson called a cabinet meeting on March 20. The cabinet agreed that there was no course except to declare war.

America Declares War

A light rain fell as President Woodrow Wilson, escorted by a squadron of cavalry from Fort Myer, went from the White House up Pennsylvania Avenue to the Capitol on the morning of April 2, 1917. Wilson had called the Congress into special joint session to ask for a declaration of war against Germany. Both sides of the chamber stood up and applauded. Some cheered. Wilson's tone was matter of fact and somewhat dry as he reviewed the submarine crisis, saying that an intercepted note to the German minister in Mexico was eloquent evidence that Germany meant to stir up enemies against the United States at its very doors. A declaration of war, said Wilson, would involve an immediate addition to the armed forces of at least a half-million men as already provided for in the law. Wilson's voice became more vibrant when he reached the words, "The world must be made safe for democracy."

The debate in the Senate lasted a day and resulted in a vote of eighty-two for, six against, and one abstention. In the House there was more opposition, with two full days of debate, but at 3 AM on April 6 the resolution was passed, 373 to 50, and was sent to the White House for signature. Daniels, the navy secretary, began preparing the navy and Marines for all-out war.

The Navy Department at War

To this point the navy secretary and his assistant had executed most of the operational and major administrative decisions for both the navy and the Marines, a process exemplified by Secretary Gideon Welles and his assistant Gustavus Fox in the Lincoln administration during the Civil War. Civilian dominance of the uniformed sea services was not quite as absolute in 1917. Congress had established the position of Chief of Naval Operations in 1915, and the Marines had a legislative provision dating from the 1830s that authorized the president to detach them to the secretary of war for extended operations with the army if necessary—a process soon to be executed. Nor did General Barnett shrink from presenting the case for his Corps directly to members of Congress. Yet in the spring of 1917, Secretary Daniels, secure in his post as a member of Wilson's cabinet, and his "virile-minded, hard-fisted" (as described by the *Chicago Post*) assistant, Franklin Delano Roosevelt, issued most of the marching orders to the Corps.

The personalities of Daniels and Roosevelt represented a study in contrast. A temperance man, Daniels, homespun and mild mannered except when he was on the speaker's stump, had alienated much of the officer corps with his prohibition in 1914 of alcoholic beverages in the ships of the navy. He had tried, producing more resentment than results, to democratize the navy, challenging the social chasm that separated officers from enlisted men. He had incurred the enmity of the Navy League and some of the Congress, but he had a way of getting sizable naval appropriations bills enacted.

The secretary was short, paunchy, and a delight to the cartoonists of the age. He wore old-fashioned black frock coats in winter and rumpled white suits in summer, always with a black string tie. One cartoonist drew him as Little Lord Fauntleroy reading a book entitled *How to Tell Ships from Automobiles*. He had grown up poor in Wilson, North Carolina, where his mother, widowed by the Civil War, was the postmistress. From his father, who had been a ship's carpenter, Daniels inherited a chest of tools. That was about as much as he knew of the navy or the sea. He had worked as a newspaperman for most of his life, and his politics were those of an agrarian reformer.

The much-different Franklin Roosevelt—tall, slender, exuberant, and elegantly tailored—was a sharp visual contrast to the rumpled Daniels. It was not love at first sight, at least not on FDR's part. Daniels always seemed fonder of his young assistant than his young assistant did of him. Daniels showed a fatherly affection for Roosevelt. FDR, in turn, almost mischievously, took every opportunity to move into Daniels' place as acting secretary.

Roosevelt swore the oath of office as assistant secretary on March 17, 1913. Before his appointment Franklin had been an obscure New York state senator, but one with good connections and strong ambitions. The youngest assistant secretary of the navy in history, he was thirty-one years old when appointed, seven years younger than his distant cousin, Theodore Roosevelt, had been when the latter had occupied the same desk—nineteen years younger than Daniels and not much more than half the age of most of the admirals. FDR took cousin TR as his model of an activist assistant secretary.

Roosevelt early formed special bonds with the Marine Corps. On the day following his swearing-in, he lunched with Lt. Col. and Mrs. Charles L. McCawley. McCawley was the Marine Corps' entrenched assistant quartermaster, a seemingly permanent fixture on the Washington scene, former aide to President Theodore Roosevelt and son of the eighth commandant of the Marines. A few weeks after the luncheon, he was promoted to colonel and elevated to the statutory position of quartermaster of the Corps, then in 1916 became a brigadier general at the same time as John Lejeune. McCawley became a favorite golfing partner of FDR's.

The tall and athletic Roosevelt, who had a particular interest in the gentlemanly sport of shooting, provided an indirect stimulus to Marine Corps marksmanship. A new rifle range was opened down the Potomac at Winthrop, Maryland, in April 1915. Going down the river to shoot known-distance firing with the Springfield with friends became a favorite Roosevelt pastime.

General Barnett's senior aide, Capt. Thomas Holcomb, became a close Roosevelt friend through their mutual interest in marksmanship. One of Holcomb's duties at headquarters was to serve as inspector of target practice, a position he held from October 1914 until his detachment in August 1917. From a Delaware family, he had been commissioned at age twenty-one in the Marine Corps in 1900. His affinity for rifle marksmanship was immediate. He shot in the international Palma Trophy Matches in 1902 and 1903 and was a perennial member of the Marine Corps Rifle Team from 1901 to 1911. His friendship with FDR would last and would benefit the Corps decades later when he became commandant during President Roosevelt's administration.

Speaking in 1944, Roosevelt would claim, with some exaggeration, "At that time in the Navy Department the Secretary didn't have charge of the Marines, the Assistant Secretary did. . . . I was in complete control of the Marine Corps . . . for eight years."

Roosevelt in the Caribbean

FDR, like his cousin, TR, had an intense personal interest in American adventures in the Caribbean. On January 21, 1917, he left Washington for an inspection visit of navy and Marine forces in the region. Cuba was still an American protectorate, and his first port of call was Havana. The destroyer *Wainwright* took his party from Havana to Port-au-Prince, where seventy-two ships of the Atlantic Fleet were lined up for Roosevelt's inspection. Each ship fired a salute as the *Wainwright* passed through the parallel lines. Franklin loved it.

Ashore at Port-au-Prince, FDR, always concerned about dressing for the occasion, changed into top hat and cutaway to address Haitian president Dartiguenave Sudre and his cabinet, which he did in French. Afterward he reviewed the Gendarmerie d'Haiti, a USMC-led native constabulary created in 1916 and commanded by

Maj. Smedley Butler (with local rank of major general). Butler, already a certified hero with adventures going back to the Boxer Rebellion, impressed him mightily.

The Marines had landed in Haiti in July 1915, and the force had been built up to a 1st Provisional Brigade. Roosevelt, determined to visit as many of the far-flung Marine detachments as possible, trekked northward to Cap Haitien. The 160-mile horseback ride, over a rough road in some places nothing more than a track, took four days. "General" Butler went along, providing an escort of fifty Marines and 150 Haitian gendarmes. Roosevelt wore a Marine uniform and rode comfortably in his own London-made saddle sent down from Hyde Park. On the last day of the visit Butler took him up to see Fort Riviere. Butler told him how a year earlier he and eighteen Marines had crawled through a drainpipe to take the fort, then held by three hundred Haitian "bandits." (Roosevelt was so impressed that when he got back to Washington he recommended a Medal of Honor for Butler. It was the second Medal of Honor for Butler, the first having been given him for his role as a battalion commander at Veracruz in 1914. At this time the Medal of Honor was the only medal authorized for heroism, and it was given quite freely—too freely, in Butler's opinion.)

Roosevelt's party reembarked at Cap Haitien and moved on to Santo Domingo. On the evening of February 3, FDR was having dinner in Santiago de los Caballeros with Col. Theodore P. "Tippy" Kane, commander of the Northern District, when a coded radio message from Secretary Daniels reached him: "Because of political situation please return Washington at once. Am sending ship to meet you and party at Puerto Plata tomorrow morning."

As a souvenir, Roosevelt took home a sixteenth-century Spanish cutlass. He was back in Washington by the afternoon of February 8 and learned that Wilson had broken diplomatic relations with Germany.

The Navy Department and the Marines

The accelerated war mobilization planning of Daniels and Roosevelt brought both officials in more frequent contact with Adm. William Benson, the first Chief of Naval Operations, and Major General Commandant George Barnett.

In 1914, the nomination of a new Marine commandant to replace the early-retiring William P. Biddle in 1914 had been one of Daniels' first battles as navy secretary. The two Virginia senators had pressed him to name Col. Littleton W. T. "Tony" Waller, the consummate expeditionary commander and favorite of many of the rank and file. But Waller had smudged his record while in the Philippines in 1901 when he had convened a drumhead court-martial on the island of Samar to try eleven Filipino bearers he suspected of treachery and had ordered the Filipinos shot. For this he was tried for murder by an army court-martial but was acquitted, the proceedings being thrown out on a technicality.

The Virginia senators, not getting satisfaction from Daniels, went around him and urged President Wilson to name Waller. Daniels himself believed that John A. Lejeune, then a colonel, was the best man for the job, an opinion reinforced by a half-hour interview in October 1913, but in those days of ironclad seniority Lejeune was too junior. The name of Col. George Barnett came to Daniels' attention. Daniels was not immediately convinced, considering Barnett neither as vigorous as Waller nor as learned as Lejeune.

With some reservations Daniels accepted Barnett as a compromise candidate and convinced Wilson to name him as Biddle's successor. Barnett received his appointment on Valentine's Day in 1914. Daniels at first found him capable and agreeable. In future years he would come to rue his choice. Meanwhile, in the hectic days of late spring 1917, Daniels and Barnett worked together to establish a meaningful role for the Marines in the European theater.

The Marines of 1917

General Barnett had inherited a corps still trying to modernize its mission, even while expanding to the highest strength level in its 140-year history. Throughout the nineteenth century the Marine Corps never mustered more than five thousand enlisted men in its ranks. The number abruptly doubled in 1910, and the Naval Appropriations Bill enacted in 1916 authorized a Corps of six hundred officers and nearly fifteen thousand men. Barnett's problems then became issues of barracks and "maneuver fields" on which to train new recruits.

For their relatively few numbers the Marines had garnered disproportionate public esteem in the two decades preceding their deployment to France. In the Spanish-American War, Marines served with distinction on board the ships of Adm. George Dewey's Pacific Squadron at the Battle of Manila Bay and later landed to establish a naval base at Guantanamo Bay, Cuba, on a site defended by a regional force of Spanish regulars. Many of the same Marines earned acclamation for their roles in the relief of the Peking foreign legations during the Boxer Rebellion of 1900 and during the protracted war of Philippine Insurrection—notwithstanding Maj. Tony Waller's court-martial for murder. In 1914, Marines had been the first to land in Veracruz in support of newly inaugurated President Woodrow Wilson's orders to prevent a delivery of machine guns and ammunition by a German ship to a Mexican regime deemed inimical to U.S. interests. Among the senior Marine officers who fought door to door in the port city were future leaders of the Marine brigade in France, including Col. John A. Lejeune, Lt. Col. Wendell C. "Buck" Neville, and Lt. Col. Albertus W. Catlin—the latter two recipients of the Medal of Honor for conspicuous bravery in the street fighting.

There was plentiful employment for Marine Corps expeditionary forces elsewhere. In April 1916 an intervention began in the Dominican Republic, the Spanish-speaking country that shared the island of Hispaniola with French-speaking

Haiti. Companies from Haiti and Marine detachments from the fleet were landed, followed in June by the 4th Regiment from San Diego. These operations were not entirely painless. In 1916, three Marines were killed and fourteen wounded in Haiti, and four were killed and nineteen wounded in the Dominican Republic. The Marines mourned their dead, but none could foresee the unspeakable casualties they would suffer in France two years later.

The Marine Corps at the outbreak of World War I was still searching for a meaningful twentieth-century mission. Its traditional role of manning the "fighting tops" and boarding parties of the old frigate navy had long been eclipsed by technology. Development of an "advanced base" defense doctrine with the expanded fleet showed promise, and both Barnett and Lejeune had commanded the fledgling outfit so configured, but the recurring demand for Marine expeditionary forces in the Caribbean and the Pacific drained the resources needed for systematic training. The Marines had also been developing the first elements of a combined-arms force. An "aeroplane" detachment had joined the Marines, albeit tardily, at Veracruz; new trucks and tractors now towed artillery pieces; a primitive armored car was available—yet these capabilities were not yet fully developed. The best the Marines could offer the nation facing combat on the western front in June 1917 would be a regiment of exceptionally experienced riflemen and a battalion of hard-nosed machine gunners.

"First to Fight"?

Among the challenges facing Daniels and Barnett following the U.S. declaration of war was the problem of securing sealift for the initial Marine forces to accompany the much larger army contingent to France. The army needed all of its available transports to deploy its divisions of regulars and their combat-support elements. The Marines would need at least three transports to move a single regiment, and the prospects were not encouraging.

There was progress of a sort under way. In June 1916, the USS *Henderson,* the first new troop transport built expressly to support Marines, was launched at the Philadelphia Navy Yard, sponsored by Miss Genevieve W. Taylor, the great-granddaughter of Brig. Gen. Archibald Henderson, USMC, a hero of the War of 1812 and the Seminole War, and Marine Corps commandant from 1820 to 1859. The navy commissioned the *Henderson* on May 24, 1917. Her abbreviated shakedown cruise would barely be finished by the time the first contingent of troops would be ready to embark. She was badly needed. Two older, much smaller navy transports, veterans of much expeditionary service with the Marines, were the *Prairie* and the *Hancock.* The first was worn out, and the second was continually undergoing repair.

Earlier, President and Mrs. Wilson visited Daniels in his handsome Navy Department office. The president said that he had been thinking about the German ships interned in the United States and had come to the conclusion that Marines should be placed on board to prevent sabotage. Daniels said he would take care of it.

One of the interned German ships, SMS *Cormoran,* was in San Luis de Apra Harbor in Guam, halfway around the world. In 1914, at the war's beginning, the Germans had captured her from the Russians and converted her into an auxiliary cruiser at their naval base at Tsingtao, China. Armed with eight 4.1-inch guns, *Cormoran* for four months had dodged British and Japanese men-of-war before exhausting her supply of food and coal. On December 15, 1914, chased by the Japanese cruiser IJN *Iwate,* she had put into Guam. Here the ship was interned and partially disarmed by the governor of the island, a U.S. Navy captain, who allowed the crew to continue to live on board. She lay immobilized under the antique but still menacing guns of the shore batteries.

In April 1917, two hours after the cablegram reached Guam announcing that a state of war existed, the governor sent his executive officer, Cdr. Owen Bartlett, with a boarding party of Marines and sailors to take possession of the ship. Bartlett's party, chugging toward the *Cormoran* in a steam launch, could make out a party of Germans departing the ship in a small boat. Bartlett ordered Cpl. Michael B. Chockie to fire a warning shot with his Springfield, probably the first shot to be fired by an American after the entry of the United States into the war.[3] Although the Germans hauled down their colors, they soon scuttled and sank their ship in the harbor.

Two interned liners that escaped scuttling, the *Kron Prinz Wilhelm* and the *Prinz Eitel Friedrich,* were in the back basin of the Philadelphia Navy Yard. The industrious German crews had built a squatters' village out of packing cases on the Back Basin dock. They found it amusing that some of the guns of the Reserve Fleet were kept trained on them.[4]

Josephus Daniels talked to the president about renaming the two interned German warships. Why not, as he noted in his diary, "Change *Kron Prinz Wilhelm* to *Von Steuben* and *Eitel Frederick* to *De Kalb*—good German names of men who helped us win our battle for independence?" The president agreed.

Of special interest to the Marines, the *Prinz Eitel Friedrich* became the *De Kalb* on May 12, needing nothing more than a coat of gray paint and a familiarization of the crew with the German engines to convert her into a troop transport.

In Washington, Barnett, certain that the fighting would be largely on land, went to Daniels to apprise him of the fact that the law gave the president in time of war the authority to transfer by executive order all or part of the Marine Corps to the army. Daniels authorized Barnett direct liaison with the secretary of war, Newton D. Baker, to see what might be worked out. "We had used the slogan 'First to Fight' on our posters, and I did not want that slogan made ridiculous," recalled Barnett, "so I felt it essential that some marines must be gotten over with the first

AEF outfit sailing for France. I received assurances that one regiment of marines would be included in the first outfit to sail from New York under Naval convoy."[5]

To make good on Barnett's promise, the Marine Corps had to assemble a regiment for duty on the western front. As Lejeune put it: "We had no organized regiments in the United States, all of our organized forces, except a few small companies, were in Haiti, Santo Domingo, and eastern Cuba."

The British and French Missions

The American ambassador in London had cabled a request on March 23 asking that a high-ranking naval officer be sent to establish liaison with the British Admiralty. The Chief of Naval Operations, Admiral Benson, chose Rear Adm. William S. Sims, president of the Naval War College in Newport, Rhode Island, to go. Benson was an elderly Georgian with a white mustache, a deliberate southern manner, and a distrust of the British. He told Sims that he was to go secretly, under an assumed name, and not even take his uniforms. In sending him off, Benson said, "Don't let the British pull the wool over your eyes. It's not our business pulling their chestnuts out of the fire. We would as soon fight the British as the Germans."

Sims arrived in England two days after the U.S. declaration of war. The matter of convoys topped Sims' agenda. He found Britain in serious danger of defeat. Allied merchant ships were being sunk by German submarines faster than they could be built, yet Adm. Sir John Jellicoe, the First Sea Lord, told him that no British destroyers could be spared from the Grand Fleet for convoy duty.

Both the British and the French dispatched missions to Washington with proposals for the use of raw American manpower. A British mission, headed by the foreign minister, Arthur J. Balfour, reached Washington on April 23.[6] The British, citing the wishes of Gen. Sir Douglas Haig, their commander in chief in France, requested that "500,000 untrained men [be sent] at once to our depots in England to be trained there, and drafted into our armies in France."

The French mission, headed by Marshal Joseph J. Joffre, arrived in the cruiser *Lorraine II* on April 24 in Hampton Roads off Fort Monroe, Virginia. The mission was met by a delegation from Washington that included Maj. Gen. Hugh L. Scott, chief of staff of the army, and Assistant Secretary of the Navy Franklin Roosevelt ("a name doubly dear to every French heart," said Joffre). After a welcoming ceremony full of flashing swords and gold braid on the battleship *Pennsylvania,* the mission boarded the presidential yacht *Mayflower* for the voyage up the Chesapeake Bay and then the Potomac, particularly beautiful in the springtime, to the American capital. Unnoticed in the passing was the small town of Quantico on the Virginia shore, but Joffre stood respectfully at the salute as the yacht passed General Washington's plantation at Mount Vernon.

"Papa" Joffre had enormous prestige in the United States. As a lieutenant Joffre had fought the Germans in the Franco-Prussian War and as a general had commanded the French on the western front for two and a half years. After the horrendous losses at Verdun and on the Somme in 1916, he was given the baton of a marshal of France and placed on the shelf. Americans were only hazily aware that command of the French army on the western front now rested with the supremely self-confident Gen. Robert Georges Nivelle, hero of Verdun. Nivelle on April 16 shifted the weight of French forces from the blood-soaked Somme to a great offensive in the Chemin des Dames ("The Ladies' Way") zone of action in a movement designed to break the stalemate. Even as the *Lorraine* crossed the Atlantic, wireless dispatches carried to the ship word that the Nivelle offensive was faltering.

Official visits began on April 26. Senior officers in the city, including Barnett and Lejeune, met Balfour and Joffre at a reception held in the Pan-American Building. Marshal Joffre told General Scott that he thought the United States was "quite capable of organizing a great army" but that first, perhaps, considering the smallness of the American army, it would be better to send men, not armies—men organized into small units, such as companies and battalions, that could be incorporated into French regiments. Officers above the rank of captain or major would not be needed. It was possible, said Joffre, "to make a soldier in a few months, officers—above all, those in the higher grades—and staffs cannot be improvised." An immediate shipment of eighty thousand men was suggested, none above the rank of captain, as "auxiliary troops."

Marshal Joffre and Lord Balfour soon began to realize that America was not going to send men as individuals or in small units to France to be under French or British command. Joffre, being a practical Frenchman, shrewdly adjusted his thinking. When on May 2 he met with President Wilson and the president asked him his opinion on how best to use the American army, Joffre prefaced his reply by noting that both the Germans and French had called to the colors the Class of 1918 conscripts. This would yield four hundred thousand new Germans in uniform but only 170,000 Frenchmen. He then recommended that the United States send a division to France at the earliest possible moment. "The division," Joffre told the president, "could leave the United States almost immediately; its training could be completed in France in the space of a month; after this period of intense training, it could be gradually worked into a sector on the front." The French could teach these American soldiers trench warfare behind the lines, Joffre told the president. It was much simpler than warfare of maneuver, he said.

Agreement was soon reached: a first U.S. division of sixteen to twenty thousand soldiers would embark on or about June 1 for France. The division would be composed of four regiments of infantry, twelve batteries of field artillery, and six batteries of heavy artillery, along with corresponding services.

Before returning to France, Marshal Joffre was introduced to the officer who had just been named to command the American Expeditionary Forces going to France,

Maj. Gen. John J. Pershing. Joffre found him a fine-looking soldier. Joffre sailed for France with the feeling that he had played his last important role in the war.

Pershing Takes Command

Pershing had come to Washington the morning of May 10 from Fort Sam Houston, near San Antonio, Texas, where he commanded the Southern Department of the army. The previous year he had led his command—which eventually numbered over fifteen thousand men—into Mexico in pursuit of the revolutionist general Francisco "Pancho" Villa, in reprisal for Villa's night raid into the cow town of Columbus, New Mexico. The so-called Punitive Expedition, which included some experimentation with airplanes and motorized transport, had gone on for a year. It was a mixed success. Pershing did penetrate some four hundred miles into Mexican territory, Villa's "bandits" were scattered, and Villa himself was wounded, but overall it was a clumsy expedition with no permanent results. Pershing withdrew to north of the Rio Grande in February 1917.

General Scott now asked him to designate four infantry regiments and one artillery regiment for service in France. Pershing nominated the 16th, 18th, 26th, and 28th regiments of infantry and the 6th Field Artillery. He came to Washington expecting to be given command of the division. Secretary of War Newton Baker informed Pershing that he was instead to be the commander in chief of the American forces in France. Pershing was agreeably surprised, or so he says in his memoirs; five other major generals were senior to him.

Pershing was dead set against the U.S. Army being used as a manpower pool for either the French or the British. He came to a definite understanding with Baker that a distinctively American army would be built as rapidly as possible.

General Barnett, with Daniels' backing, continued to argue for a Marine presence in the expeditionary force being assembled. He was successful. On May 16, Secretary of War Baker asked President Wilson for a Marine regiment, equipped as infantry, for duty in France.

On May 24, Baker and Pershing called on President Wilson for what was Pershing's first meeting with Wilson. He would not see him again until after the Armistice. Three days later, the day before his sailing, Pershing received a letter of instruction from the secretary of war advising him formally that the president had designated him "to command all land forces of the United States operating in Continental Europe and in the United Kingdom of Great Britain and Ireland, including any part of the Marine Corps which may be detached for service there with the Army."

Pershing's advance party, in secrecy, assembled at Governors Island, in New York Harbor, and in civilian clothes went on board the British steamship *Baltic*. Fifty-nine officers, sixty-seven enlisted men, fifty-six clerks, five interpreters, and three war correspondents accompanied Pershing. He had chosen Maj. James G.

Harbord to be his chief of staff. Harbord had enlisted in the army as a private in 1889. Pershing had first known him as a first lieutenant in the 10th Cavalry. Harbord's rise in rank and importance would be meteoric. Included in Pershing's entourage also were two Marine Corps lieutenant colonels—Logan Feland and Robert H. Dunlap. They too would figure large in events to come.

The 5th Regiment of Marines

Daniels, somewhat belatedly, on May 29 signed a directive to Barnett instructing him to "organize a force of Marines to be known as the Fifth Regiment of Marines for service with the army as part of the first expedition to proceed to France." The Marine Corps had four small regiments of a thousand men or less, minute by the standards of the western front, in being in the spring of 1917. The 1st Regiment, stationed at Philadelphia, had recently been reorganized, under Col. Charles G. "Squeegee" Long, as a fixed defense force. The 2d Regiment was in Haiti. The 3d and 4th regiments were in the Dominican Republic. The expeditionary regiments were on the old model, not much changed since the Civil War—nominally consisting of ten companies of a hundred men each, although they were seldom up to strength and companies moved in and out from under a headquarters that was then called the regiment's "field and staff." Companies from these four regiments would be gathered together as the building blocks for the new wartime regiment.

Capt. Frederic M. Wise ("Freddie" or "Fritz" to his friends, "Dopey" behind his back) had returned from Haiti on Christmas Day, 1916, and, with a promotion to major, was promised command of a battalion in Squeegee Long's 1st Regiment at the Philadelphia Navy Yard. Wise liked the good things of life, and his rotund figure showed it. On May 5, 1917, Major Wise married Ethel Sewall Hardy in a high-society wedding at St. Martin's Church in Radnor, on Philadelphia's Main Line. On Wise's return from his honeymoon, Lejeune telephoned him that he would have one of the battalions being readied for service in France, adding that Col. Charles A. Doyen would relieve Squeegee Long in command of the regiment and that Wise's friend Lt. Col. Logan Feland, currently assigned as an observer with Pershing's advance party, would become second in command.

The new 5th Regiment of Marines was already on its way to being fully organized. Barnett was bringing together his scattered companies to form them into battalions. The 1st Battalion, made up of the 17th Company, brought up from Pensacola, and the 49th, 66th, and 67th companies, gathered together from around Norfolk, was activated at the newly acquired camp at Quantico, Virginia, during the last week of May, under the command of Maj. Julius S. Turrill.

The 2d and 3d battalions were formed from eight companies of Marines that arrived at the Philadelphia Navy Yard on May 30 from the Caribbean as drawdowns from the expeditionary regiments. The 23d Company from Haiti and the 43d, 51st, and 55th companies from Cuba became the 2d Battalion, 5th Marines, under Major Wise. The 16th Company, from Haiti, and the 8th, 45th, and 47th companies, from the Dominican Republic, became the 3d Battalion, under Maj. Charles T. Westcott. The companies were weeded down to about forty men each and then filled back up with recruits to the new wartime strength of two hundred. "Although the majority of them was raw," said Wise, "the material was the best in the world."

Wise's four company commanders—Henry M. Butler, Joseph D. Murray, Lloyd Williams, and George Osterhout, all captains—were seasoned campaigners. Wise rejected some of his enlisted old-timers as being too old (and perhaps too alcoholic) for the western front. An exception was 1st Sgt. James Gallivan of the 43d Company, who was too tough an Irishman to be left behind.

Gallivan had come to Holyoke, Massachusetts, from County Kerry, Ireland, in 1884 at age seventeen, worked as a boilermaker for ten years, and then enlisted in the Marine Corps. Sea duty in the cruisers *Marblehead* and *Minneapolis* took him to the Mediterranean, the Adriatic, the Black Sea, to Germany for the opening of the Kiel Canal, and to Kronstadt, Russia. As a corporal he landed with Robert W. Huntington at Guantanamo Bay in 1898. As a sergeant he chased *insurrectos* in the Philippines, with a side excursion to march to the relief of the legations in Peking in 1900 during the Boxer Rebellion. In 1905 he was detailed, with the stripes of a first sergeant, to Guam, where he aided an island missionary in making better Catholics of the Chamorros, but was reduced to sergeant for drunkenness. Next year there was a stint, still as a sergeant, in the pacification of Cuba. Coming out of Cuba, he was stationed in Boston, slid down a notch to corporal, went absent without leave, was reduced to private, broke arrest, and was declared a deserter. He came back, the mark of deserter was removed, and by 1909 Gallivan was first sergeant of the Marine detachment in the battleship *New Hampshire*. In the years 1914–15 there was more sea duty, in the battleships *New York* and *Wyoming*. He landed at Veracruz in 1914, and when the Marines went into Santo Domingo in 1916 he was with them.

When Captain Murray reorganized the 43d Company in 1916 at Philadelphia for service in the Caribbean, he picked Gallivan to be his first sergeant. His physical exam for July 1916 showed him to be sixty-eight and a half inches tall, 183 pounds in weight, and to have a chest thirty-nine inches around expired and forty-three inspired, vision 20/20, hearing 15/15, and all his teeth but one. Blue eyes, dark brown hair, and a ruddy complexion—there was also a large mustache. He had married a nurse, his beloved "Kate," and was about to retire with twenty-three years' service when the United States came into the war. He promptly reenlisted and asked to stay with the 43d Company. Gallivan was then fifty, and Wise told him he was too old. Gallivan took affront and, his brogue thickening with anger, said, "There's room in France for both of us, sir."

Gallivan, seeing other noncommissioned officers, or NCOs, being made officers, asked Wise what his chances were for a commission. Wise told him he was too old but recommended that he apply for the new warrant-officer grade of Marine gunner. Gallivan sent in his application on June 4.

Wise used 1st Sergeant Gallivan to teach the ways of the Corps to the young lieutenants that he was getting. One of them was 2d Lt. Lemuel C. Shepherd Jr. of Norfolk, Virginia. His father, a doctor, had been named for an uncle, Lemuel Cornick, killed at Chancellorsville. Young Lem went to Virginia Military Institute to study electrical engineering and then switched to civil engineering. He had a cousin working in Nicaragua as a civil engineer, and it sounded interesting. After the expansion of the armed forces authorized by the National Defense Act of 1916, VMI was allotted a quota of ten army and ten Marine Corps commissions. The day after war was declared Lem presented himself to VMI's superintendent and asked that his name be added to the Marine Corps list of candidates. The Major General Commandant, George Barnett, had delivered the commencement address the previous year, and both the man and his blue uniform had impressed Lem. All on the list were ordered to the Marine Barracks in Washington for examination.[7]

They reported at 9 AM, April 11. The physical examination came first. Shepherd was afraid he might not pass as he weighed only 123 pounds, and the minimum for his height was 135 pounds. But the old navy surgeon, after taking his blood pressure, asked him just two questions, both too indelicate to be repeated. Shepherd's answers were satisfactory, and he was certified physically fit for duty in the field. The examining board considered anyone graduating from VMI to be professionally qualified. The president of the board told the candidates to raise their right hands; they were sworn in as second lieutenants and told to return to VMI and await orders. VMI obliged with an early graduation on May 3, and Shepherd was called to active duty.[8]

Shepherd was sent to the School of Application at Paris (not yet Parris) Island, South Carolina, for two weeks' indoctrination, most of it spent on the rifle range. He volunteered for duty with the 5th Regiment of Marines, then forming in Philadelphia. He arrived at the Navy Yard on June 5 and was assigned command of the 4th Platoon of the 55th Company in Wise's 2d Battalion. He had his khaki uniforms, but his officer's forest-green uniform had not yet arrived from the tailor. He cut a wedge out of the legs of a pair of enlisted trousers to make them fit into his puttees.

Embarkation for France

In late May or early June, Secretary of the Army Baker wrote Barnett a personal note that there would be no room in the first convoy for the regiment of Marines. Barnett wrote back that Baker should not be troubled; other arrangements for the transport of Marines had been made.

Barnett's reply was disingenuous. Only an inspired effort by Daniels and Roosevelt had provided, barely, enough sealift in time to embark the single Marine regiment. The nineteen-year-old *Prairie* had been found unfit for the Atlantic passage, while the fifteen-year-old *Hancock* had scarcely passed her inspection and would be consigned to the slowest ships of the convoy. Top-level Navy Department pressure and a compressed shakedown period hastened the four-year construction of the Marines' new transport, *Henderson*. Daniels' earlier conversation with President Wilson helped ensure that the newly converted *De Kalb* (nee *Prinz Eitel Friedrich*) would become a navy, vice army, transport. Navy transports were assigned to the Cruiser and Transport Force, Atlantic Fleet, a curious combination of ship types that kept the navy transports from being lumped together with army transports.

Close by the berth of the *De Kalb* in the Philadelphia Navy Yard, the 5th Regiment continued to assemble. On June 7, Colonel Doyen assumed command. Doyen was a classmate of George Barnett's, having graduated from the Naval Academy in 1881. As a second lieutenant he had taken the Marine detachment from the gunboat *Galena* ashore at Colon, Panama, in 1885, where revolutionaries were burning much of the city, to guard the U.S. consulate. He was now fifty-eight years old. He had been a colonel since 1909 and was in command of the Marine Barracks in Washington, D.C., when the war broke out. His new regiment, rounded out with a headquarters company and a supply company, totaled about 2,600 men.

Doyen with his regimental headquarters boarded the *Hancock* on June 8 at the Washington Navy Yard. On the same day Turrill's 1st Battalion arrived at the yard by rail from Quantico. On the afternoon of June 10, at one end of the Navy Yard parade ground, a baseball team from one of the battleships was practicing. Across the street from the parade ground a small boy in rompers was playing with a fox terrier on the lawn of the quarters of the commander of the Marine Barracks. Major General Commandant Barnett, dressed in summer khaki, field hat, and polished boots, came out of the quarters and took position on the curb. He was somewhat round shouldered, and his slight paunch pushed out the front of his jacket. With him was a small party of officers, including Brigadier General Lejeune and Colonel Doyen. A quartermaster sergeant trotted across the parade ground, set up a motion picture camera, and began to crank away.

At precisely 2:30 PM, Turrill's 1st Battalion, 5th Regiment of Marines, in khaki and heavy marching order, came swinging down the street. The battalion's officers left the column and joined Barnett at the curb. He had a few words for them, almost inaudible, something about sending them to join Pershing's army and that they must uphold the traditions of the Corps.

The battalion officers saluted and returned to the column. The battalion marched out the main gate and filed into a line of day coaches on the railroad siding. The regimental mascot, a small black goat, stuck his head out a train window and peered around with a look of mild but dignified curiosity. No colors were unfurled. No reporters or press photographers were present. No drums or bugles sounded. The regimental band went to war with their instruments cased and rifles over their shoulders.

The baseball team continued to practice. A half-hour later Wise's 2d Battalion came down the brick-paved street and formed on the parade ground. Westcott's 3d Battalion followed. The two battalions marched off in the direction of the docks. Barnett shook hands with Doyen. The QM sergeant stopped cranking his camera, folded its tripod, and, along with a still photographer, went off at the double to join the regiment as it embarked at the pier.

Wise's 2d Battalion boarded the *Hancock* and Westcott's 3d Battalion the *De Kalb*, and at noon, June 11, the two ships sailed for New York, where the convoy was making up. In New York the 1st Battalion joined the 3d Battalion in the *De Kalb*. To Wise's relief, his battalion and the regimental headquarters were transferred from the venerable *Hancock* to the brand-new *Henderson*, commissioned just three weeks earlier.

The convoy, twenty ships in all, got under way on June 14, the ships grouped into units depending upon their speed of advance. The *Henderson* and *De Kalb*, at fourteen knots, were in the second unit. The aging *Hancock* struggled in the slowest echelon. The *Henderson* had all the faults of a newly commissioned ship not yet completely shaken down and with a green crew. There was a great deal of firing of its 5-inch guns at real or imagined submarines. Colonel Doyen gave Wise the tiresome job of troop commander. Wise came down sick with *la grippe*, forerunner of the Spanish influenza that was to come, but managed to get around on his inspections.

Secretary of War Baker and the senior leadership of the U.S. Army could hardly have been pleased with a *New York Times* headline that proclaimed, "2,600 Marines to Go with Pershing." The front-page story virtually ignored the twenty thousand army troops preparing to embark; its effusive praise for the Marines included a photograph and biography of Colonel Doyen, the highlights of Marine Corps expeditionary history—even the words to the "Marines' Hymn," including the unauthorized "4th verse," a bit of doggerel that had emerged from the protracted Philippine Insurrection:

> From the Pest Hole of Cavite
> To the ditch at Panama,
> You will find them very needy
> Of Marines—that's what we are.
> We're the watchdogs of a pile of coal
> Or we dig a magazine.
> Though he lends a hand at every job,
> Who would not—be a Marine?[9]

CHAPTER TWO

Fivefold Expansion

Generals Barnett and Lejeune could not afford to bask in the favorable publicity that befell the Marines for their timely delivery of an infantry regiment to the first contingent of American troops to deploy to France.[1] In making good on their promise to the Wilson administration and General Pershing, they had preserved their institutional claim of being "First to Fight." Yet launching the 5th Regiment had required an exhausting effort. Further, while General Pershing publicly welcomed another regiment of regulars among his advance guard, he likely regarded the cocksure Marines as an uneven fit—disciplined riflemen for certain but at best light infantry, unaccustomed to large-unit warfare and requiring disproportionate firepower and logistic support. Barnett and Lejeune realized that the steady buildup of army divisions in France would eventually diminish the Marine contingent to the point of irrelevance. Indeed, the army historian Brig. Gen. S. L. A. "Slam" Marshall would describe the Marines in the American Expeditionary Forces as "that little raft of sea soldiers in an ocean of Army."

The senior Marines considered it imperative to raise and deploy a second regiment as soon as possible, to contribute at least a full brigade to the war in France. The Corps would also need to deploy large replacement battalions to ensure that army soldiers would not be used to restore Marine combat and operational losses.

Forming a second regiment, the 6th Marines, would take twice as long as the initial surge. For one thing, Barnett had assigned so many veteran NCOs to the ranks of the 5th Regiment that few experienced sergeants remained available stateside to provide basic recruit or advanced infantry training to the unprecedented numbers of new troops swelling the camps and barracks. The Naval Appropriations Act of 1917 had authorized a record enlisted strength of fifteen thousand Marines—but even this generous ceiling would increase fivefold in the next several months. It was an embarrassment of riches for the Marines, and they were hard pressed to find the training bases and "maneuvering grounds"—or the NCOs—with which to indoctrinate and train so many new riflemen without diluting their traditional standards.

The Marines also faced ongoing, conflicting demands: waging counterinsurgency campaigns ashore in Central America and the Caribbean; providing Marine detachments on board each new capital ship of the navy; testing the emerging mission of advanced-base defense; and providing ready forces along the Mexican border—a region still simmering from the 1916 Pancho Villa raid on Columbus, New Mexico, and the inflammatory plot revealed in the Zimmerman Telegram. Each commitment required experienced officers and NCOs, further diluting the resources available to establish a second, full-strength infantry regiment.

Preparing for Expansion

Barnett, Lejeune, and their three gifted staff assistants at headquarters had struggled to facilitate the expansion expected to come when America went to war. A summer-long effort by Lejeune and Ellis ensured that the all-encompassing Naval Appropriations Act of 1916 authorized a Marine Corps Reserve and established the warrant grades of marine gunner and quartermaster clerk, with twenty of each authorized.[2]

The Major General Commandant's 1916 annual report, in words likely drafted by Ellis, expressed the need to equip the Corps with plentiful automatic weapons, observing, "The existing war in Europe has demonstrated conclusively the great importance of the machine gun." Considering it important that all officers and men of the Marine Corps be trained in its use, Barnett requested "that the War Department allow officers of the corps to take the course of instruction at the Army Machine Gun School at Fort Sill, Okla."

In October 1915, the navy turned over to the Marines an underutilized disciplinary barracks at Port Royal, South Carolina, for use as a recruit depot in lieu of cramped space already being used at the Norfolk Navy Yard in Virginia. Port Royal was on "Paris" Island; not until 1918 would the spelling "Parris" become generally used. The new recruit depot, commanded initially by a captain, could accommodate a thousand recruits.

On the West Coast, an inspection trip by Barnett had satisfied him that a suitable site on the edge of San Diego's harbor could be obtained for about $250,000. The money for the San Diego site was put in the budget, and the purchase would be made in June 1917 of a 232-acre tract. Building would start as soon as possible. In the meantime, Marines stationed at San Diego were occupying several buildings in the Exposition Grounds.

Next, and of vital importance, was a similar "maneuvering ground" on the East Coast. Strategic considerations, said the 1916 annual report, demanded "a site on the shores of the Chesapeake Bay, or one of its tributaries."

On the day that war was declared, General Barnett had appointed a board to find a site near Washington "for a temporary training camp and maneuver field" large enough to accommodate about 7,500 Marines. After several false starts, the board on April 17 went to Quantico, Virginia, a fishing village on the Potomac some forty miles south of Washington that had been a stopping place for riverboats and was currently enjoying a boomlet from a small wartime shipyard. There was ample land available, U.S. Highway 1 went close by, and there was a pier on the river, as well as a railroad siding. The board reported to the commandant that the site had everything that was needed for a "concentration and training camp" and met all the requirements for a permanent post except that it was not on deep water. After some negotiations with the landowners, the Quantico Company, 5,300 acres were leased.

On May 2, General Barnett formed another board, this one headed by Lejeune, to lay out the campsite. Initial building plans called for a headquarters, hospital, kitchen, mess hall, bathhouses, barracks, and storehouses sufficient to provide for 3,500 men, but first off there would be a tent camp. Across the river, the existing rifle range at Winthrop, Maryland, was operating at full capacity. The Winthrop range could handle about 350 Marines at any one time, working from first light to sunset.

On May 14, the 9th Company, Artillery Battalion—four officers, ninety-one Marines, and two navy hospital corpsmen—arrived from Annapolis, went into tents, and "Marine Barracks, Quantico" was open for business.

Exploiting the "First to Fight" Appeal

"The slogan, 'First to Fight'—a line of the Marines' Hymn—attracted the adventurous, the patriotic and the brave," said Lejeune. "Its use was the happy thought of Major McLemore, the Officer in Charge of Marine Corps Recruiting."

By the war's beginning Albert Sidney McLemore was a lieutenant colonel and soon would be a colonel. McLemore had been born in 1869 in Franklin, Tennessee, site of one of the last great battles of the Civil War. He grew up on stories of that battle, of how the Confederate general John Hood had wrecked his army in valiant but futile charges against Union lines. A Naval Academy graduate, McLemore received his commission as a second lieutenant in the Marine Corps in 1893. He won a brevet promotion to captain for valorous service with Huntington's battalion in the taking of Guantanamo, Cuba, in 1898. In the Philippines in 1909 he came down with malaria and typhoid fever and was sent home to the naval hospital at Mare Island in San Francisco. For nearly a year he was in and out of the hospital.

Although eventually pronounced fit for duty, perhaps it was his dubious health that caused McLemore to be named, as a major, officer in charge of Marine Corps recruiting in 1911. It was a felicitous assignment.

McLemore did not in fact originate the motto "First to Fight," but he publicly hammered home the point that the Marine Corps was prepared for the European war, just as it would always be prepared for any war.

The Marines in 1917 had twenty-six officers and 428 enlisted men assigned to recruiting duty at 374 recruiting stations. For prospective Marines who did not find a recruiter or recruiting station immediately accessible, local postmasters had limited recruiting authority. Recruiting posters stood on A-frames in front of most post offices.

General rates of pay were as prescribed in 1908 for both the army and Marines. Privates enlisted at fifteen dollars a month. Congress doubled this with "war pay" on May 18, 1917.[3]

Attracting Recruits

The peripatetic Colonel McLemore's greatest resource was the Recruiting Publicity Bureau at 117–119 East 24th Street, New York City, which he expanded from what had been a very small office. Handsome Capt. Ross E. Rowell, who sometimes posed for recruiting posters, served as officer in charge of the Publicity Bureau, which functioned as a news bureau and had its own compositors and presses. Rowell was also editor of the *Recruiters' Bulletin,* a slick, thirty-two-page monthly magazine.[4]

Marine recruiters borrowed elephants from Barnum & Bailey Circus to display Marine Corps recruiting flags in a "Wake Up, America" parade held in New York on April 19, 1917. That same day, a Philadelphia recruiter, Sgt. Samuel Katcher, at five feet seven inches, 145 pounds, boxed the world's heavyweight champion, Jess Willard, in an exhibition match.

The Marine Corps had bought several King armored cars for service in Haiti. Capitalizing on this, a Marine "recruiting station" was set up in the King Car Company's office in New York. The Fifth Avenue Coach Company gave the Marine Corps permission to display specially prepared placards on the sides of all Fifth Avenue buses.

An instant organization called the "Patriotic League of the United States Marine Corps" sponsored a gala entertainment held on May 20 at the Hippodrome, New York's largest theater. A Marine drill team performed. General Barnett spoke of the aims and duties of the Marines and got a rousing ovation. There was a succession of performances by "stage folk," some of them with names still remembered: Marie Dressler, Lew Fields, Elsie Janis, Annette Kellerman, the Dolly Sisters, and Leon Errol. George M. Cohan sang "one of his songs of the flag"—presumably, "It's a Grand Old Flag." The affair raised five thousand dollars—a huge amount for the day—from the sale of seats and programs.

In a much-publicized ceremony, Edwin Denby, a navy gunner's mate in the Spanish-American War and a member of Congress from 1904 to 1911, enlisted in Detroit, where he was a prominent attorney. He was forty-seven years old, stood six feet tall, and weighed 254 pounds. General Barnett waived his overage, over-weight, and marriage disqualifications.[5]

The Marines made special efforts to recruit college athletes, particularly foot-ball players. Johnnie Beckett and "Brick" Mitchell joined from the University of Oregon, Robert V. Ignacio from Washington and Lee. Nathan Dixon McClure, captain of the Yale soccer team, enlisted. So did Joseph E. Magnus, the grandson of the late Adolphus Busch, the St. Louis brewer. Apparently not to be outdone, Harry A. Pabst, nephew to the Pabst brewer, enlisted. So did Harold E. Kellogg, nephew of the breakfast cereal king.

John Joseph McDermott had been court-martialed out of the Corps nearly ten years earlier for drunkenness and insubordination. "It was the whisky that did it," he said, writing to General Barnett from the Salvation Army barracks in Seattle and asking for a chance to rehabilitate himself. Barnett gave his permission, and the thirty-nine-year-old reenlisted on May 27.

Sgt. Maj. Michael McNamara, born in County Mayo in 1866, had retired in 1913 to Ireland. With America in the war, he came back to the United States, pay-ing his own way across the Atlantic, and reported for duty at Headquarters, Marine Corps. Retired gunnery sergeant James McMahon, age fifty-eight and working as a U.S. marshal in San Juan, Puerto Rico, read in the *Army and Navy Journal* that the Marine Corps was being supplied with Lewis guns and steel helmets. He wanted to wear one of those helmets, so he wrote to the Major General Commandant on May 4, "I am in excellent health and feel as young as I did ten years ago and the only disability under which I labor is that I am subject at times to rheumatism in my ankles, but not withstanding this, I am at the call of my superior officers and the old Flag."

During the month of May, 5,295 Marines were enlisted, a recruiting record. Careful calculations for 1917 recruiting costs showed that Marines were being enlisted at a cost of only $9.97, exclusive of transportation. Transportation to the recruit training camps ran up the cost to $31.17.

Barnett and McLemore scheduled a National Marine Corps Recruiting Week for June 10–16 and solicited prominent Americans for endorsements. Secretary Daniels led off with, "There are no better soldiers in the world than those in the United States Marine Corps." Theodore Roosevelt, familiarly known as "the Colo-nel," had not been that fond of the Marines when he was president, but now he came in with, "There is no finer body of men in the world than the U.S. Marine Corps."

George Horace Latimer, the editor of the *Saturday Evening Post,* managed a capsule history of the Corps in one sentence: "It will be a big thing to fight this great world battle for freedom with the Corps that served under John Paul Jones, that repelled boarders on the old *Constitution,* that stormed the heights of Chapultepec, that carried its battle-torn flags through the Civil War, that was at Guantanamo, at Santiago and Manila, that was in the van of the march on Peking, and in the thick of the fight at Tientsin."

The president of Yale University, Arthur T. Hadley, wrote, "No branch of the service has a more honorable record than the Marine Corps and none today offers as varied prospects of immediate and active service."

In Chicago on June 11, John Philip Sousa led the Navy Band from Great Lakes Training Station in the first public playing of a new march, dedicated to the Marine Corps, that he had dashed off: "The First to Fight." Sousa wrote: "I was Bandmaster of the U.S. Marine Corps in Washington from 1880 to 1892, and the love I bore the Corps during that period has remained with me ever since. . . . The Marine Corps is a wonderful branch of our United Service, and particularly appeals to the man who desires action with intelligence and consummate team work."

Artists and illustrators, including many big names, hastened to offer their services. James Montgomery Flagg led off with a painting that became a famous poster: a Marine captain in summer khaki uniform, pistol poised, standing in front of an American flag. Capt. Ross Rowell was the model. Sidney H. Riesenberg, already known for his flag paintings, came in with three more to be used as posters: *Rally 'Round the Flag, Active Service on Land and Sea,* and *First to Fight.* L. A. Shafer, a maritime artist, did a poster painting, *Spirit of 1917,* showing a four-Marine color guard determinedly advancing in a conscious imitation of the "Spirit of '76." Fred C. Yohn, a famous military artist in the Spanish-American War, executed a highly imaginary battle scene. Gilbert Gaul, whose war paintings dated back to the Civil War, portrayed a party of Marine "bombers" working their way through a barbed-wire entanglement. John Coughlin came forth with a painting of a Marine in tin helmet charging forward with a Lewis gun. A bit later Howard Chandler Christy and Charles Dana Gibson would come in with their own work as well.

In 1916 the Marine Corps Publicity Bureau had made and released a two-reel film, *The Peacemakers.* The first reel shows Marines enjoying life and training in barracks and such exotic places as the Legation Guard in Peking, China. General Barnett sends a message to the commanding officer, Marine Barracks, New York Navy Yard, to embark a company of Marines to join the brigade en route to Haiti. There are shipboard scenes, and in the second reel the Marines are ashore in Haiti battling rebels until a peace conference is forced on the Caco chiefs, after which all is serene.

Boot Camp

From the declaration of war on April 6 until June 30, a total of 12,108 men were brought into the Corps. Mare Island, California, and Paris Island, South Carolina, were swamped. Using tent camps, the recruit depots at Paris Island and Mare Island were expanded almost immediately to capacities of six thousand and 2,500 recruits, respectively. This was still not enough, and temporary recruit training camps were opened at Philadelphia Navy Yard for 2,500 recruits and at the Norfolk Navy Yard for five hundred more.

Wrote Lejeune: "Deficiencies in clothing at Parris Island caused no suffering, owing to the hot weather; temporary buildings and oyster-shell roads were constructed with the help of the recruits; food in plenty could be obtained, but there was a dearth of cooks. Men who could cook didn't want to admit it, because they had enlisted to fight and not to prepare food for fighters."

The recruit camp at Philadelphia was on League Island, adjacent to the navy yard. The recruits from there marched straight to the 2d and 3d battalions of the 5th Regiment just before the regiment sailed for France.

By July, the population at Paris Island had swollen to fourteen thousand. Most recruits, enlisting in the first flush of patriotism after Wilson's declaration of war, expected a more welcoming site than coastal South Carolina in midsummer. "This island is nothing but sand, sand, sand," wrote Pvt. Sheldon R. Gearhart to his parents in Wilkes-Barre, Pennsylvania. "You can grit your teeth any time, I don't care when, and grate on it. It's in your chow, on the sheets, and in your eyes." Pvt. James T. Hatcher, a Texan, had first tried to enlist in the cavalry but then "fell a willing victim to the marine recruiting sergeant down by the historic old Alamo." Hatcher's arrival at the Port Royal station was a rude shock. "As soon as we stepped off the train we were promptly taken in charge by a busy sergeant of the marines. . . . [W]e did not like that fellow's attitude; he did not show us the courtesy we felt was due young men taking up arms to 'make the world safe for democracy.'"

When war was declared, Martin "Gus" Gulberg was a shipping clerk in Chicago. Six weeks later he enlisted in the Marine Corps and was marched with about ninety others to the Union Depot for a two-day rail trip to Paris Island, South Carolina. He arrived at Port Royal on May 25 and was taken by navy cutter to the island. Next day his first meal, in a mess tent, was salmon salad ("gold fish, army style"), applesauce, bread, and muddy coffee. Processing took three days. Gulberg was assigned to Company 34-N; Sergeant "Hard-boiled Mac" McFellan was in charge.

At first McFellan's recruits lived in tents and slept on cots without mattresses or pillows. The days were hot and the drilling strenuous. Punishment for minor offenses was severe. A dropped rifle meant finding and picking up a thousand burnt matches. Another punishment was to carry bucketsful of seashells from the beach a mile away to surface the company streets. On June 23 Gulberg's company moved into real barracks with spring beds, mattresses, and pillows. In back of each bunkhouse was a washhouse with shower baths and tanks for washing clothes. Most of the training was close-order drill. There were also vaccinations and shots for typhoid.

Rifle Marksmanship Training

Marksmanship proficiency had become a primary Marine Corps virtue since the turn of the century. Long-range rifle accuracy had improved dramatically when the hard-hitting, Mauser-type, caliber .30-06 Springfield M1903 bolt-action rifle began replacing the Krag-Jorgensen in 1906. The Corps completed the rearming process by 1912. Firing for initial qualification or annual requalification became almost an obsession. As incentives there were silver badges and shooter's pay: five dollars a month for those qualifying as expert, three dollars for sharpshooter, two dollars for marksman. Marines called it "beer money," although temperance-minded Josephus Daniels was doing his best to dry up the camps and their surroundings.

It was a measure of the Marines' devotion to marksmanship that despite the pressure to process thousands of new recruits for overseas combat in rapid order the Corps still committed two full weeks of its nine-week recruit curriculum to rifle training. The large influx of recruits severely taxed available rifle-range facilities. Most of the recruit firing was done at Paris Island, Mare Island, and Winthrop, Maryland. Some shooting was also done at the Wakefield range in Massachusetts and the navy ranges at Virginia Beach, Virginia, and Charleston, South Carolina. To the consternation of General Barnett the percentage of recruits qualifying with the rifle as marksmen or higher fell off. By the end of June 1917, with a total of 10,093 Marines firing, the percentage had fallen from 59.5 percent in 1916 to 37.9 percent, an unacceptable dilution of fundamental combat skills.

Private Gulberg's company moved to the rifle range on July 9. The recruits were put to "snapping in"—dry shooting with empty chambers. They learned the shooting positions: standing, kneeling, sitting, and prone; they learned how to set their sights, how to use their rifle slings, both "hasty" and "deliberate." There were hours of lining up a sight picture and squeezing the trigger. "Squeeze it gentle," said the range coach. "Just like you were squeezing your girlfriend's tittie."

"Live firing" with real ammunition began on July 20 and, on the 25th and 26th Gulberg's company shot for record. The wind was blowing hard. Gulberg did poorly on the two-hundred-yard slow-fire kneeling and the five-hundred-yard rapid fire but still shot a score of 222 out of a possible 300, barely qualifying as a "marksman."

Helped by the likes of Private Gulberg and his line coaches, Corps shooting began to return to prewar standards. By August 1917, with a cumulative total for the year of 13,819 shooters, the percentage of qualifiers had climbed to 46.2 percent.

From Boot Camp to Quantico

Gulberg and his company left Paris Island on August 13, 1917, for the overnight train ride to Quantico for advanced military training in preparation for the war in France.

Pvt. James Hatcher's view of boot camp mellowed in time. "After three months on the sun-baked sand dunes of Paris Island," he recalled, "the hard work and close attention to detail demanded by our instructors had transformed us from a group of sallow-faced 'boots' to a snappy drill company, ready for advanced training." His company boarded a lighter for the trip up the coast to the new Marine base at Quantico, where they joined the 84th Company, and eventually the 3d Battalion, 6th Regiment of Marines.

A new rank of "private, first class" was authorized in the fall of 1917 so that the grade and pay structure of the Marine Corps would be the same as that for the infantry in the army as established a year earlier. The chevron was a single stripe. Old-timers lamented that the new grade made obsolete the hoary practice of naming a private performing the duties of a corporal a "lance corporal."[6]

The standard and best-known Marine Corps uniform was the blue uniform of the nineteenth century. But by 1917 that uniform had become the "dress blues," issued only to seagoing detachments and other special posts and stations. Recruits arriving at Paris and Mare islands in the spring and early summer of 1917 were lucky to receive an issue of expeditionary khaki, cotton trousers, cotton or wool flannel shirt, and a broad-brimmed hat. Khaki had come in for tropical use during the Spanish-American War. There was a khaki coat with a standing collar, but few if any of the new recruits received it. The hat, properly a "field hat," but more often called a "campaign hat," was a new model introduced in 1912. The soft hat with the fore-and-aft crease had been replaced with a hat made with a stiffer felt, a narrower brim, and a four-dent "Montana peak" crown. The same year saw the introduction of a forest-green winter service uniform, blouse and breeches made of fuzzy wool kersey (a more elegant serge or "elastique" for officers). By the end of summer recruits would get this uniform, if not at boot camp, at least before they left Quantico for France.

The 6th Regiment of Marines

The final echelon of the Marines that had shipped out in midsummer 1917 with Colonel Doyen was the 5th Regiment Base Detachment, organized at Quantico under the command of Lt. Col. Hiram I. "Hike 'em" Bearss, one of the Corps' already legendary leaders, whose exploits in the Philippines were widely known. Intended as a replacement draft, the organization of the 5th Regiment Base Detachment was virtually identical with that of the new wartime infantry battalions—four rifle companies and a machine-gun company, 1,200 Marines in all. In late July, Bearss and his battalion left Quantico for France by way of Philadelphia.

Barnett and Lejeune feared that the army would find no place for a separate regiment, such as the 5th Marines, except as line-of-communications troops in the rear echelon, so they prevailed upon Daniels to get the president's approval for a full brigade of Marines to be part of the AEF.

Lejeune set his heart on commanding the expeditionary brigade that he thought should be sent to France, and he began earmarking regimental commanders and staff officers. He wrote to Smedley Butler in Haiti, asking if he wanted to go with him, presumably to command of one of the regiments. Butler, of course, responded with an enthusiastic yes.

In July, Secretary Daniels, pursuing the objective of a Marine brigade, offered Secretary of War Baker another regiment of Marines for service in France. The offer was accepted, and on July 26 the 6th Regiment of Marines was activated at Quantico under command of Col. Albertus W. Catlin, with Lt. Col. Harry Lee as his second in command. Majors Thomas Holcomb, Bertron W. Sibley, and John A. Hughes became battalion commanders.

Catlin, born in New York State in 1868, had gone in 1886 from Minnesota to the Naval Academy, where he was halfback on the football team for three years and captain of the team his last year. After graduating in 1890 and spending the customary two years at sea as a passed midshipman he chose a commission in the Marine Corps in 1892. As a first lieutenant he commanded the Marine detachment in the battleship *Maine,* surviving her sinking in Havana Harbor in 1898. Catlin's conspicuous valor in command of a composite regiment of fleet Marines at Veracruz in 1914 resulted in his being awarded the Medal of Honor. As a colonel, he graduated from the Army War College a month after the war began. In 1917, at age forty-nine, he was a powerfully built man (admitting to 215 pounds), of medium height and with iron gray hair. An admirer said that he had "face as weak and effeminate as Plymouth Rock" and that it was largely jaw.

The regiment's second in command, Lieutenant Colonel Lee, had come down to Quantico on August 1 from Portsmouth, New Hampshire, where he had commanded the Naval Prison. The troops called him "Light Horse Harry," but the rumor that he was a direct descendent of the Light Horse Harry Lee of Revolutionary War fame was unfounded. Born in Georgetown, District of Columbia, in 1872, Lee had nearly seven years service, 1892 to 1898, in the D.C. National Guard before being commissioned a second lieutenant in the Marine Corps in August 1898. He was of stocky build and had a strong nose, a rather imperious manner, and a reputation as something of a boxer and wrestler. Early in the century he had expeditionary service in the Philippines and had been with the Legation Guard in Peking. Also behind him was service in the Caribbean, where he had smelled gunpowder at Coyopete, Nicaragua, in 1912 and in minor altercations in Cuba, Haiti, and Santo Domingo. There had been sea duty in a string of battleships including the *Wisconsin, New Hampshire,* and *Louisiana* and time spent afloat with troops in the transport *Hancock.*

Compared to the 5th Regiment, the 6th Regiment had only a handful of old salts. Sergeants, gunnery sergeants, first sergeants, quartermaster sergeants, and sergeants major were brought in from wherever they could be found. The privates, for the most part, came straight from Paris Island or Mare Island. "In consequence," said Lejeune, "the Sixth Regiment had a somewhat different character from the Fifth Regiment. There were very few old-timers. Its early training was, therefore, somewhat more difficult, but it soon found itself, and when the stress of battle came no difference between the two Regiments could be perceived by unprejudiced eyes. Both were unsurpassed. So it was, too, with the Sixth Machine Gun Battalion."

Training Officers at Quantico

At the war's beginning, the sources of Marine Corps officers, in apparent descending order, were graduates of the Naval Academy, meritorious noncommissioned officers, the Marine Corps Reserve, the Marine Corps Branch of the National Naval Volunteers, and civil life.

The Marine Officers' School reopened at Norfolk, Virginia, at the outbreak of the war with a class of thirty-two student officers going through a very quick course. This did not work out well, and the Marines moved the school to Quantico and expanded its student body to six hundred. Length of the course was originally to be a leisurely twelve months. The first class began instruction on July 15, 1917, comprising entirely meritorious noncommissioned officers and graduates of colleges in which military training had formed part of the instruction. Training consisted primarily of military topography, military engineering, applied minor tactics, the principles of open warfare—all of which were traditional—and then something new: "an intensive application of the principles of modern trench warfare, simulating as closely as possible the conditions with which our allies are confronted on the European front."

The first class, at what was also called the "Officers Camp of Instruction," consisted of 345 new lieutenants divided into four companies. The planned twelve-month course of instruction was compressed into three months.

One of the new second lieutenants was Clifton Bledsoe Cates of Tiptonville, Tennessee. The twenty-five-year-old lieutenant had gone to the Missouri Military Academy and then to the University of Tennessee, where he received his bachelor of laws degree in 1916. He was studying for the bar when war was declared and had reported for active duty at Paris Island on June 13, 1917. After two weeks, much of it spent in close-order drill or on the rifle range, none of which he thought was much good, he was sent to the Officers' School at Quantico. More than half his time in Officers' School, or so he claimed, was spent learning Morse code and semaphore, neither of which would prove of more than incidental use to a second lieutenant. There was also a great deal of close-order drill and digging of trenches. The Scottish and Canadian instructors, there for trench warfare instruction, scared Cates and his classmates to death with stories of gas warfare. "If you get one sniff of mustard gas," they were told, "you'll die."

The "bible" for training infantry officers was the slim, blue-bound *Infantry Drill Regulations, 1911,* "corrected to April 15, 1917," and made small so that it would fit into a shirt or tunic pocket. The Marines skipped lightly over much of "Part I—Drill" of the IDR, because their close-order drill, slightly different, was set forth in the navy's *Landing Party Manual.* The instructions for "bugle signals" to be used on the battlefield probably gave them pause. There were three prescribed calls: "Fix bayonets," "Charge," and "Assemble, march." Bugle calls for "Commence firing" and "Cease firing" were reserved for "exceptional cases" and were not to be used by units smaller than a regiment. Whistle signals were for the use of platoon and squad leaders. A short blast from the platoon leader's whistle was to gain the squad leaders' attention; a long blast meant "suspend firing." All other whistle signals were prohibited. Arm signals were provided for nearly every exigency of the battlefield from "Forward, march" to "Swing the cone of fire to the right, or left." Company musicians were to be equipped with signal flags and taught two-armed semaphore to be used—when they were not bugling—to send such useful messages as "Artillery fire is causing us losses."[7]

"The advance of a company into an engagement," said the IDR, "is conducted in close order, preferably in column of squads, until the probability of encountering hostile fire makes it advisable to deploy." Also, prophetically, "The advance in a succession of thin lines is used to cross a wide stretch swept, or likely to be swept, by artillery fire or heavy, long-range rifle fire which cannot be profitably returned." Nothing is said here about machine guns, but much later in the manual there is a section entitled "Miscellaneous" that begins: "Machine guns must be considered as weapons of emergency. Their effectiveness combined with their mobility renders them of great value at critical, though infrequent, periods of an engagement."

Graves B. Erskine arrived at Quantico on July 5 with a probationary commission. Erskine had just passed his twentieth birthday and was freshly graduated from Louisiana State University. He had worked his way through LSU, in part by joining the National Guard, and had served as a sergeant trumpeter with the 1st Louisiana Volunteers on the Mexican border. His grandfather had been a fiery Confederate, seriously wounded in the Civil War. His father was a dirt farmer. The tall Louisianan's southern accent was so thick that most of his classmates in Officers' School professed that they could not understand him. Erskine did not think much of the instruction he was getting and attempted to resign his commission so as to go to Canada to join the Black Watch. Lt. Col. Presley M. Rixey, by then the commanding officer of the Officers' School, did not bother to forward his request.

The first class was to graduate in October, but many of its members were pulled out early to provide platoon leaders for the new 6th Regiment. On August 28, Cates was ordered to report to the 96th Company, which was being activated that day, of the 2d Battalion, 6th Regiment. Cates was given the 4th Platoon. Capt. Donald Duncan was the company commander and FDR's friend Maj. Thomas Holcomb the battalion commander.

Holcomb had been sent down to Quantico in August from headquarters, specifically to take command of a battalion in the 6th Regiment. Behind him, in addition to his involvement in rifle marksmanship, were tours in the Philippines and in China, where, attached to the Legation Guard in Peking, he had been a Chinese-language student.

Erskine was detailed to the 79th Company, then forming, another unit of Holcomb's 2d Battalion, 6th Marines.

Most of the first graduates of the Officers' School would be used to flesh out the platoon leader ranks of the new regiments being formed, but some would go into Marine aviation. Walter S. Poague was one of these. Twenty-six years old, he had graduated from the University of Chicago in 1914. At the war's beginning he was the manager of the real estate mortgage department of a bank. He was also something of a poet and writer of short stories and plays, one of the latter, "Who's Looney Now?" having been produced regionally. Poague had barely heard of the Marines. He had never seen one. A friend who was joining told him that they did something on ships and were "first to fight." That sounded good to Poague. When he left home on June 20 for Quantico, his father said to him, "Well, son, you're going to war now. Be true. Don't ever do anything to disgrace the name."

The 1st Machine Gun Battalion was activated, under Maj. Edward B. Cole, on August 17 with two companies, the 77th and 81st, and a complement of sixteen Lewis guns. Two more companies were added later. They trained initially under British instructors brought over from France. Cole, the leading machine-gun expert in the Corps, was the ideal choice to command the new battalion.

Intensified Training

All summer long the air at Quantico was filled with the sound of thudding hammers and the whine of saws and the resinous smell of fresh-cut yellow pine. Construction was of the simplest possible type, but the buildings were screened and double floored. The "barracks," although little more than long, low huts, housed fifty men each. Every company had its own mess hall, galley, and washhouse. By late summer a camp capable of holding seven thousand men had been built. The reservation, now totaling six thousand acres, included provision for both a small-arms and field-artillery range. In late summer 1917, the Marines abandoned the range at Winthrop and moved its equipment across the Potomac River to the new range at Quantico.

Pvt. Gus Gulberg, on arriving at Quantico from Parris Island, was assigned to the 80th Company, 2d Battalion, 6th Marines. Training was mostly in trench warfare, with emphasis on the use of the bayonet. "This war business began to grow more and more serious," Gulberg wrote in his diary.

The Marine Corps, growing rapidly, activated the 7th Regiment at the same time as the 6th, but it was an old-style, 1,100-man, expeditionary regiment destined for duty in Cuba under command of Col. M. J. Shaw. Ostensibly it was going to Cuba because of good training facilities there. Actually, it was being sent to protect the sugar harvest from revolutionary unrest, fomented, it was believed, by German agents.

The 8th and 9th regiments were formed in the fall of 1917 for service with the Advance Base Force as counters to the fears, unfounded in retrospect, that the German High Seas Fleet would somehow break loose and descend on the Caribbean or that there would be further German-fomented troubles with Mexico. Col. Lawrence H. Moses took command of the 8th Regiment in November and, with forty officers and 1,200 Marines, moved to Galveston, Texas, where his regiment would be poised for any disturbances that might threaten the flow of oil from Mexican oil fields. The 9th Regiment, under Col. Frederick L. Bradman, joined the 7th Regiment, already in Cuba, where they were brigaded together in the 3d Marine Brigade under Col. James E. Mahoney.

One of the new lieutenants, John H. Craige, arriving in August 1917, retained an indelible first impression of Quantico. "In the area of the Marines' reservation," he said in a later interview, "there was not a single brick or stone building except the old hotel, a relic dating back almost to the Civil War. . . . Only a few fathoms of concrete had been laid on Barnett Avenue destined to be Quantico's Main Street. . . . Everywhere else was mud, a slippery, red, gumbo-like variety, into which the foot sank ankle-deep after a rain."

Maj. Smedley Butler, newly arrived from Haiti and saltier than ever, observed, "Quantico . . . was then little more than a filthy swamp."

Butler's assessment rang true. Mosquitoes were a big problem. Hundreds of Marines worked at filling in swampy areas and spraying with oil. Another immediate problem was sanitation. There was no sewer system or provision for garbage disposal. Burying of garbage in large pits was tried, and so were various kinds of incinerators. Pits could not be dug as fast as the garbage accumulated. Moving the garbage by lighter down river and dumping it was not popular with Virginia authorities. Finally a huge incinerator was built. At first all potable water had to be hauled in by cart.

The summer of 1917 at Quantico was one of the hottest on record. The red mud, when it dried out, generated dense clouds of red dust. Most of the acreage was in cornfields or second-growth Virginia woods. Only along the river was it particularly flat and good for such things as drill fields and tent camps. The hotel on the hill, built in the 1880s, was one of the few places within thirty or so miles offering accommodations. It became Marine Corps property in 1918 and was used as a club and as bachelor officers' quarters. Generations of Marines to come would remember it as the "Waller Building."[8]

Lejeune Takes Command

With Catlin going to France, there was a need for another senior officer to command at Quantico. Lejeune broached the subject with Barnett of his replacing Catlin, as a first step in going himself to France. There was a stiffish discussion: Barnett wanted him to stay, Lejeune wanted to go. "If you are leaving because you feel that you want to be free to work for appointment as my successor as Commandant when my term expires next February," said Barnett, "I am perfectly willing for you to stay here and do so."

Lejeune vowed that he did not want to be commandant during the war; his one desire was to go to France, and duty with troops at Quantico would prepare him for that. In his opinion, Barnett should continue to serve as commandant for the duration of the war. Barnett said he had no one in mind to relieve Lejeune. Lejeune recommended Squeegee Long, then still in Philadelphia. Somewhat mollified, Barnett approved Lejeune's transfer and brought Long down from Philadelphia to take his place at headquarters.

Lejeune took command at Quantico on September 27, 1917. Later he recalled: "The lack of housing facilities for married officers at Quantico was a serious handicap, as it was necessary for all but a few who obtained rooms at the small hotel there to seek shelter for their families in Fredericksburg, Alexandria, or Washington, and to commute to Quantico. I was one of those who made frequent journeys back and forth to Washington. This custom became very trying during the bitterly cold winter of 1917–18. I never felt colder weather anywhere."

Maj. Pete Ellis, as usual, had accompanied Lejeune to Quantico, to serve as training officer. Also on Lejeune's staff was John Craige, speedily promoted to first lieutenant. Graves Erskine's name came up on the roster as "fire patrol officer," and he was told he should report to the commanding general. With all the éclat he had learned in the Louisiana National Guard he uniformed himself immaculately, reached the doorway of Lejeune's makeshift office, and stood there waiting to be noticed. Lejeune, himself in baggy breeches and dirty puttees, eyed the immaculate fellow Louisianan, let him wait for about five minutes, and then said, "All right, Napoleon, come in and tell me what you want."

Shipping Out the 6th Regiment

By the time of Lejeune's arrival, the 6th Regiment of Marines, Colonel Catlin commanding, was in process of shipping out. Catlin was proud of his new regiment: "The officers, from captain up, and fifty or so of the non-commissioned officers were old-time Marines, but the junior officers and all of the privates were new men." Many of the new men were former college athletes, including the current holder of the world record in the mile run, "Johnny" Overton of Yale.

There were two Overtons who arrived at Quantico that summer as newly minted second lieutenants. One was the runner, John W. Overton of Yale, Class of '17; the other was Macon C. Overton, former corporal, U.S. Marine Corps. The freshly graduated Johnny Overton was a sports celebrity, remembered at Yale as the captain of the track team and an extraordinary runner. Born in Nashville, Tennessee, in 1894, he had won the intercollegiate cross-country championships in 1915 and 1916. At the Meadowbrook Games in Philadelphia in 1917 he set a new indoor record of 4:16 for the mile. After two weeks on the rifle range at Winthrop, he arrived at Quantico on July 18 as a new second lieutenant in the Marine Corps Reserve.

The other Overton, whose nickname for unexplained reasons was "Dick," had enlisted as a private on November 19, 1913. Born in Georgia in 1890, he likewise was something of an athlete, although hardly nationally known, having played second base for the "All-Marine" baseball team in 1916. As a meritorious NCO, he was discharged as a corporal on the 4th of July in 1917 at Marine Barracks, Washington, D.C., and next day was commissioned a provisional second lieutenant in the Marine Corps Reserve and almost immediately assigned to the new 6th Regiment.

On Sunday morning, September 16, the 1st Battalion of the 6th Regiment, under Maj. John A. Hughes, left Quantico by rail and that evening boarded the USS *Henderson* at the Philadelphia Navy Yard. A navy band serenaded them with march music as they went up the gangplank. On the top deck a covey of Red Cross girls cheered them enthusiastically. The *Henderson* reached New York the following day and spent the next six days swinging at anchor while the convoy was being made up. Sailing for Europe was on Sunday, September 23.

Colorful, short-tempered "Johnny the Hard" Hughes was already a legend in the Corps. The thirty-seven-year-old Brooklyn native had enlisted in 1900 and had been commissioned from the ranks (with Pete Ellis) a year later. He had fought in the bush wars of the Philippines, Panama, Cuba, and Nicaragua in the first decade of the new century, had received a Medal of Honor for Veracruz in 1914, and had been severely wounded in Santo Domingo in 1916.

Hughes assigned Dick Overton to the 76th Company. Johnny Overton, helping with the physical training program, would stay on at Quantico until February 1918, when he would sail with the 119th Replacement Company.

Colonel Catlin, with his regimental headquarters, his supply company, and his 73d (Machine Gun) Company sailed for France on October 16 in the *De Kalb.* "The crossing was no easy matter," remembered Catlin.

Maj. Bertron W. Sibley's 3d Battalion, 6th Regiment, left Quantico next and sailed on October 30 in the *Von Steuben.* The thin, handsome Sibley, one of those experienced officers who arrived at Quantico in August for duty with the 6th Regiment, had served in the 1st Vermont Infantry in the Spanish-American War. Commissioned in the Marine Corps in July 1900, he subsequently saw service in such places as Cuba, the Philippines, and China.

Embarked as a passenger in the *Von Steuben,* headed for France along with the 3d Battalion, 6th Regiment of Marines, was a slender, sharp-faced North Carolinian, Lt. Col. William Belo Lemly. Born in 1875 and a Marine officer since 1899, Lemly was Brigadier General McCawley's senior assistant quartermaster. With the organization of a Marine brigade imminent, Barnett and McCawley were sending Lemly to France as a fact finder with respect to supply and material matters. Lemly left Washington with the understanding that before he was to return to the States, the Marines in France would be concentrated, "the two marine regiments with the 9th and 23d Infantries, and other necessary organizations, to form the Second Division, American Expeditionary Forces."

A Letter from General Pershing

There had been rumblings of discontent coming back to Marine headquarters from France over Pershing's use of the 5th Marines as line of communication troops, so much so that Pershing apparently felt it diplomatic to write Barnett a personal letter:

> Dear General Barnett:
> Your Marines having been under my command for nearly six months, I feel that I can give you a discriminating report as to their excellent standing with their brothers of the Army and their general good conduct. I take this opportunity also, of giving you the reasons for distributing them along our Line of Communication which, besides being a compliment to their high state of discipline and excellent soldierly appearance, was the natural thing to do as the Marine Regiment was an additional one in the Division and not provided for in the way of transportation and fighting equipment in case the Division should be pushed to the front. When, therefore, service of the rear troops and military and provost guards were needed at our base ports and in Paris it was the Marine Regiment that had to be scattered, in an endeavor to keep the rest of the organized division intact.
>
> I have been obliged to detach a number of your officers as assistant provost marshals in France and in England, all of which I take it you will agree with me was highly complimentary to both officers and men, and was so intended. I can assure you that as soon as our service of the rear troops arrive, including a large number of officers and men for the specific duties now being performed by your men, the Marines will be brought back once more under your brigade commander and assigned to the duties which they so much desire in the Second Regular Division, under General Bundy.

General Pershing ended his letter with a flourish: "It is a great pleasure to report on your fine representatives in France. With expressions of my highest esteem, I am, sincerely yours, John J. Pershing."[9]

The letter no doubt heightened Barnett's anxiety to ship a second fully manned and ready regiment to France to form the Marine brigade as soon as possible. It helped that the vanguard division that went with Pershing was still undergoing advanced training and not as yet committed to combat on the western front. Unlike the 5th Marines, who deployed essentially intact, Barnett had to dispatch the 6th Regiment in increments, by battalions.

Last to Go

John W. Thomason Jr. was one of the new lieutenants converging on Quantico for the next session of the Marine Officers' School. He came from Charleston, South Carolina, where he had been on active duty since almost the outbreak of the war.

Thomason, born in Huntsville in 1893, came from an old and warlike Texas family. His grandfather on his mother's side had been a major on James Longstreet's staff. He taught young John to ride, hunt, and fish and filled him with tales of the Confederacy. His father was a doctor, a deacon in the Methodist Church, and a prohibitionist. Dr. Thomason also had a large library, and it was his habit in the evening to read aloud to his family. Early in life, young John got liberal doses of the King James Bible, Shakespeare, Scott, Hugo, Balzac, Dumas, and others, including Kipling—particularly Kipling. From early on, he liked to sketch and to draw. He drew wherever he was and with whatever was at hand, most often with pen, pencil, or charcoal, but sometimes watercolors. By the time he was twenty-one he had gone to three colleges with mixed success, had finally been certified as a teacher, and had done some teaching in country schools.

But Thomason wanted to be an artist, not a teacher. With his mother's connivance, his disapproving father agreed to a year at the Art Students League in New York City. During this year in New York, World War I began in Europe. Thomason returned to Texas and found a job as a cub reporter with the *Houston Chronicle*. The pay wasn't much, but on the strength of it he proposed to the girl, Leda Bass, who lived next door in Huntsville and whose father ran the Texas state penitentiary.

On the day that war was declared against Germany, Thomason quit the *Chronicle* and walked into a recruiting station that had been set up in the Rice Hotel to enquire about a reserve commission in the Marine Corps. In a fog of confusion he enlisted in the Marine Corps branch of the Texas Naval Militia and set off two days later with a company of militia to Marine Barracks, Charleston, South Carolina. In August he received a bona fide commission in the Marine Corps Reserve. His fiancé was in New York with her parents. They met in Washington and were married. In November he was transferred to the Marine Officers' School at Quantico.

At Quantico, Thomason met Laurence Stallings, a fellow student officer and a kindred spirit. Born in Macon, Georgia, in 1894, Stallings had grown up steeped in the lore of the "War between the States." After three years at Wake Forest College in North Carolina, he had worked on the *Atlanta Journal* as a reporter before being appointed a second lieutenant in the Marine Corps. There had also been some service in the Georgia National Guard.

As Thomason and Stallings worked their way through the accelerated basic course at Marine Officers' School, the frigid winter of 1917 began to set in. A light snow fell, and Lt. Graves Erskine went out in front of his quarters on Barnett Avenue to shovel clear the pathway. Major Holcomb came along and said, "Just what do you think you are doing?"

Erskine replied that he was cleaning off the walk. "Let me tell you something, young man," said Holcomb. "You are a commissioned officer; you get paid to use your brain and not your hands. Now put the shovel away and get an orderly to do it."

Erskine never forgot that lesson.

It was a very cold winter. Temperatures went as low as fourteen degrees below zero. Shells—including giant, 14-inch battleship shells—fired across the river from the Naval Proving Grounds at Indian Head, Maryland, would skip on the frozen surface. Marines would go out on the ice and drag the shells back as decorations to be placed along the company streets. During that cold winter, the 10th Regiment, formed as an artillery outfit, spun off a cadre to form the 11th Marines (Advanced Base Artillery) under Col. George Van Orden.

Quantico became a temperance camp, thanks to Secretary Daniels. The YMCA and Knights of Columbus huts were used to capacity as warm places to write letters and to get coffee, soft drinks, sandwiches, and doughnuts at a small price. The YWCA built a hostess house as lodgings for the visiting families.

Major Cole's machine-gun battalion sailed for France in December. All of Catlin's 6th Regiment was now in France except the 2d Battalion. Major Holcomb's wife was pregnant. A rumor, widely believed, went through the ranks that the battalion would not be sent overseas until the child was born. Coincidence or not, when the child was born the battalion received its sailing orders. Holcomb's 2d Battalion, 6th Regiment, left Quantico on January 18, 1918, for Philadelphia and sailed the next morning in the *Henderson*. It was another rough crossing.

Units were now leaving Quantico for France at the rate of about one battalion a month. After the departure of the last of the 6th Regiment, replacement battalions were sent out at monthly intervals, the first three under Maj. Ralph S. Keyser, Lt. Col. Harold C. Snyder, and Lt. Col. R. P. Williams, respectively.

Williams' 3d Replacement Battalion sailed in April, embarked in the now famous *Henderson*. On board, as members of the battalion, were Lts. John Thomason and Laurence Stallings.

CHAPTER THREE

New Frontiers

T hree weeks after the congressional declaration of war, the U.S. Marines landed in St. Thomas, in the Virgin Islands.[1]

"The natives gazed with wonder and amazement as the Marines landed guns, ammunition, trucks, track, cars, stores and all the Advance Base equipment," wrote Lt. Col. Jay M. Salladay in a 1918 *Marine Corps Gazette*. Eighteen months earlier, as a major, Salladay had commanded the battalion that on April 26, 1917, landed at St. Thomas, one of the three major Virgin Islands, the other two being St. Croix and St. John, just purchased from Denmark for $25 million.

"Our ship, the USS *Prairie*, was 'loaded to the gunwales' when we left Santo Domingo for St. Thomas," Salladay said. "The guns, ammunition, and equipment, trucks, stores, and supplies of all kinds were scattered about the ship in holds, magazines and on deck; two companies for Saint Thomas were on board, bag and baggage; [plus] the signal company from Haiti."

It took Salladay's Marines six days to unload the *Prairie*. Battery emplacements had been picked out, but it was pick-and-shovel work for the Marines to lay the track by which the flatcars, twenty-four of them, would take the guns and equipment to their positions. Salladay established his headquarters at St. Thomas.

One company of Marines was already on St. Croix, having landed as a precautionary measure on March 29. The United States had been thinking about buying the islands, which lay just east of Puerto Rico, since 1867, but it took the war scare that the Germans might use them for a secret submarine base to bring about the purchase. The Danes, clinging to their independence from their hulking neighbor, Germany, were in no position to haggle. The Marines strengthened their shore batteries with the addition of searchlights and such and practiced firing the 5-inch guns, but the German submarines or surface raiders never came.

This was the kind of small operation—the defense of an advance naval base—that the Chief of Naval Operations, Admiral Benson, and Major General Commandant Barnett both understood. Just before the outbreak of the war, the Marines replaced the fixed defense companies in Haiti and Santo Domingo with rifle companies and brought them back to the Philadelphia Navy Yard. Here, as the 1st Marines, they were drilled, under Brig. Gen. Tony Waller and Col. Squeegee Long, as infantry and light and heavy artillery, and in mining, signals, and aviation.

The Advance Base Force at Philadelphia lost sixteen of its 5-inch guns early in 1917, when they went to the arming of merchant ships, but as replacements a like number of 8-inch howitzers were expected from the army in early November. The artillery battalion being trained at Quantico was intended for advance base work, as were the 7th, 8th, and 9th regiments.

In Haiti, the 1st Provisional Brigade of Marines working with the new Garde d'Haiti effectively kept the peace in 1917. In neighboring Santo Domingo, the 2d Provisional Brigade of Marines was by the end of the year optimistically reporting the repression of banditry and the establishment of a fair state of peace and good order after earlier fighting against various "bandit" groups that cost four Marines killed and fifteen wounded. Plans progressed to establish a Guardia Nacional Dominicana along the pattern of the Garde in Haiti. Some six hundred Dominicans were enlisted and twenty officers were appointed from among the officers and NCOs of the brigade. In Cuba, during the first half of 1917, the endemic revolution caused battalion-sized landing parties from the fleet to be put ashore at various places in Oriente and Camaguey provinces and the eventual deployment of the 6th Marine Brigade.

Emerging Capabilities

The Marine Corps found itself changing even before the catalyst of World War I. The previous 140 years' service as shipboard landing parties and naval station security guards had given way to more substantial military proficiencies beyond the beaches. The Marines' role in sustained combat operations ashore in the Philippine Insurrection and the gritty street fighting in Veracruz had disclosed a small but aggressive force of trained riflemen, useful for their readiness as well as their resourcefulness.

The navy's concurrent need for a well-armed advance naval base defense force—spurred by the acquisition of overseas colonies in the Spanish-American War and subsequent competition with the fleets of other colonial powers—provided a viable new mission for the Marine Corps. The Marines gradually developed the doctrine, organization, equipment, and training program to facilitate the advance base mission, but the nature of World War I in 1917–18 offered few opportunities to put it to use. With French ports firmly in Allied hands and strategic priority accorded the western front, there was little need to seize and defend advance naval bases. Navy-Marine operations of this nature that occurred in the Virgin Islands and the Azores were professionally executed but quickly became sideshows.

From the first, the Marine Corps integrated its fledgling air arm into advance base defense planning. A small aeronautical unit formed part of the advance base defense force that deployed to Veracruz in 1914, although finding a ship with the right booms to embark and debark the frail float planes took so long that the fighting had long since ceased when the detachment finally arrived. The lingering crisis in Mexico obscured the arrival of a new, expeditionary aeronautical capability on foreign shores, but the event signified that the Marines were already serious about aviation and advance base operations.

Aviation Pioneers

Four months before the United States entered the war, Marine aviation consisted of just five officers and eighteen enlisted men. Most were in a detachment assigned to the Advance Base Force at Philadelphia Navy Yard. Others were at Pensacola and San Diego. Marine aviation had no organization of its own but was simply part of naval aviation.

In his 1916 annual report, Major General Barnett had informed the secretary of the navy, the abstemious Josephus Daniels, that he planned to organize a "Marine Aviation Company of ten officers and forty men, organized for duty with the Advance Base Force." They were to have both seaplanes and land planes. On February 26, 1917, 1st Lt. Alfred A. Cunningham received orders at the Philadelphia Navy Yard to form the company.

The Atlanta-born Cunningham had served in a volunteer army regiment during the Spanish-American War. After a tour of occupation duty in Cuba he came back, was mustered out, and for the next ten years sold real estate. He made two flights in the wicker basket of a gas-filled balloon in 1903, the same year as the Wright brothers' historic first flight at Kitty Hawk, North Carolina, and landed a "confirmed aeronautical enthusiast."

In 1909, at age twenty-seven, he was commissioned a second lieutenant in the Marine Corps. After two years of routine service ashore and afloat, he was promoted to first lieutenant and transferred to Philadelphia for duty and instruction at the Advance Base School. Intrigued by the possibilities of flight, he joined the Aero Club of Philadelphia and rented at twenty-five dollars a month a supposed flying machine, a pusher-type "aeroplane" (a craft with its engine mounted behind the pilot's seat, "pushing" from behind) with a two-cycle, four-cylinder engine. Cunningham thrashed about on an open field at the Navy Yard but could not get "Noisy Nan," as he called the contraption, off the ground.

"I called her everything in God's name to go up. I pleaded with her. I caressed her. I prayed to her, and I cursed that flighty Old Maid to lift up her skirts and hike, but she never would," said Cunningham.

In May 1912, possibly helped by politically connected friends in the Aero Club, Cunningham received orders to report to the U.S. Naval Aviation Camp at Annapolis "for duty in connection with aviation." He reported on May 22, and the Marine Corps celebrates that day as the birthday of Marine aviation.

From Annapolis Cunningham received further orders to the Burgess Company at Marblehead, Massachusetts, which had airplanes and civilian instructors. After two hours and forty minutes of instruction, Cunningham took off in a hydroplane, circled the bay several times, and came down to a safe landing in the water, becoming the Marine Corps' first aviator.

Between October 1912 and July 1913, Cunningham managed to make almost four hundred flights in the first Wright aircraft purchased by the navy, the B-1 seaplane, or "Bat Boat." It had been wrecked several times before Cunningham got it and rebuilt it again.

"I built it from parts of the Burgess F and the Wright B," wrote Cunningham, "which are not exactly alike and nothing fitted."

First Lt. Bernard L. "Banney" Smith was the second Marine to qualify as an aviator. He had come into the Marine Corps the same year as Cunningham. He arrived at Annapolis in September 1912, and after flight training he, in time, went on the list as "Naval Aviator no. 6." Second Lieutenant William M. "Mac" McIlvain soloed in December 1912 and became Naval Aviator no. 12. The parallel navy and Marine numbers are confusing. Their significance lies in the fact that three of the first dozen naval aviation pioneers were Marine officers.

The navy's "Aviation Camp" at Annapolis, including Cunningham and Banney Smith, went to the annual fleet maneuvers in the Caribbean in January 1913. More than 150 naval and Marine Corps officers, including Lt. Col. John Lejeune, were taken aloft in orientation flights from Guantanamo.[2]

Cunningham's aviation career had an interruption. In August 1913, he requested detachment from flight status: "My fiancée will not consent to marry me unless I give up flying." He was assigned to the Washington Navy Yard for duty and temporarily passed from the Marine Corps aviation scene, such as it was.

In January 1914, the "Marine Section of the Naval Flying School" at Annapolis, consisting of Lieutenants Smith and McIlvain and ten enlisted mechanics, with two pusher aircraft, a Curtiss C-3 flying boat and an Owl amphibian, embarked in the USS *Hancock* to join the Advance Base Brigade at Culebra for the annual Atlantic Fleet exercises. In less than a month Smith and McIlvain logged fifty-two flights.

The Annapolis camp moved to Pensacola, but by the beginning of 1915 the Marine Section was down to one pilot—Mac McIlvain. Banney Smith had been siphoned off for duty with the navy. Cunningham, presumably with his wife's permission, reported in April for refresher training and flight duty. With his seniority he moved to the top of the section.

Naval aviators began training in land planes in August 1915 at the army's Signal Corps Aviation School in San Diego. McIlvain went to the first class, and Cunningham followed him in 1916. For the first time Cunningham flew in a cockpit inside of a fuselage instead of on an open-air seat in front of the wings of a pusher. He later wrote that he would "never forget the feeling of security I felt to have a fuselage around me."

On November 8, 1916, Cunningham was hurled aloft off Pensacola in a Curtiss AB-2 seaplane by a catapult on the stern of the battleship *North Carolina*, possibly the first such catapult shot. The plane flipped over and plunged into the Gulf of Mexico. Cunningham was fished out of the water with an injured back that troubled him for the rest of his life.

Two other Marine Corps officers came into the picture at about this time. First Lts. Francis T. "Cocky" Evans and Roy S. Geiger were the fourth and fifth Marines to qualify as naval aviators.

Cocky Evans had gone to Pensacola for flight training early in the summer of 1915 as a first lieutenant and was already famous in aviation circles. Flying a Curtiss N-9 on February 13, 1917, he attempted a loop, considered impossible with a seaplane, weighted down as it was with heavy pontoons. The N-9 stalled and went into a spin; no American aviator had yet figured out a way to get out of a spin. Instinctively, Evans pushed his control wheel forward to gain speed and kicked his rudder to counter the turning motion. It worked. He repeated the sequence: trying to loop, stalling, spinning, and coming out of the spin. Finally he achieved the loop. To prove his point, he demonstrated the maneuver before an audience. Years later he received a Distinguished Flying Cross for his contribution to the technique and safety of flight.

Roy Geiger was thirty-two in 1917, having left a successful law practice in eastern Florida in 1907 to enlist in the Marines, later earning a commission and leading troops in combat at Coyotepe and Barranca, Nicaragua. He seemed ordained for the barnstorming life of the early Leatherneck aviators. As an eight-year-old adventurer, he had broken his arm trying to "fly" off a roof with turkey wings wired to his wrists. Flying the fragile old "stick and string" aeroplanes with an iron fist, Geiger made up for his lack of finesse with an uncanny sense of navigation. Claimed one longtime crewman, "the Old Man's got homing pigeon blood." Geiger always regarded himself as a line officer additionally qualified as an aviator. No Marine officer, ground or air, could conduct a formal guard mount as smartly as Geiger, who had learned the art as a corporal in the ceremonial platoon at Marine

Barracks, 8th and I ("Eye") streets, in Washington, D.C., and as a captain commanding the Mounted Detachment at the Marine Legation in Peking, China.

By the summer of 1917 and with America at war, Cunningham found himself straddling two missions. Originally, the Aviation Company at Philadelphia, redesignated as the Marine Aeronautic Company, was to train in seaplanes for antisubmarine patrols. But now Barnett had secured tentative approval for the creation of a Marine squadron to provide reconnaissance and artillery spotting for the Marine brigade that was about to be organized in France. This new squadron, authorizing eleven officers and 178 men and roughly patterned after the army squadrons then being organized, was to have six fighter planes, six reconnaissance planes, and four kite balloons. The Army Signal Corps was to furnish most of the equipment and training.

To fill his two embryonic and very different units Cunningham screened the officer candidates flooding into Quantico. There were plenty of volunteers. One was Karl Day, who later recalled: "[Captain Cunningham] told us that we were going to have an aviation section, that we would go to France, and that he was down there to talk to anybody who was interested in becoming a pilot."

Lawson H. M. Sanderson, a former University of Montana football star who played on the Mare Island Marines team that won the wartime-constrained 1918 Rose Bowl, also volunteered: "Well, hell, I thought I can ride better than I can walk. So I volunteered for aviation. . . . I'd only seen about two airplanes in my life, but I'd rather ride than walk."

Another of the new lieutenants recruited by Cunningham was the young banker and aspiring playwright Walter Poague from Chicago, who would join the Marine Aeronautic Company.

Altogether Cunningham took eighteen of these newly commissioned second lieutenants. They became members of something called the "Marine Corps Reserve Flying Corps," which had been authorized in the all-encompassing Naval Appropriation Act of 1916.

By October 14, 1917, the loosely knit assemblage had begun flight training at Philadelphia in two Curtiss R-6 seaplanes and an antiquated Farman land plane. On that date the aggregation split firmly into the two planned aviation units. The 1st Aeronautic Company, ten officers and ninety-three men, would continue to train in seaplanes for the antisubmarine missions. The 1st Aviation Squadron, twenty-four officers and 237 men, would prepare itself to support the brigade that was being formed in France.

The 1st Marine Aeronautic Company, commanded by Cocky Evans, now a captain, moved with the two Curtiss R-6s to Naval Air Station, Cape May, New Jersey, to continue its training in coastal patrolling. Despite its inauspicious beginning, Evans' small company would become the first Marine force to conduct combat operations in Europe.

Mission to the Azores

The British had been guarding the Portuguese-owned Azores islands in the mid-Atlantic (about 970 miles due west of Lisbon) against their possible use as German submarine bases. They turned over the task to the U.S. Navy in September 1917. A couple of U.S. cruisers and a few submarines were based at Punta Delgado. The Portuguese lightly defended the harbor. In December the navy decided to develop it as an advance base and tasked the Marine Corps with its shore-based defense.

General Barnett alerted the 1st Marine Aeronautic Company, under Cocky Evans, to prepare for a move to the Azores. A seacoast artillery detachment of two 7-inch guns was formed at Philadelphia under the command of Capt. Maurice G. "Don Mauricio" Holmes. Evans' 1st Marine Aeronautic Company and Holmes' seacoast artillery battery went on board the transport *Hancock,* docked in Philadelphia, on December 29, 1917.

Sailing was delayed. Lieutenant Poague used his theater-circuit connections to introduce Captain Holmes to the actress Forrest Winant, and the three had dinner at the Ritz the night of January 3. Poague and Holmes then saw the play *Turn to the Right,* in which Miss Winant was appearing. Afterward the threesome and another "pretty little actress" went out on the town. Next day Holmes and Poague had the two actresses on board the *Hancock* for lunch and a tour of the ship, an occasion the crew and Marines likely appreciated more than the visitors.

The *Hancock* finally sailed on January 9, 1918, dropping down the Delaware and passing Cape May at 4:30 in the afternoon. The seas were rough, and there was the usual sighting of a periscope, which in this case turned out to be a barrel. Two weeks later they arrived at Punta Delgado.

"First impressions are charming—verdant, precipitous hills, a half-moon harbor, white houses with tiled roofs," Lieutenant Poague told his dairy. "I am going to love this place."

Before long he would change his mind.

Captain Holmes mounted a 7-inch gun on each side of the entrance to the harbor. Evans' company began flying antisubmarine patrols on Saturday, February 16. "Crowds lined the streets, docks, water front and house tops," wrote Poague. "A municipal holiday was declared, quite a grand occasion."

Poague's own first flight in the Azores, an hour-long hop, occurred five days later. "It is now two and a half months since I have flown, and yet the former control came to me as easily as ever," he wrote in his diary. "Flying is like swimming, I am sure, or skating, or riding a bicycle, in that once it is learned and the muscles become adapted, it is never forgotten."

Operating eighteen floatplanes and flying boats, the company worked up to thirty-two scouting flights a week. Submarine sightings, expected daily, proved to be extremely rare. Poague flew most often with Lt. Harvey B. Mims. Off-duty hours he spent as often as he could horseback riding in the hills. He soon became bored: "The Azores, peaceful and pleasant, are stifling."

On February 27 Mims and Poague came into the bay at a hundred miles an hour, too fast for a landing, and, facing a rock cliff, nearly side-slipped into the dock. "A close shave—exciting and a lot of fun," wrote Poague.

The admiral commanding the Azores advance base directed Poague to work up a vaudeville show to benefit the Portuguese Red Cross. "It will be great fun to get among the drops again and with the odor of greasepaint," wrote Poague. Almost in the same breath he told his diary, "Our first smash-up occurred when Mims wrecked a new N-9 (100 H.P.) at sea. He had a fist full of alibis and deserted the plane rather than get wet."

The vaudeville show was given on April 6, and Poague considered the whole performance a glorious success, particularly when an attractive woman, draped in the American flag, sang the national anthem.

On May 23, Captain Evans tested Poague for his naval aviator's wings. The test consisted of landing in a rough sea and getting away again. Poague plowed into a buoy, which took the bottom off one of his pontoons, but he got aloft. As he wheeled over the beach where his company commander was standing, the water spilled out of the back of the pontoon and drenched Evans. Evans passed him anyway. The final test came on June 4: Poague had to spiral down from three thousand feet and land within 150 feet of a target ten feet square. He made it.

A few days later the Marines in the Azores learned that a huge battle (Belleau Wood) was raging in France. "The two regiments of Marines have lived up to the best of our traditions," Poague told his diary. His subsequent notes reflected the exaggerated preliminary rumors of that day ("scuttlebutt" in navy-Marine lingo): "Six thousand Marines officially are credited with taking 6 miles by 2½ of trenches from 30,000 Germans and another 30,000 Huns were called to stop them. It is as I expected. We have the finest body of fighting men in the world."

On June 19, 2d Lt. Rollins "Rollie" Harger went down in the water twelve kilometers out. Capt. David Brewster, Poague, and a doctor sped to the rescue in a fast motorboat. Harger was unhurt; the plane was a wreck. To salvage the engine, Poague dived down about twenty-five feet to put a line around the propeller hub. He was cut up quite badly and afterward bled at the mouth and nose, but the line held. They towed the machine onto the beach, where the engine and instruments could be salvaged.

The Spanish influenza reached the Azores in early July. Brewster, Boynton, and Poague were among those taken sick. The hospital was under canvas, with the patients held in tents. A tame rabbit there pleased Poague. He recovered and got back to flying. On July 23 he set two island flying records, a flight of two hours seven minutes' duration and an altitude of 6,300 feet. Half the officers of the company, including Evans, left the camp that night to return to the States, where it was presumed they would be instructors or cadre for new flying companies.

On September 2, three beautiful new Curtiss HS-2L flying boats, with seventy-four-foot wingspans, telephones between pilot and gunner, and four-hundred-mile cruising ranges, arrived. They had come, in Poague's opinion, just in time. The old machines, he wrote, were "utterly rotten." His joy was short-lived. The new planes had arrived without their 12-cylinder, 360-horsepower Liberty engines. Next day, a promotion to first lieutenant made him feel better.

On Sunday, September 8, Poague noted in his diary that he had made over a hundred flights. He now seldom mentioned his flying in his diary—"Flying is too monotonous, too repetitious to be entered."

Poague was now flying with GySgt. Walter B. Ziegler as his mechanic and gunner. On September 11 they got a clear sight of a submarine, or so they thought, at about sixty feet depth. They let go a bomb, but it failed to explode. On the following day they had a motor failure and had to make a forced landing, setting down in a rough sea. "Not a thing broken!" crowed Poague.

There was a stunt that Poague and Ziegler had wanted to try, exchanging places while in midair. On Saturday, September 28, they did it at "a thousand feet above the sea with the most glorious sunset of flame and purple" as a backdrop. Poague missed his footing and hung by his hands over the sea until he could work his way back into the aircraft.

Poague's nerves were beginning to fray. He wasn't sleeping well. On Wednesday, October 9, he and Ziegler took off at sundown for a flight in "old 328, which was on its last legs." The plane lost power at twenty-five feet. Poague slewed it over on its side to avoid hitting a buoy, and it went into the water at sixty-five miles per hour, taking off the pontoons, wings, and propeller. Ziegler and Poague got off with nothing worse than an unscheduled swim.

All now knew that Germany was about to cave in. On October 16 Poague told his diary: "I am cheated out of action if this war is called off." He had a touch more of influenza. By October 21, of the seventy remaining members of the company, all but twelve were in the hospital with the disease. Flight operations ceased. "The Portuguese are dying like flies, daily more," wrote Poague.

A well-liked corporal, "Daddy" Evans, died on October 25. Next day Poague commanded the escort at his funeral. More were to die. The last entry in Poague's diary is for October 27 and ends with: "Where have they gone? Why were they here? What is it all about?"

On November 5, 1918, less than a week before Armistice Day on the western front, Poague and Zeigler started out on a sunrise patrol, taking off in a downwind of twenty-five miles per hour. Poague got up to flying speed with difficulty. His pontoons caught on the crest of a wave. The plane turned over twice. Poague and Ziegler were left hanging head down under water. Ziegler kicked his way free and found "Mr. Poague" crushed between the top wing and cockpit. Ziegler somehow got him loose and held him afloat until a fishing boat picked them up, but his pilot was dead. "On Nov. 5 I can say I lost the best friend I had in the U.S.M.C.," Ziegler later wrote to Poague's father.

Poague had said many times that he did not want to be buried in the Azores. All the caskets made up of sheet lead had been used up because of the influenza epidemic. The company's metalsmiths made him a coffin of the copper used to tip the wooden propellers. The navy doctor embalmed the body. The Portuguese Red Cross gave him a posthumous certificate of merit and a medal for his work with the vaudeville show.

As it turned out, the only enemies faced by the 1st Marine Aeronautic Company and the advance base force coastal artillery detachment were boredom and Spanish influenza. Many Marines, like Lieutenant Poague, felt "cheated out of the action" by the scarcity of German U-boats or sea raiders in the Azores. As one crewman, Cpl. Christian F. Schilt, recalled the experience at the end of a distinguished forty-year career in Marine aviation, "We saw a few [submarines] out there; in fact we dropped a few bombs, but as far as we know we didn't damage anything." Yet the Leathernecks' willingness to undertake naval combat missions in foreign waters on short notice bolstered their claim of "First to Fight" and helped Marine aviation survive the postwar downsizing that ensued.

Forming the Northern Bombing Group

Under an agreement reached between Captain Cunningham and Col. Henry H. "Hap" Arnold of the Army Signal Corps, the 1st Aviation Squadron was to train at Hazlehurst (later Roosevelt) Field at Mineola, Long Island. Then it was to move to the army's advance school of flying at Houston, Texas. After this, "the Squadron will . . . be ready for service in France and the Army will completely equip it with the same technical equipment furnished their squadrons." So reported Cunningham to Barnett on October 10, 1917.

The 1st Aviation Squadron, under Capt. Mac McIlvain, moved to Mineola on October 17 and went into tents near the runway. Flight instruction was in Curtiss JN-4B Jennies with civilian instructors, not all of whom were satisfactory. Karl Day remembered that one instructor "was scared to death. He wouldn't let anybody touch the controls. I had four or five rides with him, and he never once let me touch the throttle, the wheel, or touch the rudder. So we raised hell about him, and he got fired."

Cunningham's motley force was also to have a balloon contingent, useful for peering over the lines on the western front and adjusting artillery fire. In November a detachment of six officers went to Fort Omaha, Nebraska, to learn the elements of aerial observation. Capt. Roy Geiger found he loved the freedom and silence of ballooning. Restless for action and impatient to experience aerial combat in any form, Geiger volunteered for temporary duty as a U-boat spotter in late 1917, riding a kite balloon tethered to the battleship *North Carolina* while escorting a convoy across the North Atlantic.

Cunningham himself left for France in November to pin down a definite mission for the Marine Corps squadron intended for Europe. Cunningham visited French and British air bases and flight schools and managed to fly on several missions over the German lines. Relations with the U.S. Army were less cordial. Cunningham tried to extract a promise that the Marine squadron would be attached to the Marine brigade, but in his postwar words, the army aviation authorities "stated candidly that if the [Marine] squadron got to France it would be used to furnish personnel to run one of their training fields, but that this was as near the front as it would ever get." The army had vigorously developed its own aviation support capability and saw no incentive for diluting its wartime contributions by making space for the upstart Marine squadron. Cunningham's vision of Marine air flying close air support for Marine infantry would not be realized until 1919 in Haiti.[3]

Cunningham turned to the navy. During conferences with U.S. Navy officers at Dunkirk and with officers of the British destroyer patrol, he perceived a need for day bombers to fly patrols over Belgium's English Channel coast and to attack German submarine pens at Zeebrugge, Bruges, and Ostend.

In Cunningham's absence, Major General Barnett organized an Aeronautic Detachment at Philadelphia in December under Captain Geiger, back from his frigid crossing of the North Atlantic. Its mission was uncertain, but apparently it was intended for service with the Advance Base Force.

By December 1917, with the coldest winter on record and temperatures on Long Island diving to sixteen below zero, flight conditions at Mineola had grown impossible. Captain McIlvain, on his own initiative, loaded his squadron onto a train and headed south on New Year's Day.

The train stopped briefly in Washington while McIlvain visited Headquarters, Marine Corps, and asked where he might go. Phone calls were made, and he was directed to go to Lake Charles, Louisiana. Backdated orders were drawn up to that effect. Armed with these orders McIlvain took his squadron to Gerstrier Field at Lake Charles, but the base commander refused to receive the squadron, because he had no instructions to do so from the War Department. For several days the Marines continued to live on board their train, cadging meals from a friendly army mess hall. The base commander eventually, and somewhat reluctantly, allowed the Marines to unload and set up.

Instead of the wheel-controlled Jennies they had flown at Mineola, McIlvain's flyers transitioned into the more modern, stick-controlled JN-4D. More exciting was the S4-C Thomas-Morse Scout. The single-placed little "Tommy" resembled the celebrated French Nieuports, and like the Nieuports it had a rotary engine. In a rotary engine—not to be confused with a radial engine, which it resembled superficially—the engine rotated around the crankshaft rather than standing still. This imparted a wicked torque that would throw the Scout into a spin the instant the pilot relaxed his attention.

Cunningham returned to the United States in late 1917 and presented his plan for a land-based force of navy and Marine planes for use against the German U-boat bases to the General Board of the Navy. The board approved the formation of a Northern Bombing Group, to include a Marine element. On March 11, 1918, Major General Commandant Barnett ordered Cunningham to organize and take command of the 1st Marine Aviation Force, to be formed at Miami, Florida, by combining McIlvain's squadron from Mineola and Geiger's detachment from Philadelphia.

Cunningham's exhausting quest to establish a clear combat role for his high-spirited aviators was far from over. Influenced by inputs from Admiral Sims' headquarters in London as well as from the French and British authorities, the prospective Northern Bombing Group underwent several changes of planned mission and aircraft. Originally it was to bomb U-boats in shallow coastal waters and conduct antisubmarine patrols, with Marine fighter planes flying escort for navy patrol bombers. This got changed to Marines flying daylight bombing raids in British-designed DeHavilland DH-4s and the navy flying night-bombing missions in big Italian-built Caproni bombers.

Captain Geiger received orders to move his detachment from Philadelphia to Naval Air Station, Miami, Florida, on February 4, 1918. Three days later he was packed up and on his way. On arriving in Miami, Geiger, charged with finding a field big enough for the entire 1st Marine Aviation Force, moved from the main navy field at Coconut Grove to a small sandy airstrip owned by the Curtiss Flying School at the edge of the Everglades. With no specific authority to do so, Geiger took over the school, requisitioned its Jennies, and promised the civilian flight instructors commissions in the Marine Corps Reserve. Cunningham, arriving from Washington, found his first task that of legitimizing Geiger's peremptory actions.

On April 1, McIlvain's squadron arrived from Lake Charles. It was now visualized that the squadron and a half would be expanded to four squadrons. The indefatigable Cunningham went traveling to find the needed pilots and mechanics for his burgeoning force. He visited Quantico and picked up more second lieutenant volunteers and sent them down to Miami for flight training. There were volunteers from elsewhere. Said Ford Rogers, they were "strays that Cunningham . . . picked up. I don't know where he got them." Enlisted ground crew members also appeared, some of them skilled mechanics, electricians, carpenters, and blacksmiths, and some "just good Marines who had little more than basic military training."[4]

Cunningham visited the naval air stations at Pensacola and Key West, proselytizing naval aviators, most of them young reservists anxious to go to France. Of the 135 Marine aviators who eventually flew in France, seventy-eight were former naval officers.

Colgate W. Darden Jr. was one of those who joined from the navy. Darden had dropped out of the University of Virginia to drive an ambulance for the French. He saw heavy action at Verdun and Champagne and was hospitalized for a long time, not for wounds but with a serious illness. Convalescing, he returned to the United States and on America's entry into the war joined the navy to be a pilot.

Another was Ralph Talbot, of Weymouth, Massachusetts. At Weymouth High School he had played baseball and football, edited the school paper, and chaired the debating team. One of his teachers, a woman, later remembered him in a letter to his mother, "He was tall for his age with the head and at times, the bearing of a young prince." His father was dead. His widowed mother kept a scrapbook, the way mothers do. After Weymouth High he went to Mercersburg Academy, where he made a reputation for his whimsical verse, edited his class yearbook, and was an honor graduate in 1916. From Mercersburg he went to Yale College and completed a year, but then war was declared. He had been taking private flying lessons. He considered going in the Army Air Service, to the point of filling out half of the application form, but then veered off in the direction of naval aviation. He enlisted as a seaman, second class, in the navy on October 26, 1917. Flight training followed, and on April 8, 1918, Talbot was enrolled as an ensign in the Naval Reserve and assigned to Naval Air Station, Miami. He succumbed to Marine Corps blandishments, was disenrolled on May 25, and next day was commissioned a second lieutenant (provisional) in the Marine Corps Reserve Flying Corps and assigned to active duty with the 1st Marine Aviation Force. He was five feet, nine and a half inches tall and weighed 148 pounds, the right size to be a high school quarterback, or a pilot.

Curtiss Field was renamed the Marine Flying Field, and it grew into a complex of hangars, storehouses, machine shops, and tent camps. The training schedule went from daylight to dark. Would-be Marine pilots had to first qualify in seaplanes, a necessary requirement in order to get their navy wings—the familiar gold wings were first authorized in 1918. Next came elementary land-plane training in the ubiquitous Jenny, including formation flying, aerobatics, and the rudiments of aerial tactics, gunnery, bombing, and reconnaissance. Some enlisted men were trained as gunners and observers. Sand and dust caused engine problems. Because of the swamps of the bordering Everglades, every crash caused a major rescue problem. Four officers and three enlisted men were killed in training accidents.

The ultimate strength of Marine aviation was set at an ambitious 1,500 officers and six thousand enlisted men, an exponential growth in barely eighteen months. The first class of twenty-five enlisted candidates entered the new pilot's program on July 10, 1918. Having passed the physical and education requirements, they were given the temporary rank of gunnery sergeant.

First there was a ten-week academic course at Massachusetts Institute of Technology at Cambridge, Massachusetts, near Boston, followed by flight training at Miami. Those who successfully completed their training were commissioned second lieutenants in the Marine Corps Flying Corps. Enlisted training was largely accomplished at the navy schools at Great Lakes Training Station, north of Chicago, and at San Diego.

The 1st Marine Aviation Force came officially into being on June 16, 1918, with Cunningham in command, a headquarters detachment, and four squadrons. Captains Geiger and McIlvain commanded Squadrons A and B, respectively. Capt. Douglas B. Roben was given Squadron C, and 1st Lt. Russell A. Presley got Squadron D.

A British officer sent to Miami to appraise the squadrons cheerfully announced them fit for combat. At least one Marine flyer disagreed. Said Ford Rogers, "We had flown nothing but Jennies. We got one DH-4 and all of us got one flight. . . . Our gunnery training had consisted of getting into the rear seat and using a Lewis gun, shooting at targets on the ground. None of us had ever fired a fixed gun in our lives. None of us had ever dropped a bomb in our lives."

The 1st Marine Aviation Force finally received orders on July 10 to proceed to France. Squadrons A, B, and C entrained for New York three days later. For the moment, Squadron D was left behind. There was a stopover in Philadelphia, arguably the "birthplace" of Marine aviation, for bit of a celebration. On July 18 the 107 officers and 654 enlisted men of the three squadrons sailed from New York in the much-used *De Kalb*. The fourth squadron completed its training at Marine Flying Field, Miami, and departed for France ten weeks later.

Cunningham and his force would encounter even greater frustrations upon arrival in France. Forced to start virtually from scratch, Cunningham would work tirelessly to provide aircraft, airfields, and indeed a legitimate mission for his impatient flight crews.

CHAPTER FOUR

"Over There"

Inspired by Woodrow Wilson's appeal to Congress for a declaration of war against Germany, the celebrated Broadway entertainer George M. Cohan wrote the words and music to the song "Over There" while riding a train from New Rochelle to New York.[1] Instantly popular, the song caught the wave of patriotism that flourished in America in 1917. Cohan's words in the chorus reflected the spirit of the times: "The Yanks are coming, the Yanks are coming, the drums rum-tumming ev'rywhere," and ending with the promise, "We'll be over, we're coming over, and we won't come back till it's over—over there."

The Yanks were indeed coming. Beginning with General Pershing's advance party, closely followed by the first division-sized deployment, including the 5th Regiment of Marines, the East Coast ports of the United States launched ever more frequent convoys of men and material to France.

The first Americans to enter the war zone were appalled to see the devastated French countryside. "The ruin wrought cannot be described," Marine major Robert L. Denig wrote his wife in 1917. "It is just a country swept clean. The land a mass of shell-holes, every tree killed, all houses down, and this from the English Channel to Switzerland and at least fifty miles wide."

General Pershing Arrives

The British steamship *Baltic,* with General Pershing's party, reached Liverpool the morning of June 7, 1917, after a ten-day passage. Pershing was met on the pier by a guard of honor drawn from the 3d Battalion, Royal Welch Fusiliers, a regiment that had fought against the Americans at Bunker Hill. This action had been balanced by fighting side by side with the Marines and the U.S. Army at Tientsin during the Boxer Rebellion, seventeen years earlier.

Pershing had an audience with King George V, smartly turned out in the uniform of a field marshal, on June 9. The king told Pershing and his staff, Marine lieutenant colonels Logan Feland and Robert Dunlap among them, "The Anglo-Saxon race must save civilization."

Pershing and his party crossed the English Channel to Boulogne by steamer on the morning of June 13. Here the honor guards were French colonials in field uniform. Pershing proceeded to Paris, where Marshal Joffre and General Ferdinand Foch met him at the station. It was Pershing's first meeting with Foch, who had become more important in the scheme of things than Joffre. Foch had commanded resolutely in the earlier bloodbaths of the First Marne, Somme, and Ypres campaigns. Now chief of the French General Staff, he would soon take command of all allied troops fighting in France. Later Pershing met Gen. Henri-Philippe Petain, newly appointed commander in chief of the French army.

The Marines Land in France

On June 27, ten days after Pershing's party arrived in Boulogne, the *Henderson* and *De Kalb* with Col. Charles Doyen and the 5th Regiment of Marines on board docked at St. Nazaire on the Bay of Biscay. As a VMI-trained civil engineer, 2d Lt. Lem Shepherd was ordered to lay out a tent camp for the regiment. Shrewdly, he found some old-time sergeants who knew how to do such things, and by the time the regiment disembarked the site had been properly staked out.

By July 2 all of Doyen's regiment was ashore, marching eight kilometers through the rain to their muddy camp. Doyen reported his regiment present for duty, and—significantly—it passed from navy to American Expeditionary Forces (AEF) control, being assigned to the army's 1st Division, which had been activated on June 9 and was being assembled in France. With four of its own regiments in the division—the 16th, 18th, 26th, and 28th infantry, as recommended by Pershing—the army had no real need or desire for a fifth infantry regiment, particularly if it was a Marine outfit. Pershing's GHQ (general headquarters) chopped up most of the regiment into small parcels and sent them off to mostly line-of-communications duty. On July 9 the 5th Regiment began performing guard and provost duty.

At about this time, General Petain concluded: "The Allies will not acquire numerical superiority until the American army is in a position to send a considerable number of divisions into the lines." Pershing's AEF, after considerable negotiations with the French, had been given a prospective sector near the middle of the western front, which then extended across northern France from Switzerland to the North Sea.

On July 16 the 5th Regiment—or the 5th Marines, as it was already being called—less Major Westcott's 3d Battalion, which stayed at St. Nazaire in the Loire

River estuary, proceeded to Gondrecourt. The Marines traveled for the first time in the much-despised "40 hommes 8 chevaux" French railway boxcars, meaning suitable transport for forty men or eight horses. Officers rode more comfortably in a coach car.

Maj. "Fritz" Wise's 2d Battalion drew the village of Menancourt as its billeting area. The townspeople turned out to greet them, children presented bouquets of flowers, and the band of the Chasseurs Alpins played the "Star-Spangled Banner." The Marines were billeted in houses, stables, haylofts, or almost anything with a roof. Wise and his headquarters officers had a house and their own mess. Wise's reputation as an officer who dined often and well had preceded him. His personal orderly, Pvt. John McKeown, who had been with him since Santo Domingo, was in charge of Wise's mess, which soon became famous throughout the 1st Division, particularly after Wise acquired a French chef.

Enlisted messing was more spartan. The company galleys were set up in stable yards, and the troops ate in the open. Boiled and baked beans figured large in the enlisted menu. Luckily, there was splendid summer weather.

Training for the Western Front

The Marines, as part of the 1st Division, began their training under Chasseurs Alpins—the "Blue Devils," wearers of a large blue beret and a darker blue uniform than the horizon blue usual to the French army.[2] The scheme of training, coming down from Pershing's headquarters through the 1st Division, was that the French would teach the techniques of trench warfare but that tactical training would be under the regiment's own officers.

Wise's 2d Battalion, 5th Regiment, paired off with the 115th Chasseurs Alpins. The Blue Devils' camp was five kilometers away. British instructors arrived to give the Americans training in bayonet fighting.

"The British at that time were crazy about the bayonet. They knew it was going to win the war," remembered Wise. "The French were equally obsessed with the grenade. They knew it was going to win the war. So we also got a full dose of training in hand grenade throwing. . . . Hour after hour we threw those grenades into the 'enemy trenches,' ducked, and waited for the explosions."

First Sergeant James Gallivan, whose thirty-three years of active service qualified him for membership in the mythical "Old Corps," was delighted to find his name on the lengthy promotion list for Marine gunners and quartermaster clerks signed by Franklin Roosevelt, as acting secretary of the navy, on October 22. Promoted a week later, Gallivan bought his officer's uniforms, added the bronze bursting-bomb insignia of his new rank and Sam Browne belt, trimmed his sweeping mustaches to something approximating the more stylish military brush being worn by Pershing, and on November 25 went off for a month-long course at the

Infantry School at Gondrecourt, where earnest young second lieutenants would teach him the fundamentals of making war.

Wise's battalion stood in ranks all day on August 1, 1917, awaiting inspection by General Pershing and Marshal Foch. Late in the afternoon the two great men arrived and trooped the line, accompanied by Pershing's chief of staff, James Harbord, now a colonel.

Foch shook Wise's hand after the inspection and said, "Major Wise, the Marines seem to be the Chasseurs of the American Army." Or so Wise remembered.

Later there was a grand review of the entire 1st Division at Gondrecourt, and Georges Clemenceau, soon to become prime minister, came to it. French artillery treated the Americans to a demonstration of a "rolling barrage," the tightly coordinated concentration of fire that preceded and protected an infantry advance against a fortified position.

The AEF was being funneled into France through the Bay of Biscay ports, in order to relieve the congestion of the Channel ports caused by French and British shipping. Lieutenant Colonel Hiram Bearss' Base Detachment arrived in France in August. The Base Detachment, along with 3d Battalion, 5th Regiment, already so assigned, was given guard and provost duties under the newly formed Service of Supply (SOS) in the vicinity of St. Nazaire.

Bordeaux would become a key port. Bearss took command of Base Section no. 2 at Bordeaux on September 8. His headquarters and three of his companies joined him in October. Part of his 7th Company was sent to SOS headquarters in Paris. His 30th Company was transferred to Chaumont, where Pershing had now established the General Headquarters of the AEF.

An old campaigner, Frederick A. Barker, with a temporary promotion to major, reported to Paris on GHQ orders in September as an assistant provost marshal. Barker was one of the sturdy souls who had joined the 5th Regiment in Philadelphia from Haiti. He arrived in Philadelphia on May 28 by way of the old protected cruiser *Charleston* and was assigned to command of the 47th Company in the regiment's 3d Battalion. Born in Charlestown, Massachusetts, outside of Boston, in 1880, Barker had served a hitch as a sergeant in the 1st Regiment of Cavalry, 1899–1902. Appointed a second lieutenant in the Marines in 1904, he had gone through the School of Application at Annapolis and served much of his time as a junior officer at sea. He had landed as a captain at Cap Haitien in 1916 and had fought the Cacos in the north of Haiti at such places as Haut de Cap and Fort Riviere. That same year, 1916, he landed as a company commander with the 4th Regiment of Marines at Monte Cristi, Santo Domingo, and in the march to Santiago fought the Dominican rebels at Las Trencheras and Guayacanes. For this service Major General Commandant Barnett had cited him for "conspicuous courage and skill."

At the end of the summer the Chasseurs Alpins left the Gondrecourt area to move up into the line in the Champagne. Rumors rippled through the 5th Regiment that they were to be detached from the 1st Division and made part of a new 2d Division.

In a September 1, 1917, cable, now lost, Pershing apparently stated that he found the 5th Marine Regiment indigestible and asked that no more Marines be sent to France. On September 17, the War Department overrode his objections:

Reference your cablegram of September 1 about the Marine regiment in France, the President has directed an additional regiment (the 6th) to be sent and it is now impossible to change the arrangements. This regiment combined with the one already with you will form a brigade and become part of the 2nd Division which will then consist of one brigade of regulars and one of Marines. The Marine brigade will be commanded by a general officer of Marines about to be nominated and while serving in France will be part of the army under your command. About one thousand two hundred of the 6th Marine Regiment sails today.

Forming the 2d Regular Division

On September 20, 1917, Maj. Gen. Tasker H. Bliss, the army's chief of staff, published the "composition of the 2d Regular Division for service abroad." The order was hurriedly drawn. There were mistakes in the typing and some in substance, most of the units listed did not yet exist, but it would serve.

The headquarters of the 2d Division was to arrive in France in September. In keeping with the organization then favored by the U.S. Army, the division would be arrayed in the "square" (vice "triangular") mode, containing four infantry regiments constituting two brigades. The Marine Corps was to provide one of its two infantry brigades. One of the regiments would be the 5th Marines. The other regiment, the 6th Marines, had yet to arrive. In the AEF's orderly way, the two brigades of the 1st Division were the 1st and 2d. Hence, the two infantry brigades of the 2d Division would be the 3d Brigade of Infantry and the 4th Brigade of Marines.

The 2d Division headquarters was organized in the summer of 1917 at Fort Ethan Allen, Vermont, from details drawn from the 2d Cavalry Regiment. Brig. Gen. Omar Bundy, a small, dapper officer then commanding the 1st Brigade, 1st Division, with a promotion to major general, was to command the new division.

Its 3d Brigade would have two regular army regiments, the 9th and 23d infantry. When the war began both the 9th and the 23d were down on the border in Texas. They were stripped down to provide cadre for other new units and then built up to the new, big, wartime strengths.

The 9th Infantry held many battle honors. It had marched and fought with William T. Sherman in the Civil War, battled the Sioux in the Indian Wars, and was at Santiago in the Spanish-American War. In the Far East the regiment fought the *insurrectos* in the Philippines and was with the China Relief Expedition in the Boxer Rebellion. In the battle for Tientsin, July 13, 1900, the 9th Infantry was brigaded with the 1st Marine Regiment. It lost ninety-five of seven hundred men but gained a regimental motto, "Keep up the fire!"—the last words of the regimental commander. In 1901, at Balangiga on Samar, Filipino insurrectionists surprised Company C, 9th Infantry, at their Sunday breakfast and massacred most of them, killing all the officers, with only a remnant brought out by a sergeant. It was Tony Waller's Marine battalion that avenged them, leading to Waller's celebrated court-martial.

The 23d Infantry was almost as old and scarcely less honored than the 9th. It did not get its number until 1866, but its antecedents fought in the Civil War with the Army of the Potomac from the Peninsula through Petersburg. In the Indian Wars it was with the 9th against the Sioux. It was at the siege for Manila and stayed on in the Philippines for the insurrection.

The 9th and 23d infantry sailed for France in September 1917, with an average strength of fifty-six officers and 3,430 men. Twelve percent of the 9th Infantry and 10 percent of the 23d Infantry had more than one year's service at the time of sailing.

The strength of the 5th Regiment when it arrived in France was seventy officers and 2,689 men. Thirty-four percent of the Marines were "old-timers," in that they had more than one year of service. Twelve percent had four or more years' service. No other regiment of the AEF had that much seasoning. Unlike the 5th Marines, only 7 percent of the strength of the 6th Regiment being accumulated at Quantico had over one year's service and a mere 3 percent four or more years.

The division's 2d Engineers—and army engineers were always highly regarded by the Marines—was organized as a regiment in Mexico in 1916, but its roots, as a company and a battalion, went back to the Mexican and Civil Wars.

A 2d Division concentration area was assigned near Bourmont, in eastern Haute-Marne, about sixty-five kilometers behind the front at Verdun. The 5th Marines, less detachments, including its regimental machine-gun company, which stayed with the 1st Division for advance training, moved to Bourmont on September 24. The regimental headquarters and Wise's 2d Battalion were billeted in the village of Damblain, about sixteen kilometers away. Wise's men were billeted half in barracks, half in houses. Wise got a house and swiftly augmented its kitchen.

The balance of the regiment remained scattered to the four winds. One company of the 5th Regiment was doing guard duty at Nevers, in the Burgundy region on the banks of the river Loire. Westcott's 3d Battalion remained in the vicinity of St. Nazaire doing port duties. In late September the 67th Company of the 1st Battalion redeployed to Southampton, England, to organize American troops passing through.

The French and British instructors presumed it was their duty to train the Americans to do things exactly as they were themselves. The history of the 2d Division reports that friction soon developed: "Americans were not Frenchmen nor Englishmen, and their ways were not our ways. . . . They had lost the idea, so highly developed during our Civil War, that entrenchments are merely the indispensable instrument to enable troops to advance again. . . . They never had a high estimate of the value of rifle fire, and their esteem for this weapon had fallen to a point where it was regarded as only a bayonet handle."

Intensified Training

Pershing and his staff preached a doctrine of an aggressive offensive and open warfare. This objective was not being met by the training, centered on trench warfare, being given the AEF by the French and British. Weeks of short-tempered discussion followed.

It was also a time of temporary and rapidly shifting command arrangements. Charles Doyen, with his promotion to brigadier general, was confirmed in command of the incomplete Marine brigade and, on October 26, was given temporary command of the embryonic 2d Division. Major General Bundy assumed command three weeks later.

General Pershing arranged a new system of training under the French. Battalions, as soon as they had a modicum of training, would be sent to quiet sectors of the front to serve under French tutelage and command. The division would then reassemble for larger unit training before being certified ready for combat.

That fall the 5th Regiment was reorganized once again. A regiment now consisted of twelve rifle companies, a machine-gun company, a supply company, and a headquarters company. The strength of the rifle companies went up from two hundred to 250. Six officers were allocated to each company, a senior and junior captain and four lieutenants, one for each platoon.

The 6th Regiment of Marines

The 6th Regiment began arriving a battalion at a time. The 1st Battalion, 6th Marines, under Maj. "Johnny the Hard" Hughes, came into St. Nazaire on October 5 after an eighteen-day passage. It was a bright sunny day. The battalion disembarked the following day, and the first Frenchman Pvt. Martin "Gus" Gulberg met offered to exchange his money (Gulberg did not know the rate and decided to wait) and to sell him some pictures of naked women.

The 1st Battalion, 6th Regiment, went into Camp no. 1, a new camp not quite completed. It rained. Gulberg's bunkhouse lacked bunks, and the roof leaked. The next day a French truck delivered mattress ticks and straw to fill them. Until December 2 the 75th Company worked as stevedores on the docks and with the 17th Engineers, who were building a railroad and a reservoir. The next day the 75th reported to the provost marshal as military police. "The M.P. is the most hated man in the army," bemoaned Gulberg.

The battalion continued the ordeal of guard and police duties there and at Brest and Le Havre until the end of the year, in Colonel Catlin's words, "to help the engineers and stevedores bring order out of the chaos of the port."

Colonel Catlin, the regimental commander, arrived at St. Nazaire with his headquarters and supply and machine-gun companies on the first day of November. His 3d Battalion, under Major Sibley, came in at Brest on November 12, and together he and Sibley went to Bordeaux.

One of Catlin's Marines wrote to his father: "Write to Quantico and tell Nelson Springer to take salt-water soap with him when he crosses. . . . I didn't worry about U-boats nor the fact that I had to sleep under a life-boat, completely dressed and burdened with a life belt and a canteen filled with fresh water. Nor has the fact annoyed me the least bit that I never took my clothes off after we started for France. But having to wash in salt water, and none too much at that, was the nearest approach to a hardship I experienced."

As for food on board ship, the young Marine continued: "The food was about what we got at Quantico, but we had to stand in line half the day to get a look in. After eating we would stand in another slowly moving line to wash the mess gear. I used bread to clean mine and found it served the purpose admirably. Lines of men wound all over the ship, a large part of them below decks. Only the fittest survived, and you may guess that I didn't miss a meal."

It was raining, a winter rain, that cold winter of 1917–18, and the young Marine was writing in his "pup tent," two shelter halves buttoned together. "My tent mate has lifted the poncho on the open end of the tent. The inference is that he will soon come in and then all my time will be taken by seeing that he does not touch my side of the tent roof, for if he does it will start leaking. In some miraculous way we manage to keep the four-by-six-foot spot under the tent fairly dry. He is taking off his shoes so that the mud won't get on the blankets."[3]

Logistic Support for the Marine Brigade

Lt. Col. William Lemly, the Marine Corps assistant quartermaster, had made the crossing in the *Von Steuben* with Sibley's 3d Battalion, 6th Regiment, and then gone his separate way. He reported to the AEF headquarters at Chaumont after a call on Maj. D. B. Wills, the brigade paymaster, who had his offices in the Equitable Building in Paris.

Lemly spent the next two weeks at Chaumont and in visiting Damblain, headquarters of the Marine brigade, and Breuvannes, headquarters of the 5th Regiment. In the field Lemly learned that the Marines were either billeted in French homes or buildings or quartered in Adrian barracks, which were prefabricated, one-story frame buildings with tarpaper roofs and, sometimes, wooden floors.

Such a building was supposed to hold ninety-six men "comfortably." The double-decked bunks arranged parallel to the side walls had chicken-wire springs and bed sacks filled with straw. The barracks were lighted with oil lanterns and warmed with wood-burning stoves. Each company had an additional Adrian barracks for use as a kitchen and mess hall. Each battalion had an extra one for use as an infirmary. Enough Adrian barracks were waiting in neighboring towns for the arrival of the 6th Regiment.

The regimental quartermaster of the 5th Marines told Lemly that there was no difficulty in getting rations but that clothing was in short supply. Enough English-type helmets and French-type gas masks had been received for the regiment, but woolen socks, leggings, and rubber boots were urgently needed. Rolling kitchens—an innovation welcomed by all hands—and water carts had not yet been received. The Jeffrey trucks belonging to the Marine Corps were most satisfactory, but spare parts were lacking. Most of the rest of the transport, including some that had been set aside for the 6th Regiment, consisting of escort wagons, draft and pack mules, horses, motorcycles with sidecars, and bicycles, was in place.

The Marines told Lemly that the felt field hat, the broad-brimmed "campaign" hat, which, worn with khakis, had been the hallmark of a Marine campaigning in the Caribbean, was not standing up to the rains of northern France. A flat cap similar to the "overseas" cap being worn by the army was needed. It packed easily and could be worn, if needed, under the helmet.

The Marines' winter service uniform trousers did not work well with their canvas leggings, but it was expected that all Marines in France would soon be in army uniforms, which had breeches instead of trousers. The army was also adopting wrap puttees, nothing more than long pieces of woolen cloth, which were de rigueur for the French and British in the trenches.

Lemly wanted to see how things were done on the British front. Pershing's headquarters obligingly arranged for him to visit the 147th Brigade, the Duke of Wellington's Regiment, which held the front about eight kilometers north of Ypres, with two battalions on line and the other battalions in reserve. Those on the front lines were living in shell holes, those in reserve in ruined buildings, huts, dugouts, tents, and Nissen huts. The Nissen huts were hemispherical structures made up of heavy corrugated steel over a frame.[4]

Lemly marveled that despite the dirt and squalor, the officers and men of the 147th Brigade managed a smartness of appearance, with their equipment giving every impression of being well taken care of:

> Every morning the division train, horse drawn wagons very similar to the escort wagon, would load at the railhead, where the supplies were distributed to the different battalions. . . . Rations for the officers and men at the front were sent forward daily, packed in sand bags and transported each afternoon

before dark as far as possible in limber wagons, water in water carts, then packed upon pack mules and taken in after dark as near the front as possible, from which point carried in by the men. The cooking was done in rolling kitchens, some of which were within a mile of the extreme front, protected as well as possible from shell fire, and on the first line small oil stoves and solidified alcohol provided means of warming the food and even cooking in a limited way. . . . When the supplies go forward each day to the men on the forward line an extra pair of clean woolen socks per man is sent in waterproof bags. The worn socks are sent back, then thoroughly washed, a powder composed of powdered talc and camphor dusted into them, and [they] are ready to be sent to the front line again.

Lemly found the rations issued to French and English troops very similar to American army rations, "with the exception that both the French and English rations include tobacco or cigarettes, the French ration wine and the English ration rum."

Lemly learned that the English officer's tunic, with its turn-down collar and flat lapels, was considered the most comfortable coat for field service. Many Marine officers favored its adoption.

Lemly returned to New York on January 8, 1918, and submitted his long list of recommendations to General McCawley, the quartermaster general. Among his recommendations, Lemly believed that the individual entrenching tools being issued were unsatisfactory. Many more long-handled shovels, picks, and crowbars were needed. The wire cutters were entirely too small; the French used two-hand wire cutters. Instead of a sight cover for the front sight, the '03 rifle should have front-sight-protecting studs, one of each side of the sight. Despite these shortcomings, Lemly wound up his report by saying, "The Marines are the best equipped troops in the AEF."

McCawley forwarded the report to Barnett with an endorsement that agreed with most of Lemly's recommendations. Specifically, he recognized that the field hat was unsatisfactory and said that the Depot Quartermaster in Philadelphia would be charged with developing a suitable distinctive cap for the Marines along the lines of the French forage cap. McCawley also recommended that a service coat along the lines of the British tunic be adopted.[5]

Marine Firepower

Maj. Edward B. Cole arrived with the 1st Machine Gun Battalion headquarters and two companies in December 1917. He picked up the two machine-gun companies left by the 5th Marines at Gondrecourt, and his battalion was complete. In accordance with the AEF's tidy numbering system, the battalion was redesignated the 6th Machine Gun Battalion.

Machine gunners were a kind of aristocracy of the infantry. The 6th Machine Gun Battalion edged out even the 5th Marines in seasoning. Thirty-six percent of Cole's Marines had more than a year's service. Thirteen percent had more than four years.

When the 5th Marines first came to France, there was a machine-gun company in each of the infantry battalions. As now reorganized, there was a four-company machine-gun battalion immediately under command of the brigade commander and a regimental machine-gun company in each of the infantry regiments. Major Cole, commanding the machine-gun battalion, was also the brigade machine-gun officer and as such the brigade commander's advisor on the tactical use of the guns.

Edward Cole was exceptionally well qualified for this responsibility. The thirty-eight-year-old Boston native was considered the premier machine-gun expert in the Corps, a self-acquired distinction. Most of his fourteen years of commissioned service had been routine—tours in Cuba, China, and Puerto Rico; brief combat in Veracruz; and expeditionary service with the Advance Base Force. Serving often as the adjutant or quartermaster in field units, Cole developed a keen interest in crew-served automatic weapons, studying in particular the employment of heavy machine guns by the antagonists fighting in France from the start of the war. As a captain in late 1916, he represented the Marine Corps on the interservice Machine Gun Board, hastily convened by the War Department shortly before the United States entered the war. Few Marines at the time had imagined the use of preassault barrage fire by massed machine guns or the employment of machine-gun carts to provide mobile support to an infantry advance in rough terrain. Cole brought this perspective to his command of the 6th Machine Gun Battalion, along with a fierce commitment to provide first-class fire support to the infantry.

The machine-gun companies came to France armed with the drum-fed Lewis light machine gun fitted with a bipod. The prime mover was the "Cole machine-gun cart," a light wagon with two bicycle wheels, earlier designed by then-Captain Cole to be pulled by two Marines. The machine gunners later had their hand-pulled Cole carts supplemented by French mule-drawn carts, but they would find the animals could not always get all the way to the front.

On arriving in France the machine-gun companies saw their familiar Lewis guns replaced by French Hotchkiss heavy machine guns, to conform to AEF practice. The Marine gunners were resentful. Observed ordnance historian Col. Brooke Nihart, "The [Lewis] guns were badly needed to arm Army Air Service planes—or so the story went."

At first the Marines did not much like the air-cooled Hotchkiss, which weighed seventy pounds and required a seventy-pound tripod, but with time they came to appreciate it as a dependable weapon with greater range than the Lewis. The Hotchkiss machine gun, Model 1914, was fed with brass strips of twenty-five cartridges, originally of French 8-mm caliber. These were replaced with guns chambered for the U.S. 30-06 cartridge. The five cooling rings at the base of its heavy barrel made the gun instantly recognizable.

"Its big fault," said Maj. Littleton W. T. Waller Jr., "was the fact that its being air cooled, which on prolonged barrage fire cut down its rate of speed to approximately 25 rounds a minute."

Major Waller was the son of the fabled "Tony" Waller of Samar fame, now sitting out the war in Philadelphia; after Belleau Wood "Tony Junior" would succeed Major Cole as the brigade machine-gun officer. The Marines found more to admire in British machine gunnery than in the French. In accordance with British practice, in the attack machine guns were usually grouped into batteries for delivery of preparatory fire. As the attack progressed, control of the machine guns became progressively decentralized. Later it would become practice to have at least one company of machine guns attached to each attacking infantry battalion.

There was also a liberal issue of Chauchat machine rifles, Model 1915, one to a squad. Marines viewed the "Sho-Sho" with contempt, making invidious comparisons to the Lewis gun they might have had. (Although the air-cooled Lewis weighed three pounds more than the Chauchat, the better-balanced Lewis was more easily handled as a machine rifle.) Rumor had it that the French built the Chauchat in bicycle shops, charged Uncle Sam eight dollars apiece, and at that price still made a profit. Originally chambered for the French 8-mm cartridge, a new model came along chambered for the U.S. 30-06 cartridge. There was a semicircular or half-moon-shaped sixteen- or twenty-round magazine. It had a flimsy bipod that was usually used only in the defense. In the attack the "Sho-Sho" would be most often fired from the hip, in a kind of marching fire. According to Colonel Nihart, "The Marines said it was about as accurate fired from the hip as fired from the shoulder—'spray and pray' for a hit."

The Marines knew dimly that the division artillery that was to support them was training somewhere else. The artillery regiments of the 2d Field Artillery Brigade were all new formations, although from 10 to 16 percent of the gunners had at least a year's service. The 15th and 17th field artillery sailed for France in December 1917. The 12th Field Artillery, which would most often support the Marines, followed in January 1918.

Moving Up

The odds against the Allies on the western front were widening. The collapse of Russia made it possible for Gen. Erich Ludendorff to thin out the German's eastern front. From December 1917 to March 1918, ten divisions a month, as many as the efficient German railroads could carry, arrived in the western front. As the 1918 campaign season opened, the French estimated that the Germans would have two hundred divisions against the Allies' 180, counting the four American divisions (1st, 2d, 26th, and 42d) each as two divisions because of their size.

By now the Marines had a different look. They had come to France wearing their customary expeditionary outfits—broad-brimmed felt field hats (commonly called "campaign hats") and trousers with canvas leggings. Now, for the most part they wore breeches with wrap puttees and flat "overseas caps."[6] Marines joining the 2d Division at Bourmont received their steel helmets (the British M1917 "tin hat") and gas masks. These two items were the hallmarks of the western front.

In China, Col. Wendell Neville, who had teamed effectively with John Lejeune during the street fighting in Veracruz, finally received Headquarters, Marine Corps, approval of his persistent requests for a transfer from command of the Legation Guard in Peking to a regimental command in the Marine Brigade. He assumed command of the 5th Regiment from Lt. Col. Hiram Bearss on January 1, 1918. Neville, born and raised in Norfolk, was an 1890 graduate of the Naval Academy. Nicknamed "Whispering Buck" for his thunderous voice, Neville, forty-seven years old, had spent nearly half his life as a Marine officer. He wore the Medal of Honor from Veracruz.

The Base Detachment that Hiram Bearss had brought over remained at Bordeaux until early January, when it was detached from the SOS and consolidated with the 5th Marines, as a way of providing each battalion with four rather than three rifle companies. Two separate rifle companies arrived from Quantico. Westcott's 3d Battalion rejoined from St. Nazaire at the end of January, and except for the 67th Company, still at Southampton, the 5th Marines was complete.

Lt. Col. Logan Feland became chief of staff of the 2d Division, but he would return to the Brigade in March to serve as second in command of the 5th Marines.

Catlin's 6th Marines were relieved of their port duties early in January and went by rail to the 2d Division training area, moving into the billets reserved for them in the Bourmont area northeast of the 5th Marines.

On the night of January 1, the 1st Battalion, 6th Marines, pulled out of St. Nazaire on a French military train. "The signs on the freight cars read 'Hommes 40,'" wrote Gulberg, "but they always managed to squeeze in about sixty men. The scenery was fine, so they told me—all I saw was the four walls of the car." Pvt. James Hatcher, the Texan who had originally sought to join the U.S. cavalry, recalled his experience crammed into a French boxcar as "a nightmare for anyone not supplied with a generous sense of humor. . . . As the cars pitched and cavorted we hung on for our lives."

After a two-day trip the 1st Battalion, 6th Marines, reached Damblain, near Bourmont, on a cold, wet morning. "Here, under French tutelage," wrote Gulberg, "we engaged in the hardest kind of intensive training. It was winter, the weather was cold and often stormy, but this did not make any difference. We were subject to rush calls during the night, such as forced marches to the trenches, occupations and relief, patrol work, gas and raid signals, sham raids, and other details of trench warfare, such as developed in this war. When we got through we were as hard as nails."

The reality of the villages was less romantic than their poetic names. The best that the writers home could say in any case was "Somewhere in France." That sounded romantic enough to thrill girlfriends and impress proud parents with their blue-starred flags (some of which would soon change into gold-starred flags) in their front windows.

The Marines were billeted in farm country. The French, in their way, did not live in isolated farmhouses but in little villages, with their farms outside them. The 5th Marines was billeted in four little villages, the 6th Marines in five. The inhabitants were mostly old men, women of all ages, and young children, with the pinch of war everywhere in evidence. The younger men were in the army, and many of the young women and girls were off somewhere working in munitions plants. The prosperity of the villages, the Marines were told, was measured by the height of the communal manure pile.

Every Marine, it seemed, smoked cigarettes. They were much more convenient than a pipe and they were cheap, usually five cents a pack. Camels were a favorite brand, but some of the old-timers still rolled their own, shaking out flake tobacco into a cigarette paper from a small cloth "Bull Durham" bag.

Holcomb's 2d Battalion, 6th Marines, did not arrive in France until the 5th of February. It went directly to the 2d Division training area.

The 119th Replacement Company also arrived that month. One of its members was the Yale runner, 2d Lt. Johnny Overton. He was sent off to the Officers Training School at Gondrecourt.

For two months the brigade trained hard under a battalion of the French 77th Infantry. Three English-speaking French officers, a captain and two lieutenants, were assigned to each regiment as advisors. The 6th Marines drew as its senior advisor Capt. Tribot Laspierre, a charming man who had campaigned in North Africa as well as on the western front. Emphasis was on trench warfare. The Frenchmen showed the Marines how to develop a trench system, thoughtfully close to their own billeting, which was from thirteen to twenty-one kilometers from the American cantonments, so that the Marines had to march as many as forty-two kilometers a day, with full packs and entrenching tools. Training concentrated on forced marches and practice at patrolling, raids, and gas attacks. When General Pershing came to inspect the brigade at Bourmont he is supposed to have said, "I only wish I had 500,000 of these Marines!"[7]

The last Marine unit to be drawn into the brigade training area was the 67th Company, which returned from Southampton on March 10. The 4th Brigade's aggregate strength was 280 officers and 9,164 enlisted men, making it by far the largest tactical unit of Marines ever assembled until that time.

The Marine brigade that assembled near Bourmont in March 1918 still retained a considerable percentage of old campaigners, but the majority of the men and junior officers had come in for just the duration of the war. Some of the company commanders and all of the field-grade officers were regulars. Some junior officers had been promoted from the ranks. Some had been appointed from civilian life since the outbreak of the war. Some would fail. Some officers would prove physically incapable of meeting the demands upon them. Some would succeed brilliantly. A great many would become casualties.

The 2d Division was now fully formed, and its infantry brigades were almost ready for duty at the front. Rumors crackled that the division would soon be moving up into the lines. When the orders came on March 5 they said that the division was going into a quiet part of the Verdun front for its next phase of training. The rival 1st Division had already moved up and would be the first to see serious action, at a place called Cantigny. The 2d Division was moving at the same time as the 42d and 26th divisions, all considered now almost combat ready.

Colonel Catlin had no doubts about the readiness of his 6th Marines. By the time they gone through their training in France there was no newness about them. "They acted like veterans; they thought like veterans; and all because of that training and the material they were to start with."

CHAPTER FIVE

The Trenches of Verdun

The Marines approached the Verdun battlefield with curiosity and uneasiness.[1] Although relatively quiet in the spring of 1918, the fortified hilltops east of the Meuse River had been the scene two years earlier of a nightmarish battle in which the Germans and French inflicted more than a million casualties on each other in ten months of unremitting slaughter. The battle ended as a bloody draw, with neither side gaining a mile of new ground. Each new artillery barrage, it seemed, exposed more bleached bones, glistening in the craters.

The French planned to distribute units of the 2d U.S. Division among the divisions of the French X Corps, commanded by a General Vandenberg, in the area southeast of Verdun-sur-Meuse. The region was in Lorraine, between St. Mihiel and Verdun, along the Meuse River, which here ran nearly north and south. The Germans held St. Mihiel. The French held Verdun. The distance between the two cities was about thirty-two kilometers. There had been heavy fighting here in the fall of 1914, when the Germans had broken through to form the St. Mihiel salient, which they still held; more heavy fighting in the spring of 1915, when the French retook the ridge at Les Eparges; and again in the spring of 1916, when the Germans launched their massive attack against Verdun. Now the area was quiet, a place for exhausted divisions on both sides to live and let live.

Pershing, not wanting his troops parceled out as companies, suggested, rather strongly, that a complete American battalion relieve a French battalion in the front line but agreed that the French would remain entirely in tactical command until the relief of the French battalions was complete.

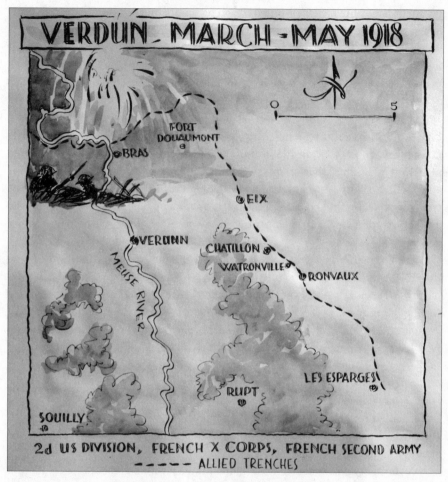

VERDUN - MARCH - MAY 1918

FORT DOUAUMONT

BRAS

EIX

VERDUN

CHATILLON

WATRONVILLE

RONVAUX

MEUSE RIVER

LES ESPARGES

RUPT

SOUILLY

2d US DIVISION, FRENCH X CORPS, FRENCH SECOND ARMY
– – – – – ALLIED TRENCHES

It wasn't quite "Verdun"—the trenches around Les Eparges were about twenty-three kilometers southeast of the 1916 battle's epicenter at Fort Douaumont—but the Marines would always call it such. Also, while their three-month commitment to the trenches near Verdun could hardly compare with the abject misery experienced by the original combatants, the Marines would learn enough of mud, rats, artillery barrages, poison-gas shells, and nocturnal raids into "no-man's-land" to last a lifetime.

The movement from the Bourmont area began on March 13. Except for the motor transport elements, all troops moved by rail. Through long practice the French had optimized the procedure. The standard French military train had thirty boxcars, seventeen flatcars, a coach for the officers, and a caboose or two for the train crew. This standard train could carry a battalion of infantry or a battery of artillery. Fifty-eight trains were needed (twenty-six for the artillery alone) to move an American division, twice the size of a French or British division. An infantry regiment needed five trains—one for each battalion; one for the regimental head-quarters, headquarters company, and machine-gun company; and one for the supply company. The railhead and regulating station was at Souilly, a small town about twenty-four kilometers south of Verdun and of little consequence except to the people living there. It lay just within the fan of longer-ranged German guns.

The Germans

Like the British and the French, the Germans had successively reorganized their divisions since 1914 to give them more firepower with fewer men. By the spring of 1918 the German division consisted of an infantry brigade of three regiments and a field artillery regiment. Command of a division called for a lieutenant general (*generalleutnant*) and each of the brigades a major general (*generalmajor*). The average age of a German lieutenant general was a grizzled sixty-one, of a major general fifty-seven.

The German infantry brigade had three regiments, each organized much like the U.S. Army and Marine regiments, nominally commanded by a colonel (*oberst*) but by 1918 more usually by a major (*major*). A battalion, of which there were three to a regiment, was now usually commanded by a captain (*hauptman*) and a company, four to a battalion, by a lieutenant (*oberleutnant* or *leutnant*). Platoons were led by *offizierstelvertreter* (acting officers) or *vizefeldwebel* (roughly equivalent to Marine gunners).

After the battle of the Somme in 1916, the Germans virtually abandoned the tactical movement of corps, using their corps instead as semipermanent "groups," often named for their commanding general, that stayed in place and controlled their two, three, or four divisions, which moved in and out of their sectors as the situation required.[2]

A German divisional artillery regiment rated six four-gun batteries of 77-mm field guns and three batteries of 105-mm field howitzers, all horse drawn. British intelligence estimated that the German army in early 1918 had 2,900 field artillery batteries, as compared to 2,300 infantry battalions. Corps or "foot" artillery, of which the Germans had a plentitude, tended to stay fixed in its sectors. By 1918 the Germans had 2,250 batteries armed variously with 150-mm and 210-mm howitzers and 100-mm, 130-mm, 150-mm, and 240-mm guns, as well as a mélange of naval guns and captured French and Belgian artillery pieces. The rough ratio was three high-angle-of-fire howitzers to one long-range, flat-trajectory gun.

Trench Fighting

The 2d Division moved forward at night. The Germans picked up the movement, and there was shelling as the Marines and soldiers unloaded at Souilly. The Marines had no personnel casualties, but the 5th Marines' band took a direct hit on its bass drum.

By the time Wise's 2d Battalion, 5th Regiment, detrained it was broad daylight, and his Marines watched curiously at the minuet being danced in the sky: toylike airplanes being chased by the white puffs of exploding antiaircraft shells. Their French guide said they should certainly move away from the station, as they were sure to be shelled. Wise's Marines marched across the Meuse over a pontoon bridge and were billeted in wooden barracks by early afternoon. They were shelled for about twenty minutes that night but took no casualties.

As neatly drawn on situation maps well to the rear, the western front epitomized French logic and nomenclature. A division in the line occupied a "sector." Brigades or regiments were given one or more "subsectors." A "subsector" consisted of one or more "centers of resistance" (CRs). Infantry battalions usually occupied each CR, being made up of "strongpoints" occupied by companies. The front line itself was not a straight line, and it was not filled shoulder to shoulder with men but was held by "combat groups"—squad- or platoon-sized detachments under lieutenants or NCOs—at from fifty- to 150-yard intervals. Half the men were supposed to be awake at all times.

The western face of the St. Mihiel salient ran southeast from Verdun to St. Mihiel. The French Second Army held the Allied front here, with Vandenberg's X Corps as its right flank element. The corps had three divisional sectors—Toulon, Rupt, and Troyon (why so named no one remembered). Toulon, the left sector of the X Corps front, where the Marines would be introduced to battle, had a frontage of about ten kilometers along the eastern crest or ridgeline of the Cotes de Meuse, about eleven kilometers east of the river.

Field fortifications were an elaborate system of trenches and dugouts; communications trenches, called *boyaux,* running from front to rear; and connecting trenches going out to the flanks. The frontline trench was perhaps six feet deep and three feet wide, revetted with timber or sandbags. Firing steps were cut into the front wall. Dugouts for men not on watch were dug into the rear wall. Dugouts came in various sizes, some large enough to accommodate thirty to forty men, some barely big enough for three or four. Most of the larger dugouts had two entrances in case one was caved in by shell fire. To the rear of the front lines was a support line, held by a second battalion of the regiment holding the subsector, and to the rear of that was a reserve camp for the remaining battalion.

Major Cole assigned the brigade's six machine-gun companies to the six infantry battalions and supervised the laying of their guns so as to fire "final protective lines" along the barbed-wire entanglements in front of the trenches.

The Americans were to be supported by French artillery at first and then by their own batteries. Light field guns, the famous French 75s, were positioned within a mile or so of the front line. Heavy artillery, the 155-mm howitzers and long-barreled guns, was farther back. The 2d Division's batteries arrived, one every four hours, by rail, and by March 23 all were present, portioned out behind the X Corps' three sectors and moved into old French emplacements. Carefully constructed fire plans called for the delivery of standing barrages in front of any threatened point in the line. Patrols going forward of the line could be covered by "curtain" or "box" barrages. It was all very logical, and sometimes it worked quite well.

General Bundy collocated his 2d Division headquarters with that of Vandenberg at Sommedieue on March 17. Within the Toulon sector the 6th Marines was assigned to subsector Bonchamp, center of resistance Mont-sous-les-Cotes; the 5th Marines to subsector Les Eparges, CR Montgirmont.

Bundy agreed with Vandenberg that one battalion of each American infantry regiment, after a few days' orientation, would relieve a French battalion in some center of resistance and come under the command of the French regimental commander. Reliefs were always made at night.

Wise's 2d Battalion, 5th Marines, the first to occupy a center of resistance, entered CR Montgirmont, located at the point of a large salient near the center of the Toulon sector, the night of March 17/18. Turrill's 1st Battalion took position in support in the secondary line. Westcott's 3d Battalion, in reserve, moved into camp to the rear and continued training.

The morning after his arrival at the railhead, Wise, with details from each of his companies, looked over their section of CR Montgirmont. The hike to the front lines was up three kilometers of communication trench. Wise was taken to the dugout of the French major commanding, who explained that in this sector there was no continuous trench system but a series of strongpoints. Montgirmont itself was a hill about a hundred meters high and about three kilometers in circumference. It was divided into four company sectors. Three company positions faced the Germans; the other was on the reverse slope.

"It is a very, very quiet sector," said the French major. "Like being in rest billets. You'll have no trouble here."

Every afternoon, from two to five, the Germans would shell Montgirmont.

"We never saw a German," said Wise.

Catlin's 6th Marines' dispositions were similar. Major Sibley's 3d Battalion, 6th Marines, began its move into the trenches at CR Mont-sous-les-Cotes, at 9 PM on March 18 and was in position by 4 AM.

The ground in front of the leading edge of the Marines' trenches sloped away until it rose to meet the corresponding German front line. No-man's-land in the Toulon sector, shell churned and barbed-wire laced, was sometimes as narrow as a hundred meters, but for much of its length the lines were a kilometer apart. Cautiously viewed through periscopes and loopholes, no-man's-land was desolate and forlorn, with the wreckage of little villages and farmhouses, for this area had been the scene of heavy fighting in 1915. Now there was little action, by mutual, unspoken consent, except for the intermittent German shelling and an occasional raid.

Where the lines were the closest, listening posts pushed out in front were manned at night. Where the distances were greater, there were observation posts out in front or a sketchy outpost line made up of strongpoints manned by one or

Brig. Gen. Smedley Butler and Maj. Gen. John Lejeune, two of the most prominent Leathernecks of the first three decades of the twentieth century, officiate at a postwar Marine baseball game in Washington in 1925. (USMC #521996, History Division, Marine Corps University [hereafter HD/MCU])

Alfred A. Cunningham, pioneering first Marine aviator, stands before a Curtis "Jenny" trainer at Pensacola in 1914. In 1917–18 Cunningham was instrumental in deploying primitive airplane squadrons to combat missions in the Azores and northern France. (USMC #517396, HD/MCU)

Marine Gunnery Sergeant, *1918, by Col. Donna J. Neary, USMCR. The commanding presence and personal example of such veteran NCOs enabled the 4th Marine Brigade to fight effectively against the most lethal adversaries the Corps had ever faced.* (Marine Corps Art Collection)

Marine Rifleman, *by Samuel Johnson Woolf. Painted by a civilian artist in France in 1918, the oil portrait captures the wary confidence of new veterans—at ease among the rubble but ready for the fighting to resume.* (Marine Corps Art Collection)

Brig. Gen. James G. Harbord of the U.S. Army took command of the 4th Marine Brigade amid considerable interservice resentment but won the hearts of his Marines with his stalwart leadership. "They never failed me," he said of his Marines. (Courtesy Naval History)

The Flare, *by John W. Thomason, an infantry officer in the 5th Marines who survived the 1918 battles to chronicle the Marines' combat experience with stark sketches and lively narrative in books like* Fix Bayonets. *(Marine Corps Art Collection)*

Wire Cutters, *by Lester G. Hornby, a civilian artist authorized by General Pershing to sketch U.S. combat forces. This work portrays a pair of sappers stealthily cutting German wire in advance of a raiding party.* (Marine Corps Art Collection)

With their "tin" helmets, M1903 Springfield rifles, and stripped down to light marching packs, these Leathernecks of the 55th Company, 5th Marines, are on their way to the front in 1918. (Courtesy *Naval History*)

Col. Albertus W. Catlin, who survived the sinking of the USS Maine *in Cuba and received the Medal of Honor at Veracruz, commanded the 6th Marines before being shot in the chest at Belleau Wood.* (USMC #11367, HD/MCU)

Capt. Harvey Dunn, USA, one of eight artists commissioned by the army in 1917, portrayed the high point of the German advance on Paris as the Boche attacked through the wheat toward the U.S. Marines defending Les Mares Farm. (Marine Corps Art Collection)

GySgt. Dan Daly, paragon of hard-nosed NCO leadership and recipient of Medals of Honor for China (1900) and Haiti (1915), who inspired his Marines in Belleau Wood's wheat fields with "Come on, you sons of bitches, do you want to live forever?" (USMC #515597, HD/MCU)

Maj. "Johnny the Hard" Hughes led the 1st Battalion, 6th Marines, at Belleau Wood and Soissons. Blinded by mustard gas during a German counterattack, Hughes reported, "Terrific bombardment—everything OK—can't you get hot coffee to me?"
(Hughes biographical files, HD/MCU)

Lemuel C. Shepherd Jr. was wounded three times while serving in the 5th Marines in World War I. In 1945 he commanded the 6th Marine Division at Okinawa (shown) and later became the twentieth commandant of the Marine Corps. (USMC #122-119, HD/MCU)

A German minnenwerfer *(mine thrower) captured by the 2d Battalion, 5th Marines, at Belleau Wood. Marines nicknamed the enemy trench mortar "the moaning Minnie" for the projectile's whistling trajectory.* (USMC #4975, HD/MCU)

Ground crews of the 1st Marine Aviation Force prepare three British-built DeHaviland light bombers for the next mission on a forward airstrip in northern France. (Courtesy *Naval History*)

Artist James Butcher's Bombing of Thielt, Belgium *portrays DeHaviland bombers of Capt. Robert Lytle's Squadron 9, 1st Marine Aviation Force, attacking German-held railroad yards at Thielt in October 1918.* (Marine Corps Art Collection)

Second Lt. Ralph Talbot, a twenty-one-year-old Marine pilot, received the Medal of Honor for "exceptionally merito-rious service and extraordinary heroism" in two air missions over France and Belgium. He crashed and died two weeks later. (USMC #524930, HD/MCU)

Former sergeant Gerald C. Thomas was Maj. "Johnny the Hard" Hughes' intelligence scout at Belleau Wood and Soissons, earning a battlefield commission. After brilliant service on Gua-dalcanal and in Korea, he retired as a four-star general. (USMC #522520, HD/MCU)

two platoons. Both sides used the piles of rubble from the demolished farmhouses or hamlets between the lines to construct these strongpoints.

The support trench (not be confused with the "support line," which was farther to the rear) ran fifty to two hundred meters behind the front line and was connected to it by zigzag trenches. Main supply trenches stretched back from the support trenches for as much as 3.2 kilometers, so that a man could emerge in the rear from below ground at a relatively safe distance from whatever "Fritz" might be shooting that day or night.

Marine battalions were to have ten days in each of the three positions—front line, support, and reserve—and then rotate. Accordingly the 1st Battalion, 5th Marines, and the 2d Battalion, 6th Marines, were the next to go up to the front.

Major Hughes' 1st Battalion, 6th Marines, had stayed in the Bourmont training area until March 17, St. Patrick's Day. Those Marines with Irish blood, and there were many, duly observed the day. The celebration was topped off by some filling their canteens with *vin rouge*. Private Gus Gulberg's lieutenant, inspecting rifles in the 75th Company, got a whiff of someone's breath. The lieutenant had the whole platoon uncork their canteens and went down the ranks sniffing each one. "Many quarts of *vin rouge* were spilled that day," said Gulberg.

Hughes' battalion left camp at about noon for the six-mile hike to the railway station. The American Red Cross at the station gave out hot coffee and cigarettes. A long train ride took them to the railhead at Souilly, where the French Red Cross served them more hot coffee, but this time laced with rum. After breakfasting in a field next to some dead mules, the battalion began a "long but interesting hike," moving toward a reserve position. At one point the sight of a dozen German airplanes overhead being pursued by antiaircraft fire entertained them. That night the battalion arrived in Sommedieue. The French had decorated the town in their honor.

Gulberg and five other Marines from the 75th Company were billeted in a room on the first floor of a stone house. After scouting around for some wine, stealing some potatoes from the commissary, and getting some bacon grease from a cook, they had a "big feed of fried hardtack, French fried potatoes and *vin rouge*."

Hughes' battalion spent six days in Sommedieue; quiet days except for occasional long-range shelling. The move to the front began on a Sunday night. The Marines reached the communications trenches and started in. Orders were passed: no loud talking, no smoking. The trench was in some places knee deep in mud; Gulberg stumbled and fell six or seven times. The 75th Company reached the front line at about midnight and made the relief without any trouble. Gulberg's post was a little machine-gun emplacement with a corrugated iron roof.

No-Man's-Land

The Marines began sending out patrols of two kinds. Those of one kind were wire patrols, which went out to repair the barbed wire, the other reconnaissance patrols sent to eavesdrop on the Germans. These were not raiding parties, not at first, although picking up a German prisoner was, in Colonel Catlin's words, "always welcome."

Hand-cranked telephones were the most dependable form of communication from outposts to front line to supports in the rear. Marines firmly believed that the Germans, as close as a hundred meters away, could hear every word being said, by means of powerful induction coils. Simple "shackle" codes were used to encrypt numbers, the most vulnerable part of any message. Marine wiremen labored valiantly to keep the wire intact. Shell fire cut it as often as fifteen or twenty times a day.

Other than the telephones, runners were the basic form of communication. Messages were scrawled on field message pads. Commanders sent important messages by runners in pairs, following separate routes. Runners were schooled to carry messages in the left breast pocket of their shirt or coat. If they became a casualty, that's where others were to look.

That left breast pocket was an important receptacle for other things. Patriotic Marines and soldiers were prone to carrying small, folded, forty-eight-star American flags. Religious ones were apt to have a New Testament. More worldly types used the pocket for a pack of playing cards. Whistles and watches might also vie for space in the left breast pocket. Officers and NCOs carried whistles for signaling; the whistle went into the pocket, and a chain secured it to a button or buttonhole. The officer's whistle was a shrill affair, like a London policeman's. The sergeant's whistle was of the type called a "thunderer," with a cork ball that vibrated in its chamber. Old-timers were apt to use the breast pocket to house a watch, again with a chain to a buttonhole. Thick railroad watches were prevalent. Younger officers and some well-to-do enlisted favored wristwatches, a new fashion that the war had made popular. When orders were given, there was a great to-do about synchronizing watches. It was more than dramatics. Exact time was life-important, particularly in coordinating supporting fires.

In their apprenticeship in the trenches, Marine reconnaissance patrols were schooled to go out on a definite route and on a definite time schedule. If detected by the Germans they could be protected by prepared friendly artillery fires. An average patrol might be a half-platoon, or about twenty-five Marines, led by a lieutenant.

The "quiet sector" was now quiet only in relative terms. The Germans had learned there were Americans opposing them, and their curiosity was aroused. They tended to use larger patrols than the Marines, about forty men. Clashes between Marine and German patrols were frequent but generally inconclusive.

German aircraft greatly fascinated the Marines. They were certain that the gaudily painted biplanes with the black Maltese crosses on their wings watched and reported every movement they made to the German batteries below. Sausage-shaped observation balloons ("Drachen") with wicker baskets floated above the horizon behind the German lines. Shelling by the Germans occurred daily.

After spending ten days in the line and ten days in support, Wise's 2d Battalion went into reserve, which meant an encampment of shacks well to the rear. As was his wont, Wise managed an excellent mess. In addition to the army ration of meat, potatoes, onions, and bread, there was a French commissary nearby that supplied fish, chickens, cheese, and wine. After ten days of rest Wise's battalion returned to the front, this time to CR Chantillon, with the post of command in a rock quarry. The Germans shelled Wise's position every day from two to three. There was more patrolling now, and the patrols were larger.

One of Wise's patrols got the worst of it. Lieutenant August L. Sundeval, a Plattsburg-trained Army Reserve lieutenant in the 18th Company, leading a patrol of thirty Marines ran head-on into a German patrol estimated at a hundred or more, possibly a *Sturmtruppen* company in training. The Germans were using the quiet sector as a sort of finishing school for divisions being retrained in General Von Hutier's stealthy tactics made famous earlier on the eastern front and at Caporetto. Each division was charged with developing a company-sized force of *Sturmtruppen,* specially trained for the assault.

In the melee, Sundeval was hit. Gunnery Sergeant Winchenbaugh carried back the dying lieutenant, for which gallantry he received the Croix de Guerre and was recommended for the Distinguished Service Cross. Two other Marines were missing in action. These were Wise's first combat losses.

One of Catlin's 6th Marines' larger outposts, where the lines were about three-quarters of a mile apart, was manned by a platoon, about fifty Marines, under Lt. Allan C. Perkinson. Just before midnight one night the Germans raided the outpost. Perkinson tried to signal for a box barrage, but his signal rockets were wet. Two men, Privates Sleet and Hullinger, offered to sprint back to the frontline trench, ignoring the connecting trench as too slow, to get more rockets. Both Sleet and Hullinger reached the main trench safely, and Sleet dashed back with an armful of rockets through an intense German artillery barrage. As it turned out, the rockets weren't needed; Perkinson and his men had beaten off the raid. The Germans departed after flinging a number of stick grenades into the Marine position. German shell fire continued for another spiteful half-hour. At dawn Perkinson sent out patrols. They found about five hundred "potato masher" grenades, fifty big, two-handed wire cutters, and two dead Germans. Perkinson guessed that there might have been a hundred Germans in the raiding force. He had only one casualty, a man wounded by the shell fire. Perkinson received the Croix de Guerre for the night's work, and so did the two runners.

Of these nasty little fights Colonel Catlin said, "We loved the Hun no more for that."

Rats and Cooties

The trenches had not been well maintained except for the officers' dugouts, some of which were little miracles of housekeeping improvisation. Otherwise, mud was everywhere. Most dugouts were wet with standing water and overrun with vermin in the form of "cooties" and rats. "Cooties," unforgettably pervasive in trench warfare, were small but persistent members of the louse family. "The cootie is as troublesome as shrapnel and he loves Red Cross knitting," said Catlin.

Getting back into reserve meant baths and having one's clothes steamed to give temporary relief from the louse. Rats, however, were equally omnipresent and virtually indestructible. They would eat anything and would chew their way through canvas packs to get at rations. They also made a more grisly diet of bodies left out in no-man's-land . The Marines heard that some regiments, particularly the English ones, kept terriers for the killing of rats. The Leathernecks had no terriers, but the 5th Marines had a coatimundi, a kind of raccoonlike ant bear, for a mascot and it had a reputation as a rat killer. The 6th Marines' mascot, a Central American anteater, proved ineffective in this role.

If not terriers, the Marines did have dogs. The 6th Marines' machine-gun company had a dog that had come along from Haiti. One of the regiment's battalions had a German shepherd that had been presented to it. An officer in the 6th Marines kept a sheep dog from the Pyrenees.

The Germans Break the Deadlock

The Marines heard that the Germans had launched a big push somewhere to their west. General Ludendorff's first great offensive of 1918 had begun on the Somme on March 21 and was driving toward Amiens, its axis of advance along the fault line marking the boundary between the French army and the British Expeditionary Force. Ludendorff believed that if he could split apart the two armies it would break the alliance and so end the war.[3] The Germans drove a wedge about a hundred kilometers wide and fifty kilometers deep into the front, with the apex just short of Amiens. The British and French armies did not have a common commander. Jealousies and political sensibilities had made that impossible until this critical time. On March 24, Field Marshal Haig and General Petain proposed to their respective governments a single command. On the following day, Pershing, budging from his insistence that the Americans be employed in an American army, met with Petain at Compiegne and offered the separate use of the four divisions ready for combat. On March 26, at Douellens, an agreement was reached giving General Foch certain powers for effecting coordination. Two days later Pershing visited Foch at Bombon and unreservedly placed all the American forces at his disposal. On April 3, at Beauvais, with representatives of all governments present, General Foch was designated the commander in chief of the entire front.

The Allied commanders placed constant demands on Pershing to provide the largest number of personnel possible in the smallest tactical units possible. First to go were four Negro regiments of infantry intended for the 93d Division. These regiments were placed at the disposal of the French, who scattered them from Alsace to Champagne in different French corps. They would remain so isolated until the end of the war.

French troops were pulled away from the quiet sectors, including Verdun, and sent to reinforce the lines at the point of threatened rupture. The X Corps had to extend another eight kilometers north from the old limiting point at Eix to cover the departure of two divisions. Patrol activities increased.

The 5th Marines moved to the left, with Turrill's 1st Battalion filling CR Eix on the extreme left and Westcott's 3d Battalion moving into CR Chatillon on the right, a stretch of five and a half kilometers along a railroad track that ran parallel to the Meuse. Neville held Wise's 2d Battalion in reserve. The 6th Marines stretched out to the left, with Hughes' 1st Battalion taking over CR Montgirmont. Colonels Neville and Catlin reassumed tactical command of their regiments from their French counterparts.

On March 26, Major Westcott, who had brought the 3d Battalion, 5th Marines, to France, gave up command to Maj. Edward S. Sturdivant. Westcott was sent off to command an army outfit, the 1st Battalion, 104th Infantry, 26th U.S. Division. Six weeks later, Sturdivant would yield command to Maj. Benjamin S. Berry and transfer to the 3d U.S. Division to command the 3d Battalion, 30th Infantry. Berry, tall and slender, had received the Croix de Guerre as a captain in the Verdun sector two months earlier when his company repulsed a German night raid.

On April 2 the 6th Marines made further adjustments, giving the brigade a contiguous front, four battalions on line, two in reserve, and the 12th Field Artillery in direct support. Wrote Colonel Catlin:

> This placed the Sixth next to the Fifth and brought our brigade of Marines together in the region of Les Eparges. At this new position of the Sixth the woods jutted farther out upon the plain, and at one point the opposing trenches were only 150 yards apart. Here we had listening posts in the old French trench just outside our first line of wire.
>
> During those days and nights in the trenches the Quartermaster's outfit had as hard a time of it as any of us. Hard work and little glory was their lot, but they stood to their task . . . and the boys in front were fed. The supply company was located three miles in the rear and every twenty-four hours the commissary detachments had to get adequate supplies to the battalion dumps at the front whether the roads were shelled or not. It all had to be done at night and the weather had no place in the calculations. Food was taken to the front line every night by the battalion Quartermaster and his men on mule carts, pack mules. . . . [T]here is none of the excitement and uplift of battle in driving mules at night.

Poison Gas

Catlin moved his PC to a hill overlooking his regimental positions and named it "Rome." In ancient times the hill had been the site of a fortified Roman camp, and a trace of the old earthworks—a grass-covered mound ten feet high—still ran across the hill. A few gas shells fell near PC (post of command) Rome, and Catlin clapped on his gas mask.

"A gas mask, by the way," wrote Catlin, "is a thing one is anxious to take off at the first opportunity. It is a hot and stifling thing and seems to impede the faculties; the wearer takes in the air through his mouth, after it has been sucked through the purifying chemicals. His nose is not trusted and is clamped shut. Imagine yourself fighting with a clothespin on your nose and a bag over your mouth and you may be able to get some notion of what a gas mask is like."

The old tactic of infantry advancing behind clouds of nonpersistent gas had failed. Now, through German chemical wizardry, there was a new agent. The Bayer Company, of the aspirin people, was in the forefront of war gas technology. Mustard gas was the new agent.

"Gas was the worst evil we had to encounter," wrote Catlin, "We learned to dread the deadly smell of mustard."

The Germans called it "Yellow Cross" from the markings on its shell casings. Bombardments sometimes mixed "Yellow Cross" mustard-gas shells with "Green Cross" diphosgene. By and large, mustard did not kill; it incapacitated. Diphosgene killed. In one of the war's nice little ironies, it smelled like fresh-cut hay. A third major agent was a family of arsenical compounds encased in "Blue Cross" shells, but the effectiveness of arsenical compounds proved disappointing.

On the night of April 12/13, Capt. Adolph B. Miller's 74th Company, 1st Battalion, 6th Marines, was in reserve at Fontaine–St. Robert, about a mile behind the front line and fairly comfortably billeted in prefabricated, wooden Adrian huts, in this case sunk about three feet into the ground in a ravine. There was no overhead cover except for the flimsy roofs. The Marines were sleeping, sixty to a hut, in double-decked bunks with chicken-wire springs. During the predawn hours of April 13 the Germans unleashed a sudden bombardment of some two thousand mustard gas shells into the ravine. One of the first shells exploded inside a hut filled with sleeping men. Partly due to severity of shelling, partly due to the inexperience of Marines who were slow in getting on their gas masks, losses were horrific: 295 casualties, including all the 74th Company's officers. Forty Marines died.

The sudden bombardment of sleeping men in reserve positions was a common tragedy along the western front, but the incident shocked the Marines, who in a matter of minutes suffered more combat casualties than the Corps had sustained in all four years of the American Civil War. Pvt. James Hatcher's 84th Company, 3d Battalion, 6th Marines, had recently occupied the very barracks hit by the mustard gas barrage. As Hatcher remembered the catastrophe, "That company was almost annihilated. Some of the poor fellows who were not killed outright, rushed out on the hills to escape the gas, and then, crazed by the poison, they wandered for days before being found."

The 5th Marines took casualties in action the night of April 17. In the confused fighting 2d Lt. Max D. Gilfillan and Sgt. Louis Cukela of the 66th Company, 2d Battalion, would be honored with the French Croix de Guerre for distinguished valor. For the twenty-nine-year-old Cukela, a Croatian émigré and former army corporal, the citation would mark the beginning of an enviable string of combat awards from a half-dozen countries in 1918, culminating at Soissons, where he would receive Medals of Honor from both the army and the navy for the same action.

On the night of April 20/21, a platoon of the 45th Company of the 3d Battalion, 5th Marines, under 2d Lt. Edward B. Hope, occupied the commanding high ground on the extreme left flank of the division. After a heavy bombardment, the Germans hit the platoon with one of their specially trained *Sturmtruppen* parties. The Marines beat them off. The Germans left behind the bodies of two officers and a soldier. One wounded soldier was taken prisoner. Hope lost three killed and eleven wounded. He received the Croix de Guerre, becoming, with Gilfillan and Cukela, one of the first Marines to receive the award.

The same night as the raid against the 45th Company, the 84th Company, 6th Marines, fought off a raid made by the Germans with flamethrowers and grenades.

Both sides became increasingly edgy about these nocturnal excursions between the trenches, and the slightest disturbance triggered immediate artillery barrages. During a particularly heavy barrage the regimental dental officer for the 5th Marines, Lt. Cdr. Alexander G. Lyle, U.S. Navy, rushed into the firestorm to assist a badly wounded Marine, Cpl. Thomas Regan. Doctor Lyle administered first aid to Regan while shielding him with his body and then carried him safely back to the trench line. Both men survived. Lyle received the Medal of Honor.

Rumors and Concerns

Spring came, and the land turned green once again. Catlin remembered "a hillside that was white and fragrant with a great mass of lily-of-the-valley." The benign season notwithstanding, a general spirit of concern prevailed among the Allied troops. Ludendorff's series of offensives had unleashed the Germans from their trenches, and once again large, mobile forces threatened to penetrate far into the interior of France.

More French divisions departed the Verdun sector for emergencies elsewhere along the line. Pershing was not keen on further trench employment for the 2d Division, or for that matter on further training of his divisions by the French. He had decided that American divisions would do any training in trench warfare for the new regiments now arriving from the states. Pershing expressed these concerns and also set a deadline for the return of the 2d Division to American control in a terse letter to the chief of the French Military Commission on the last day of April.

Five days later the 2d Division received orders to regroup in the Combles area southwest of Bar-le-Duc and then entrain for movement to the Chaumont-en-Vexin training area. They would be there only two weeks.

General Harbord Takes Command of the Marine Brigade

During this baptism in the lines Pershing replaced Brig. Gen. Charles Doyen as the 4th Brigade commander with his own chief of staff, army brigadier general James G. Harbord. In Pershing's judgment, the fifty-eight-year-old Doyen wasn't physically up to the rigors of the western front. Doyen was not alone in being relieved. The U.S. Army commanders of the 3d Brigade and the 2d Field Artillery Brigade were also replaced. Pershing was merciless in relieving senior commanders he considered less than fully competent. The same winnowing process was happening throughout the AEF.

The Marines did not take kindly to having their veteran brigade commander, Doyen, relieved by an army officer, even one as personable and industrious as Harbord. Some brigade staff officers spoke darkly about Pershing's motives in suppressing the free spirit of the Marines by removing their leader. For his part, Harbord seemed to realize the awkwardness of the situation. He was no Marine, and he had very limited command or combat experience. Yet he worked hard to understand and preserve the distinctive pride and culture of his Marines, and soon the grumbling ceased. It turns out that there was a lot to admire about Harbord's innate leadership.

Harbord and Catlin had been members of the same class at the Army War College, and Catlin found him to be a splendid soldier: "Though not a Marine himself, General Harbord fully understood and appreciated the traditions of our Corps, and it was said of him that he became as pro-Marine as any Marine."

Hard-nosed Capt. Holland M. Smith (the media would not saddle him with the nickname "Howlin' Mad" until 1943) also developed a liking for the new brigade commander. Earlier in the year Smith had become the first Marine officer to graduate from the Army General Staff College in Langres, France, and he was brigade adjutant when Harbord assumed command. "Harbord was one of America's great soldiers . . . of the same soldierly breed as Pershing," Smith stated later. "I always took Harbord as a model."

Lt. Lucian H. Vandoren of Holcomb's battalion wrote to his father, "General Harbord, former Chief of Staff for General Pershing, has, as you probably know, been given command of the Brigade of Marines now serving in France. The other night he dined with us and we found him every inch the soldier, very interesting and likeable. He, in responding to a toast to 'our new Marine,' said that he was very glad to be a Marine and added that General Pershing, in turning the Brigade over to him, had said that he was 'giving him the finest command in France.'"

Moving Northwest

On a bright day early in May there was a ceremony in a wooded spot behind the Verdun lines. Two companies of Marines and two of soldiers formed a hollow square in the glade. A French band played martial airs, and a French general passed out the Croix de Guerre to about twenty-five Marines and doughboys and a like number of French poilus. The ceremony was a kind of graduation exercise marking the readiness of the 2d Division for more serious employment. Between the 9th and 16th of May the French relieved the 2d Division in position.

"We rejoiced," said Catlin, "for the order meant a rest from trench digging, relief from the nightly peril of No Man's Land, a fond farewell to the mud and rats and cooties. . . . Eagerly we climbed out of the damp and narrow trenches, fought one more battle with the cooties, and looked for the last time on 'the misty mid-region of Wier' which was No Man's Land."

This time in the trenches had taught the Marines many things. They learned the art of night reliefs. They learned to coordinate the fires of battalion weapons and attached machine guns with mortars and artillery. They learned to patrol in no-man's-land—to repair barbed-wire entanglements, to repel German raids, to raid German positions. They got a bitter taste of gas warfare.

The Marines left the soggy Verdun sector without regrets. They had no way of knowing that they would be returning to the St. Mihiel salient, those of them who survived, in the late summer. The division moved by foot, truck, and train to a training area near Bar-le-Duc and just northeast of Vitry-le-Francois.

The Germans, having nearly cut the western front in two at Amiens, next attacked the British on the Lys and drove them back. The French shifted a number of divisions to support the British. The Marines read the censored news in the *Stars and Stripes* and heard rumors of what was going on elsewhere on the western front. They fidgeted impatiently. Why weren't they being used on a more active front? Said Catlin: "We learned that the First Division had been sent in at Cantigny, and this did not add to our contentment."

The 2d Division moved by train on May 18 and 19 to Pontoise and then marched to a reserve position at Chaumont-en-Vixen near Beauvais, which was about halfway between Paris and Amiens. They skirted Paris, but there was no liberty for the men. The division completed this movement on May 23, dimly aware that the war had changed since Ludendorff's first offensive in March and keenly anxious to get into the fighting.

At Chaumont-en-Vixen there was vigorous, last-minute training in expectation of the division taking its place at the front. In the new training area there was no trench work but constant drilling, route marching (a Marine's heavy marching order weighed about sixty pounds), and field problems in open warfare at the battalion, regimental, and brigade levels.

The 2d Division, as now assembled, was an imposing sight. In the 6th Regiment, Colonel Catlin was allocated 332 mules to pull his wagons—rations, water, ammunition, rolling kitchens, and so forth. The regiment's transport included the colonel's touring car, three motorcycles for messenger service, and fifty-nine riding horses (the British called them "chargers") for the commanders and staff officers of the regiment and its battalions. The automobile would go to the front but not the horses. The horses were kept in perfect condition but were of little use.

The 6th Marines also had "Lizzie," or more formally, "Elizabeth Ford," a Ford car given the regiment by New York socialite Mrs. Elizabeth Pearce. Lizzie came equipped as an ambulance and had been used as such in Bordeaux when the regiment had camped eight kilometers outside that city. When the 6th Marines joined up with the 2d Division, the division had ambulances enough, and Lizzie became a mail carrier and a general-purpose hauler. Up by Verdun she got smashed up in a ditch, and the ambulance top was lost. The Marines pulled her out of the ditch and converted her into a sort of pickup truck. Lizzie remained the regiment's motorized mascot. In the words of one popular verse from the ranks, the Ford was "a cute little jinny, all noise and tinny, but full of American pep." As Catlin later described the vehicle at Belleau Wood, "one wheel wobbled and she was full of shrapnel holes, but she still ran."

The 3d Replacement Battalion joined the 4th Brigade at Chaumont. John Thomason, now a first lieutenant, was assigned as second in command of Capt. George W. Hamilton's 49th Company, 1st Battalion, 5th Marines. Laurence Stallings went to Capt. Philip T. Case's 47th Company, 3d Battalion, of the same regiment. Thomason would be with the 49th Company for the remainder of the war. Stallings would be less lucky.

Brigade maneuvers were held on May 29. A rumor rippled through the ranks that they were going up to relieve the 1st U.S. Division at Cantigny. Maj. Gen. Robert L. Bullard's 1st Division had launched the first American offensive of the war on May 28, a regimental-sized assault that seized the fortified high ground near Cantigny, and had then held on against a heavy German shelling and waves of counterattacks. The tactical victory provided the Allies a rare bright spot in an otherwise dismal week of defeat and retreat. The Marines hoped their own trial by fire would come soon.

CHAPTER SIX

"Retreat, Hell!"

Once again turmoil swept northern France.[1] Ludendorff's offensives had caused tens of thousands of refugees to flee westward, pitiful columns of families, struggling with their enormous bundles and their terrified children. German long-range guns began bombarding Paris in random patterns, heightening the sense of panic. Rumors and despair became increasingly rampant.

Soldiers and Marines of the 2d Division champed at the bit. Many of them—the 5th Marines, 6th Machine Gun Battalion, and both regiments of the 3d Infantry Brigade—had already spent nearly a full year in France, doing little more than training. The men were impatient to fight, to prove themselves against the Germans, to make a difference in the war.

Strength returns for the 2d Division issued with suspect exactness from the post of command at Chaumont-en-Vixen on May 29, 1918, reported 1,063 officers and 25,602 men available for duty. Ammunition on hand was reported as "belts and combat trains filled" for small arms and "combat trains" and "ammunition trains" filled for the hungry guns of the artillery. Omar Bundy's division, Marines and doughboys alike, their appetites whetted by the Verdun experience, were armed and equipped for a serious fight. It looked as if their time had finally come.

The commanding general of the French Group Reserve Armies had requested that the division be moved into the Beauvais area, the movement to be made by marching, commencing the morning of May 31, and to be completed in two days.

The 30th of May was Memorial Day, and in the 2d Division there were observances. The regimental bands were ordered to play "Departed Days" at noon, while the staffs worked on the march tables and administrative orders that would govern the two-day movement to Beauvais.

But in the afternoon all these preparations were canceled. On May 27 the Germans had jolted the Allies with their third big offensive of the year, breaking through the French lines on the Champagne front. The ancient province of Champagne, with Picardy to its west, Lorraine to its east, and Burgundy to the south, had been quiet since the failure of the Nivelle offensive the previous spring, a failure so disastrous that much of the French army had mutinied. After 1917, the French, now under Gen. Philippe Petain, were reliable only in defense. Even then, Petain had authorized a "flexible defense"—essentially permitting his commanders to give up ground at their discretion.

At 5 PM a French staff officer arrived at the 2d Division headquarters, his dust-covered automobile evidence of hard driving. The division was to start for Meaux, which was on the Marne about forty kilometers west of Chateau-Thierry and ninety kilometers from Chaumont-en-Vixen. French camions would be provided beginning at 5 AM the following morning for the infantry. There was no transportation available for the combat-support units or supply trains.

Foch had thinned out his forces in the Champagne region to meet the demands of Picardy. The Chemin des Dames front was considered very strong, which is the reason it was used to rest exhausted French and British troops. The French Sixth Army (General Duchene) held the front with six French and four British divisions, all badly worn. On the German side, General von Boehn's Seventh Army occupied the front.

The movement of the Marine brigade began during the night. Harbord's headquarters broke camp at 4 AM the morning of May 31. The weather was clear and warm. Regiments embarked in camions during the night and morning and traveled all day. At French Sixth Army headquarters at Trilport, verbal orders were given that the infantry was to concentrate near May-en-Multien, northeast of Meaux, and there await the arrival of the artillery and animal transport.

Paris Threatened

In late April Ludendorff had approved Operation "Blucher," which would put Crown Prince Wilhelm's army group into the attack on a twenty-two-mile front with the objective of reaching the line Soissons–Rheims. Crack divisions that had been used on the Somme and on the Lys would be used again, but they could not be ready until the end of May. The scope of the German offensive was meant to be limited. The line of the Vesle River was as far as it was expected to go.

Once again the Germans showed great skill in lateral movement across the front, achieving almost complete surprise. They struck hard early on the morning of May 27, hitting the Chemin des Dames highway northwest of Rheims. By evening the Germans had advanced nineteen kilometers, reaching Fismes and attaining a line of about ten kilometers along the Vesle. The French had thrown in all locally available reserves and, with eleven divisions in the fight, began to pull in reserves from as far away as the Vosges and beyond Amiens. On May 28 the Germans crossed the Vesle and moved south along a broad front from Soissons to Rheims. The depleted French and British divisions in that formerly quiet sector were routed.

Agreeably surprised, the Germans decided to strike on for the Marne. On May 29 their attacks were pointed at Soissons and Rheims. Soissons was taken; Rheims was not. In the center a great salient bulged forward and on the 30th reached the Marne. The farthest advance of the German drive would be the much-fought-over ancient city of Chateau-Thierry on the road to Paris. The French capital was once again in danger. The Germans were confident, the French demoralized. Petain summed it up in a report to Foch on June 1: since May 27, thirty-two French and five British divisions had been engaged; of this number, seventeen were used up. Only nine more divisions could be shifted to the front, and, wrote Petain, *"Et c'est tout"* (That is all).

Pershing later wrote: "The alarming situation had caused General Petain to call on me on May 30th for American troops to be sent to the region of Chateau-Thierry."

New German Tactics

Ludendorff's 1918 offensives put an end to trench warfare as it had been fought on the western front for the past three years. German tactical innovations are generally credited in large part to the highly successful Gen. Oskar von Hutier, who had been transferred from the eastern to the western front. Key to the Hutier tactics in the attack was the novel use of small combat groups that moved their light machine guns swiftly to the front. In defense, heavy machine guns were used in even greater numbers than before, not to hold a rigid front line but disposed in depth in mutually supporting positions. The English-speaking Allies called these clusters of water-cooled Maxims "machine-gun nests." Riflemen became little more than ammo bearers for the machine guns. German long-range guns had great propaganda value in shelling Paris, but German artillery doctrine called for masses of medium and light artillery well up to the front in both the attack and the defense.

German artillery preparations for the Chemin des Dames offensive were enormous. The German artillery virtuoso Col. Georg Bruchmuller, called out of retirement in 1916, orchestrated the bombardment by nearly four thousand guns. In the initial attack on May 27, Bruchmuller had drenched the Chemin des Dames with gas, using Yellow Cross and Blue Cross gas shells by the hundreds of thousands.

During the winter of 1917–18 Bruchmuller had conducted some interesting trial shoots with gas shells, reporting the results directly to Ludendorff. To be effective, gas had to be persistent, unaffected by the weather, and dispersed evenly. Bruchmuller's experiments, including tests with animals and human "volunteers," indicated that dichlorodiethyl sulphide might be the perfect agent. It was a yellowish liquid that evaporated slowly and, in minute droplets, clung to vegetation, equipment, and uniforms. A vesicant, it caused blisters. It affected the eyes, causing severe conjunctivitis and often at least temporary blindness. It ravaged the throat and lungs. It looked something like and smelled something like mustard.

The Germans first used "mustard gas" operationally in July 1917, but not until the spring of 1918 did they use it in quantity. Under Bruchmuller's tutelage, German artillery had mastered the technique of delivering gas shells. Gas shells made a gurgling sound in flight and exploded with a "plop." A direct hit, such as was needed with high explosive, was unnecessary. Mustard in heavy gaseous form rolled into low places, including dugouts and shell holes, and lingered for days.[2]

Allied Countermoves

The 2d Division chief of staff, Col. Preston Brown, U.S. Army, went ahead by car and found the roads around Meaux clogged with refugees. He drove on to Trilport, headquarters of the French Sixth Army. Brown suggested to General Duchene, its very tired commander, that the 2d Division convoys be rerouted north of Meaux to May-en-Multien and that the division occupy a line along the Clignon Brook, facing north toward Soissons. This would put the division in the area of the VII Corps. General Duchene approved the change with a Gallic shrug.

French motor trucks called *camions* arrived at four o'clock the next morning. Camions had bench seats along the sides and canvas covers like prairie schooners. They moved in serials of about fifty vehicles, each serial enough to lift a battalion. The Marines thought the drivers were Chinese; actually, they were Annamites and Tonkinese from French Indochina.

The last day of May was clear, bright, and sweltering hot. The Marines fell in at dawn, ate breakfast from rolling kitchens, and climbed into the trucks. Thirty or so Marines, with rifles and sixty-pound packs, crowded into each truck. A French officer rode with each battalion convoy in an automobile and took the battalion commander and his staff with him. The first serial moved out at 5:30 AM, with Lieutenant Colonel Wise's battalion embarked.

Wise saw his men loaded into the trucks and then went to the head of the column in a little car belonging to the French transport officer. Outside Meaux, Wise saw for the first time civilian refugees streaming down the road. "All looked terror stricken."

Colonel Catlin waited until his last squad had moved out and then followed in his staff car. It was 120 kilometers to his destination. The roads were generally good, but the drivers, who had been at their wheels for three days and nights, had the exciting habit of falling asleep. The Marine passengers behaved as though they were going to a picnic. The French villagers dutifully cheered them and threw flowers as they passed. Small American flags were furiously waved.

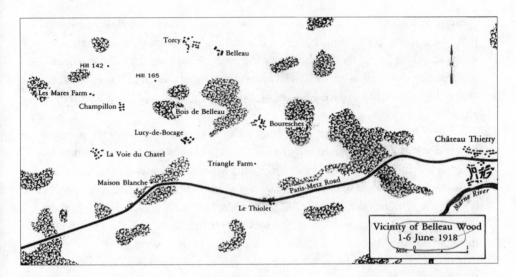

Vicinity of Belleau Wood
1–6 June 1918

"We were jammed into French trucks and started out," wrote Lt. Clifton Cates of the 96th Company to his mother and sister a few days later. "We rode all day and all night—it was an awful cold and dirty trip. If you can, imagine about one thousand trucks lined up behind the other and running as fast as possible. We passed thru the outskirts of gay Paree and on thru numerous towns. The French people would cheer us as we passed thru the towns, and the children would throw us worlds of flowers—it is a sign of good luck."

"It was more like an enormous bridal procession than a column of fighters going to face a terrible death," said Colonel Catlin.

Few Marines knew their destination—most assumed they were off to relieve the 1st Division near Chateau-Thierry—but they welcomed the speedy advance toward the front. Aboard one of the trucks carrying the 84th Company of the 3d Battalion, 6th Marines, Pvt. James Hatcher recalled that the driver "informed us that the Germans had broken through along the Chemin des Dames and that they were now nearing Paris; that the French were unable to stop them . . . that we were going in to fill a breach in the line, and . . . most of us had but a few hours to live." Yet, Hatcher added, "our spirits refused to be dampened."

The ancient town of Meaux is on the Paris–Metz road, about halfway between Paris and Chateau-Thierry. Many armies, through history, have marched through Meaux—in both directions. Now retreating French soldiers and refugees so clogged the town that it could not be used as an assembly area. Leading units were rerouted, as recommended by Colonel Brown, to May-en-Multien to the northeast, and once there the French XXI Corps ordered them on to Montreuil-aux-Lions.

Concentration at Montreuil

During the afternoon of May 31 an order arrived for Bundy from General Duchene, commanding the French Sixth Army, informing him that the 2d Division had "been placed at the disposal" of his army "for the initial purpose of closing the gap" that had opened in the front lines and instructing him "then to counterattack as soon as possible." Next day Duchene would formalize the assignment in an imperious manner with a Sixth Army special order: "The American 2d Division is placed at the disposal of the French XXI Army Corps with headquarters at Montreuil-aux-Lions."

Wise's battalion arrived at May about six in the evening. Most of the population had fled the village. An officer from division headquarters gave him orders to take his battalion to Gandelu. Wise assembled his battalion and started down the road. A mile and a half out of May, an anxious motorcycle courier caught up with him with a written order, "Return to May at once. The Germans have already taken Gandelu." Wise's battalion countermarched and pitched their two-man "pup tents" in a field outside May. Every half-hour other units of the division rolled in.

About ten in the evening Wise bumped into General Harbord. "The Germans have broken through and are coming toward Paris at the rate of about fifteen miles a day," said Harbord. "The French are not able to hold them. The Second Division is to be thrown in to back up the French, but just when and just where I don't know now."

By now all roads were choked with troops and refugees streaming to the rear. The 9th Infantry, in the lead, took up a position across the Chateau-Thierry–Paris road. Being at the rear of the column and the situation being somewhat tense, the 6th Marines assumed a position near Le Thiolet north of that road, across from the 9th Infantry. Major General Bundy held the 23d Infantry and the 5th Marines in reserve.

Troops began arriving at Montreuil just after dawn on June 1, the 9th Infantry still in the lead. Firing could be heard both from the north (Soissons) and east (Chateau-Thierry).

Chateau-Thierry lies on both sides of the Marne. While the 2d Division marched to Meaux, the motorized 7th Machine Gun Battalion from the U.S. 3d Division rushed forward to defend the old stone highway bridge that crossed the river in the center of the town. The German column came down to the bridge, and on May 31 the machine gunners and a battalion of French colonials stopped them.[3]

After being stopped at the bridge at Chateau-Thierry, the Germans did not attempt to advance further down the Paris–Metz road, choosing instead to swing to the west and come down perpendicularly to the road from the north.

Lt. Graves Erskine from the 79th Company had been sent off for a month-long school in automatic weapons and "musketry" (the conduct of rifle fire) at Gondrecourt. When he learned that the 2d Division was moving up he took abrupt leave of the school and caught up with the 2d Battalion, 6th Marines, at Meaux. He told a skeptical Major Holcomb that he had completed the course, and Holcomb sent him on to his company.

Catlin arrived in Meaux about 8:30 PM on May 31 after a hard day's drive. His regiment had already passed through the town. Catlin reported to division headquarters and was given written orders and maps and told to proceed north. About ten o'clock he was overtaken by a French staff officer, who sent him off in the direction of Montreuil-aux-Lions. "I was a lost Colonel, hunting around in the dark for his command, and hunting with an anxiety that, in this crisis, approached panic," remembered Catlin.

Harbord's Marines arrived during the night and early morning of June 1. The men were stiff and tired after twenty-four hours spent in the camions. Harbord used his automobile as his headquarter until he could open a PC.

Camions were going forward, and camions were coming back. Units were intermingled. (Catlin's regimental band, whose members would serve as stretcher bearers, would not get to the front for two days.) The traffic moving to the rear thickened with more refugees and French soldiers.

"For the most part everything and everybody seemed to be hurrying away from the battle line except the Americans," said Catlin. He found his regiment, or a good part of it, at Montreuil, about 6.5 kilometers behind the line of contact. His Marines had been in the camions from nineteen to thirty hours, depending upon their luck and route. Some had to hike the last kilometers in. All were gray with dust and "looked more like miners emerging from an all-night shift than like fresh troops ready to plunge into battle."

"General, These Are American Regulars"

Major General Bundy and Colonel Brown reported to General Degoutte, commanding the French XXI Corps, on the morning of June 1. Degoutte had fought his corps for five days against greatly superior numbers. He had retreated, but his retreat, in Bundy's opinion, had been an orderly one. He had saved his artillery and his transport.

The French had been sending fresh troops in as fast as they arrived, whereupon "overwhelmed by numbers, they evaporated immediately like drops of rain on white-hot iron." The French proposed to do the same with the American regiments as quickly as they arrived. Colonel Brown demurred. The division's machine guns and artillery were not up yet; the men were tired from an all-day truck ride and an all-night march. He suggested a defensive line behind the French rear guards with a counterattack to follow. General Degoutte reluctantly agreed to a line astride the Paris road just east of Coupru but remained doubtful. Could the Americans hold?

"General," promised Colonel Brown, "these are American regulars. In a hundred and fifty years they have never been beaten. They will hold."

Orders to the brigades came early on June 1. The 9th Infantry was to form a line with its left flank at Le Thiolet on the Paris–Metz road, its right extending almost to the Marne. The 6th Marines was to follow behind the 9th Infantry and then deploy to the left or north of the Paris–Metz road in the sector of the French 43d Division.

Harbord and his regimental commanders tried to sort out the havoc. Somewhere to the left was the right flank of the French 43d Division. In front, the French 164th Division was falling back. The XXI Corps order said, "We have lost Le Genetrie and the enemy is gaining ground in the direction of Bouresches."

The 6th Marines, following behind the 9th Infantry, deployed as ordered to the left or north of the road in the sector of the 43d Division (Michel) on a front of 6.4 kilometers. Harbord ordered Catlin to put two battalions into the line at once. Actually, there was no distinct line, except as the Marines might themselves establish it. At 2:30 PM on June 1, the 6th Regiment began the march forward along the Chateau-Thierry road. Having sent his infantry marching to the front, Catlin then commandeered twenty-five trucks and, riding with them, took forward his regiment's baggage and ammunition.

Six kilometers of marching brought Catlin's regiment to within eight hundred meters of the line of contact. For two days his Marines had had nothing but reserve rations of hardtack and bacon. Each man carried two days of such rations in his pack, a pound of bread and three-quarters of a pound of bacon per day.

The Battlefield

The countryside was sun-drenched rolling farmlands, mostly wheat fields drained by small streams and with woods on the hills. These were prosperous farms with thatched-roof stone houses and big, substantial barns. Virtually every farm was enclosed by a stout stone wall, which gave it the defensive strength of a minor fort. The Ourcq River to the west flowed in a curved line to join the Marne at Meaux. To the north, a small stream, known to the 2d Division as Clignon Brook, flowed westward into the Ourcq. Clignon Brook was at no point very wide or very deep, but it did flow through a deep ravine that made it a natural obstacle.

The French 43d Division was trying to hold a line along the Clignon but was being driven back. The French attempted a stand in the villages of Gandelu, Bussiares, Torcy, Belleau, and Bouresches, but the Germans pushed them out. Two corridors of approach were now open to the Germans: through Bussiares and through Belleau, a very old village, dating back to the eleventh century. Both roads offered the Germans a decent alternate route to bypass the Allied resistance encountered at Chateau-Thierry and continue the advance on Paris. Belleau Wood, a large, overgrown hunting preserve lying between the two routes, served their purposes admirably as an assembly area concealed from Allied observation aircraft, a launching point for renewing the attacks westward, or, if needed, a defensive strongpoint against Allied counterattacks, should that event materialize.

At 4:10 PM on June 1 Harbord from his position in Lucy-le-Bocage informed division: "Have reported to CG French 43d Division and established liaison. Troops arriving by camion going in between Le Thiolet and Lucy-le-Bocage. Important that available engineers with plenty of tools come in as soon as the infantry finish with camions. . . . Hurry them."

Catlin showed his battalion commanders his map, indicating the points to be defended, and told them the line was to be held at all costs. With "Johnny the Hard" Hughes away on detached duty, Maj. Maurice E. Shearer now temporarily commanded the 1st Battalion. Shearer's battalion, stretched thinly, took a position northwest of Lucy-le-Bocage, facing Hill 142 and extending to the southeast as far as Lucy.

"Lucy"

Before the war Lucy-le-Bocage had been a pretty, prosperous village, most of it built of cut limestone, some of it plastered over, the roofs of dull red tile or sometimes heavy corrugated iron painted red. The village church was considered particularly beautiful and was a landmark and an excellent artillery registration point that could be seen across the rolling wheat fields from many kilometers away.[4]

In front of Lucy was a wood marked on the map as the "Bois de Belleau." Holcomb's 2d Battalion extended the line to the southeast from Lucy through Triangle Farm to Le Thiolet on the Paris–Metz road. Cole's 6th Machine Gun Battalion was to be distributed along the length of the line but was not as yet fully in position. Sibley's 3d Battalion, 6th Regiment, went into brigade reserve about a mile and a half behind the line in the vicinity of La Voie du Chatel.

The Marines moved up under light artillery fire. Accustomed to the deep trenches near Verdun, the Marines responded to orders to "dig in" by scraping shallow rifle pits or expanding existing shell craters. Scrunching down, they made themselves as comfortable as they could and ate their hardtack and raw bacon. The propensity of German artillery commanders to deliver harassing and interdiction fires against likely Allied reserve areas soon caused a fervent renewal of digging efforts. Deeper fighting holes—dubbed "foxholes"—quickly replaced the Marines' Civil War–era rifle pits along the front.

The Germans were coming through the French at the rate of ten or eleven kilometers a day, and nowhere were the French holding. The retreat of the French 43d Division left the support line being formed by the 9th Infantry and the 6th Marines to cover the whole front of the XXI Corps, with nothing much between them and the Germans.

"The Dutchmen were about fifteen hundred yards away when we came on the scene," Pvt. John C. Geiger of Jasper, Florida, wrote later from his hospital bed, as recorded by Catlin. "We got orders to dig in. We used the lids of our mess gear and bayonet for tools. . . . You'd be surprised to know just how much digging you can do under those circumstances."

At midnight June 1/2 Degoutte telephoned Bundy to inform him that a gap of nearly four kilometers existed in the line near Gandelu and that a German attack might be expected at any moment. Bundy ordered Col. Paul B. Malone, U.S. Army, commanding officer of the 23d Infantry, to proceed with his regiment plus Major Turrill's 1st Battalion of the 5th Marines, the 5th Machine Gun Battalion, and Company I, 2d Engineers, to the vicinity of Gandelu to take a position as directed by General Michel, commanding the French 43d Division. The doughboys and Marines were roused from their sleep and made a forced march through the shell-lit darkness to their destinations. The regiment, temporarily detached from the 2d Division and assigned to the French 43d Division, was in position by daylight, June 2. General Michel's orders to Turrill were to fill the substantial gap from Bois de Veuilly west to the right flank of the French VII Corps.

The 2d Division on June 2 was still technically in support. Supply trains were arriving, and the machine-gun battalions and artillery were coming up. The 5th Marines, having bivouacked at May-en-Multien, marched forward and was held in reserve. The actual front lines were still occupied by badly worn elements of the French 43d (Michel) and 164th (Gaucher) divisions.

Late in the afternoon on the second, word came that a fresh German division was expected to attack with two regiments north of the Paris–Metz road and one to the south. Colonel Catlin moved the 97th Company, from Maj. Bertron W. Sibley's 3d Battalion, 6th Regiment, into the line to reinforce Holcomb's thinly held position. A short time later, still concerned, Catlin moved another of Sibley's companies, the 82d, into Holcomb's line.

A considerable gap remained between the 23d Infantry and the 6th Marines. To fill this gap, Wise on the morning of June 2 received orders to move his 2d Battalion, 5th Marines, from its bivouac near Pyramides Farm to a position about one and a half kilometers north of Marigny. The orders enjoined him to establish a defensive line that was to be held to the last.

A Day of Confusion

The second of June was a day filled with suppositions and contradictions. At 10:20 AM, the peripatetic Harbord, who had been making his own reconnaissance northwest of Marigny in the Bois de Vaurichart, sent a lengthy message to Colonel Malone from Pyramide. Harbord told Malone he had asked Neville to fill the gap between Hill 142 and the northeast corner of Bois de Vaurichart with Wise's 2d Battalion, 5th Marines. Meanwhile Catlin had reported heavy shelling around Triangle and Lucy.

Wise had his four rifle companies move up separately, as his battalion was to occupy a broad front and German artillery was already very active. The 55th

Company, under Capt. John Blanchfield, halted in the woods just above Champillon while the company commander and his officers went forward to reconnoiter. Blanchfield was a "mustang"; he had cut his teeth as an enlisted Marine, and his permanent grade was marine gunner. The crude French maps and constantly changing orders perplexed him. By now it was about 4 PM. The German artillery fire seemed to be coming from the vicinity of Bussiares and Torcy. There was little or no counterbattery fire, as the American guns had not yet come up and the French 75s were displacing to the rear. Some French soldiers were passing to the rear by the way of the Champillon–Bussiares road. They said the Germans were right behind them. Captain Blanchfield sent a runner back to his waiting company with orders that it was to come forward at the double.

As his company came up, Blanchfield formed a skirmish line with its right touching the Champillon–Bussiares road and its left resting on Les Mares farmhouse. He was tied in on his right with the 51st Company, but he worried about a five-hundred-yard gap in the battalion lines that remained on his left flank, beyond the farmhouse.

Meanwhile, Degoutte, commanding the XXI Corps, issued instructions, timed 10:30 and dated June 2, to the generals commanding the 2d, 43d, and 164th divisions:

Thanks to the arrival of the American 2d Division, it has been possible to stiffen the entire front of the army corps, by means of a solid line, occupied at present by the American regiments. . . . It should be well understood that all the French elements which are in front of that line should hold desperately against all hostile attacks. . . . The American regiments should fully understand that they are to hold in place and that French elements driven back by hostile attack are to be allowed to pass through the American lines, in order that they may be reorganized under the protection of their American comrades.

About this time Harbord, still at Pyramide, sent a cautionary message to Neville: "French consider it very important that you get in line at the earliest possible moment. . . . Cole is sending a M.G. Co. via the Lucy–Champillon Road. Be sure and close gap between you and Turrill. I have had no word at all of any kind from him."

In early afternoon Harbord continued muddying the command lines with a message to Neville: "Please close gap between your line and Turrill, incorporating the two small French battalions if they remain as they probably will. Feeling a little uncertain about Turrill's position as belief that he extends to northwest corner of Bois de Vauricourt is based on order I sent him to do so, and I have heard nothing from him since he left last night. Get in touch with him, include him in your command."

A bit later (2:40 PM) it was Catlin who received a cautionary message from Harbord. The French division headquarters had reported that his line was giving way a little at Triangle. "We are ordered to hold that place at all costs. If report is true get word to Holcomb and stiffen your lines there a little." Holcomb bristled at the implied rebuke and sent a zinger back up the line to the brigade commander. Harbord was not above eating a bit of humble pie, reporting to division, "Report that right was giving way was false. French now acknowledge that it was withdrawal of a working party that they saw. Telephone direct with battalion commander [Holcomb] at Triangle says that when his outfit runs it will be in the other direction. Nothing doing in the fall-back business."

At Les Mares Farm, Captain Blanchfield's Marines dug in for the night. French stragglers coming back through his line reported that the *Boche* were now on the reverse slope of Hill 165. As darkness came the desultory German shelling ceased for a time and then was renewed, with particular attention to the positions around the farmhouse.

Buck Neville had established his regimental PC in a quarry three hundred meters northwest of the village of Marigny. He was left with little to do. Turrill's 1st Battalion was off with the 23d Infantry. Berry's 3d Battalion was in corps reserve near La Loge Farm. Only Wise's battalion, in line to his front, was of immediate concern.

The Germans Close the Range

Harbord's messages increased in frequency as the Germans bore down on the cluster of farms, villages, and woodlots north of the Paris–Metz highway. At 4:30 PM on the second of June he instructed Catlin:

> Turrill's [1st] Bn., 5th Marines is being brought back to replace Berry near here as brigade reserve. Berry's battalion becomes corps reserve, to be held in rear of junction between you and 9th Inf. Pass word to your line to be on lookout for any indications of attack and to report in quickest way possible. Your M.G. Co. is marching overland about a distance of 30 miles. Would ordinarily arrive tomorrow evening. Division undertaking to get trucks to bring guns and men tonight.

The 23d Infantry had extended the line held by the division as far as the village of Gandelu. This gave the 2d Division a total frontage of some seventeen kilometers, from which, according to the XXI Corps order for June 2, "No retirement will be thought of on any pretext whatsoever." The 23d Infantry had been the first to see close-in action, beating off two German attacks in the Bois de Veuilly.

French aerial reconnaissance reported that as of about 8:45 PM approximately one German regiment had come out of the woods and had crossed south of the Belleau–Torcy road, "pushing back our [French] foot troops along the small stream north of Lucy-le-Bocage." French artillery had taken the *Boche* under fire.

The 6th Marines had taken several casualties during the day. Catlin credited the 6th Machine Gun Battalion with stopping the German advance several times during the morning.

Shearer, in command of the 1st Battalion, 6th Marines, at midnight June 2/3 sent a lateral message to Wise that he was holding the front line from Hill 142 to Lucy, inclusive, and that Captain Stowell's 76th Company rested on Hill 142.

Collision Course

The rampant confusion of June 2 continued the following day. At 1:35 AM a XXI Corps message informed the 2d Division that Bussiares, Torcy, and Belleau Wood had been lost to the Germans and that General Michel was preparing to counterattack.

Harbord had already heard from Michel. At 1 AM on June 3, he was advised that the French had received orders to retake the position they had just lost. Yet the French counterattack failed to materialize. At 3:20 AM Neville sent Catlin a message by courier that the French on his right flank had withdrawn, leaving a gap between the 5th Marines on Hill 142 and the 6th Marines' left flank.

The Germans believed they had effectively bypassed stubbornly defended Chateau-Thierry and now prepared to break through the understrength French divisions still blocking their path to Paris. By the morning of June 3 the French retreat had become general, and the Marine support line had become the front line. After a none too restful night, the Marines awoke to find the last of the French falling back through their lines. "Fini la guerre," the retreating French soldiers called out to the Marines. "Pas fini," the Marines replied—"not yet." They braced themselves for the German onslaught.

All that morning a French officer stood near Catlin's post of command trying to reorganize some part of the tattered torrent that was falling back. With a few stout souls he made an effort to make a counterattack of his own that afternoon but was driven back, and his little party of Frenchmen melted away behind Catlin's lines.

"When the Crown Prince drove toward the Marne at Chateau Thierry, the French lines opposing him were so thin that they had to give way," said Logan Feland in a talk three years after the war. "No troops could have done better than the French did there. There were too few of them and no help could be sent them. Their falling back was not disorderly, although they had suffered the severest losses and were weary to the point of exhaustion. The First Battalion of Chasseurs passed through our lines with two officers and thirty-four men left out of a strength of some thirty officers and 600 men with which they entered the fight."[5]

If field messages are accepted literally, they present a very muddled picture of the front. At 6:15 AM Neville elaborated on his frontline positions in another message to Catlin. Wise had gone out at first light and had made contact with Shearer, but his right-flank company (Williams) had not been able to get in touch with Shearer' left company. Wise was told to extend to the right. Key to Wise's position on the Marines' left flank was Les Mares Farm, held by the 55th Company. In front of the 55th, a kilometer away, was Hill 165, and behind the hill were Bussiares Wood and the village of Bussiares.

On the right flank of Wise's battalion, Shearer's battalion picked up at Hill 142 and extended to the southeast to Lucy-de-Bocage. From Lucy to the southeast ran Holcomb's battalion, with its right flank on the Paris–Metz road at the village of Le Thiolet.

In front of Lucy was the woods marked on the map as the "Bois de Belleau." Belleau Wood began less than eight hundred meters northeast of Lucy on rising ground that stood above the surrounding wheat fields. Roughly kidney shaped, it was three kilometers from north to south and about eight hundred meters wide at its widest part. The French told the Americans that the wood was lightly held. They were wrong. By June 3 the German 237th Division occupied the wood in strength.

Holcomb had set up his battalion headquarters in a stone farmhouse. A shell struck the house, killing five of his men. He moved to the cover of the woods.

The French on the left of Wise's battalion pulled out. Catlin filled in with three of his reserve companies from Sibley's battalion, leaving him only one company in regimental reserve.

By the third of June the 2d Division's artillery was in position to support: the 12th and 15th artillery with 75s, the 17th with 155s; and the light guns about two kilometers behind the lines, the heavies about five kilometers back.

The Fight for Les Mares Farm

The 55th Company still held Les Mares Farm, about three kilometers northwest of Lucy. The morning of June 3 brought heavy German shelling, and a German attack seemed in the making. Lt. Lem Shepherd's fourteen-man outpost hunkered in the wheat on the small knoll three hundred meters forward of the farmhouse, watching the dark woods to their front.

About noon on the third, Sibley's 82d Company (Capt. Dwight Smith) was sent in to reinforce the line northeast of Champillon, a hamlet between Lucy and Les Mares and a mile south of Torcy.

At 3:10 PM on June 3, Capt. Lloyd W. Williams, commanding the 51st Company, 2d Battalion, 5th Regiment, dispatched this message to Lieutenant Colonel Wise:

> The French Major gave Capt. Corbin written orders to fall back. I have countermanded the order. Kindly see that French do not shorten their artillery range. Send 82nd and 84th Companies on their way to fill gap on right of this company.

Someone, and there are many claimants, said, "Retreat, hell! We just got here." The best claim for the remark is that of Captain Williams, a popular, hard-bitten officer.

When Williams' message reached regiment, "Whispering Buck" Neville apparently repeated Wise's oral endorsement, probably with a few additional expletives. Whoever said it first, "Retreat, hell! We just got here" became a war cry that has echoed down through time.[6]

Lloyd Williams was killed ten days later in Belleau Wood.

The attack on June 3 came first against the French who were still in front of Wise's battalion on the left flank. Catlin could see it clearly from his observation post at La Voie du Chatel. The Germans came down an open slope in "platoon waves" through a wide field of wheat in which poppies "gleamed like splashes of blood in the afternoon sun." The French fell back. The Germans came in two columns, "steady as machines," Catlin later recalled.

The Germans then turned their attention to the Allied troops in unfamiliar uniforms defending the strongpoint identified on their French maps as "Les Mares Ferme."

As the afternoon sun began to sink below the treetops in Belleau Wood, German artillery fire against Captain Blanchfield's lines increased in intensity. Shortly a formation of gray-clad infantry emerged from the distant woods, advancing purposefully through the wheat toward the farm. Maj. Frank Evans, regimental adjutant, stood next to Catlin in their PC and observed the attack unfold. "When the Germans attacked at 5 PM we had a box seat," he reported. "They came out . . . in two columns across a wheat-field. From our distance it looked flat and green as a baseball field, set between a row of woods on the farther side, and woods and a ravine on the near side. We could see the two thin brown columns advancing in perfect order."

Lem Shepherd's much closer view of the advancing columns was less picturesque. From his outpost hillock the Germans seemed full of menace and endless in number. Determined to lead effectively in his first combat, he ordered "Battle sights!" and kept his men from firing until the lead files closed to 275 meters, then opened up a steady fire. With the initial recoil of their Springfields against their shoulders the riflemen settled into the ingrained mantra of their range coaches, the seamless cycle of breath control, aiming at center mass, and squeezing the trigger. The Germans hesitated as their front ranks tumbled, then directed their machine-gun crews back at the edge of the woods to rake the half-hidden outpost. One of the first Maxim bullets struck Shepherd in the throat, narrowly missing his artery, spinning him to the ground. His men maintained their spoiling fire until they were in danger of being outflanked. Shepherd, grateful to be spitting saliva, not blood, scrambled to his feet to lead the survivors back to the 55th Company's main line.

Blanchfield's riflemen covered Shepherd's withdrawal, directing a deadly fire against the Germans converging on the farmhouse. Rarely in the war would the

Marines enjoy such advantageous firing positions. Kneeling behind the farm's stone walls they aimed carefully at the dark figures silhouetted against the golden wheat, knocking them down at ranges close to five hundred meters. Colonel Catlin, observing the fight, described the Marines' rifle fire as "terrible in its effectiveness." Shepherd would never forget this first battle. "A Marine with a rifle, that's all in the hell we had," he said, "but we held our lines."

The Germans withdrew, stunned by the intensity of the Americans' defense. Their veteran officers studied the farmyard defenses more carefully and ordered a second attack, this time aiming for the gap beyond the farmhouse. Some few stouthearted Frenchmen had been used as gap fillers between Blanchfield's left flank and the Bois de Veuilly. They, apparently thinking the farmhouse had fallen, now fell back. Blanchfield moved a section from his right flank platoon over to "refuse" (rotate back) his exposed flank. To his front and to the left of the farmhouse was a wheat field, through which the Germans were working their way.

This time Blanchfield received more help from his neighbors. The German flanking movement drew long-range fire from the adjoining elements of Wise's battalion. At the same time, the 2d Division's 12th Field Artillery Battalion found the range, dropping 75-mm high-explosive shells in the fields beyond the farmhouse. Catlin, observing from his catbird's seat, said, "The German lines did not break," he said. "They were broken." The Germans fell back in disorder to a distant line on the edge of Bussiares.

The disciplined rifle fire of the Marines, combined with the 12th Field Artillery's timely support, made for an auspicious first major engagement for the 2d Division, yet no one believed the battle to be over. The Germans consolidated machine-gun positions in the woods, puzzling over their unexpected setback. An hour earlier the road to Paris had seemed theirs for the taking.

At some time during the fight a Maxim machine-gun bullet smashed into the thigh of Marine gunner James Gallivan of the 43d Company. The bullet hit just above Gallivan's knee, and he went down hard. Wise, seeing Gallivan being carried to the rear on a stretcher, accused him jokingly of shooting himself in the leg. According to Wise, Gallivan raised himself on one elbow, shook his fist at his battalion commander, and shouted, "The only thing that saves you from a beating is me inability to rise!" Wise would not see Gallivan again for a long time.

Afterward a wounded Marine from Toledo wrote home from the hospital: "I got your Dutchmen for you . . . lots of them, not over three hundred yards away, and one with a pistol for good luck. He's a good Fritz now. They couldn't kill me, but it was almost as bad. I've still got both my hands and legs, but my head is all to the bad even yet."

The Toledo Marine had helped take a wounded man back to the dressing station and was returning up the road when a shell struck close by. "How do I feel?" he wrote from the hospital. "Sometimes I'm all right and again I'm not. I have spells in which everything leaves me for hours at a time and I can't tell for the life of me what I did during that time. And when I go out in the sun I get dizzy and bleed at the nose and my head feels like scrambled eggs most of the time."[7]

Consolidating the Front

At 5:40 PM on June 3, Harbord sent Bundy a resume of the day's activities. The Germans were reported massing in the neighborhood of Bouresches. "The French line has fallen back nearly to our line, practically on our whole front. In one case, a retreating French officer gave an order in writing to an American officer to fall back from the position we have been holding. The order was not obeyed."

Harbord asked for heavy interdiction fires by newly arrived American 155-mm artillery during the night to impede German movement. "French artillery from motives of economy of ammunition, are not registering on these points."

Intermittent machine-gun and rifle fire continued until dark. By then one more of Sibley's companies, Capt. Alfred H. Noble's 83d, had joined the 97th and the 82d. Sibley went up to command his three frontline companies. This left just the 84th Company, already pummeled by the shelling, in brigade reserve. German patrols probed the Marine position that night, and Blanchfield's own patrols reported Germans in the Bois des Mares and Bois de Baron. Sounds of spadework told him that the Germans were digging in the wheat field as well. During the night he finally received a section of much-needed machine guns.

Heavy German shelling took its toll, particularly on the remainder of Sibley's battalion in its reserve position. The reserve, Capt. Mark Smith's 84th Company, taught a lesson by the shelling, dug in more seriously. Catlin inspected them and found: "Each man had dug a hole six feet long, two and a half feet wide, and three feet deep. Even the battalion commander had his hole. . . . They were arranged in rows like graves in a Potter's Field or a soldier's cemetery. . . . When I saw them each was filled with the motionless form of a sleeping man. It was a gruesome sight."

Trucks were arriving with rations, but there was neither time nor place to cook them. The Marines did the best they could with bread, cold bacon, and "monkey meat," as they called the dubious canned beef—a French ration in small blue cans, widely believed to have come from the jungles of Madagascar, foul smelling and with strange orange flecks Actually it was Argentine beef, and the orange flecks were bits of carrot. Drinking water had to be brought up in canteens from a mile away.

On the afternoon of the third, the mule-drawn supply trains, supervised by Maj. Henry Manney of the 6th Marines and Maj. Bennett Puryear of the 5th Marines, had reached Montreuil. The mules had been driven eighty-eight kilometers in twenty-two hours. The 6th Marines' beloved Lizzie Ford was with them, "backfiring and steaming." The rolling kitchens moved up to within three kilometers of the lines, and from June 4 on there would be at least one hot meal and hot coffee each night.

The Marines worked on their positions all through the night of June 3/4. Outposts were pushed into the smaller woods near Belleau. The last of the French left that night.

Meanwhile the Germans, following close behind the French, made a violent attack on the portions of the sector held by the Wise's 2d Battalion, 5th Marines, and Sibley's three companies of the 3d Battalion, 6th Marines. With daylight Captain Blanchfield and his 55th Company could see Germans coming across the crest of Hill 165, moving into Bois des Mares. This was reported to the artillery, and the distant woods were shelled heavily all day. Blanchfield put snipers into the upper windows of the Les Mares farmhouse and barn. They found targets among the Germans investing the wheat field.

The Germans had brought up their 150s. During the day on June 4 German observation aircraft and "sausage" balloons were active, and the artillery fires, once registered on likely targets, continued intermittently. Crossroads were prime targets. In twenty-four hours the Marines lost twenty dead and 195 wounded to shell fire. Gas shells were mixed in with the high explosive. Casualties were heaviest in the woods to the rear, where the reserves were concentrated. Lucy-le-Bocage was heavily bombarded. Catlin said that the shells fell so thickly on Lucy "that you could scoop up handfuls of shrapnel bullets in the streets, round pellets about the size of marbles."

Preparing to Counterattack

On June 4 the division front was tidied up into two brigade sectors, with the Marine brigade on the left. All four infantry regiments of the 2d Division were now on line, each with a front of about 2.8 kilometers, two battalions on line, one in reserve, properly grouped by brigade. The reserve battalion of the 5th Marines was at Harbord's disposal, but the reserve battalion of the 6th Marines was in corps reserve. With the help of several French batteries of light guns, the 12th Field Artillery with its French 75s continued in support of the 4th Brigade, with the 17th Field Artillery and its heavier 155s in general support.

Opposite the 2d Division, the German IV Reserve Corps, sensing a coming counteroffensive, prepared defensive positions. A patrol had picked up the corpse of a Marine from the 6th Regiment, giving the Germans their first positive identification that the enemies to their front, in both olive drab and green uniforms, were Americans.

On the night of June 4/5 the French 167th Division (General Schmidt) relieved the 43d, allowing Malone's 23d Infantry to return to 2d Division control. The 23d marched to the southeast and went in on the left of the 9th Infantry, narrowing the front of the 6th Marines. More French came up, relieving Wise's battalion and taking over as far eastward as Hill 142, further shortening the Marines' line. Major Berry's 3d Battalion, 5th Marines, was sent in to take over from Hill 142 to Lucy, and Shearer's 1st Battalion, 6th Marines, was pulled back to a support line. Holcomb moved his left flank over until it joined Berry at Lucy.

That night, June 4, Lt. William Eddy, a German-speaking intelligence officer of the 6th Marines, went forward with two men through the German lines almost as far as the village of Torcy. They lay in a clover field, watching the Germans march past and listening to their talk. Eddy already had the reputation of being a daredevil for his patrol work in the lines near Verdun. The son of a missionary, he had been born and raised in Asia Minor.

The Germans had not entirely given up on Les Mares Farm. At noon on the fifth, a lookout, possibly Lieutenant Shepherd, reported to Captain Blanchfield that he could hear digging to his front. Cpl. Francis J. Dockx volunteered to go out to take a look. Three other Marines went with him. GySgt. David L. Buford and two more Marines followed them. Crawling forward for about fifty meters into the wheat field, they intercepted a party of about thirty Germans with two machine guns. It was mostly automatic pistols at close range. The Germans broke and ran. Buford killed seven of them—spectacular shooting with the service automatic pistol, whose maximum effective range was generously said to be twenty meters. Those who were not hit at close range fell to Marine riflemen as they attempted to reach the cover of the woods. Corporal Dockx and one other Marine were killed. One machine gun was destroyed. The Marines carried the other weapon back to the lines, along with several wounded prisoners.

To the north of the line and west of Belleau Wood the Germans were still troublesome, particularly the shell fire coming from the reverse slope of Hill 165. During the day Catlin moved his PC once again, leaving Mont Blanche and returning to Lucy.

Albertus Catlin was no stranger to combat. As we have seen, he had commanded the Marine detachment on board the USS *Maine* when the battleship blew up in Havana in February 1898, and he wore the Medal of Honor awarded for his command of the 3d Regiment at Veracruz in 1914. Yet the pending assault troubled him. Belleau Wood, he later observed, "loomed up before us like a heavy, menacing frown in the landscape." As he eyed the objective from the ruins of Lucy, Catlin would recall, "we were nearer to the woods on the south than on the west, and on both sides open wheat fields lay between our lines and the forest. From without it appeared almost impenetrable, and there were those open spaces to cross."

CHAPTER SEVEN

Belleau Wood

The three-week struggle for Belleau Wood ranks as one of the greatest battles of the twentieth century for the U.S. Marines, a touchstone that compares with Iwo Jima in 1945 and the Chosin Reservoir in 1950.[1]

On June 6, 1918, the moment they launched their first assault on the dark woodland, the Marines abruptly left behind fourteen decades of small-scale skirmishes with insurgents, pirates, and light infantry regiments and entered the industrialized world of massive firepower and wholesale slaughter. Costly mistakes in command, intelligence, and communications reflected their difficult transition. In the end, the Marines' stubborn pride and affinity for close combat—the same die-hard aggressiveness that had characterized their old ship-to-ship boarding parties—helped them prevail over a veteran foe, surprising the Germans and bolstering the flagging morale of the French at a crucial moment in the war.

The Germans had chosen their ground well. The sprawling hardwood forest was a labyrinth of underbrush, fallen logs, rock ledges, and ravines, ideal for a defense dominated by Maxim machine guns and trench mortars. The woods occupied more than a square mile of terrain, deep enough to absorb several battalions fighting each other at extremely close ranges and convoluted enough to confuse their commanders for days at a time. Indeed, the fighting for small, bitterly defended Belleau Wood would presage future Marine landings on such bloody Pacific islets as Tulagi, Gavutu, Betio, and Engebi. The similarities between the Marines' advance through the fire-swept wheat fields towards Belleau Wood and the next generation of Leathernecks wading ashore under heavy fire at Tarawa are haunting.

The battle for Belleau Wood was not well fought. It was a confused crisscross-ing of battalions and companies stumbling blindly through gas-choked woods and suffering horrendous losses from German machine guns and field artillery. The Marines would lose almost half their men, but they would beat the best the Ger-mans had to offer.

Taking the Offensive

All through the fifth of June the Marines watched and waited, braced for an attack they thought was sure to come. It did not materialize. The German success in the Aisne offensive had exceeded General Ludendorff's expectations, but he could not sustain a further exploitation of the thirty-five-mile breakthrough north of the Marne. He halted the advance and ordered a temporary defensive. General Degoutte, commanding XXI Corps, sensed the change in momentum and has-tened to launch a counteroffensive as early as June 6.

The evening of the fifth found the Marine Brigade holding a shortened line, with Turrill's battalion of the 5th Marines on the left flank (minus two rifle companies, detached in support of the neighboring French division), Berry's battalion of the 5th and Holcomb's of the 6th in front, and Sibley's of the 6th in immediate support.

Degoutte ordered an early morning attack to seize stronger ground at Hill 142, cut the Torcy–Bussiares road, and to "straighten out the line." The first attack would be led by the French 167th Division on the Marines' left. The 1st Battalion, 5th Marines (Major Turrill), would lead the advance on Hill 142, with a frontage of about eight hundred meters cut by two ravines. Turrill was to advance about nine hundred meters, conforming to the advance of the French. The 3d Battalion, 5th Marines (Major Berry), on Turrill's right, was in turn to pivot forward and deploy its left to accommodate Turrill's advance. The attack would be preceded by a half-hour artillery preparation by all the artillery in the division. In addi-tion, a company of Major Cole's 6th Machine Gun Battalion, with Hotchkiss heavy machine guns, was to be attached to Turrill's battalion. Both of Turrill's detached rifle companies were to be returned well in advance.

The plan, hastily conceived and poorly coordinated, had too many moving parts to be executed in the hours of darkness leading to the 3:45 AM assault. Nei-ther the missing rifle companies nor the machine-gun company arrived in time. Turrill had no choice but to initiate his attack with but half his battalion. The two rifle companies, the 67th and 49th, made the most of a bad situation. Lt. John Thomason, leading one of the assault platoons, later described the initial advance as "a beautiful deployment, lines all dressed up and guiding true. Such matters were of deep concern to this outfit."

The Germans saw Turrill's understrength outfit coming. Intense artillery fire severely hindered the advance of the French division on his left and that of Berry's battalion on his right, leaving Turrill badly exposed on both flanks and generally unsupported.

The fierce momentum of Turrill's attack enabled the Marines to seize the crest of Hill 142 and the road beyond, but holding it proved problematical. Exceptional leadership by Capt. George Hamilton and the surviving NCOs in the ranks salvaged a tactical victory, but by the time Colonel Neville could rush the missing companies, machine gunners, and other reinforcements forward, the hillside was dotted with clumps of fallen Marines.

Capt. Keller Rockey, Turrill's adjutant, appraised George Hamilton as "well qualified professionally, sound, brave, a fine leader respected by his men." While extremely glad to have Hamilton leading the assault, Turrill was beside himself in frustration over his exposed flanks, missing units, poor maps, sporadic artillery support, and slow delivery of ammunition, stretchers, and water by Neville's headquarters. Hamilton's blunt report reached Turrill about 10 o'clock: "Our casualties are very heavy. We need medical aid badly. . . . We will need artillery assistance to hold this line tonight. Ammunition of all kinds is needed. . . . All my officers are gone." Turrill sent one blistering message to Neville that began, *"Need ammunition!"* Neville and Feland delivered "30,000 [rounds] Springfield, 20,000 Hotchkiss, and 20,000 Chauchat" to nearby Champillon, but it did Turrill little good. He had no men available to hump the boxes forward to Hamilton's toehold on Hill 142, nearly two kilometers north.

The Marines were learning the hard way how much more difficult and costly offensive operations are than defensive ones. In this morning's work the 5th Marines lost ten officers and about four hundred men in killed and wounded, a bloody start to what would become an exceptionally bloody day.

Turrill's attack had hit at the boundary between the German 197th and 237th divisions. They reported the action as severe, and two more battalions and a battery were sent up from the IV Corps reserve to take position behind the 197th. Immediately in front of Turrill and Berry were two infantry battalions of the 237th Division. Also engaged were two battalions from the 197th Division, one from the 7th Saxon Jagers and one from the 273d Regiment.

Tactical communications within the Marine Brigade had been poor. Brigadier General Harbord, new to battle command, believed the initial, secondhand reports of an easy victory and forwarded them unchallenged to his division and corps commanders. The early reports pleased General Degoutte. By the time Harbord learned the facts of the ragged attack, piecemeal commitment of forces, and heavy losses sustained in taking Hill 142—"straightening the line"—it was hours later and Degoutte had already ordered a second, larger, and more ambitious advance against Belleau Wood and Bouresches.

Objective: Belleau Wood

Turrill's advance left the Germans holding a decided salient of their own with its apex pointed at Lucy-le-Bocage. At about noon, Degoutte directed the 2d Division to reduce the salient. General Bundy concluded it would be necessary to take the town of Bouresches and at least part of Belleau Wood to straighten the American line from its advance position to the northwest down to Triangle Farm.

Bundy passed the requirement to the 4th Brigade. Harbord had virtually no intelligence on the enemy's strength or dispositions but was under the impression that Belleau Wood was lightly defended. He concluded that it could be taken with a surprise attack without much artillery preparation. Belleau Wood being longer than it was wide, he also judged that it would be easier to take it from west to east rather than plunging straight ahead.

Harbord later assessed his intelligence-gathering shortcomings at the start of the battle: "No reconnaissance or scouting appears to have been done by the companies in front of their positions between June 4th and 6th, the responsibility having been ours since the withdrawal of the French on the 4th. This was probably due to inexperience. Maps were scarce."

Harbord decided to make his attack in two stages. First, he would take Belleau Wood, and second, he would establish a line tying in with the French near Bussiares and then running through Torcy and Belleau to the town of Bouresches.

The orders to attack were written at brigade headquarters, about three kilometers to the rear, at 2 PM. Colonel Catlin of the 6th Marines was given local

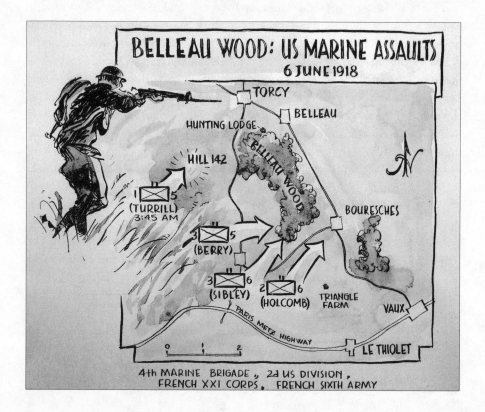

command of the attack, but General Harbord would dictate the scheme of maneuver, battalion by battalion. Berry's battalion of the 5th Marines was to come under Catlin's command for the attack.

Catlin assumed that Belleau Wood "was a typical piece of well-kept French woodland, which the foresters had thinned and cared for so that the timber was of fairly uniform size and the underbrush fairly well cleaned out inside," as he later wrote, elsewhere noting with grim self-satisfaction that "this bitter struggle for a bit of ground smaller than Central Park marked the turning point of this whole war."

But Catlin himself never got into the wood, and his mental picture of it was wrong. Bois de Belleau, the hunting preserve of the Chateau Belleau located on the north side of the wood, was not a tidy woodlot such as the Marines had seen before and would see again. Of all the small woods that dotted the pastoral countryside, Belleau Wood was the largest and the most convoluted. Once into the wood, the Marines would find their visibility limited to as little as fifteen to twenty feet. Its tumbled mass of rocks, fairly tall trees, and thick underbrush and the heat of the day would have reminded their grandfathers of the Devil's Den at Gettysburg.[2]

Something was going on inside the wood, and the intelligence report that came down from division said the Germans were organizing defenses and consolidating their machine-gun positions.

Berry's 3d Battalion, 5th Marines, was to face around ninety degrees and attack east on a front of about one and a half kilometers. The 3d Battalion, 6th Marines, under Sibley, was to advance on a narrowed front on Berry's right from just north of Lucy-le-Bocage and go through the southern end of wood. Once he had taken the southern half of the wood, Sibley was to continue on to Bouresches. To his left, Berry was to advance to the ridge west of Torcy, keeping contact with the French. If all went well the two battalions would wind up holding a new front running from Bouresches across the northeast edge of Belleau Wood to the village of Torcy. On the extreme left, Major Turrill's 1st Battalion, 5th Marines, was to conform to Berry's advance, while on the right, the 2d Battalion, 6th Marines (Major Holcomb), was to conform to Sibley's advance.

Holcomb's battalion was to act as the hinge connecting the Marines of the 4th Brigade to the soldiers of the 3d Brigade. Holcomb was ordered to send one company to Turrill's battalion. In the second phase Catlin was to retain command of Berry's and Sibley's battalions, and Lieutenant Colonel Feland, second in command of the 5th Marines, was to oversee Turrill's attack that was to carry on into Torcy.

At this point, Harbord had no notion that immediately in front of him in Belleau Wood was the 461st Regiment, 237th Division, strength twenty-eight officers and 1,141 men plus a few attachments, Major Bischoff commanding. Because of the tangled nature of the terrain, Bischoff, an old colonial soldier who had seen much bush fighting in Africa, had elected to defend in place rather than by counterattack. He had positioned two battalions, well reinforced with machine guns and trench mortars, along the western and southwestern edges of the wood. His reserve battalion was in the northern half of the wood.

The German divisions of 1918, like the French, had three infantry regiments and three battalions of artillery. By now the Germans were making up for their shortage of infantrymen by increased numbers of machine guns and masses of light artillery employed close to the front.

Not until 3:45 PM, not much more than an hour before jump-off time, did Harbord's aide, Lt. Norris Williams, arrive by motorcycle at the 6th Marines headquarters with a copy of the attack order for Catlin, who then met immediately with Holcomb and Sibley at Holcomb's headquarters, some 450 meters behind the line.

"Holcomb's battalion was ordered to hold the line, while Sibley's was to come up, pass through it, and make the attack on the southern section of the woods, starting in on the western side," remembered Catlin. "The objectives for the first attack mentioned in the orders were the eastern edge of the woods and Bouresches. Berry's battalion was to attack from the west of Sibley's left."

"It was a clear, bright day. At that season of the year it did not get dark till about 8:30, so we had three hours of daylight ahead of us." As Catlin stood there, issuing his orders, Sibley's battalion was filing past into a ravine, getting into its jumping-off position. Holcomb and Sibley left to give oral orders to their company commanders.

Berry and his battalion were in a wood, nearly two kilometers away, out of reach. Catlin wrote later that he went back to Lucy for two reasons: first, because he thought he could best see the action from there, and second, because he was anxious about Berry and thought it necessary to get as close to Berry's battalion as possible.

As he went through Lucy, Catlin went around the left of Sibley's battalion, waiting in shallow trenches, ready to go "over the top." They had picked up that phrase from the British; later it would get shortened to "going over," or, more frequently, the terse "going in."

"When Marines go into line they travel in heavy marching order," Catlin stated, "but when they go in to fight it is light marching order, with no extra clothing or any blankets. They carry twenty-odd pounds then. . . . The machine guns were in position, both those of the machine gun company of the Sixth and those of two companies of the machine gun battalion attached to the brigade. They were just back of the front line. Each company had eight automatic rifles and eight in reserve; all were used."

To Catlin, "The men seemed cool, in good spirits, and ready for the word to start."

Catlin spoke to a number of them as he passed. "I am no speech maker," he later said. "If the truth must be told, I think what I said was, 'Give 'em Hell, boys!'"

Catlin tried to phone Berry's PC from Lucy, but heavy shelling had prevented the running of a telephone line to Berry. Catlin sent runners but was not sure that

Berry could be reached before the attack had to be made. As it happened, Berry had received orders from the 5th Marines headquarters and knew the role his battalion was to play. Catlin reached the right flank of Berry's battalion. They too seemed to be ready.

So were Bischoff's Germans. They had watched the Americans form up and knew an attack was coming. Bischoff had called for reinforcements, and two battalions of the corps reserve were moving forward.

As a prelude to the attack, the French and American artillery shelled the wood and the roads and ravines behind it for about a half an hour. In Catlin's mind it was not a proper preparation: "They had no definite locations and were obliged to shell at random in a sort of hit-or-miss fire. It must have been largely miss."

Through the Wheat

General Harbord had ordered the attack to get off at 5 PM. The attackers jumped off more or less as scheduled, with the shrilling of many officers' and NCOs' whistles, on the heels of the ineffective bombardment. Catlin's two assault battalions, Berry's and Sibley's, went forward in four skirmish lines, precisely dressing right and left, in the kind of attack that the British and French might have preached but had not practiced since the horrendous losses of 1916 and 1917. The scene reminded more than a few observers of a smaller version of Pickett's charge on the third day at Gettysburg. The Germans later reported that the Americans offered excellent targets.

Berry had 350 meters of open wheat field to cross. Catlin did not believe he would be able to reach the woods. To him it looked as though Sibley's battalion would have to bear the brunt of the attack.

"No one knows how many Germans were in those woods," said Catlin. "I have seen the estimate placed at 1,000, but there were certainly more than that. It had been impossible to get patrols into the woods, but we knew they were full of machine guns and that the enemy had trench mortars there. . . . Sibley and Berry had a thousand men each, but only half of these could be used for the first rush, and, as Berry's position was problematical, it was Sibley's stupendous task to lead his 500 through the southern end of the wood clear to the eastern border if the attack was not to be a total failure. Even to a Marine it seemed hardly men enough."

Because of poor communications the attacks of the two battalions were virtually independent. Catlin knew only in a general way what was happening to Berry's battalion. In front of Berry was an open wheat field four hundred meters wide. It was winter wheat, still green but tall and headed out. Berry's Marines, crossing the field with the ripening wheat almost up to their waists, took terrible losses, mostly to German machine guns.

Floyd Gibbons, the flamboyant but fearless correspondent of the *Chicago Tribune,* was with Berry and saw it all. It was flat, open country with no protection at all except the bending wheat. It was as if, said Gibbons, the air were full of red-hot nails. German machine guns and shells cut great gaps in the line. The surviving Marines quickly abandoned the parade-ground formation, hit the deck, fanned out, and began advancing in rushes. "Sometimes a squad would run forward fifty feet and drop," observed Gibbons, himself hugging the earth, "And as its members flattened on the ground for safety another squad would rise from the ground and make another rush."

The final hundred meters to the edge of the woods were the toughest. German machine-gun fire hit Berry in the left arm near the elbow, the slug ripping down the length of his forearm, blood running down his sleeve. Berry, in excruciating pain, continued on.

Floyd Gibbons saw Berry struggling and tried to reach him. Twice clipped by bullets, Gibbons resorted to crawling but was hit a third time, reporting later from a field hospital that "a bullet striking the ground immediately under my left cheek bone had ricocheted upward, going completely through the left eye and then crashing out through my forehead, leaving the eyeball and upper eyelid completely halved . . . and a compound fracture of the skull."

The line wavered. A voice of a sergeant, possibly that of GySgt. Dan Daly, was heard to shout: "Come on, you sons of bitches! Do you want to live forever?"[3] A few Marines reached the edge of the woods with Major Berry and bayoneted some of the German machine gunners who had tormented them. The remnants of the shattered battalion hugged the ground and waited for darkness so they could pull back.

Sibley's battalion fared better. On Sibley's left there was open grassland, perhaps two hundred meters wide; his right was close to the woods. Catlin watched them go in, saying later that it was one of the most beautiful sights he ever saw. "The battalion pivoted on its right, the left sweeping across the open ground in four waves, as steadily and correctly as though on parade. There were two companies of them, deployed in four skirmish lines, the men placed five yards apart and the waves fifteen to twenty yards behind each other. They walked at the regulation pace, because a man is of little use in a hand-to-hand bayonet struggle after a hundred yards dash. . . . Oh, it took courage and steady nerves to do that it the face of the enemy's machine gun fire. . . . In this frame of mind the soldier can perhaps walk with even more coolness and determination than he can run."

Sibley's Marines swarmed into the southern edge of the wood. Then his left flank came up against the German main line of resistance and was stopped. His right flank continued to advance, so that, in effect, his battalion pivoted a quarter-turn to the left. First Lt. Alfred H. Noble, the twenty-four-year-old Marylander commanding the 83d Company in Sibley's battalion, later described his first encounter with the interlocking bands of Maxim heavy machine-gun fire: "We went in bare-handed and we got slaughtered."[4]

Catlin had taken position on a little rise in the ground, about three hundred meters from the woods, screened a bit by some bushes. It was near a road where Sibley's left flank had touched Berry's right. He had no field telephone. He watched through his field glasses as the first wave reached the edge of the woods and then plunged in.

Just about the time Sibley's Marines reached the woods, a sniper's bullet hit Catlin in the chest. The bullet spun him around and knocked him to the ground. The bullet had drilled a hole straight through him, going through his right lung. Catlin later said that it felt like a sledgehammer had hit him. He felt little pain, but his right side was paralyzed. His French liaison officer, Capt. Tribot Laspierre, a little man, dragged Catlin, no small burden at 215 pounds, head first back to a shelter trench some twenty feet to the rear.

Catlin did not lose consciousness. Laspierre laid him down in the bottom of the shallow trench and did what he could do. Catlin had him send a runner back to Lucy, where his rear regimental headquarters could be telephoned and his executive officer, Lt. Col. Harry Lee, summoned to the front.

Lee got there by a combination of automobile and foot, and Catlin turned over command of the regiment. The regimental surgeon, Dr. Farwell, came up from Lucy and administered first aid. Farwell brought stretcher bearers with him, but the artillery fire was too heavy for them to move Catlin to the rear. There were gas shells mixed in with the high explosive. Farwell fitted a gas mask to Catlin's face, which was not pleasant for a man gasping for breath with a lung full of blood.

When the artillery fire let up, Catlin was carried back to Lucy, and here an ambulance took him first to Meaux and finally, after eight hours in the ambulance, to a hospital in Paris. He remained in the hospital until July 22, when he was discharged and sent home on leave. Catlin was out of the war, but the battle for Belleau Wood had just begun.

Floyd Gibbons' "Last Dispatch"

Floyd Gibbons' uncensored and hyperbolic account of this day's assault created a windfall of favorable publicity for the Marines and a half-century of enmity from the U.S. Army. The cocksure correspondent had posted a preliminary account of the opening assault of June 6 even before the jump-off ("I am up front and entering Belleau Wood with the U.S. Marines"), intending to embellish the story further after the action. When initial reports that Gibbons had been killed reached the chief AEF censor—a personal friend of the reporter—he decided to let what purported to be Gibbons' dying dispatch go forward untouched, despite its forbidden mention of specific units ("The Marine Brigade"). The account also included favorable mention of Gibbons' observations earlier in the week of the initial U.S. Army units fighting at Chateau-Thierry, but since he failed to identify their service or organization, his many readers back home got the false impression that the Marines had done it all, including stopping the Germans at the Marne. "U.S. Marines Smash Huns, Gain Glory" proclaimed the headlines of the June 6th edition of the *Chicago Daily Tribune,* while the *New York Times* opened with "Our Marines Attack . . . Foe Losing Heavily" the following day. The unintended omission of army achievements rankled tens of thousands of soldiers, including General Pershing. Writing eighteen years after the event, Major General Harbord admitted that the uncensored Gibbons dispatch had "lit fires of professional jealousy that still smolder."

Seizing Bouresches

Sibley's battalion had a precarious hold on the southwestern corner of the wood. Feland with Turrill's battalion was standing fast to the north. Holcomb's battalion was being stretched between the moving 4th Brigade and stationary 3d Brigade. Holcomb detailed Capt. Donald F. Duncan's 96th Company to close up on Sibley's right. When Sibley pivoted to the left, this lone company continued on into Bouresches.

As Lieutenant Cates of the 96th wrote to his mother, "at 4:35 PM we received word that we were to move into position and to attack a certain town at 5 PM. . . . We moved across an open field and stopped in a small woods and my platoon was in a wheat field. The Boche machine guns and artillery had opened up on us and it was some party. At a certain time and signal we got up and swept over a ground literally covered with machine gun bullets—it was my first charge, and Mother it is a wonderful thrill to be out there in front of a bunch of men that will follow you to death. A lot of men went down; most of them only wounded, but a few dead. About three fourths of the way over a bullet hit me solid: it knocked me cold, but it did not go thru my helmet."

Casualties in the 96th Company were heavy. Captain Duncan, the company commander, and 1st Sgt. Joseph A. Sissler were killed early in the attack. First Lt. James F. Robertson, the second in command, took over.

When Cates recovered consciousness he tried to put on his helmet. It was difficult, because there was a big dent in it. He saw three Marines off to his right in a ravine and started toward them, falling down several times. They caught him as he stumbled into the ravine. To revive him, Sgt. Aloysius P. Sheridan (called "Jack" by his friends) poured champagne onto Cates's head from a bottle he had been treasuring. Cates convinced Sheridan that he would rather drink the wine than have it poured on his head, and after a big swig he felt better.

Cates could see about twenty Marines with Lieutenant Robertson on the western edge of the town. He attracted their attention by yelling and blowing his whistle and then went forward to join them. Robertson returned the platoon to Cates and directed him to finish cleaning out the town while he went back for reinforcements. With twenty-four Marines, Cates drove what he estimated to be a German company and five machine guns out of the town.

"I killed my first German," he wrote home a few days later. "After we had entered the town a Boche put a bullet thru the brim of my helmet, another bullet entered the shoulder of my coat [just grazing the skin]."

Holcomb's 79th Company under Capt. Randolph T. Zane followed the 96th into the town. In getting into Bouresches, Lt. Graves Erskine's fifty-eight-man platoon shriveled away—by casualties or men just plain lost—until he was down to five or six men. He overran a machine gun left with a solitary gunner. He kicked the gunner in the leg to get his attention and told him he was a prisoner. The gunner got to his feet, tall and arrogant, refused to take his slung rifle from his shoulder, and without invitation pulled Erskine's canteen from its holder and took a drink. An annoyed Erskine, pistol in hand, disarmed the prisoner and sent him to the rear under guard of one of his Marines. The Marine was back in a suspiciously short time. Erskine accused him of shooting the prisoner. The Marine readily admitted that he had. Erskine asked him why. "I can't go back to Minnesota and tell them I didn't kill a German," was the miscreant's reply.

Interlocking German fire stopped Erskine's small group in its tracks. He sent a messenger back to Captain Zane, reporting that he was pinned down. "About an hour later," said Erskine, "this poor kid crawled back to report the captain's words: 'Goddammit, continue the advance.' This was at early nightfall. We continued the advance."

Sibley, hearing from Holcomb that his men in Bouresches needed support, sent the right half of his battalion into the village so that by midnight some six hundred Marines were in the town. A volunteer party with a Ford truck reached them with rations. In a wild ride after dark, Lt. William Moore and Spanish-American War Medal-of-Honor veteran Sgt. Maj. John Quick delivered a truckload of ammunition and engineering tools to the outpost.

Erskine, with what was left of his platoon, reinforced with fifteen or twenty men from the 2d Engineers, was given a little sector in the northeast of Bouresches to defend. He dug in behind a seven-foot hedge, individual foxholes that in time his men developed into a shallow trench line.

Holcomb's position in Bouresches was tenuous at best and under heavy machine gun and artillery fire, but the Germans did not attempt to retake the town. Cates found himself "safe and sound; all except two bum fingers and a face which is skinned up; caused by a rifle exploding when I was trying to put a V.B. rifle grenade into a Boche machine gun emplacement."[5]

Lt. Col. Harry Lee had gone forward at about 6 PM to take Catlin's place. Harbord, hearing nothing from Lee, sent him further orders at about 9 PM to push forward the attack. Lee reached Berry's battalion's right flank company. He sent a runner back to Harbord reporting these positions. Harbord received the message at about 11:10. He ordered Lee to dig in, sending forward two companies of engineers to help.

The Marine brigade's losses for June 6 were thirty-one officers and 1,056 men killed, wounded, and missing, chiefly in the rifle companies, the heaviest day in casualties by far that the Marine Corps had ever experienced in all its 142 years of war and expeditions. Hundreds of wounded men swamped the dressing stations and field hospitals behind the lines. A battalion surgeon recorded that the wounds he treated on June 6 were mainly the "tearing, lacerating, crushing, and amputating types."

It had been a bloody day for the Germans also. The German 237th Division had lost thirteen officers and 268 men. The German 197th Division to the northwest, engaged by the French 167th Division and, on its left flank, by Turrill's battalion, had lost heavily. The German 10th Division at Bouresches had lost about 150 men.

Early in the afternoon the 2d Division's 3d Brigade had been ordered to conform to the attack of the 4th Brigade by advancing the 23d Infantry. Soon hotly engaged immediately south of Bouresches by the 398th Infantry of the 10th Division, the 23d Infantry had suffered twenty-seven doughboys killed and 225 wounded or missing. During the night the 398th Infantry was reinforced with two battalions of the 6th Grenadiers.

Fighting in the Woods

The seventh of June was relatively quiet. The Marines got ready to resume the attack. The Germans were in process of relief, the 197th and 10th being replaced by the 5th Guards and 28th Division, respectively. The 237th Division stayed in place but with a shortened line. Elements of the 28th Division took over the southwestern corner of the wood facing Sibley. The Americans shelled the wood during the night, but without much effect, because the shells burst high in the trees.

Capt. John Blanchfield, whose 55th Company had defended Les Mares Farm so creditably on June 3, was killed on the seventh, and for a few hours 1st Lt. Lem Shepherd commanded the company. Then he went down with a bullet through his leg. Kiki, his little dog, followed the stretcher bearers to the aid station. An orderly tried to separate Shepherd from his dog. Shepherd said, "Either you take my dog or you leave me here."

In the predawn morning of June 8, the Marines heard movement to their front and took a light shelling. At 4 AM Sibley, supported by Stokes trench mortars, attempted an advance. He made little progress against Bischoff's Maxims, disposed in depth. At about noon Sibley came back to his original line. "They are too strong for us," he admitted. "Soon as we take one machine gun, another opens up." In the afternoon, by order of Harbord, Sibley came out of the wood entirely so that the artillery could have free play.

Under the mistaken assumption that the Marines held the southern half of the woods, an order came down from division, which presumably had gotten it from

BELLEAU WOOD ATTACKS
10-11 JUNE 1918

BELLEAU WOOD

HILL 181

WISE
11 JUNE

WHEAT
FIELDS

BOURESCHES

LUCY-LE-
BOCAGE

1 6
(HUGHES)
10 JUNE

corps, to clear the rest of the wood. The artillery brigade commander came up to work out the plan of fires. The artillery would pound the wood all day on the ninth. The 1st Battalion, 6th Marines (Major Hughes, who had just returned to reclaim his command from Major Shearer), until now in reserve, was to be in the assault. Hughes moved after dark into an attack position facing the south edge of woods. His orders were to attack straight to the north on a front of about nine hundred meters. The 2d Division's artillery, reinforced by the fires of the French 164th and 197th divisions—thirty light batteries and twelve medium batteries—was scheduled to deliver twenty-eight thousand rounds of 75-mm and six thousand rounds of 155-mm.

Hughes jumped off at 4:30 AM on June 10. Guns from Maj. Edward Cole's 6th Machine Gun Battalion laid down a barrage on the road east of wood. The regimental machine guns went forward with the attack. All seemed to go well. At seven o'clock Hughes reported to brigade that the artillery had "blown the Bois de Belleau to mince-meat."

An hour later Hughes reported his day's objective taken at a cost of about forty casualties, an ill-advised and premature report that at face value delighted General Harbord. Hughes then "cleaned out" a nest of machine guns that had been bypassed to his right rear, at a cost of about twenty-five more casualties. This was not a minor mop-up operation. Hughes' 75th Company experienced desperate, point-blank fighting. "Machine guns were everywhere," Cpl. "Gus" Gulberg recorded in his diary. "We had to rush each gun crew in turn. . . . It was a furious dash from one nest to another." In this fighting, Major Cole, the brigade's machine-gun battalion commander, once again moved forward to direct fire from his teams supporting the infantry attacks. When platoon and squad leaders fell in the melee, Cole took up the charge. A German grenade exploded at his feet, wounding him grievously. "Fragments of the grenade went through both arms, both legs, and in his face," his brother, an army brigadier general, wrote home. "He lost a tremendous amount of blood . . . and was twice transfused." General Cole reported the amputation of his brother's right hand yet hoped he would survive. He did not. Major Cole died eight days after the attack, his loss a serious blow to the Marine Brigade.[6]

Hughes thought he had reached the narrow neck of the woods. He was wrong. Actually he had just reached the German main line of resistance, where Sibley had been stopped three days before. Unfortunately, Harbord clung to the false hope of Hughes' earlier reports and had shared his optimism with the division and corps commanders.

Wise's 2d Battalion, 5th Marines, which had relieved the 3d Battalion in the Bois de Champillon, was now ordered to attack at 4:30 the next morning and, together with Hughes, clear out the whole wood. The two battalions, once joined, were to push on to the northeast to the far edge of the wood. Hughes's left flank was supposedly on Hill 169.

Wise was to have his left flank guide on a road marking the west edge of the wood, starting on a frontage of five hundred meters, which would widen out to a thousand meters. In support, he was supposed to have all of the division's artillery. It did not turn out that way. With even less artillery support than before, the 2d Battalion, 5th Marines, attacked early on the morning of June 11. Wise put his left flank along the road that skirted the western edge of the wood, expecting that on the right flank he would meet a battalion of the 6th Marines at the narrow neck of the woods. But Hughes' left flank was not where it was supposed to be. Wise, in searching for it, veered to the right and did not extend his front the planned thousand meters. His attack struck the boundary between the 28th and 237th divisions. The frontline regiments were the 40th Infantry of the 28th and the 461st Infantry of the 237th. Wise continued to echelon to the right, looking for Hughes's battalion, until his left flank was pulled loose from the road and was where his right flank was supposed to be. Hughes' 1st Battalion, 6th Marines, then caught up with him, and together they held the narrow waist of the wood. The northern half of the wood, however, remained firmly in German hands.

Marine losses for the day were seven officers and 222 men, mostly from Wise's battalion. The 40th Infantry, 28th Division, had been pretty much driven out of the wood, but Bischoff's 461st was still in position. German losses were seventeen officers and 763 men, including many prisoners, mostly from the 40th Infantry.

The night of June 11/12 was quiet. The Germans counterattacked early in morning in half-hearted fashion and failed to regain their lost ground. Harbord, meanwhile, had called his commanders together for a conference. Wise, who had received 150 replacements and had been reinforced with two companies of engineers, was confident that with sufficient artillery support he could take the remainder of the wood.

The attack plan was simple. The 12th Field Artillery would shell the northern half of the wood for an hour, commencing at 4 PM. Wise would jump off at 5:00 and attack straight to the north. In execution, Wise was dissatisfied with the weight of the artillery preparation and asked that it be extended for another half-hour. This was done, but the little 75-mm shells in whatever number did not get down through the trees and into the German emplacements effectively.

When Wise went forward at 5:30 PM, the reinforced 461st Infantry was waiting for him. His front widened, and his line broke up into small groups, which unexpectedly turned out to be fortunate. He had stumbled unwittingly into a workable technique for taking out German machine guns. Small groups of squad or platoon size, each under an officer or NCO, went forward, firing their Chauchats and Springfields from the hip until they could close on the machine gun with grenades and bayonets. The 461st Infantry was smashed into fragments, some of which continued to fight on among the boulders. A battalion of the 110th Grenadiers that had come forward to replace a battalion of the 40th Infantry was likewise shattered. Elements of Wise's battalion broke through to the open ground beyond the north edge of the wood before stopping at about 8:40 PM to reorganize and defend for the night.

While Wise's battalion was consolidating its new position, a wounded German officer and forty-two men came through under a white flag. From these prisoners Wise learned that the Germans planned a counterattack the following morning. Wise was in an attenuated position. He had extended his flank to make contact with Hughes. He had lost 150 men; Hughes had lost fifty-four. In two days' fighting the Marines had taken four hundred prisoners, sixty machine guns, and ten *minenwerfers,* the German spigot mortars. Aside from replacements, Wise was down to three hundred men of his original battalion, with one officer to a company. Wise's left flank was hanging in the air, so he bent it back into a position that came to be known as "The Hook." Hughes was still fairly strong, with seven hundred men.

Holcomb's battalion was still in Bouresches. On the tenth of June, with German shells dropping on the town at the rate of about one a minute, Cates had written home to his mother and sister: "I am sitting here writing on a dining room table and trusting a shell doesn't hit near. I am pretty well worn out, I have only had four hours sleep the last four days. . . . We are to be relieved soon. . . . I lost 32 men out of my platoon of fifty-six; only two or three dead—the others wounded—most of them slightly. I am very proud of my men and they deserve a lot of credit."

The Marine line, roughly defined by foxholes, was fairly solid to the northeast but not to the north. The German counterattack came, behind a heavy artillery bombardment fired by the batteries of all three of their divisions, at 4 AM on June 13, across the northeastern edge of the woods and hitting most seriously at Bouresches. The Germans got into the town but could not take it. The rest of the day was filled with harassing artillery fire, a mixture of high explosive and mustard gas. The night that followed was fairly quiet.

The battalions of the 5th and 6th Marines were now thoroughly intermingled. Wise's battalion was down to one-third its original strength. He had lost 615 men and nineteen officers since May 31. Turrill's 1st Battalion, 5th Marines, to his left in the companion wood, the Bois de Champillon, joined up with him by extending a company in a thin line into the western half of the woods. Holcomb's 2d Battalion, 6th Marines, held on in Bouresches. The Germans attacked Lieutenant Erskine's position three times. The hedge proved a blessing. The Germans had to lob their grenades high in the air to get them over the hedge, and they exploded well behind Erskine's line. Erskine's platoon stayed there until the 2d Battalion was pulled out of Bouresches.

Exhaustion

To the Marines it seemed that the Germans were sending in a steady flow of reinforcements. Actually, the German IV Reserve Corps was nearly used up. On June 13 the frontline strength of the entire 237th Division, which had begun the battle with 3,200 infantrymen, was down to forty-seven officers and 1,482 men. On the previous day Bischoff's 461st Infantry had just nine officers and 149 men present and fit for duty. On the 14th the division commander of the 237th scraped together two officers and 349 men from his division rear and sent them forward. Nor were the units on Bischoff's flanks in any better condition. The Germans would try no more major counterattacks but would limit their future actions to artillery fire and gas attacks.

The Marine brigade, in turn, was near exhaustion, with no relief in sight. To ease the situation General Bundy, the 2d Division commander, ordered the 3d Brigade to extend its zone to the left so as to shorten the Marine line. The 23d Infantry's line was now to extend from Le Thiolet to Bouresches, facing nearly east. The 3d Battalion, 23d Infantry, moved into Bouresches. During the relief the Germans shelled the village heavily with high explosive and mustard gas. The effects were devastating. The Marines took 400 casualties, the soldiers 150. The gas attack was particularly heavy against Hughes's battalion and also Holcomb's battalion. "Johnny the Hard" Hughes, who had fully lived up to his nickname in Belleau Wood, had to be evacuated. His 74th Company, the unit that had suffered so heavily in the predawn gas shelling of its reserve barracks near Verdun, suffered even worse gas casualties near Bouresches.

At this low point in the battle, Buck Neville handed General Harbord a pair of Marine Corps collar insignia and brusquely growled, "Here, we think it is about time you put these on." Harbord was unabashedly thrilled.

Harbord attempted to sort out his regiments. Drawing a north–south boundary line through the woods, he gave the right sector to the 5th Marines and the

left to the 6th Marines. The 3d Battalion, 5th Marines, on coming out of Bouresches was to go into brigade reserve at Lucy. Holcomb's 2d Battalion, 6th Marines,
was supposed to replace Wise's 2d Battalion, 5th Marines. Wise's battalion, when
it came out of the line, was to go into division reserve farther to the west. But the
moves did not work out as planned.

Casualties from the gas attack were so great that Holcomb did not have enough
men to complete the relief. Wise consequently refused to take his battalion out of
the line. Both battalions stayed in the woods, with Holcomb placing the remnants
of his battalion in the eastern edge of the woods between Wise's battalion on the
left and Hughes' battalion on the right.

In the 79th Company, Captain Zane was seriously wounded, and Graves
Erskine found himself, as senior surviving lieutenant, the acting commander. He
was still the company commander when the 2d Battalion came out of Bouresches
and went into Belleau Wood. The 79th Company was given a position just in front
of the hunting lodge. Erskine's outfit, with thirty or forty effectives, had taken over
its share of the line when an immaculately uniformed middle-aged gentleman in
a French helmet visited it. Erskine, not too politely, asked him who he was. The
gentleman in the French helmet replied, "I am your brigade commander."

"You are not. I know the brigade commander," shot back Erskine, unaware
that Harbord had replaced Doyen. Harbord found the whole incident vastly amusing and promised, jumping over the prerogatives of regimental and battalion commanders, that when the company came out of the wood Erskine would stay in
command.

Battalions, tattered by the fighting, continued to shift back and forth. For the
most part Harbord continued to deal directly with his battalion commanders. Neville and Lee, the regimental commanders, were playing little or no tactical role.

In Holcomb's battalion, Cates, as soon after the gas attack as he could manage it,
stripped down to the skin and scrubbed himself with a heavy lather of soap and
aired his clothing as best he could. He wound up with bad blisters between the legs,
around his neck, and on his forehead where his helmet rubbed.

Earlier in the campaign—ages earlier, it now seemed—Maj. Maurice E. Shearer
had been one of the officers on the 4th Brigade staff who had protested too publicly the abrupt replacement of Colonel Doyen by the army officer, Brigadier General Harbord. Shearer could have faced a court-martial, but Harbord dropped the
charges and made good use of his former opponent. Shearer commanded 1st Battalion, 6th Marines, in Hughes' temporary absence during the frantic positioning
of units to block the Germans' advance. Next Shearer had replaced the wounded
Major Berry in command of 3d Battalion, 5th Marines, now moving out of Bouresches into brigade reserve, as planned, at Lucy. The village with the pretty name
was by now completely destroyed. Major Turrill, relatively inactive in the Bois de

Champillon with his 1st Battalion, 5th Marines, held a thin line facing east. Wise's and Hughes' battalions along with Holcomb's battalion were still in the Bois de Belleau. Lt. Col. Logan Feland, second in command of the 5th Marines, was given direct charge of the three battered battalions and reorganized their positions. However, with Belleau Wood dripping with mustard gas, Harbord did not think the Germans would be counterattacking into it.

Respite

To the rear, the corps and division commanders continued to debate the relief of the Marine brigade. Bundy felt that he had done all that he could do by extending the front of the 3d Brigade to the left. On the night of June 15/16, Degoutte, the commander of XXI Corps, extended the right flank of the French 167th Division so as to relieve Major Sibley's 3d Battalion, 6th Marines, south of Bussiares. This left four battalions of the Marine brigade on line.

That same day Degoutte moved up to command of the French Sixth Army, and General Naulin took over XXI Corps. Naulin suggested that the 3d Brigade take over the entire division front. Bundy thought that would be unsafe. He urgently requested the attachment of the 7th Infantry, U.S. 3d Division, which was being held in army reserve. He was given the use of the untried regiment for a week, June 15–22.

One battalion of the 7th Infantry was to go forward each night. Of the four Marine battalions coming out, one would go into division reserve; the other three would go into the rest area being vacated by the 7th Infantry. All machine guns and transportation were to remain in place and temporarily exchanged with the relieving units.

On the sixteenth of June, Cates wrote again to his mother: "It has been a living hell since I started this. We were shelled all night with shrapnel and gas shells. . . . We wore our gas masks for four hours. It was mustard gas and a lot of the men were burned. . . . I now have two notches on my pistol grip, and I hope I can make it fifty. . . . I am in charge of my company now, as I am [the] only officer left."

On that night an army unit relieved Cates' 96th Company in the front lines. The movement caught the Germans' attention and brought down a heavy shelling. Overall, however, the relief went smoothly. On the first night, the 2d Battalion, 7th Infantry, occupied the right half of the Marine line in Belleau Wood. On the second night, the 1st Battalion came up and took over the left half, including "The Hook," and extending farther to the west. On the next night the 3d Battalion moved into the line on the north edge of the Bois de Champillon.

Relief completed, the three army battalions held the entire brigade line, with Colonel Neville in command of the front line and Lieutenant Colonel Feland remaining in immediate command in the woods. The colonel commanding the 7th Infantry, without active command, stayed forward as an observer.

General Lejeune Arrives

Brig. Gen. John Lejeune disembarked from USS *Henderson* at Brest on June 8, 1918. He immediately sought news of 4th Brigade of Marines at navy headquarters. His friend Rear Adm. H. B. Wilson briefed him on the military situation: "It is worse than it has been any time in the twelve months that I have been in France. The defeat of the Allied forces on the Chemin des Dames was a disaster of far greater proportions than the general public has any idea of." Wilson told Lejeune that the 2d Division had gone into the lines west of Chateau-Thierry and north of the Marne to fill a great gap in the French lines and that the Marine brigade in a brilliant attack had taken the southern part of Belleau Wood. The bitter fighting in Belleau Wood still continued.

Lejeune next went to report to the local army headquarters. The adjutant, after riffling through Lejeune's orders, told him that his instructions were to send all officers not attached to combat units to the Officers Reclassification Camp at Blois to await assignment by Pershing's headquarters. Lejeune had been warned that Blois ("Blooey") was a good place to avoid.

Lejeune put up a great front of carrying messages of immense importance that must be taken personally to Pershing's GHQ at Chaumont. After many phone calls and considerable bluffing, he gained permission to proceed to GHQ by way of a Cadillac he had providentially included in his hold baggage in the *Henderson*. With him went Maj. Pete Ellis and two aides. The Marines arrived in Paris on the second day and took rooms at the Continental Hotel. There was an air raid, but Lejeune had been told that a bomb had never hit the Continental, so he stayed in bed while the sirens shrieked and hundreds of antiaircraft guns blazed away at the sky. Lejeune had also heard that the Germans had a gun that could shell the city from ninety-seven kilometers away.

Lejeune visited in the Paris hospitals the Marines wounded from Belleau Wood. He was touched when these Marines spontaneously sang the "Marines Hymn" when they saw who he was. Lejeune found Colonel Catlin among the officer wounded. Catlin insisted that he was nearly well enough to return to his regiment. Major Berry, his arm shattered by machine-gun fire, was also there. Catlin and Berry told him of Maj. Edward Cole's charge against a machine-gun nest that had cost him his life.

Next morning Lejeune left on the all-day drive to Chaumont, reporting the following morning to Brig. Gen. James W. McAndrew, who had replaced Harbord as Pershing's chief of staff. McAndrew told him bluntly, "The Marine Corps has no authority over you while you are on duty with the AEF. Your assignment to duty is entirely in the hands of General Pershing."

Lejeune replied that his chief reason for coming to Chaumont was to offer Pershing a Marine division, complete in all its parts. McAndrew said that he would bring the matter to General Pershing's attention. Hours later Lejeune was pleasantly surprised to receive an invitation to dinner with General Pershing. The AEF commander greeted him cordially and gave him a good meal. He said that he remembered meeting Lejeune at Baguio in the Philippines and knew about his service at Veracruz and his attendance at the Army War College. Pershing had high words of praise for the Marines' performance at Belleau Wood, but he made no mention of the possibility of a Marine division in France.

General McAndrew held Lejeune at arm's length for the next several days before finally granting him an appointment with Pershing. Lejeune marshaled all of his arguments. Pershing responded that the service of the 4th Brigade was splendid and that he would welcome individual officers who were detailed to the AEF but that he could not approve of a Marine division, because it would interfere with his plans for a homogeneous army. A cable to that effect would be sent to Headquarters, Marine Corps.

Lejeune, dismayed, retreated to the outer office and asked McAndrew what duty he might expect. McAndrew said all he could offer for the moment was duty as an observer with the 35th Division. Lejeune bit his tongue in disappointment and then asked permission to visit the 2d Division en route to the 35th Division.

Early on the morning of June 19 Lejeune and his aides left Chaumont in the Cadillac. Just before sunset on a pleasant summer evening, they crossed the Marne and joined a group of Marines at a chateau being used by Wise as his battalion headquarters during the temporary respite from Belleau Wood. Maj. Ralph E. Keyser, who had been one of Major General Barnett's aides, was also staying at the chateau while in the process of relieving Wise of command of the 2d Battalion, 5th Marines. He and Wise insisted that Lejeune spend the night with them. Next morning Lejeune inspected Wise's battalion and found his companies, just relieved at Belleau Wood, no stronger than platoons. From here Lejeune drove on to the 2d Division headquarters, missing Brigadier General Bundy but finding Lieutenant Colonel Lee, the 6th Regiment's commander. Together with Lee he visited Holcomb's and Sibley's battalions, bivouacked in the woods. He then went on to Harbord's headquarters. Harbord brought him up to date on the situation. After absorbing replacements and resting about a week, the brigade would be going back into Belleau Wood. Lejeune next visited his old friend Buck Neville, who was exercising tactical command of the 7th Infantry, and then Hughes' and Turrill's battalions, before making a long night's drive through the pouring rain back to Chaumont. Lejeune reflected on the Marines' commendable performance and heavy losses to date. He was anxious to return as their brigade commander.

Back to Belleau Wood

The Germans had made their reliefs at the same time as the Americans. Seventh Army orders of the thirteenth of June terminated any further offensive and authorized assumption of a defensive posture pending a new offensive elsewhere. The

87th Division was assigned to the IV Reserve Corps. The 87th was to move into the lines between June 15 and 19, not only relieving the pulverized 237th but also extending its line to the south as far as Bouresches so as to relieve what was left of the 110th Grenadiers of the 28th Division as well. Ordered to defend in depth, the 87th nevertheless put all three regiments on line. The two flank regiments classically put one battalion on line, one in support, and one in reserve. The center regiment, the 347th Infantry, was given Belleau Wood and deployed one battalion in the wood, one to the west of it, and held one in reserve. The division commander asked permission to withdraw altogether from Belleau Wood, drawing a new line through Belleau village, but the corps commander disapproved. Wishing to keep his commitment to the woods itself at a minimum, the division commander calculated that with two weeks work he could make the defenses on the northern edge of the wood strong enough to be held by two companies, enabling him to pull back one company to Belleau.

The Marines had begun work on wire entanglements on June 14. The 2d Battalion, 7th Infantry, continued this but otherwise stayed stationary. The army battalions on the flanks did reconnaissance patrols and on the night of June 18/19 attempted to straighten the line. The 1st Battalion in the left half of Belleau Wood went forward, banged into the German main line of resistance, and after losing twenty men came back to its original positions. The same battalion made a more substantial attack on June 20 and lost 180 men without much gain. The 3d Battalion did better, reaching the Torcy–Bussiares road against no resistance and echeloning its right flank back toward Bois de Belleau.

The time limit on the loan of the 7th Infantry was running out. The Marine brigade had recuperated remarkably. During its brief respite, the Marine battalions were pumped up with about 2,800 replacements and after a little rest were considered ready to go back into the line. An Alsatian deserter gave division headquarters and Harbord a clearer picture of the German defenses in Belleau Wood.

The relief of the 7th Infantry was accomplished on three consecutive nights. On the night of June 21/22 Major Shearer took his 3d Battalion, 5th Marines, into position in the northern part of the woods. The next night Major Sibley's 3d Battalion, 6th Marines, went in on the east. On the third night, June 23/24, the 2d Battalion, 5th Marines, now under Major Keyser, moved in on the extreme left of the brigade and division sector.

Belleau Wood was a tough place for any new regiment to experience its first major combat. To its credit, the 7th Infantry had fought well, gave up no ground, and gained precious time for the Marines to rest and rearm. The army regiment had lost some three hundred casualties while in the line, mostly in the 1st Battalion.

All the accumulated horrors of the battlefield greeted the Marines as they eased back into the lines. The woods and surrounding wheat fields smelled ghastly. Hundreds of American and German bodies lay where they had fallen earlier, decomposing badly in the June sun. Pvt. James Hatcher, with Sibley's 3d Battalion, recalled: "Our next turn on the front line was in a position taken by our 5th regiment on June 6th. Many of the dead still lay unburied upon the ground and the place had a most horrible stench. . . . A wheatfield lay between us and the German positions, two hundred yards distant. That wheatfield was littered with German corpses." Hatcher was grateful for his gas mask.

On the twenty-third of June, Lieutenant Cates wrote his sister, Katherine, from his bivouac in the Bois Gros Jean, "The 96 Co. [is] a complete new company now—a new captain named Woodworth [Capt. Wethered Woodworth] and a Lt. Duwaine [1st Lt. Robert L. Duane] from N.Y. We three will be the only officers for the time being. . . . I sent Mother the brass bar that had been hit by the machine gun bullet. I have a lot of souvenirs that I will bring home—German shoulder bars, pistol, bayonet, pack raincoat, helmet and maps. . . . I appreciate you trying to send me the candy and cigarettes—just write me letters—that is enough, as we are getting a lot of tobacco and chocolate free, thru the Y.M.C.A. and Red Cross."

The objective now was to drive the Germans from the northern edge of the woods. Shearer, given the order, attacked at seven o'clock on the evening of June 23. After an ineffective preparation fired by trench mortars and rifle grenades, all four of his companies went forward in the assault. Shearer's tactic was to have grenadiers out in front, followed by riflemen in skirmish line. His companies ran into a battalion of the 347th Infantry fully organized for defense. When a machine gun was overrun, the crew would usually escape, and the captured position would come under fire from other supporting guns. The attack faltered to a halt with no ground gained. The battalion ebbed back to its old positions by midnight, having taken 104 casualties.

Second Lt. Laurence T. Stallings was a platoon commander in 47th Company in this assault. The former *Atlanta Journal* reporter had joined the 3d Battalion, 5th Marines, at the beginning of the fighting at Belleau Wood and fought well at Bouresches. Stallings recalled in his postwar book, *The Doughboys,* the horrors of leading his support platoon through the windrows of casualties from the futile attacks of June 23: "Men in supporting platoons, inching forward to plug the gaps in a decimated company where there was no artillery roar to drown the cries of human beings, sometimes thought this duty the worst of war's alarms . . . crawling forward hugging the ground, the blood of other men on their sleeves, their hands, their faces." Shearer decried his losses and the paucity of artillery support in a message to Harbord, saying, "Infantry alone cannot dislodge enemy guns."

Harbord and Bundy agreed that stronger artillery support was needed. The preliminary bombardment for the next attack would be fired by the entire 2d Field Artillery Brigade, plus nine light batteries and nine heavy batteries borrowed from the French. Shearer pulled his battalion back slightly to give the artillery a free hand. The shelling began at 3 AM on the twenty-fifth and went on until 5 PM—fourteen hours. The French batteries dug deep into the German rear areas. The American guns, light and heavy, concentrated on the northern end of the wood. This was by far the most effective Allied preassault shelling of the battle. German records speak of the violence of the bombardment and the destruction of many of their Maxim machine guns, the heart of their defenses. The trees in front of Shearer's position were shelled into splinters. As the barrage rolled forward, the Marines jumped off precisely at 5 PM. From left to right it was the 16th Company, the 47th Company, two platoons of the 45th Company, and the 20th Company. Two platoons of the 45th Company were held back in reserve.

The Germans resisted stubbornly. In front of Shearer was the 1st Battalion, 347th Infantry, and to the west, part of the 2d Battalion, 347th. They had long before learned how to hole up during an artillery bombardment. Once the fires were lifted, they popped up out of their holes and got behind their remaining machine guns.

Lieutenant Stallings had become the senior surviving officer and acting commander of the 47th Company. Colonel Neville did not quite trust him in this role, so he assigned an old-timer, Capt. Gaines Moseley, to oversee his actions. The 47th Company reached the center portion of its objective. Moseley found Stallings sick from gas. A shell fragment had lodged in his leg, and to get at it the corpsman had unspiraled his wrap puttees and cut away the lower part of his beautiful forest-green breeches. A potato-masher grenade had burst at Stallings' feet, driving his tin hat into his right cheek. The Maxims were chattering out in front of him. Captain Moseley advised that the platoon on the left needed help. Stallings went with nine men and stumbled into a German company. He charged a machine-gun nest and took a bullet that tore off his right kneecap. He threw a grenade that finished the nest. Eight months in the hospital would follow, as doctors tried to save the leg.

"Woods Now U.S. Marine Corps Entirely"

At 9:30 PM Shearer reported that he had the whole wood except for a few scattered machine guns. He was organizing for defense on the north edge of the woods but doubted that he could hold against a serious counterattack. Harbord directed Neville to support Shearer with both of the battalions on his flanks.

There would be no counterattack. The German battalion commander had called for reinforcements but did not get them—two companies from another regiment—until almost midnight. By that time it was too late. By then his division commander was thinking not of a counterattack but of a withdrawal to the Torcy–Belleau road—beyond the woods. When morning of the twenty-sixth came, Shearer's Marines took care of the few remaining die-hard machine gunners. Harbord, with great satisfaction, relayed Shearer's terse message to division: "Woods now U.S. Marine Corps entirely."

In this last action the Germans lost seven officers and 423 men, including 260 captured, and twenty-five machine guns. This prompted a reprimand from the high command to the division and corps commanders for allowing so many men to be trapped in such a position. American losses in this last attack were four officers and 119 men killed and wounded.

On that same twenty-sixth of June, Cates wrote his mother from a support position in the woods northwest of Lucy: "Last night I took fifty-two men out to put up some barb wire—the Boche spotted us about midnight and began to shell us—I withdrew my men and waited until they had stopped and then started back to work; just as we renewed work they started again, so I brought my men in—no one was hurt. We found coffee, ham, steak, bread, and potatoes waiting for us—we get one hot meal a day here. They bring it in big thermos cans on a Ford truck. They also bring canned meat, bread, bacon, sugar, candles, and solidified alcohol. During the day we take either the alcohol or candles and cook the bacon in our mess gear; then fry the bread in the bacon fat, and put sugar on it—it's a swell dish. We either heat the canned meat or eat it cold. The water is brought in large water carts. Of course, we are not so lucky while we are in the front line—the 'chow' gets shot up real often, and we have to go without."

Cates went on: "I wish you could see your son with his equipment on—dirty, torn, ragged suit; wrapped puttees, shoes, that used to be boots, but are now cut off; steel helmet, with a hole thru it and a big dent; pistol belt and suspenders; first aid packages and cover; pistol and holster; canteen, cup and cover; knapsack, which holds toilet articles, maps, message books, extra cartridges, etc; field glasses and case, two extra pistol clips and cases; German gas mask (which saved my life); French gas mask; big German Luger pistol and holster; big musette bag with cigarettes, chocolate bars, magazines, writing paper, condiment can, malted milk tablets, comb, little clothes brush, alkaline tablets (for gas) and other junk; a blanket roll which contains a poncho, blanket, air pillow, handkerchiefs, socks, underwear, etc; and a German raincoat slung over my arm. A nice load, but I need every bit of it."

The clearing of Belleau Wood ended the offensive for the Marines. The Marines went into the deliberate defense. By July 2 each regiment—the 6th Marines in Belleau Wood itself and the 5th Marines on the ground to the west of it—had only one battalion left on line.

The 3d Infantry Brigade, in a tidy operation, attacked and took Vaux to the east on the evening of July 1. The 2d Division then began the deliberate organization of its zone of action into a defensive sector, organizing in considerable depth in the new way with sufficient elasticity to absorb the shock of Ludendorff's new-model attacks. *"Pas Fini"* was the nickname for the sector, and this became its official designation.

On the evening of July 3, once again in a support position, Cates was told to pick out twenty men from the 96th Company and take them to Paris to participate in the long-anticipated Fourth of July parade. He selected as many of the old-timers as possible. The march to the rear in the broad daylight of the late summer evening attracted a few German shells. A truck and a train got them to Paris by dark. They went into a good camp, where there were shower baths and bunks to sleep in. Cates and his men were up early on the morning of the fourth, trying to make themselves look halfway presentable. ("We still looked like a bunch of bums.") At eight o'clock they left the camp and formed up for the parade. Cates found himself the platoon commander of a composite platoon of eighty Marines.

In the crowd were many convalescing American wounded. Cates saw several members of the old 96th Company, and joyous yells were exchanged. Most of Paris witnessed the parade, and there was great enthusiasm for the Marines. Cates wrote his mother, "They literally covered us with roses."

Shepherd, after evacuation through a series of Red Cross hospitals and an infection that nearly killed him, was hobbling around Paris on crutches, conspicuous in his tin hat and bloodstained breeches and with Kiki on the end of a chain. He found a uniform of greenish cloth in a tailor shop. It looked something like a Marine uniform, so he bought it. By the Fourth of July he felt well enough to go see the big parade he had heard the French were having for the Americans. He and Kiki found a spot on the Place de la Concorde from which to watch. To his delight he saw some men from the 55th Company go marching by. He joined them on his crutches.[7]

Belleau Wood was especially hard on the Marine machine gunners. Not attached to any particular infantry battalion, they stayed in the line as the infantry battalions came and went. Two companies were on the front for twenty-two days without relief.

The 2d Division was long overdue for rest and refitting. The Marine brigade had taken about four thousand casualties, about 55 percent of its original strength, the largest number of casualties suffered by a single American brigade in the entire war. In turn, the brigade had inflicted a loss upon the Germans of about three thousand, including prisoners.

When relieved by the U.S. 26th Division on July 6, the 2d Division moved to a reserve battle position about ten kilometers behind the front. Cates reported that a rumor was threading its way through the brigade that General Lejeune had recommended to General Barnett that a division of Marines be sent to Italy.

The rumor had some substance to it, although the proposal had not originated with John Lejeune. In January 1918, Admiral Sims' Naval Planning Section in London proposed an allied landing to attack German submarine bases along the Sabbioncello Peninsula on the Adriatic Sea. The planning staff (which included Col. Robert H. Dunlap, USMC) proposed an Allied landing force of about thirty thousand troops, mostly Italian soldiers, augmented by units "trained in landing operations; for instance American marines." Senior members of the Inter-Allied

Council were reviewing the proposal in March when General Ludendorff launched his first great offensive. The ensuing crisis on the western front halted consideration of such peripheral operations.

The French Sixth Army on June 30, 1918, issued an order that changed the name of Bois de Belleau to Bois de la Brigade de Marine.

German intelligence reports assessing the Americans began to change from contempt to begrudging respect. "They fight like devils," a German lieutenant of the 40th Infantry opposing the 5th Marines in Belleau Wood recorded in his diary on June 10. By the time the 2d Division came out of the line, the Germans had classified it as a "shock unit." Nothing in their records, however, shows that they ever bestowed the accolade *"Teufelhunde,"* or "Devil Dogs," upon the Marines.[8]

The Marine Brigade's tactical victory at Belleau Wood, combined with the adjoining U.S. Army successes at Cantigny and Vaux, demonstrated to their Allies and the Germans that American forces could fight, sustain losses, and prevail. This provided a significant psychological turning point on the western front. The Germans were by no means beaten. Yet after Belleau Wood there was a sense of the tide finally beginning to turn. And hundreds of thousands of fresh American forces were on their way to France.

CHAPTER EIGHT

"In Every Clime and Place"

W hile several thousand "Devil Dogs" of the 4th Brigade fought the Germans tooth and nail in Belleau Wood in the early summer of 1918, most Marines were serving elsewhere—at sea, in the air, and on many foreign shores.[1]

On June 30, 1918, the same day the French army renamed Belleau Wood "Les Bois de la Brigade de Marine," the Marine Corps reported an active-duty strength of 1,503 officers and 51,316 enlisted men. The following day Congress authorized an increase to the seemingly stratospheric level of 3,341 officers and 75,500 enlisted. The Corps would come close to attaining those authorized figures by year's end.

The distribution of troops in hundreds of small units and detachments around the world in 1918 reflected the multiplicity of roles and missions assigned to the Corps.

Many Marines, swayed by Floyd Gibbons' sensational accounts of Leatherneck derring-do in Belleau Wood, began to favor the inland, shock-troop role, regardless of whether such a main mission would duplicate the U.S. Army's role or imperial the Marines' vital ties with the navy. These proponents may not have realized that a large number of the thirty-two thousand Marines who served in France during the war never saw combat on the western front. Postwar leadership in the Corps would reflect these realities—a relatively small number of officers who had fought the Germans and the majority who wanted that honor but instead manned other ramparts around the world. Those in the first group had experienced a massive, industrialized war, featuring heavy artillery, aircraft, and newfangled tanks—a war where they rubbed shoulders with troops of a dozen Allied armies and fought against a deadly efficient and well-armed enemy. Their counterparts, by contrast, fought bandits in the Dominican Republic, Caco night-fighters in Haiti, or the occasional Bolshevik revolutionary in Siberia. The succession of eight Marine commandants over the thirty-five-year period following the war represented both experiences. John Lejeune, Wendell Neville, Thomas Holcomb, Clifton Cates, and Lemuel Shepherd had fought with distinction on the western front; the other three had served in the Caribbean during the period of World War I (Ben Fuller in the Dominican Republic, John Russell and Archer Vandegrift in Haiti).

The Quest for a Marine Division

Earlier in 1918 President Woodrow Wilson had reappointed George Barnett to a second four-year term as Major General Commandant. For much of the year Barnett sought to gain approval from the Wilson administration to provide General Pershing's AEF with a Marine division. Assembling a full-blown division for combat service in France was difficult, despite the unprecedented number of new Marines authorized by Congress. In addition to matching the existing 4th Brigade with an additional brigade of two new infantry regiments, Barnett would also have to furnish a full regiment of artillery, machine-gun and engineer battalions, and the entire range of combat logistic support units and equipment—plus a large pool of trained replacements poised for rapid deployment.

The idea died stillborn. Pershing made it quite clear to Lejeune at Chaumont in June that he would not accept a Marine division in the AEF. He was building a homogeneous army, he said. His numbers were growing exponentially. A million doughboys had arrived in France by mid-summer. The total would double again by autumn. The significance of the Marines' influence within the AEF diminished with the arrival of each new army division. In June 1917 the 5th Regiment of Marines had represented 20 percent of the first regular infantry troops arriving in France, and one year later the Marine Brigade had fought at Belleau Wood with spectacular savagery, contributing a critical boost to the Allied cause. Yet by the summer of 1918 the Marine Brigade represented less than 1 percent of the AEF, truly fitting "Slam" Marshall's description of "a little raft of sea soldiers in an ocean of Army."

Pershing had no particular need for a Marine division, with its unique supply requirements, tenuous troop-replacement pipeline, inexperienced general staff officers, and a disruptive hunger for recognition. He conveyed this conclusion to the secretary of war. Neither Secretary Baker nor President Wilson chose to overrule Pershing on the issue.

Deployment of the 5th Marine Brigade

Barnett, rebuffed, lowered his sights. Working through Navy Secretary Daniels, he sought President Wilson's permission to send at least one additional Marine brigade to France. Wilson acceded, and on September 5, 1918, Barnett ordered the formation in Quantico of the 5th Marine Brigade, composed of the newly established 11th and 13th regiments of Marines and the 5th Machine Gun Battalion. Brig. Gen. Eli Cole commanded the new brigade. Cols. George Van Orden and Smedley Butler commanded the 11th and 13th Marines, respectively. The officers and men, impatient for orders overseas all year, embarked swiftly, and the brigade's lead elements began landing in France less than three weeks after the commandant's warning order. Cole's Marines had high hopes for action on the western front, where their counterparts in the 2d Division were then on the move toward Blanc Mont.

The War Department advised General Pershing he could use the 5th Marine Brigade as best needed. Pershing promptly did so, deploying the newly arriving Marines as "line-of-communications troops" in the Service of Supply. To their chagrin, Cole's Marines would see no combat, serving instead in a hundred scattered detachments as dock and warehouse guards, provost marshals, fire marshals, military police, convoy escorts, and prison wardens. Smedley Butler, the flamboyant sparkplug with his two Medals of Honor from Haiti and Vera Cruz, became at thirty-seven the youngest brigadier general in the Corps and eventually relieved Brigadier General Cole in command of the 5th Brigade. Butler's collateral but more significant duty became that of commander of the Pontanezen Camp at Brest, a transient facility that became after the Armistice the largest embarkation camp in the world. Butler chafed at his rear-echelon duties ("to sit in the rear and run this filthy mudhole") but performed remarkably well, receiving the army's Distinguished Service Cross for nine months of an otherwise thankless mission.

Barnett was not without influence in Washington, but he was powerless in regard to Pershing. Moreover, he and his small staff had their hands full coordinating the deployment of the balance of the Marines in sixteen countries and on board sixty ships. In addition to the two brigades and, eventually, the 1st Marine Aviation Force in France and the 1st Marine Aeronautic Company in the Azores, the Corps maintained prewar-configured brigades along the Mexican border, as well in Cuba, Haiti, and the Dominican Republic, as well as the advance base force in the Virgin Islands and on call in Philadelphia. Marines also defended remote coaling stations, naval ammunition depots, and radio stations. Marine trainers served at bases and ranges around the country, including a newly established School of Machine Gun Instruction at Utica, New York. At Parris (as now spelled) Island, Congress authorized the Marines to take control of the entire island, increasing the space usable for recruit training from seventy-eight to three thousand acres.

The First Women Marines

Earlier Barnett secured authorization to establish a Marine Corps Reserve for the duration of the war. Barnett took advantage of the opportunity to enlist, as reservists, the first women into the Marine Corps. Barnett's motives may have been more practical than altruistic—women clerks could free male clerks to deploy to the far-flung brigades—but in doing so he boldly broke down the centuries-old barrier. Secretary Daniels, on August 8, 1918, approved Barnett's request to enlist women in the Marine Corps Reserve to perform clerical functions. Five days later, Opha M. Johnson, a civil servant at headquarters, became the first female to enroll in the Corps. Eventually three hundred women served as Marines during the war, almost exclusively in Washington. Although they did not experience boot camp, the women wore long-skirted green uniforms and received instruction in military discipline and close-order drill, including the difficult eight-man squad choreography ("Right front into line . . . *march!*").

Male Marines struggled with how to address their new female counterparts, seeking a name more suitable than their official classification, "Reserves (F)." *Leatherneck* magazine described them as "the Marine girls." Someone dubbed them "Marinettes." Other nicknames were insulting. A high-spirited New York woman, Martha L. Wilchinski, wrote her views on the subject to her sweetheart serving in France. "I'm a lady leatherneck," she said, "I'm the last word in Hun hunters; I'm a real, live, honest-to-goodness Marine!" Nor did Wilchinski suffer fools in regard to the unflattering nicknames being circulated. "I hear some people are giving us nicknames," she said. "Isn't it funny the minute a girl becomes a regular fellow somebody always tries to queer it by calling her something else? Well, anyone that calls me anything but 'Marine' is going to hear from me. 'Marine' is good enough for me."

Marines like Private Wilchinski freed enough of their male counterparts to form the equivalent of a small battalion. Though they were terminated with the war's end, the women established a valuable precedent. Twenty thousand Women Marines would serve in World War II, freeing enough men to form an entire division.

America in 1918

The issue of equal rights for women was one of a number of new initiatives sweeping wartime America in 1918. The initial wave of patriotism that followed President Wilson's declaration of war in April 1917 had subsided after the first year and had been replaced with impatience at the slow buildup and training of the AEF, followed by shock at the butcher's bill for the first battles involving American troops and a growing watchfulness over future international commitments. As most wars do, this one accelerated social and political changes.

Wilson's vision of a league of cooperative nations and an end to all wars first inspired the populace and then evoked its cynicism. The 1918 congressional mid-term elections reflected the shifting public sentiment. The Democrats had ruled both houses for eight years. In 1917 President Wilson had asked Republican leaders for a "political moratorium" for the duration of the war emergency. The Republicans pretty much toed the bipartisan line for the first year and a half, both for

actical reasons, not wanting to be painted as disloyal to the war
n two weeks before the midterm election, however, Wilson com-
;ious political blunder, calling for the continuation of a Democratic
ssential to the nation's security." Many voters considered the president's public questioning of Republican patriotism a cheap shot—a new factor that
combined with a growing disillusionment with America's emerging role as a global
superpower to carry the Republicans to a two-seat majority in the Senate and a
forty-one-seat majority in the House, setting the stage for the bitter defeat of Wilson's Treaty of Versailles after the Armistice.

The scourge of a deadly influenza pandemic stalked the world in 1918. The
"Spanish Flu" would kill millions of people worldwide by 1920. In the United
States, the flu and its accompanying pneumonia struck twenty million citizens.
One in four died. More than 193,000 Americans died in the single month of Octo-
ber 1918. Half as many U.S. troops died in homeland training camps as died in
combat overseas.

The unprecedented death rate among the civilian population made the sharply
increasing combat deaths all the more painful. Among prominent Americans slain
on the western front was the renowned poet and journalist Joyce Kilmer, best
known for his poem "Trees," published in the book *Trees and Other Poems* in 1914.
Sergeant Kilmer, a soldier in the 69th Infantry, was thirty-one years old when he
was killed during the Second Battle of the Marne on July 30, 1918.

The gulf between President Wilson's idealistic pursuit of an equitable peace
and the average American's growing pessimism and isolationism became manifest
in several ways. The best-selling novel in America in the spring and summer of
1918 was the gritty, antiwar book *The Four Horsemen of the Apocalypse,* by Spanish
author Vicente Blasco-Ibanez. The *New York Times Book Review* edition of December 22, 1918, described the book as "the greatest novel the world has seen in many
years . . . the one novel of the war that will be more valued as the years pass."

The mood of the populace was further manifested in virulent anti-German
prejudice. In 1912 the distinguished German conductor Karl Muck became music
director of the Boston Symphony Orchestra. Muck was considered one of the
world's greatest interpreters of the works of Richard Wagner, but by 1918 his pref-
erence for German music and his refusal to play the "Star-Spangled Banner" led
to his arrest under the Alien Enemies Act. The government imprisoned Dr. Muck
in Fort Oglethorpe, Georgia, until the end of the war and then deported him back
to Germany.

In 1918 the total population of the United States exceeded 103 million. In the
same year, the government introduced Daylight Saving Time, established regular
airmail service between New York City, Washington, and Chicago, and began sell-
ing the first airmail postage stamps. The Wilson administration struggled to support the two million U.S. troops fighting in France and provide food, equipment,
and munitions for the Allies as well. The war's ever-increasing costs in blood and

treasure caused Wilson to emphasize a "Work or Fight" policy, primarily aimed at able-bodied, adult, white males. A popular pro-government song written by Edward Laska in 1918 concluded with these verses: "If you want to do what's right / You must either 'work or fight' / So get busy 'Over Here' or 'Over There.'"

The somber "get busy" mood affected college sports in America, with many of the best athletes volunteering for service overseas and a general malaise spreading among the stay-at-home fans. The annual Rose Bowl football game, already a tradition, seemed to be in jeopardy in 1918 when tournament officials offered to cancel the event in deference to the serious business of waging war. President Wilson bestirred himself to intervene, stating, "I think the normal life of the country should be continued in every way possible." Officials agreed to produce a modified tournament game between two military teams (each containing a goodly share of former all-star collegians), with net profits going to the American Red Cross. The Mare Island Marines and the Camp Lewis Soldiers played the 1918 game in Pasadena's Tournament Park (about three miles from the present site of the Rose Bowl). The Marines prevailed 19–7, with fullback Hollis Huntington, the former University of Oregon All-American, garnering Most Valuable Player honors by gaining 111 yards in twenty bone-crushing carries.

In other sports highlights in 1918, former world heavyweight champion John L. Sullivan died, and the current U.S. heavyweight champion Jack Dempsey defended his title with a fourteen-second knockout of contender John Morris. The thoroughbred Exterminator won the Kentucky Derby. Thirty-year-old Knute Rockne became the head football coach of Notre Dame's "Fighting Irish."

In a lightly attended World Series played entirely in September, in deference to the war effort, the Boston Red Sox defeated the Chicago Cubs, four games to two. The championship was the fifth in fifteen years for the exultant Red Sox. Boston's sensational left-handed pitcher, twenty-three-year-old George Herman "Babe" Ruth, won two games in the Series, surrendering two runs in seventeen innings, and belted a two-run triple. Boston would trade the talented but troublesome Ruth to the New York Yankees at the end of the following season, incurring what became called "The Curse of the Bambino," the excruciating eighty-six-year span until its next World Series victory.

As in all wars, Marines assigned to overseas duty or service with fleet hungered for current news of the war, their hometowns, or national sports. In 1918, General Pershing ordered the U.S. Army to publish an overseas newspaper for all servicemen serving in Europe. Beginning on February 8, 1918, editions of *The American Soldiers' Newspaper* began appearing weekly under the title *Stars and Stripes,* resuming the tradition of the Civil War newspaper of the same name published by Illinois troops in Bloomfield, Missouri, in 1861. Straight talk and lively writing by gifted journalists such as sports editor Grantland Rice helped *Stars and Stripes* attain a peak circulation of 526,000 readers by the war's end.

Marines with the Atlantic Fleet

In September 1918 Major General Commandant Barnett embarked on a navy ship to begin a month-long inspection of the Marines in Europe. The Atlantic crossing gave Barnett a rare opportunity to visit with some of the two thousand Marines assigned to staffs and detachments of sixty warships, principally battleships and cruisers. Many had filled these seagoing billets since before the U.S. declaration of war in April 1917. Typically, a cruiser, such as the USS *Charleston,* warranted a Marine detachment of two officers and sixty-two enlisted men, while a battleship, like the USS *Wyoming,* rated two Marine officers and eighty-six troops.

Division 9 of the Atlantic Fleet, under the command of Rear Adm. Hugh Rodman and consisting of the battleships *New York* (flagship), *Wyoming, Florida,* and *Delaware,* rendezvoused in Lynnhaven Roads, Chesapeake Bay, on November 24, 1917, and sailed the following day with destroyer *Manley* as an escort. The destination was Scapa Flow in the Orkney Islands for service with the British Grand Fleet. The voyage took thirteen days, four of which, including a miserable Thanksgiving on November 29, were spent weathering a ninety-knot gale off Newfoundland. The battleships went their separate ways in the storm. The ships reassembled on December 7, when the British light cruiser *Blanche* and ten destroyers arrived as escorts for their entrance into Scapa Flow. The U.S. battleships were given a rousing welcome, a "hearty three cheers" for the Yanks.

Rodman's division Marine officer and aide was Maj. Nelson P. Vulte, and so he would remain throughout the division's service with the Grand Fleet. Marines in battleships traditionally stood watch in the open gun tubs of the 6-inch secondary batteries, and for them the best part of getting to Scapa Flow was getting out of the North Atlantic winter weather.

First duty for the Marines after dropping anchor was to join the sailors in recoaling the battleships' empty bunkers. Said one sea-going Marine:

> At this time the Marines first became acquainted with the small regulation bags of the British Navy holding about 200 pounds. The colliers looked sort of unfriendly and the coal itself was a fiendish mixture of fine, lung-filling dust, smothering lumps that defied the shovels and maddened the shovelers. A bitter wind added to the misery, while cutting snow-squalls were unwelcome visitors. It was an all-night sort of horrible nightmare and the stuff seemed to go aboard the ships with pitiful slowness. As one Marine remarked: "It was a new game, strange coal and stranger colliers, and we did not handle it well at first, but before long we had that darned Welsh coal trained so it would roll over and play dead."

Rodman's division received the designation of Sixth Battle Squadron of the British Grand Fleet. After ten days in Scapa Flow's "wet gloom," they moved in company with the Grand Fleet's Fifth Battle Squadron to Rosyth Naval Dock Yard near Edinburgh, Scotland. The fleet's commander in chief, the handsome and popular Adm. David Beatty, led the way in the *Queen Elizabeth*. The U.S. Marines looked with awe at the British dreadnoughts, all veterans of Jutland and all capable of turning up twenty-five knots. Ruefully the Americans noted that they were all oil burners, unlike the labor-intensive, coal-fired U.S. ships.

Distinguished visitors were piped aboard the *New York,* not only Admiral Beatty but, separately, Adm. John R. Jellicoe, now the First Sea Lord. Some of the older Marines knew vaguely that Jellicoe had been with them in 1900 in the relief of Peking and had been badly wounded.

At the end of January the American Sixth Battle Squadron sortied with the British Fifth Battle Squadron for maneuvers in the North Sea. The vice admiral commanding obligingly sent a signal to Admiral Rodman in the *New York* that he had two German submarines dead ahead at a thousand yards. The *New York* veered, and the British destroyer screen drove the subs down with depth charges.

On February 7 Rodman's squadron sortied again, this time in company with the British Third Light Cruiser Squadron to escort a convoy of freighters to Bergen, Norway. The *Florida* and *Wyoming* narrowly missed colliding on the seventh. The next day the squadron went to general quarters with the sighting of one or more submarines. The battleships plunged along as the destroyers darted back and forth, letting go with their depth charges. *Delaware* got off one round from a port anti-aircraft gun at something judged to be either a torpedo or periscope. A torpedo missed the *Florida* by about a hundred feet.

A Marine in the *Wyoming* described the sorties thusly: "These trips gave us new ideas in endurance and discomfort, watch and watch, zigzagging steadily at 18 knots, fog, storm, and the North Sea, plus a big coaling the instant we got back to base. . . . Our first trip we flushed a sub, which let fly a 'tin-fish' across our bows and ducked. That was the memorable occasion when the Delaware broke loose and flew over the horizon like a hen in front of an automobile, her speed being estimated at 30 knots."

The *Texas* joined the squadron on February 11. Her senior Marine officer was Capt. Pedro del Valle, the first Puerto Rican to receive a Marine Corps commission, a dynamic officer whose future would include artillery command at Guadalcanal and division command at Okinawa. These short cruises became routine: a week or ten days at sea, submarine "sightings" but never a clear-cut kill.

In late April a stimulating rumor rippled through the wardrooms and mess decks that the German High Seas Fleet was "out." The British Grand Fleet steamed majestically to meet them, but another Jutland was not to be.

"A new game was tried" at the end of June when Rodman's squadron went out to cover the American minelaying squadron as it began to lay the great mine barrage from the Orkneys across the North Sea to the Norwegian coast. Occasional submarine sightings enlivened the proceedings.

The twenty-second of July was a state occasion for the British Grand Fleet: the king and queen of England came to visit. The royal guests, embarked in HMS *Oak,* passed down the line of battleships. The usual honors were rendered, with three cheers from the men manning the rails. King George V, in his uniform of an Admiral of the Fleet, and Queen Mary came on board the *New York,* which, in addition to its own complement, had details from the other American battleships present for the affair.

The American squadron went out again with the British Fifth Battle Squadron on August 8 to escort the American minelaying squadron once more. The *Florida* reported a torpedo crossing her bow, and on the ninth the *Arkansas* fired at a submarine with her 5-inch guns. The *Texas* also blazed away, and the accompanying destroyers dropped depth charges.

Back at Rosyth after only two days at sea, the Marine detachments from the five battleships were gathered together ashore on for military training as a provisional battalion under Major Vulte. Assistant Secretary of the Navy Franklin D. Roosevelt, continuing his grand tour, visited the flagship on August 29.

In the middle of October a report that German raiders were headed for Pentland Firth at high speed sent the squadron out in the hope that there would be, at last, some real action, but it proved to be another false alarm. Steaming back in the early evening of October 14, *New York* hit something submerged and damaged her starboard propeller so badly that she had to put into Newcastle-on-Tyne for repairs. The submerged object was later declared a submarine, and *New York* was credited with the destruction of the same. Admiral Rodman shifted his flag temporarily to the *Wyoming.*

The Grand Fleet celebrated the Armistice in a big way. The whole fleet assembled in the Firth of Forth the afternoon of November 11. The flagship *Queen Elizabeth* signaled "Splice the main-brace. Negative 6th B.S." The cryptic second phrase translated into "No rum for the Americans, thanks to Secretary of the Navy Daniels' General Order 99 prohibition of alcoholic beverages." The sailor-king, George V, arrived that night in his admiral's uniform to review the entire fleet. Every searchlight was turned on; every whistle blew; every siren wailed. Crews cheered. Bands played. There was much visiting among ships. Small craft appeared at American gangways to take off passengers to British ships, where Daniels' prohibition did not apply. The celebration went far into the night.

At 3:30 AM on November 21, Division 9 got under way to take its place in the north column of the Grand Fleet, which was going out to take the surrender of the German High Seas Fleet at the mouth of the Firth of Forth.

About midday Admiral Beatty sent a message to the Admiralty with the particulars: "The Grand Fleet met this morning at 9:20, five battle cruisers, nine battleships, seven light cruisers, and forty-nine destroyers of the High Seas Fleet, which surrendered for internment and are being brought to Firth of Forth."

On the morning of December 1st, Division 9—joined by the *Nevada* from Bantry Bay, Ireland, where she had been serving with Division 6—prepared to go to sea. They were going home. Admiral Beatty paid a final visit to the *New York,* passing between eight officer sideboys on the quarterdeck. He made a good speech: "The support which you have shown is that of true comradeship; and in time of stress, that is worth a great deal. You will return to your own shores; and I hope in the sunshine, which Admiral Rodman tells me always shines there, you won't forget your 'comrades of the mist' and your pleasant associations of the North Sea. . . . I thank you again and again for the great part the Sixth Battle Squadron played in bringing about the greatest naval victory in history."

The *New York,* followed by the *Texas, Nevada, Arkansas, Wyoming,* and *Florida,* all flying "homeward-bound" pennants, steamed out of the harbor. They arrived at Weymouth on December 4 and joined up with the *Utah, Oklahoma,* and *Arizona* of Division 6. Admiral Sims came on board the *Wyoming* on the twelfth, and the next morning the combined divisions went to sea to meet up with the *George Washington,* flying the president's flag to show that President Wilson was on board. The escorting battleship *Pennsylvania* flew the flag of Vice Adm. Henry T. Mayo, commander in chief of the Atlantic Fleet. A day's steaming brought them to Brest.

With President Wilson safely delivered to France, divisions 6 and 9 on December 14 sailed for home, arriving off the Ambrose lightship on Christmas Day. Next morning they sailed into New York Harbor, greeted by a tumultuous welcome. All available vessels assembled for a naval review, with Secretary of the Navy Daniels in the yacht *Mayflower* and Assistant Secretary Roosevelt in the *Aztec.*

Col. John Twiggs "Handsome Jack" Myers, the national hero of the defense of the Peking Legations during the 1900 Boxer Rebellion, was the fleet Marine officer of the Atlantic Fleet almost to the end of the war. Col. Richard M. Cutts was fleet Marine officer of the Pacific Fleet for most of the war.

Marines in Siberia

The Marines of the small Asiatic Fleet, under Rear Adm. Austin M. Knight, commander in chief, saw more action than the battleship Marines of the Atlantic Fleet. The cruiser *Brooklyn,* flagship of the Asiatic Fleet, had a regular Marine complement, under Capt. Archie F. Howard, of one more officer and about seventy-five enlisted. With orders to proceed to the Pacific coast of Siberia at the height of the Bolshevik Revolution, the flagship embarked fifty more Marines from the Cavite Naval Station and steamed north. From tropical Manila to frigid Vladivostok was a rough voyage. Howard organized and trained six machine-gun crews during the passage. The *Brooklyn,* arriving at the Siberian port on March 1, 1918, had to break through from two to four feet of ice to get alongside the dock. Once there the Marines, uncomfortable in their overcrowded quarters, stayed embarked.

China had just come into the war on the Allied side. Lt. Col. Louis McCarty Little, the fleet Marine and intelligence officer on Admiral Knight's staff, had prepared for an immediate landing at Vladivostok, but Admiral Knight sent him off to China on a secret mission, the details of which are lost.

The Japanese, from a squadron commanded by Rear Adm. Hiroharu Kato, were the first to land, going ashore on April 5. The Marines watched from the decks of the *Brooklyn* as the Japanese landing force of about 160 bluejackets pulled away from IJS *Asahi* and *Iwami.*

The Bolsheviks had only a tenuous grip on Vladivostok. The chief Red defenders of Vladivostok were subverted German and Austrian prisoners of war, more willing to fight for their former enemy than to die in his camps. Opposing them and threatening to take the port was a corps of Czechs and Slovaks, former prisoners of war, some twelve thousand of them, who had fought their way east across war-ravaged Siberia. Their objective was to reach Vladivostok and shipping that might eventually get them back to their homeland.

The combined landing parties established an "Allied Military Council" to oversee the weak Bolshevik command. Landing parties being put ashore had the specific mission of guarding the warehouses holding war materiel that the Bolsheviks might want to move inland. The U.S. Marines stayed afloat, increasingly claustrophobic and impatient.

The Bolsheviks in Vladivostok received orders from Moscow to disarm the approaching Czechs and Slovaks and send them to prisoner-of-war camps. The Bolsheviks began a movement inland on June 28, including the shipment of arms and ammunition to support the move. The Czechs retaliated with an ultimatum demanding the disarming of the Red Guards. Not getting that, they marched into the city early on the twenty-ninth. There was little or no resistance. Before the morning was over the Czechs had the city hall, post office, telegraph office, and police headquarters.

The British landed around two hundred bluejackets from the *Suffolk.* The Chinese put a party ashore from a gunboat. The British and Japanese put a cordon around the district containing the consulates but took no part in the actual fighting. A hastily organized company, called the *Frontoviki,* of former Russian officers and soldiers reinforced the Czechs.

By midafternoon the Czechs had reached the railroad station and then assaulted the Red Guard headquarters opposite the station. By then the Chinese had landed another party, this one of about sixty sailors from the cruiser *Hai-Yung.* The busy day was ending when at 5:30 PM, the *Brooklyn* began landing its Marines, including thirty designated to serve as a consular guard. The Bolsheviks and some stray Hungarians in the headquarters building surrendered at about 6:00 PM. On the following day the Czechs, evening old scores, executed a substantial number of their German and Magyar prisoners. The Americans maintained nominal neutrality while the revolution swirled around them but tilted in favor of the Czechs. An Allied patrol was formed that included Americans and the Czechs and Slovaks, as well as British, Japanese, and Chinese. The *Brooklyn*'s Marines expanded their sector to include the sprawling Russian naval base that adjoined the U.S. consulate, sharing patrol responsibilities with other Allied landing parties. Only one incident occurred: a British Royal Marine shot and killed a drunken Russian sailor.

The Czechs and Slovaks now hoped to break through the Bolshevik front to reach the main body of Czecho-Slovak soldiers, some sixty thousand of them, still somewhere in Siberia. With blatant British, French, and Japanese help, they marched off to open a section of the Trans-Siberian railroad. The Americans, whatever their personal sympathies, stayed officially aloof. The British went so far as to dismount guns from the *Suffolk,* land them ashore, and send them forward, officered and manned by the British, on railway cars to the front lines.

With the Czechs gone, the resurgent Bolsheviks set up a provisional government in Vladivostok. The Allied Military Council gave it qualified recognition.

About July 3 the Czechs fought a stiff action with the Reds. Their wounded came streaming back to Vladivostok, where they were taken in hand by the medical department of the *Brooklyn*. A hundred German and Austrian prisoners, under the supervision of ten Marine guards led by Sgt. Allen H. Lange, were put to cleaning up an abandoned Russian military hospital on Russian Island in the harbor, eight kilometers from Vladivostok.

Brooklyn put on full dress, all flags flying, for the Fourth of July. Counterpoint was a funeral cortege that paraded through the city with nine Bolshevik coffins. The funeral passed by the American consulate, and the Bolsheviks mistook the 4th of July observance for honors being given their dead. A red banner flying three times a day on the *Brooklyn*'s flag hoist—actually the cruiser's meal pennant—further deluded the Bolsheviks into thinking that there was about to be an uprising among the crew.

A large number of Japanese transports arrived laden with soldiers. Concerned about the possibility of the Japanese carving out an unwelcome sphere of influence in the key warm-water port, the War Department deployed an army infantry brigade from the Philippines to bolster the American presence. U.S. Marines continued to guard the consulate until just before the *Brooklyn* sailed away on October 10, 1918. Few, if any, Marines ever fired a round in anger during their half-year deployment to Siberia.

The 1st Marine Aviation Force in France

While the *Brooklyn*'s Marines still guarded the U.S. consulate in Vladivostok and as the 4th Brigade marched toward Mont Blanc, the main body of the 1st Marine Aviation Force—some 750 aviators, gunners, and ground crewmen—finally arrived in France. Maj. Alfred Cunningham and his three squadrons landed at Brest on July 30, 1918, expecting that their aircraft and equipment would be waiting for them when they arrived. They were not, and no one at Brest seemed to care much. Immediate problems included a lack of rapport between Cunningham, not the most tactful of persons, and Capt. David Hanrahan, USN, commander of the Northern Bombing Group.

No arrangements had been made to move the squadrons from Brest to their intended airfield near Calais, 545 kilometers away. Cunningham persuaded the French to give him a train for the two-day trip. When he sent a working party to the navy supply base at Pauillac, forty-eight kilometers from Bordeaux, to pick up his motor transport, his officer in charge, Lt. Karl Day, found, "All our . . . trucks . . . had gotten mixed up and gotten into the Army pool, and I had to go down there, drag 'em out of the pool, and find drivers, and send those things North."

Cunningham's Marines on arriving at Calais were temporarily billeted in a British rest camp while work began on the airfield sites picked out by the advance party. Cunningham established his headquarters at Bois en Ardres. Squadrons A and B were to go to Oye, a town between Calais and Dunkirk. Squadron C was to go to LaFresne, twelve kilometers southwest of Calais. The sites that had been selected were essentially flat fields planted in sugar beets.

Progress on the two Marine airfields went slowly. The Marines had no engineering equipment. The sugar beet plants yielded to Marines with spades. A borrowed navy steamroller compacted the soil. The British were generous with construction materials, including portable canvas-and-wood hangars. Housing went through three stages: tents with dirt floors, tents with wooden floors and framing, and finally portable wooden huts with stoves. There were the usual canvas cots and furniture improvised from packing cases.

Second Lts. Colgate Darden and Ralph Talbot were in Squadron C at LaFresne. Talbot, called "Dick" by his friends, shared a tent with 2d Lt. Alvin L. Pritchard.

Then there was the little matter of not having any aircraft. Before leaving for France Cunningham had arranged for the delivery from the army of seventy-two DH-4 two-place bombers. These planes, in crates, arrived at Pauillac about the same time as the Force's landing at Brest, but due to delays in assembly the first aircraft did not reach Cunningham until September 7. Even so they did not arrive in proper numbers. By some miscalculation most had been shipped to England.

In desperation, Cunningham struck a bargain with the British, who had excess DH-9A airframes but no engines. Conversely, the Americans had a surplus of Liberty engines in Europe but few airframes to put them in. Cunningham's deal, approved by the U.S. Navy (presumably by Admiral Sims' headquarters in London), was that for every three Liberty engines delivered, the British would return to the Marines one completely equipped DH-9A.[2]

The Marines were quick to identify their planes by painting the eagle, globe, and anchor insignia on the fuselages, substituting the red, white, and blue cockade or roundel (identifying U.S. aircraft) for the globe.

The Marine airfields were behind the British sector of the western front. By now the mission of the 1st Marine Aviation Force had changed. Under Allied pressure, the Germans had abandoned their submarine bases on the Channel coast. The new mission would be general aviation support of the British and Belgian—and sometimes French—armies.

Knowing that the Royal Air Force had more planes than pilots, Cunningham arranged for his idle fliers to fly with RAF squadrons 217 and 218, which were equipped with both DH-4s and DH-9s. The Marine pilots rotated through the British squadrons so that each would go on at least three raids. While so serving they picked up such British affectations as the stylish RAF overseas caps and crook-handled canes, which were being carried also by their groundling brother Marine Corps officers.

Lt. Karl Day flew with Squadron 218, a mixed lot drawn from several of the British dominions. He admired greatly the squadron commander, Maj. Bert Wemp, a Canadian. Day also remembered that in the "V" flight formations the newcomers were always the last plane on the right. If the new pilot were shot down, the loss would not disturb the main formation.

On September 28, 1st Lt. Everett S. Brewer and GySgt. Harry B. Wersheiner, flying with Squadron 218, got the Marines' first aerial kill in a dogfight over Courtemarke, Belgium. Both Marines were badly wounded in the fracas. On October 2 and 3, Marines flying with Squadron 218 flew the Corps' first aerial resupply mission. Two planes—one piloted by Capt. Francis P. Mulcahy with GySgt. Thomas L. McCullough in the back seat, the other with Capt. Robert S. Lytle at the stick and GySgt. Amil Wiman as observer—flew through heavy German fire to deliver 2,600 pounds of food and stores to an isolated French regiment near Stadenburg.

The two-seater DH-4's operational reputation preceded it to the airfields of France. On one hand, the biplane was a joy to fly, cruising at 90 mph, diving at 125, with a rated ceiling of fifteen thousand feet, and the capability of four hours aloft on a tank of gas. The aircraft was well armed for combat, with two forward-firing Vickers .30-caliber machine guns, bomb racks, and twin Lewis .30-caliber machine guns mounted on a 360-degree traverse ring in the rear cockpit. On the other hand, the DH-4 had what boxers called a "glass jaw," in the form of an unarmored fuel tank mounted between the two cockpits. Enemy gunfire—or, more commonly, a hard landing—could ignite a catastrophic fire. The nickname "Flying Coffins" reflected aviators' concerns about this vulnerability.

The DH-4 posed an additional hazard as well. To fire the rear guns in a dogfight, the gunner had to fold up his seat and stand erect, striving to swivel his guns while maintaining a precarious balance, a challenge described by one aviation historian as similar to "a man standing upright in a full gale in a waist-high wash tub." Indeed, in the desperate dogfight over Courtemarke on September 28, Gunnery Sergeant Wersheiner was pitched out of his cockpit, landed on the tail assembly, and barely managed to survive by clawing his way forward under fire to reclaim his empty station.

Cunningham's final component, Squadron D, arrived at LaFresne on October 5 with forty-two officers and 183 enlisted men, raising the strength of the force to 149 officers and 842 men. Officially, to conform to the Northern Bombing Group's numbering system, squadrons A, B, C, and D became squadrons 7, 8, 9, and 10.

Squadron 9 went out on a raid on October 8. Ralph Talbot had "the fastest ship in the squadron" and was given the job of protecting the rear of the flight as it returned from the bombing. Next day he wrote to his fiancée:

> This week has been one of intense activity, especially for me for I got my first Hun yesterday. We were ten miles inside the lines when four Fokker triplanes and five Fokker biplanes attacked us. One Hun climbed up and put a bullet into the gas tank six inches over my head, and another bullet cut the shoulder of my uniform but never touched me, and he put four into my tail before I could swing around. Then a second later my own tracers entered his machine and he began to tremble and fell over on his back and down in a spin. We had six machines in our flight and one of the boys was knocked off. The fight took place at 14,000 feet.

Talbot received a written commendation on October 12 from Cunningham as day wing commander, confirming the shoot-down of the German. He had a part in another, bigger, raid two days later.

Captain Lytle, commanding Squadron 9, took out five DH-4s and three DH-9As to strike the German-held railroad yards at Thielt, Belgium. They dropped 2,218 pounds of bombs. On the way home, twelve German fighters—eight Fokker D-VIIs and four Pfalz D-IIIs—jumped Lytle's eight DeHavilands. In the melee, the Germans singled out the DH-4 flown by Ralph Talbot with Cpl. Robert G. Robinson in the back seat. Captain Lytle's engine failed as he tried to come to Talbot's aid. Robinson was an expert gunner. With his twin Lewis guns he brought down one attacking plane. Two others closed in from below. Robinson took a bullet in his elbow. Clearing a jammed gun with his one good hand, Robinson continued to fire until he was hit twice more. With Robinson unconscious in the back seat, Talbot whipped his DH-4 around and got a second German with his front guns. He then put his damaged plane into a long dive, clearing the German lines at fifty feet and landing safely at a Belgian airfield. Robinson was taken to a field hospital. The surgeon general of the Belgian army operated on his arm and saved it.

Lytle made a dead-stick landing in front of the Belgian lines. He and his observer scrambled to safety. That night, under cover of darkness, a Marine working party dismantled his plane and brought it back in through the lines.

Talbot tested a new plane, with Lt. Colgate Darden in the back seat as observer on October 25. The engine failed. The plane crashed. Darden had not fastened his seat belt and was thrown clear and badly smashed up. Talbot burned to death.

Pritchard, Talbot's tent mate, collected his personal belongings to be sent home. He knew that Talbot had been writing war poems with a vague idea of publishing them after the war. Pritchard found some of them. Most had no titles, but there was one entitled "The Circus":

Under the main top
Spreading wide,
Under the paneled, vaulty blue,
Against some filmy heap I swoop.
I glide!
Doing . . .
Doing what my heart forbears to do.
Tenor of the bugle,
Shrilling high.
Warning siren!—Like a violin!
An undernote that stirs!—Mitrailleuse![3]
Tatting . . .
Tatting for the concert to begin.
Our circus whips and reels about
The sky!
Fantastic some,—some bizarre!
Cheers and urgings reach us from afar
Cheers!
Cheers for the superman.
The Nation's aviator.
We are the star performers!
Buffoons!
Who swing from bar to bar with ease.
Ignoring Life, ignoring Death
For honors
Beneath the Big Top
On the Big Trapeze.

Pritchard collected the poems and sent them with a labored letter to Talbot's mother: "Dick went out as he would have preferred, with the roar of a powerful motor in his ears, going out into action. Death was very merciful to him, for he felt not the slightest pain. Thus passed the best friend, the truest gentleman I ever knew."[4]

Mrs. Talbot added the letter and the verses to the scrapbook she was keeping. Both Talbot and Robinson received Medals of Honor—Talbot's, of course, posthumously. His mother received it in 1920.

Colgate Darden, badly smashed up with fractured vertebrae, a crushed face, and temporary paralysis, was hospitalized for a year. Afterward he married Irene DuPont, was elected to two terms in the House of Representatives, and was governor of Virginia, chancellor of William and Mary, and president of the University of Virginia.

In all, the four Marine squadrons carried out fourteen bombing raids, always flying without fighter escort. There were several more fights with German planes. In one of these, on October 22, the plane flown by 2d Lt. Harvey G. Norman, with 2d Lt. Caleb W. Taylor as his observer, was shot down, killing both Norman and Taylor, in what was the first loss of a Marine aircraft to enemy action.

By the time of the Armistice, with the pluses of additional acquisitions and the minuses of operational losses, Cunningham's four squadrons had a total of twenty DH-9As and sixteen DH-4s. Totaling up, they had flown forty-three missions with the British, fourteen on their own. They calculated they had dropped 15,140 pounds of bombs while with the British and 18,792 pounds by themselves. Four pilots had been killed and one pilot and two gunners wounded. They had also counted four confirmed kills of German fighters and eight "probables," including one credited to Captain Mulcahy. Four officers and twenty-one enlisted men had succumbed to the influenza epidemic, which for a while in October virtually halted operations. The force received thirty individual awards, including Talbot's and Robinson's Medals of Honor and four Distinguished Service Medals. Alfred Cunningham received the Navy Cross. Ralph Talbot would be the only Marine officer to receive the Medal of Honor in the war.

With the Armistice and the beginning of winter weather, Cunningham asked for his group's early return to the United States, arguing, "I think we could accomplish much more at home, getting our Aviation service established under the new conditions of peace."

In December 1918, having established the foundation for Marine combat aviation during its short, heated aerial campaign, the 1st Marine Aviation Force sailed for home in the USS *Mercury*.

CHAPTER NINE

Soissons: The First Day

T he surviving troops of the 2d U.S. Division dreamed of an extended liberty in Paris following their hard-won victories at Belleau Wood and Vaux.[1] It was not to be. Less than three weeks after the battle, the division was swept up in a helter-skelter counteroffensive that collided with the German army at Soissons. Marine veterans of both battles would often swear Soissons had been worse than Belleau Wood.

Soissons (pronounced "swah-SON") differed from the battle of Belleau Wood in scale, duration, and topography, yet here the Marines would experience casualty rates averaging more than a thousand a day—matching their future losses at bloody Tarawa in World War II.

Lejeune on the Sidelines

Brig. Gen. John Lejeune departed Chaumont on June 21 in search of the U.S. 35th Division, which was somewhere on the western slopes of the Vosges Mountains. He found the headquarters of the 35th in the "lovely little town of d'Arches." Still eager for a command billet, Lejeune next reported to the 32d Division, occupying a quiet sector similar to that the 2d Division had held near Verdun. He was offered command of the 32d Division's 64th Brigade. He found the 64th Brigade, the "Michigan Brigade," at Suarce, occupying a subsector under tactical control of a French division. It was a good learning experience for Lejeune. At Suarce there was not much in the way of German shelling, but there were occasional air raids. On July 14, Lejeune and his officers celebrated Bastille Day with champagne toasts in the brigade mess. After three very quiet weeks of brigade command, Lejeune received the delayed orders assigning him to command of the 4th Brigade. But before he could carry out these orders, the Marines were once again in action.

A Calm between Storms

The 2d Division, in reserve, held the support line back of Belleau Wood and Vaux until the second week in July. The less seriously wounded from Belleau Wood had begun to return to their old outfits.

On July 11, the AEF headquarters notified Harbord that he was being promoted to major general. The 6th Marines band serenaded him that evening. Neville was sick in the hospital, and Logan Feland was acting commander of the 5th Regiment. Harry Lee still had command of the 6th Regiment. The two regimental commanders gave Harbord his second silver star. Next day General Pershing took lunch with Harbord. He praised the performance of the Marine brigade in Belleau Wood and hinted that Harbord might be getting command of the 2d Division. For the moment, two major generals in the division were one too many, so General Bundy, with some asperity, authorized Harbord five days leave in Paris, beginning July 13.

That evening Harbord and his two aides dined at the Ritz and then went to the Opera Comique to hear *La Vie Boheme*. Next day, July 14, was a Sunday and, war or no war, also Bastille Day. Pershing's chief of staff informed Harbord by telephone that he was to take command of the 2d Division, and the sooner the better. Widely hailed as the senior hero of Belleau Wood, Harbord delayed his departure from Paris until the following morning, as that evening he was guest of honor at a big dinner at the Inter-Allied Club, once the residence of Baron Charles Rothschild.

The Last Great German Offensive

The sleep of the 2d Division was disturbed that night of July 14/15 by the inordinately loud sound of distant artillery fire coming from the east. Men stumbled out of barns and haystacks to stare at the unmistakable red-orange false dawn on the horizon, marking a prolonged bombardment. From Rheims to Chateau-Thierry and across the Champagne to the Argonne, the armies of the German crown prince were attacking.

Hurried along by these events, Harbord, early on the morning of July 15, drove back from Paris to the 2d Division headquarters, comfortably situated in the Chateau de Chamigny on the Marne. He arrived there before Bundy was up for breakfast. By nine o'clock Harbord had assumed command and was somewhat piqued that Bundy did not leave immediately but stayed on to have dinner.

At 6:55 that evening, Gen. Marie Emile Fayolle, commanding the French Sixth Army, to which the 2d Division was assigned, issued an order placing the division at the disposal of Gen. Charles "The Butcher" Mangin, commander of the French Tenth Army. Mangin's dispirited troops had nicknamed him "The Butcher" after their heavy losses in the Second Battle of the Aisne during the disastrous Nivelle Offensive of 1917. Yet Mangin was undeniably a fighter, so President Clemenceau had restored him to field army command in 1918. Mangin, fifty-two at the time of Soissons, would later write, "Whatever you do, you lose a lot of men."

At about 8:30 PM on July 15 a French staff officer arrived at Harbord's headquarters at Chamigny and stated vaguely that the division would be moving somewhere. Later that evening more specific orders arrived. Mounted and motor units would march overland. Infantry and dismounted elements would move by truck to an unnamed area, subject to further orders.

"In truck movements of troops, the French never tell any one where they are going," complained Harbord in his diary. "A division of twenty-eight thousand men, the size of a European army corps, had been completely removed from the control of its responsible commander, and deflected by marching and by truck, through France to destination unknown to any of the authorities responsible either for its supply, its safety, or its efficiency in the coming attack."

General Foch had begun concentrating troops north of Paris to attack the flanks of the huge German salient reaching toward Paris. Before the great counterattack could be pushed forward, the fifth and final German offensive of 1918 began, on July 15, on the Champagne-Marne front.

"The selection of the Germans of the Champagne sector and the eastern and southern faces of the Marne pocket on which to make their offensive was fortunate for the Allies," wrote Pershing dryly in his final report, "as it favored the launching of the counter-attack already planned."[2]

In General Pershing's words: "General Petain's initial plan for the counterattack involved the entire western face of the Marne salient. The First and Second American Divisions, with the First French Moroccan Division between them, were employed as the spearhead of the main attack, driving directly eastward, through the most sensitive portion of the German lines, to the heights south of Soissons."

The Allies' Counteroffensive

The offensive came to be known as the Aisne-Marne Offensive, and it lasted from July 18 until the sixth of August. Some 270,000 American troops were involved.

Harbord and his chief of staff, Col. Preston Brown, reported to General Mangin's Tenth Army headquarters at Chantilly on the afternoon of July 16. Mangin was away. There was no information as to his intentions for the 2d Division except that it would be assigned to the French XX Corps.

Harbord found Maj. Gen. Pierre E. Berdoulat, commander of the XX Corps, at Retheuil in company with Maj. Gen. Robert L. Bullard, USA. Pershing had sent Bullard, commanding the new U.S. III Corps, to observe the forthcoming battle. Berdoulat told Harbord that the 2d Division, as part of XX Corps, was to attack on a wide front extending south from the vicinity of Soissons. Harbord received a supply of maps and copies of the XX Corps attack order. The French operations officer offered to write the 2d Division attack order. Harbord declined with a bit of ice in his voice. There were many shrugs of French shoulders.

Harbord and Brown then drove to Bullard's III Corps headquarters at Taille-fontaine and here found clerks and a mimeograph machine. The two officers spent the night writing the attack order. The front would be approached through the Forêt de Retz (also known as the Forêt de Villers-Cotterets), a sprawling beech forest. The zone of action assigned the 2d Division was a plateau, about nine kilo-meters deep, opening on the eastern edge of the Forêt de Retz and cut with many ravines. Most of the land was planted in wheat, which now stood waist high. It was dotted with villages and farmhouses, built of stone from local quarries, offering the Germans strong defensive positions.

Coming out of the woods, the division would advance almost due east on a frontage of about three kilometers. The first objective would be a line running through Beaurepaire Farm. Here the axis of the attack would change from east to southeast, requiring an awkward wheeling maneuver. The next objectives would be Vauxcastille and then the village of Vierzy. The distance from the east edge of the woods to Vierzy was about five kilometers.

Harbord expected that the principal resistance would be on his right. This front he gave to the 3d Brigade, which would attack with both its regiments, the 9th and 23d infantry, abreast. The narrower left front he gave to the 5th Regiment, with the 6th Regiment held in corps reserve. The 2d Field Artillery Brigade, reinforced by a French artillery regiment, would fire the supporting barrage. The wheat fields promised good tank country. The XX Corps assigned four battalions of French tanks—Schneiders and the smaller Renaults, fifty-four tanks in all—to support the division. When dawn came on the seventeenth, Harbord left Taillefontaine by motorcar to attempt to find his division.

Moving East

While the mimeograph machine at III Corps headquarters turned out the attack order, the Marines marched from their billeting areas near Nanteuil-sur-Marne to the main highway, where they "embussed" in the now-familiar camions with the Annamite drivers. The truck convoys moved forward in total darkness except for the dim glow of an occasional tail lamp and the quick flare of a surreptitiously lit cigarette.

As then-Sgt. Gerald C. Thomas, 1st Battalion, 6th Regiment, remembered it years later:

> Foch decided that he would stop the attack on July 15th, which he did, and then he would pinch in the German pocket and threaten their line of with-drawal if he had the troops to do it by that time. They took us from this

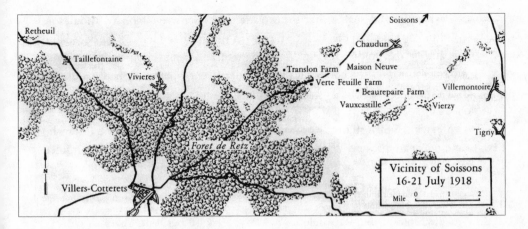

Belleau Wood front, picked us up on the afternoon of the 16th, and we rode all night. I knew we were riding around the pocket because I could always see those flashes of artillery off to the right. I knew damn well where we were going. I couldn't talk to the Annamites any more that time than I could when going to Belleau Wood, but I didn't need to because I knew we were going up the other side of that pocket.

In the morning the Marines tumbled out of the camions near spots on the map marked as Pierrefonde, Retheuil, and Taillefontaine. They learned, or at least their senior officers did, that the 1st and 2d divisions would fight as units of the French XX corps of General Mangin's Tenth Army to break the German front between the Aisne and Ourcq rivers. The XX Corps was expected to make a deep penetration at the critical point on the western flank of the salient. *2,*

The XX Corps was to attack with the 1st U.S. Division on the left, the 1st Moroccan Division in the center, and the 2d U.S. Division on the right. A division of the French XXX Corps was to be to the 2d Division's right. The 3d Brigade would advance with its two regiments side by side, the 9th Infantry on the left, the 23d Infantry on the right. The 5th Marines would attack on the left of the 3d Brigade. The 5th Marines was to detail one company and one machine-gun platoon to maintain combat liaison with the 3d Brigade. A second company and machine-gun platoon was to maintain combat liaison with the Moroccan division. A *"groupement"* of about thirty French tanks was assigned to support the 5th Regiment. The 6th Marines, along with the 2d Engineers and the 4th Machine Gun Battalion, would be in division reserve. A French squadron of ten aircraft was specifically assigned to support the division in the attack, or so XX Corps promised. To ensure surprise, there would be no preliminary artillery preparation. The attack would begin with a barrage that would roll forward at the rate of one hundred meters every two minutes.

"Very solid and businesslike the brigade was," later wrote John W. Thomason, second in command of the 49th Company in the 5th Regiment, "keen-faced and gaunt and hard from the great fight behind them, and fit and competent for greater battles yet to come. The companies were under strength, but they had the quality of veterans. They had met the Boche and broken him, and they knew they could do it again."

Merwin H. Silverthorn, who had been a sergeant in Belleau Wood (and who would retire after World War II as a lieutenant general), was now a newly minted second lieutenant leading the 4th Platoon of the 45th Company, 3d Battalion, 5th Marines. He remembered many years later:

> Going into action, we would always leave back 10 per cent. That's an old trench warfare concept. That is, if the whole organization got wiped out, then the 10 per cent that was left back would become the nucleus for the new organization. . . . Well, the 10 per cent would consist of all those who were absent, sick in the hospital or away at school and one officer. . . . There normally was an officer in the hospital or away at school, so actually leaving behind 10 per cent was a paper transaction.

The Forced March from Hell

The weather, being cloudy, rainy, and totally miserable, favored a surprise attack. The Forêt de Retz, a magnificent hardwood forest, to the north and east of Villers-Cotterets, concealed the approach march. One principal highway, with a paved center and dirt shoulders, ran through the forest, with many dirt roads criss-crossing it. During the night on July 17, by a terrible forced march through mud and rain, the 1st Moroccan Division and the U.S. 1st and 2d divisions were concentrated in the forest. As Harbord recalled the nightmarish forced march, "The roads were like tunnels in their gloom. The rate of movement through that dark forest could not have exceeded a mile per hour."

Maj. Robert L. Denig, temporarily commanding the 2d Battalion, 6th Regiment, described the forest in a letter to his wife as a place where "deer would scamper ahead—and we could have eaten one raw." Denig marveled at the amalgamation of forces. "Troops of all kinds passed us in the night—a shadowy stream, over half a million men. Some French officers told us they had never seen such a concentration since Verdun."

Thomason wrote later: "And after the 5th Marines have forgotten the machine guns that sowed death in the wheat behind Hill 142, and the shrapnel that showered down at Blanc Mont, before St. Etienne, they will remember the march to the Soissons battle, through the dark and the rain. . . . No battle ever tried them half as hard as the night road to Soissons."

Neville came back from the hospital in time to command the Marine brigade. He opened his headquarters at Vivieres at 1:30 PM on the 17th. The 5th and 6th Marines would reach the woods during the afternoon and evening. The 6th Machine Gun Battalion would arrive about 3 AM the next day.

Lt. Graves Erskine of the 79th Company had come down with the flu about the time they marched to the rear from Belleau Wood. He escaped from the camp sickbay when he learned his company was moving up once again. Erskine started for the front, catching rides on trucks where he could, until he found his company in the Forêt de Retz.

The main roads through the forest were packed with traffic moving to the front. The congestion delayed the delivery of the attack orders. There was little or no time for reconnaissance or the study of maps. For hours it was necessary for the infantry to march in single file along a ditch dug into the clay on the right of the road, each man holding on to the belt or coat tail of the man in front of him.

"In World War I our food and supply were pretty much all the way back to Civil War days," remembered Merwin Silverthorn, adding:

A man carried two days' reserve rations in his pack. Those reserve rations consisted of a package of hardtack for one thing. Now hardtack is like a soda cracker about three inches square, a quarter of an inch thick, white, just like an ordinary saltine soda cracker, only it's much tougher. It doesn't break up easily. . . . That was his carbohydrate base. Then he carried some raw sugar. Whatever he did with that, nobody knew. He had some salt and pepper. And then he had some bacon in another tin known as the bacon tin, which was a slab of bacon. How he was going to prepare it was up to him.

"We got off our trucks on the forenoon of the 17th of July. We then started to hike," remembered Lieutenant Silverthorn. "The men were separated from their equipment; that is, their rolling kitchens, their machine guns and their artillery and picked up and moved by this truck train and had to be joined together on the field of battle."

We started hiking as soon as we got out of the trucks and hiked until late that afternoon. Now we had gone over 24 hours without any food or water. Everybody had a canteen so he could drink it, but the men weren't allowed to touch the reserve ration unless it was permitted by orders of higher authority.

Now, the officers didn't carry reserve rations. They had to be carried in a pack, in certain shaped tins, and the officers didn't carry a pack. The officers carried a musette bag . . . a pouch type of thing that had a shoulder strap on it. . . . There you carried your spare clothing, which was usually a pair of socks and your shaving . . . gear; and then a miscellaneous supply of food—a can of salmon or maybe a can of pate de fois gras or maybe a can of beans or maybe not—depending on the individual. . . . I was able to get a candy bar at this YMCA truck, and that was my sole food on the 17th of July.

"Officers marched as the rear of their platoon and were responsible that no men of their platoon fell out," remembered Silverthorn. "If on the hike a man fell out, it was up to the lieutenant to talk him into falling in again or taking his pack or taking his rifle or something like that." That is, if you could see him, and Silverthorn said that in the wet darkness of the woods that was impossible.

Lt. Col. Logan Feland reported to Harbord at his headquarters late in the afternoon and received his orders for the 5th Marines. At ten o'clock he found his regiment three kilometers west of division headquarters. Feland established his regimental PC with only his adjutant and two orderlies. His communication to the front would be by battalion runner and to the rear by a telephone line.

The log of a battalion surgeon in the 5th Marines had this entry for June 17:

By mid-afternoon the canteens, filled the night before, had been drained, and acute thirst was bothering the men. Some men who had found and eaten a few canned sardines were in the utmost distress. There was no hope that either water or food would be available. Some men chewed on grass and some moistened their lips with mud. At about 2200 [10 PM] a brisk thunder and lightning storm soaked the men and the road. The rain relieved the thirst of many but made leg movement difficult. The men who could not keep going attempted to work their way toward the side of the road through darkness and an indescribably mixed mass of milling humanity. If a call for aid were answered a medical worker would lose his organization when he stepped out of the file. He would find himself in the nearby files of French, Senegalese, and Algerians.

More tanks, large and small, than the Marines had ever seen had been assembled in the forest along with troop after troop of French cavalry. There were also the Moroccans, "whose cold-blooded manner of fighting had from early days of the war struck terror in the hearts of the Germans," recalled an early history of the 1st Battalion, 5th Marines.

"The Moroccans, under the blue-eyed General Dogan, whose Croix-de-Guerre carried seven palms, were reckoned the best shock-troops of France, and the Americans understood that if they did not keep up with the Moroccans or pass them in the assault they would be dishonored," wrote Harbord.

Mangin's Tenth Army was truly a multinational force. "All of the Allied troops of the world were represented here," wrote Sgt. Karl P. Spencer, 82d Company, in Sibley's 3d Battalion, 6th Marines, to his mother after the battle. "[There were]

Americans in their khaki; Moroccans and Italians wearing a dirty brown colored uniform; the Scots in their kilties . . . Irish troops wearing tam-o-shanters; and the French wearing all the different shades of blue imaginable—here was a display of colors that outclassed the rainbow."

Maj. Julius Turrill's 1st Battalion, 5th Regiment, had been billeted in Crouttes from July 9 to the fifteenth, "worn out, but well satisfied" from their work in Belleau Wood. At 10 PM on the night of the sixteenth the battalion boarded trucks and, once again, under cover of darkness, found itself going forward through Meaux, this time toward Soissons. After an all-night ride the battalion "debussed" at 8:30 AM at a railroad station north of Brassaire. Turrill found a bivouac site for his battalion a short march away, off the side of the road two kilometers south of Taillefontaine. After the daylight hours had passed, at 9:40 PM on July 17, Turrill started the march through the forest of Retz in an effort to reach the jumping-off point before H-hour, his 1st Battalion being followed by the 2d and 3d. Each rifleman carried two extra bandoliers of ammunition. The expected French guides were not there to show Turrill the way. The road was filled with wheeled traffic. The wet clay in the ditch on the side of the road was treacherously slippery. The ditch at various points was blocked by wagons or camions that had run off the road. Horses and wagons injured several men.

"I bumped my head into the rear end of more horses than I thought existed, because you couldn't see your hand in front of your face," remembered Robert Blake, who as a first lieutenant was the second in command of the 17th Company.

Major Waller's 6th Machine Gun Battalion had started to march on the afternoon of July 16. By a combination of hiking and movement by camion the battalion reached its designated bivouac area in the Villers-Cotterets woods. Just before dark on the seventeenth Waller received the order that the battalion was to support the 5th Marines. By 10:30 PM the machine gunners were on the march again, with the men stumbling their way along the rain-soaked Villers–Cotterets–Soissons road, through the black forest, in a valiant effort to reach the front line in order to support the infantry battalions in the attack. "This march through the woods was the worst the battalion ever experienced," wrote Major Waller.

At the time of jump-off neither the 8th Machine Gun Company nor the 6th Machine Gun Battalion had arrived. "Very well," said some unknown optimist, "we will take the Boche machine guns."

Coming through the forest, Julius Turrill reached a roadblock marking the nearness of the front line and turned his battalion to the northeast. Long packs were dropped off, and the men went forward in light marching order. Turrill deployed the 66th Company on the right and the 17th Company on the left, holding the 67th Company in support. The 49th Company came up about ten minutes later, and Turrill ordered its commander, Capt. George Hamilton, to establish liaison with the French 1st Moroccan Division, which contained components from several colonial African countries.

Hamilton came back to give his company the attack order and said to his officers: "The 49th Company has the division's left, and we're to keep in touch with the French over there. They're the Senegalese—the ones you saw on the road, and said to be born fighters. The tanks will come behind us through the woods, and take the lead as soon as we hit the open."

Surprise Attack

"At 4 o'clock only one Regiment—the Ninth Infantry—was in position on the jump-off line," says the history of the 2d Division. "The attacking Battalions of the Twenty-third Infantry arrived in position at exactly 4.30, after double-timing for over a mile. The First and Second Battalions of the Fifth Marines came up on the run just as the attack started, going from column into attack formation without a halt."

In its postwar history the 5th Regiment describes the arrival at the jump-off line in this way: "No sooner had the designated position been reached than our barrage started and the companies had to deploy at once without being given opportunity to rest. The French guides, designated to meet the First Battalion, had failed to show up and the guides for two of the companies of the Second Battalion (43rd and 55th) had led them too far north and placed them in position north of the Paris–Maubeuge highway."

Attack orders were sketchy. None of the company commanders had maps; they were not given much more to go on than compass bearings of their direction of attack.

The rear elements of the assault battalions had to double-time to attack position as the rolling barrage began. The 5th Marines were advancing on a broad front, the 1st Battalion (Turrill) on the left; with the added mission of maintaining contact with the Moroccans; the 2d Battalion (Keyser) on the right; and the 3d Battalion (Shearer) in the old frontline trenches as support. The jump-off line for the regiment was about three kilometers from the eastern edge of the forest.

"The Marine Battalions came on the run as the attack started," wrote General Harbord. "Few machine-gun units go into action without guns, but ours did that morning, for the guns had not gotten up. Tired, hungry and thirsty, without machine guns, Stokes mortars, 1-pounders or grenades, armed only with rifle and bayonet, the troops swept through with an impetuosity and dash that before night carried them far in advance of the Moroccans."

The German XIII Corps

The German Ninth Army defended the Marne salient against Mangin's attacking French Tenth Army. In the sector ranging east from Forêt de Retz to the Soissons–

Chateau-Thierry Highway, the German XIII Corps, commanded by Maj. Gen. Baron von Watter, held the front. The German defensive sectors extended to the northeast. This would cause the Germans to withdraw at an angle to the Allied front. Immediately opposite the 2d Division were the consolidated 14th and 47th reserve divisions, six infantry regiments with an average effective strength of thirty officers and a thousand men, with 140 light and two hundred heavy machine guns. They had the support of light and medium artillery, about six battalions in all. Von Watter had protested that his divisions were worn thin and in no condition to hold off a determined attack. He had been told that no more troops were available. The Germans were tired, their rations short, and their morale none too good, but they had the battle-wise cunning born of four years of survival. The sudden emergence from the woods to their east of the French XX Corps came as an unwelcome surprise. Lacking the sophisticated defenses of their former trench complexes, the Germans would fight this battle with mobile tactics, trading space for time, until reinforcing infantry and artillery units could be rushed to the sector.

As the attack began the 2d Division faced the 14th Reserve Division on its right and the 47th Reserve Division on its left. Resistance was not strong at first. Two battalions lightly held an outpost line, one each from the 218th and 219th infantry. The main line of resistance was a few hundred meters behind, thinly manned by two battalions, one from the 138th Infantry and one from the 17th Infantry. The German direct support artillery was about a mile to the rear. A second, stronger defensive line ran along the ridge east of Chaudun and through Vierzy.

Ravines and Wheat Fields

The barrage began as Turrill's Marines were deploying. The Germans answered with their own barrage. The battalion endured the shelling for about twenty minutes and then went forward. Without machine guns the attack was made with rifles, bayonets, and automatic rifles. One of Capt. William L. Crabbe's 66th Company survivors, Pvt. Elton E. Mackin, remembered the intensity of the German fire many years later. "The bullets," he said, "made noises like angry hornets zeeping overhead or popped like champagne corks near our ears when they were close."

Keyser went in on the right of Turrill. His companies, from right to left, being the 51st (now commanded, with the fiery Capt. Lloyd Williams dead, by Capt. William Corbin), the 18th (Capt. Lester Wass), the 43d (Capt. Joseph Murray), and the 55th (army 1st Lt. Elliott Cooke). This is the point where Keyser's French guides took the 43d and 55th companies too far to the north so that they were on the wrong side of the Paris–Maubeuge highway. Captain Murray discovered the error and corrected his position. Cooke's company remained isolated for hours, sustaining heavy casualties. Corbin's 51st Company, on the brigade's right flank, was to maintain liaison with the 9th Infantry.

The 3d Brigade on the right attacked over open ground against little resistance. By 6:45 AM the first waves of doughboys had advanced four kilometers and were crossing open fields behind a screen of tanks toward Beaurepaire Farm. The Marine battalions, still bound by the woods, moved more slowly.

It was close to 6 AM before the assault battalions of the 5th Regiment went "over the top." The barrage continued to roll inexorably forward. The first waves, going against heavy shelling and machine-gun fire, burst through the barbed wire interlaced among the trees and overran the first German outpost line. As they hurried, so as to maintain the momentum of their surprise, the rifle companies became dispersed and fragmented by the pace, the terrain—rolling wheat fields bisected by steep ravines and thickets—and the increasingly effective German machine-gun and artillery fire.

Small, improvised groups of Marines—sometimes joined by soldiers or Senegalese—advanced randomly, often led and inspired by NCOs like Acting GySgt. Louis Cukela and Sgt. Matek Kocak, both members of, and separated from, Captain Crabbe's 66th Company in Turrill's Battalion. Both received the Medal of Honor for their extraordinary valor and initiative this day.

Lieutenant Cooke's 55th Company on the left of Keyser's battalion followed the Paris–Maubeuge highway, which led them too far to the northeast. Cooke mistook a town in the distance for Vierzy; it was Chaudun. He took his company just west of Chaudun—moving deeper into the 1st Moroccan Division's sector—and reported Vierzy as captured, causing considerable confusion at brigade and division headquarters.

On Keyser's right, the 51st Company, in attempting to keep contact with the 9th Infantry, had met heavy resistance. In the center, La Verte Feuille Farm was taken with the help of the French tanks, which, to the Marines' satisfaction, crushed most of the German machine-gun positions. Specially selected hunting parties of riflemen picked off German snipers in trees "like shooting squirrels." Fritz Wise later claimed the idea had been his legacy to his former battalion.

By sunup Turrill had also reached the edge of the forest. There had been snipers in trees and machine guns to contend with but no serious resistance. Most of his casualties were from shells bursting in the trees. With daylight, as the Marines moved out into the open, German aircraft came down to strafe and bomb.

More beneficially, with daylight Turrill's line of skirmishers received the support of seven or eight French light tanks. At about eight o'clock Turrill committed Capt. Frank Whitehead's 67th Company to fill a gap that had opened between the right of his 1st Battalion and the left of Keyser's 2d Battalion.

Writing seven years after the event, John Thomason described the panorama that unfolded to his 49th Company that morning:

The woods fell away behind, and for miles to left and right across the rolling country the waves of assault could be seen. . . . The tanks, large and small, lumbered in advance. Over them the battle-planes flew low, searching the ground. . . . The infantry followed close, American Marines and Regulars, Senegalese and the Foreign Legion of France, their rifles slanting forward. . . . And behind the infantry, straining horses with lean-muzzled 75s, battery on battery—artillery, over the top at last with the rifles. On the skirts of the attack hovered squadrons of cavalry . . . dragoons and lancers, marked from afar by the sparkle and glitter of lance-heads and sabers.

Sgt. Donald V. Paradis of the 80th Company, usually employed as a runner by the newly promoted commander of the 2d Battalion, 6th Regiment, Lt. Col. Thomas Holcomb, had a ringside seat to watch the attack of the 5th Marines: "We could see the French tanks moving from one patch of woods to the other mopping up the isolated German machine guns and infantry. Some of the tanks were put out of action by shellfire, as we watched. Two men manned these small French tanks: a driver and a gunner. Some mounted Hotchkiss machine guns and others had 1-pounder cannon on them. We called them male and female. The Hotchkiss was the female and the 1-pounder was the male."

The 9th Infantry overran Beaurepaire Farm, defended by a battalion of the 219th. With this intermediate objective taken, the direction of advance changed nearly forty-five degrees, a difficult maneuver under the best of circumstances. The change exposed the left flank of the 3d Brigade to heavy fire from German machine guns and artillery at Maison Neuve Farm. Very heavy losses resulted.

Battalion aid station wagons and ambulances were somewhere to the rear, so there were no medical instruments or supplies available except for those in the pouches of the hospital corpsmen. An entire German dressing station captured intact at Beaurepaire Farm was put to immediate use. The sturdy stone buildings offered good shelter for the wounded that came pouring in. Ambulances had still not come up, and the less serious wounded were sent back in ammunition trucks that had emptied their loads. German prisoners, some walking wounded themselves, were used as litter bearers for the more serious cases.

"The walking wounded started coming back about the middle of forenoon," remembered Sergeant Paradis. "A large contingent of German prisoners, a hundred or more, came marching back carrying American wounded, also some of their own, guarded by not more than 4 or 5 wounded Marines. [Those] Marines were what we called *bon blessé*; they could walk, but still they had a wound."

Wheeling Southeastward

The advance was rapid from Beaurepaire Farm to Vauxcastille. Not even direct fire from German 77s and 150s could stop the Americans, but losses were heavy, and units became even more intermingled. A gap opened between the 2d Division and the Moroccan Division on the left. As the advance continued, the left of the Turrill's line was enfiladed by machine guns in the woods north of Le Translon, which the Moroccans had not yet taken. Turrill pushed ahead against the stiffening resistance, veering into the Moroccan zone of action. Maison Neuve Farm was on his right, the village of Chaudun on his left. Except for a small detachment of Captain Hamilton's 49th Company that was still intact, his 17th Company, commanded by Capt. Leroy P. Hunt, a big Californian, was his left flank company.

"We were the left flank company of the division hooked up with the French Moroccan division," remembered Lieutenant Blake. "That particular unit was Senegalese troops—big, black, scar-faced panthers. They fired their Chauchats from the shoulder. They handled that Chauchat gun as if it were a toy. . . . Some of our men nearly got into fights with them, because they wanted to kill prisoners that had surrendered."

Hunt's immediate objective was Le Translon Farm, but as he advanced he lost contact with the Moroccans, leaving his flank exposed. About a kilometer east of the farm, Hunt met up with a company of the 18th Infantry, 1st Division. After an argument as to who was where, the company commander from the 18th Infantry ordered his men to dig in; Hunt continued to advance to the east until he was about three-quarters of a kilometer southwest of Chaudun. A detachment of about twenty Moroccans and a lieutenant and a few stragglers from the 2d Battalion had attached themselves to his company. Heavy machine-gun fire came out of Chaudun. Going against considerable resistance, Hunt's mixed force captured the town, together with machine guns and prisoners, at about nine o'clock. Hunt then moved to the southeast toward his original objective until he was wounded and evacuated.

At about 9:30 AM, the 16th and 20th companies (Capts. Robert Yowell and Richard Platt) came up from the 3d Battalion, and Turrill was able to form a support with these two fresh companies and a part of Hamilton's 49th Company. In the meantime, the 1st Battalion's 66th and 67th companies (Captains Crabbe and Whitehead) had reached the ravine extending from Chaudun to Vauxcastille.

Keyser's 2d Battalion had gained its objectives, having fought its way to the Chaudun-Vauxcastille ravine through heavy machine-gun fire with the aid of the French tanks. Keyser had three of his companies more or less in hand. Captain Murray of the 43d Company was wounded, and the remnant of his company was merged with Wass's 18th Company. The 55th Company had broken into parts and by 4 PM was gathering on the left of the 1st Battalion in the trenches near Chaudun. All the officers of the 55th Company, including its intrepid army commander, Lt. Elliott Cooke, were now casualties. By this time, Corbin's 51st Company, which had been maintaining contact with the 9th Infantry, had come up and joined the 18th and 43d companies in the ravine northwest of Vierzy.

By midafternoon, the division was on its final objective, except for the village of Vierzy itself, which was still strongly held by the Germans. With his front line breached and his forward artillery positions overrun, General von Watter attempted to use his corps reserve to occupy an old trench position—the Paris position—running southeast of Chaudun for about a mile, and also to build up the line running south through Vierzy. In and about Vierzy were fragments of all six regiments of the 14th and 47th reserve divisions, with miscellaneous additions. The 28th Division, which the Marines had fought in Belleau Wood, until now in reserve, was moving all three of its regiments into line. The Germans divided the defense into two sectors: a northern sector under command of the 27th Brigade, 14th Reserve Division, and a southern sector under command of the 94th Reserve Brigade, 47th Reserve Division. Von Watter's reserves in those positions finally caused the 2d Division to pause in its charge forward, to give the infantry a breather and to bring the artillery forward before resuming the attack.

The Attack on Vierzy

Brig. Gen. Hanson E. Ely, commanding the 3d Brigade, had established his head-quarters at Beaurepaire Farm. Having no telephone link to Harbord's headquarters at Carrefour de Nemours, he drove back in his staff car to report to Harbord in person. At 1:30 PM Harbord ordered him to resume the attack, with the 5th Marines as an attached reinforcement.

After giving this order, at about 2 PM, Harbord displaced his own division headquarters forward to La Verte Feuille Farm. By then the division held a line from Vauxcastille to Maison Neuve, about two kilometers to the east of Beaurepaire Farm, about halfway between the eastern edge of the Forêt de Retz and the main objective, the north–south highway connecting Soissons with Chateau-Thierry. Elements of the 5th Marines and the 9th and 23d infantry held the eastern edge of the Vauxcastille ravine, the western edge of Vierzy, and the high ground north of the town. At Vauxcastille ravine the assault battalions had halted to reorganize.

It was four o'clock before Ely could again reach Beaurepaire. Regimental commanders were sent for and received the attack order at four-thirty. The attack was ordered "as soon as possible, but not later than six PM." The French tank officer said his tanks could not possibly be ready until seven. Tanks were ordered to follow if they could not accompany.

Maj. Maurice Shearer's 3d Battalion, 5th Regiment, moving in regimental reserve, had first occupied old French trenches to the rear of the jump-off line. At about 8 AM, at Keyser's request, he sent forward Capt. Thomas Quigley's 45th Company to La Verte Feuille Farm to reinforce the battered 55th Company.

By Silverthorn's recollection, the 45th Company went into battle at something like half strength, about a hundred Marines, and by the time it went forward to join the 1st Battalion this number had been reduced by a third.

"On the 18th," Silverthorn said, "we were moving forward in open warfare, very spectacular . . . like the old European Napoleonic battles. The terrain was open. You could see for miles. There were grain fields with ripening grain . . . as we passed through these fields we would thread the heads of the grain and eat this grain, which was wheat or barley or rye or something like that. It seemed to taste pretty good."

"The French cavalry came galloping across spectacularly and came under artillery fire and then would wheel and move. It was as near as you could have to a battle portrayed by the movies," Silverthorn recalled.

Earlier, Shearer's 16th and 20th companies had gone forward to reinforce Turrill. His remaining company, Capt. Philip Case's 47th, was used to constitute a provost guard of two officers and thirty men, to escort prisoners to the rear and bring ammunition forward. With all his companies parceled out, Shearer was left with a headquarters and no battalion.

Until now Marine machine guns had been of little help.

Waller's 6th Machine Gun Battalion caught up with the 5th Marines at La Verte Feuille Farm at about 3 PM. His companies were then paired off with the assault battalions and the machine guns spread out on the line. This deployment had barely begun before the machine-gun companies were recalled to support the attack by the 3d Brigade, which Ely had scheduled to jump off at 5:30 PM. Not until evening did the supply train arrived with the remaining guns, carts, and ammunition. The machine gunners that did have their guns had difficulty keeping up with the advance, because of the weight of the guns, tripods, and ammunition.

The 3d Brigade, with a battalion of Marines attached to each of its regiments, had the mission of taking Vierzy, where Major General von Watter was forming his new line. The 9th Infantry, on the left, was to pass north of the town, and the 23d Infantry was to take the town itself.

For his part of the attack, Major Keyser received verbal orders from the 3d Brigade adjutant at La Verte Feuille Farm to join his 2d Battalion, 5th Regiment, to the 9th Infantry. His was to be the left assault battalion in the renewed attack. He proceeded to the ravine northwest of Vierzy where his 18th, 43d, and 51st companies were waiting. The 55th Company was still off by itself. Keyser sent a runner telling it to join up. After several delays, but before the 55th Company could arrive, the jump-off time came. Keyser, with neither tank nor artillery support, went forward at about 7 PM with his three depleted companies in two waves on a five-hundred-meter front. Guiding on the rate of advance of the 9th Infantry battalion to his right, Keyser had gone forward for about a kilometer and a half when his left flank company, the 51st, came up against heavy machine-gun fire. The Moroccans, who were supposed to be on his left, had not come up. While the 51st Company, with the help of the 18th Company, was reducing this resistance, the right of the 9th Infantry regimental line continued to plunge forward, taking with it a part of the 18th Company that was on the right flank.

While Keyser was working on reducing several German machine guns, six French tanks came back through his position, attracting heavy German artillery fire. This destroyed four of the tanks and caused Keyser many casualties, including the fatal wounding of that proven stalwart, Captain Wass, of the 18th Company. The loss of rock-solid Lester Wass meant that all four company commanders in the 2d Battalion who had first taken the measure of German infantry attacks on the third of June were now gone. Keyser doggedly continued his advance. The patchwork 55th Company had rejoined the battalion, and the French could be seen coming up on the left. By dusk the battalion had reached an old French trench line. German machine-gun fire from guns hidden in the wheat was growing heavier, and Keyser, with neither grenades nor tank support, wisely decided to stop for the night. Keyser's right flank by then had reached a position just south of the woods at Lechelle. The battalion halted in the old trench system and would stay there until withdrawn two days later. The 9th Infantry battalions, on his right, advanced a mile east of Vierzy before stopping for the night. Keyser had done his best, but his chosen bivouac left a dangerous gap between his right flank and the 9th Infantry.

Major Turrill did not receive the attack order for his 1st Battalion to join the 23d Infantry until 5:15 PM, fifteen minutes before the scheduled jump-off. It was a classic supporting commander's nightmare. His PC at that time was on the Paris–Maubeuge highway. Knowing that he could not possibly meet the jump-off time with his entire battalion, Turrill hurriedly gathered about those Marines closest to him, about 150 of them from the 1st and 3d battalions, and marched with this improvised company by way of La Verte Feuille Farm to Vauxcastille. On the road Capt. John H. Fay and the 8th Machine Gun Company, which had just received its machine guns and ammunition from the regimental supply train, joined him. With this pickup force and the three companies from Shearer's 3d Battalion, Turrill went forward. German machine guns at Lechelle enfiladed his advance on the left. By early evening he had taken four-fifths of Vierzy, after which the 23d Infantry entered from the northwest and took the remainder. The 1st Battalion and the 8th Machine Gun Company then went into a position to the rear of the 23d Infantry southeast of the town.

Evening of the First Day

Twilight seemed to linger indefinitely. Lieutenant Silverthorn remembered, "In northern France it wasn't real dark until 11 o'clock at night and started getting light about 0300 in the morning; you had about four hours of darkness."

By nightfall of July 18, the 5th Regiment held good positions along the ridge between Chaudun and Vierzy. That evening, Feland moved his PC to Vauxcastille and in the morning to a large tunnel in Vierzy. During the evening Maj. Alphonse DeCarre, who had been left in charge of the regimental rear, brought these Marines up to Vauxcastille. Severe bombing by German aircraft disrupted his march up.

Unlike the closed confines of Belleau Wood, the battle for Soissons occurred in largely open terrain, and both sides suffered from air attacks. Navy Pharmacist's Mate George B. Strott watched the first day's aerial battle from the 6th Marines' reserve positions. "The air at all levels was filled with aircraft of all categories," he recalled. He described "flaming observation balloons" that became "black clouds of smoke" as they fell to the ground. "Intermittently, low-flying enemy planes swooped over our lines, dropping bombs and strafing the troops with machine-gun fire."

General Harbord had retained the 6th Marines in reserve throughout the day. As the regiment advanced across the battlefield in the late afternoon to stake out their next-day jump-off positions on a slope west of Vierzy, the veterans in the ranks studied with professional interest the flotsam left by the attack of the 5th Marines. Pvt. James Hatcher of the 84th Company recalled, "Here I saw the full effects of the day's fighting. Men were scattered over the rolling fields where they had fallen, while the wheat was furrowed with little lanes where the tanks had crossed, assisting the infantry in the charge. Many wrecked tanks and aeroplanes were in evidence and most of the planes were French."

The American line for the night ran nearly north and south a mile east of Vierzy, the left bent back to face Lechelle. The 1st Moroccan Division was on the left and the French 38th Division on the right. The Germans chose not to counter-attack during the night.

At 5 AM on July 19, Turrill sent this field message to his regiment: "Five-fifteen PM yesterday, rec'd order to support 3d Brig. for an attack at that hour. Took my support consisting of parts of 49th, 16th & 20th cos. to Vierzy. Arrived before 23d Inf. and with 8th M.G. Co. attacked thro' town. When half-way thro' town 23d came up and continued the attack. Now in support to 23d Inf. Need rations. . . . Have here Capt. Platt with 40 men, Capt. Yowell—4 off. 70 men. Hdqtrs. 7 off., 35 men, 30 men of 49th Co.—total 187. Turrill."

Not until late in the afternoon did the ambulances arrive to clear the Beaurepaire dressing station of all its wounded. The aid station then moved forward to Vierzy.

"The end of the day found the 2d Division holding a line one kilometer east of Vierzy after a day's advance of eight kilometers. Several thousand prisoners, hundreds of machine guns and practically all of the artillery, light and heavy, of two German divisions had fallen into our hands," says the short history of the 2d Division. Soissons marked the first time the Marines had captured substantial field artillery pieces from any enemy.

The day's victory had come at a cost. The division's three assault regiments were done in by three days without food or rest and with precious little water. The confused and disjointed fighting had reflected the urgency of the French Tenth Army's advance to blunt the latest Ludendorff offensive and seize the Marne salient. The paucity of maps, reliable guides, advance coordination, and above all, crew-served weapons had spiked the casualty count as the troops advanced across the open countryside. The 5th Marines alone had lost more than 450 men killed, wounded, or missing. The critical highway connecting Soissons with Chateau-Thierry still lay six kilometers farther east. As the nineteenth of July dawned, the 6th Marines realized that the second day's assault would be theirs alone, a single regiment covering the same zone of action that the three spent regiments had filled during the first day's confusing battle.

CHAPTER TEN

Soissons: The Second Day

The ground taken by the French Tenth Army near Soissons on July 18 far exceeded the commander's expectations.[1] General Mangin, delighted with the success of his foreign troops, ordered a continuation of the attack to begin at 4 AM. For the 2d Division the objective would be the Soissons–Chateau-Thierry road.

At 10 PM on the eighteenth Harbord had again advanced his headquarters, this time to Beaurepaire Farm. He had outrun his communications. There was no telephone wire to the rear. At about 2 AM a French staff officer brought him the XX Corps attack order for the following morning. Harbord summoned the 6th Regiment's commander, Lt. Col. Harry Lee, to his headquarters, once again bypassing the brigade commander, Col. Buck Neville, in the chain of command.[2]

The 6th Marines, as corps reserve, had moved up to Beaurepaire Farm early on the afternoon of July 18. As then-Sergeant Thomas remembered the battlefield on the day preceding the regiment's main assault:

We were horribly short of water. The horses and men had drunk up all the wells for miles around, and there was no water. We sent off details with canteens, and they were gone eight or ten hours before they could come back with their canteens full. That day lancers and cuirassiers, the beautiful French cavalry, would go loping by. The artillery was displacing forward, at the gallop. On the side of the road the walking wounded were coming back. . . .

About three o'clock in the afternoon, our regiment moved forward and deployed on the side of a hill. Down in front of us and off to the left was a

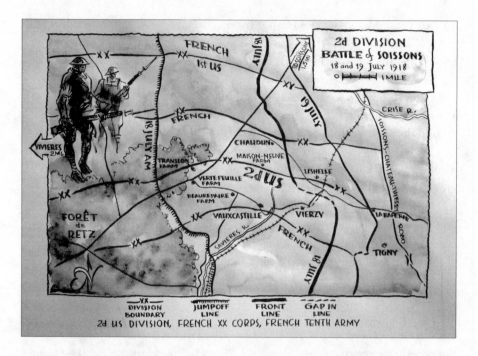

2d US DIVISION, FRENCH XX CORPS, FRENCH TENTH ARMY

line of artillery pieces as far as you could see standing hub to hub. I never saw anything like it, before or since.

Attack Orders

The Marines of the 6th Regiment were spectators, not participants, in the events of the eighteenth. The night was fairly well over before Lieutenant Colonel Lee received the attack order for the following day. At 3 AM on the nineteenth at Harbord's headquarters he learned that the 6th Marines, reinforced with the 6th Machine Gun Battalion, would take over the whole division front. The artillery preparation was to begin at 6 AM. Passage of lines would be at 7 AM. The 6th Marines would advance on a frontage of about 2,200 meters. The 1st Battalion, 2d Engineers, and the 4th Machine Gun Battalion would constitute the division reserve. All heavy tanks remaining at the disposition of the division commander would be placed under orders of Lee, the attack commander. All light tanks would be held in division reserve.

The regimental headquarters staff issued the warning order and distributed maps to the battalion commanders in the field south of Beaurepaire Farm at about 4:30 AM, telling them to advance their units to Vierzy and report for final guidance to Lee, who had gone forward to set up his PC in the railroad station. It was understood that the attack would be at 8 AM.

The senior Allied commanders were realists. General Mangin and Maj. Gen. Pierre Berdoulat, commanding the French XX Corps, had fought the Germans for four years. Major General Harbord, a relative newcomer to this business, had learned much from his three-week battle at Belleau Wood. No one underestimated the difficulty the 6th Marines would face in renewing the attack eastward on the second day. The element of surprise was gone. The German Ninth Army had reinforced its lines with artillery and infantry throughout the short night. All approaches to the north–south highway would be well covered by preregistered cannon fire and the ubiquitous Maxim machine guns.

Harbord possibly had these forebodings in mind early in the morning of the nineteenth, when he sent a lengthy message to Berdoulat. The pith of it was: "With the exception of the Sixth Marines, kept out of the fight as Corps Reserve yesterday, and the Second Regiment of Engineers, which are armed with rifles, every infantry unit was exhausted in the fight yesterday. It was necessary, therefore to make the attack this morning with one regiment, the Sixth Marines, supported by a battalion of the Engineer Regiment, a force considered by me as inadequate to the task, but no other was available."

Moving Up

The 6th Regiment moved out from Beaurepaire farm at 6 AM. Working its way up through the ravine, the column reached Vierzy without loss. Lee, at the railroad station, issued orders sequentially to his battalion commanders as they arrived: the 1st Battalion (Johnny Hughes) to go in on the right, the 2d (Thomas Holcomb) on the left, and the 3d (Berton Sibley) to follow in support.

Major Waller used two machine-gun companies (the 15th and 77th machine gun companies, to which had been attached one platoon each from the 23d and 81st machine gun companies) in the attack and two in support. One company had to cover the whole front until the other three could get into position.

Major Sibley reached Vierzy with the 3d Battalion at about 8:15. Lee ordered him to follow the 1st and 2d battalions at a distance of about a thousand meters. The 3d Battalion was to be followed by the 1st Battalion, 2d Engineers (army), in reserve. Sibley understood that he was to be supported by both the 15th and 77th machine gun companies. Sibley put all four of his companies, each in column of platoons, on line: the 97th on the right, the 84th right center, the 83d left center, and the 82d on the left. He also had weapons sections of Headquarters Company. The Stokes mortars and the 37-mm guns were somewhere to the rear with the regimental train, so the mortarmen and gunners were assigned to Sibley as extra riflemen.

Standard tactics for the "square" infantry battalions of World War I called for two companies in the assault, two companies immediately behind in support. As an example, in Holcomb's 2d Battalion, the 80th Company was the left-flank assault company, with the 96th Company following close behind in support. To their right, similarly disposed, were the 78th and 79th companies.

Thomas Holcomb, with his promotion to lieutenant colonel, was to move up to regimental second in command. He had orders to turn his battalion over to Maj. Robert L. Denig, but he elected to stay with his battalion for the attack. Denig, suddenly a supernumerary, came along as an observer. Denig, always a Marine but a first-rate journalist as well, captured the essence of this day's battle in a subsequent letter home that began: "We formed up in a sunken road . . . that was perpendicular to the enemy's front," he wrote, "Hughes right, Holcomb left, Sibley in support. . . . I heard Lieutenant Overton call to one of his friends to send a certain pin to his mother should he get hit. At 8:30 we jumped off."

Sgt. Jerry Thomas began the day as a platoon sergeant in the 75th Company of Hughes' 1st Battalion. Within hours he would assume command of his shattered company. As Thomas remembered the approach march:

> We formed right up soon after daybreak. . . . My battalion came up out of the Vierzy Ravine and deployed on the edge of a wheat field. The Germans, who were over on the right on a hill, spotted us. They were about 1,800 yards away, but they started throwing machine gun bullets at us. . . . I could see Holcomb's battalion come out of the orchard way off to our left and deploy and move out. . . . We lay there, and after a while we heard rumbling. It was the tanks. . . . When the tanks passed through, the command came, "Forward." We got up and started going with them.

Sgt. Donald Paradis was again acting as a runner for Holcomb. He remembered that the 80th Company reached the jump-off line at about 7 AM and then was ordered to lie down in the wheat field and wait for the tanks to come up. There was no sign of any heavy tanks, but four small ones came up over the ridge behind them and started down the slope. The 80th and 96th companies had not dug in. Caught by the shelling and machine-gun fire drawn by the tanks, they could only hug the ground and take it. All four tanks were knocked out. GySgt. John Schrank was killed about ten feet from Paradis: "The medics started to bandage him and First Lieutenant Clifton Cates took his pulse and said, 'don't bother, he's dead.'"

Cates was still with the 96th Company. Administration in the brigade was haphazard, and he wasn't certain if he were a first lieutenant, still a second lieutenant, or perhaps even a captain. In 1967, he remembered the opening of the second day at Soissons this way:

> So we formed for the attack and we were supposed to have had, I think it was, eight little old French tanks. So there we stayed for an hour or an hour and a half waiting for the tanks to arrive. By that time, we were getting not only artillery fire but indirect machine gun fire. . . . In fact, one hit the back of my shoulder. I thought somebody had hit me with a rock. I finally pulled it out

and it was a red-hot bullet. I went over to Major Holcomb and yelled to him, "Well. I got the first blessé. Here's the first wound," and I handed him this bullet and he dropped it, it was still hot.

"It Seemed Like a Black Curtain"

The 6th Marines began the passage of lines at 8:25 A.M. The terrain resembled the exposed approaches to Belleau Wood. The German positions were about a kilometer away, across open fields. The ground was practically level, no cover, except for the waist-high wheat. The wheat was now more golden than green, and the poppies seemed less red than on the fields, as if they had faded.

"We finally got under way and started the attack with these little old tanks," recalled Cates. " It was the most beautiful attack that I have ever seen. As far as you could see, up to the right, there were just waves and waves of men extending up two miles, I guess."

"Our company moved out in two waves, about fifty yards between waves," remembered Sergeant Paradis. As Holcomb's runner he stayed close to his commander. "Our battalion headquarters, consisting of about thirty men also moved in two waves, just back of the 80th Company's second wave. It was about a thousand yards to the German lines and as we started forward the German shellfire concentrated just a couple of hundred yards in front of their lines. The concentration was so great that it seemed like a black curtain, and it seemed to me that Colonel Holcomb was headed for the thickest and blackest part of that German line."

The 80th Company had a new commander, Capt. Egbert T. Lloyd, a small man. As a bit of bravado copied from English and French officers, many Marine officers left their Colt .45s in their holsters and went into the attack carrying crook-handled canes. Paradis could see Lloyd through the smoke with the first wave, swinging his cane and urging his men forward.

The attack moved out in perfect view of the Germans. By now Gen. Baron Von Watter, commanding the opposing XIII Corps, had firmed up his new line along the Chateau-Thierry road with the relatively fresh 46th Division. (The 14th and 47th divisions had been so badly mauled on the eighteenth that a few days later the 47th was permanently broken up and its pieces absorbed by the 14th.) West of Tigny was the 49th Division.

The American artillery preparation had been inadequate. The battle was a hopscotch kind of thing, crossing the wheat fields to reach the dubious shelter of the woodlots. The pace, because of the necessity of following the allotted French tanks, was slow. Of the fifty-four French tanks that had begun the battle the day before, only twenty-eight were still operational. During the morning eleven more would be knocked out. When Lieutenant Cates admired the "waves and waves of men extending two miles" as he began his advance, so must have the German gunners, rimming the higher ground, firing lanyards in hand, the morning sun rising behind their heads to illuminate their approaching targets. German artillery spotters, observing the American advance through binoculars from their "sausage" balloons, called down a devastating fire. The waiting Maxims, covering every crossroad, fence line, or choke point in the terrain, took up the slaughter.

"It was the hottest place in the world," wrote Sgt. Gus Gulberg of the 75th Company, 1st Battalion, and "shells of all sizes fell like hailstones." In his diary, Gulberg later recorded, "Some of our men were hit before we got started. The whistle blew and we were off behind a platoon of whippet tanks. These tanks were a great help to the infantry in cleaning out machine gun nests, but I would rather take my chances without them rather than follow them, because they draw artillery fire."

"It seemed to rain shells," recalled Pvt. Carl A. Brannen of the 80th Company, 2d Battalion. "The last glance I had of Lt. Overton he was walking backward and trying to shout something back to us. He carried his cane in his left hand and a .45 in the right. The din and roar was so terrific I didn't have any idea what he was saying, but interpreted it from his expression to be some words of encouragement. He was soon down, killed. The gunnery sergeant was killed."[3]

Denig mourned John Overton's death: "Overton was hit by a big piece of shell and fell. Afterwards I heard . . . he was buried that night and the pin [for his mother] found."

Sergeant Gulberg went forward a few hundred meters, felt a sting in his right leg, cut away his breeches, and found two holes where a machine gun bullet had gone through the flesh. He took three or four steps and was knocked down by another hit, this one in the left leg. He tried to get up but couldn't move his left leg. He dropped all his equipment except his canteen and his pistol and hugged the ground. His canteen was empty. He took a canteen from a corpse and found that it too was dry. He looked at his wristwatch. It was 10 AM.

One hour into the assault Lt. Graves Erskine, the flu-ridden escapee from the brigade's sickbay who had rejoined the 79th Company in Holcomb's battalion, was knocked out by a shell concussion. He was evacuated through a field hospital and put on a train that took him to Hospital no. 5 in Paris, from which, after making himself obnoxious to the staff, he was sent on to Nantes.

After a gain of about one kilometer the Marine line halted to reform its depleted ranks. The right of the line was stopped in front of Tigny, the left at La Raperie. A gap had opened between the 1st and 2d battalions.

Sibley's Battalion into the Gap

At 8:55 AM Sibley received a message by runner from Lee telling him to reinforce the line in the center, using two companies in waves and two in local support. Sibley sent the 84th Company in to the left of the 1st Battalion and the 83d Company to the right of the 2d Battalion to fill the reported gap. The 97th and 82d companies remained in support.

At 9:50 AM Sibley reported to Lee that his attacking line was moving forward. By 10:30 his two assault companies had pushed forward almost to the Bois de Tigny, north of the village, but had taken heavy casualties. Soon Sibley had to deploy all four companies in the main assault due to losses sustained in the 1st and 2d battalions. One of Sibley's officers reached Hughes, who said that he had only about a hundred men left and that nothing less than a regiment would drive the Germans out of Tigny.

Sibley's Marines soon experienced the full fury of the German shelling. Pvt. James Hatcher, 84th Company, recalled, "The artillery barrage descended in earnest. . . . Many [men] were falling torn and mangled beyond description. The shells seemed to come in one solid, screaming, rushing stream. The ground seemed alive with bursting geysers of smoke and dust. . . . By this time some of the enemy's artillery was firing at point blank range and one shell passed so close to my head the rush of air nearly shoved me off my feet."

"I Will Hold"

The maelstrom of bursting shells claimed two of Sgt. Jerry Thomas's best friends, one decapitated by shrapnel, the other mortally wounded. "The Germans had massed their artillery on a hill about three or four miles off in front of us," he remembered. "It was all direct fire. . . . Our attack collapsed. The attack was over."

By 10 AM Capt. Wethered Woodworth's 96th Company had reached a position about three kilometers east of Vierzy near Villemontaire and was digging in. The French colonials on the Marines' left had failed to keep up, and the 96th Company, on the left flank, suffered accordingly. In the space of about two hours the 96th had taken a total of twenty-six killed and fifty-six wounded. All the officers of the company were wounded early in the attack.

As Lt. Clifford Cates remembered:

The Moroccans that were supposed to have attacked on our left didn't appear at all. We broke the first German lines without too much trouble. By that time though we were catching billy-hell. . . . I had just remarked to this sergeant of mine close to me, "Look at Captains Woodworth and [James F.] Robertson getting right together there. That's bad business." And I hadn't any more than said it when a shell hit close to them and they both went down. By that time, the other lieutenants had all been wounded and I was the only one left out of the company. I tried to take charge, but just about that time a whole bunch of Germans jumped up out of the trench and started running and our men went after them like a bunch of coyotes. With that it was bedlam. I was never able to organize them again. I kept the attack going for about a kilometer, I guess. By that time, though, we were getting terrific fire from our left flank. . . . [T]he attack just petered out. We were up near an old sugar mill. And that's where I wrote that message . . . to Major Holcomb. I think I said, "I have twenty men out of my company or out of my battalion and a few stragglers," and I wound up by saying, "I will hold." By that time though, I had a pretty bad wound across my knee.[4]

This second wound, caused by a shell fragment, virtually tore the trousers off Cates. He tied a piece of blanket around his waist and so earned the temporary nickname "Kiltie."

The Marines had outrun their artillery support. It was almost impossible to evacuate the wounded. Casualties were so heavy that a further advance appeared impracticable. What was left of the regiment took shelter in half-completed trenches left by the Germans.

Holcomb's battalion gained the shelter of a wood about four hundred meters west of Villemontaire. Sergeant Paradis remembered their desperation and exhaustion:

> We reached the German front lines and found a series of foxholes that they had abandoned. What few of us that were left fell into these foxholes. We even piled on top of each other to seek cover from that murderous shellfire. I laid there with every muscle in my body twitching, hardly knowing what I was doing. We could hear the wounded calling for help, but very little could be done for them until after dark came. . . . Our advance had not taken long. We were in the German foxholes probably by 9 or 9:30 and from then until about 4 PM the shellfire, machine gun and rifle fire never let up.

Pvt. Carl Brannen of the 80th Company, Holcomb's Battalion, believing he was the only survivor of Johnny Overton's platoon, collapsed in a dirt road, thoroughly demoralized. "In thirty or forty minutes, our regiment had been almost annihilated," he said. "The field which had been recently crossed was strewn with dead and dying."

Maj. Robert Denig continued to shadow Holcomb. "At 10:30 we dug in —the attack just died," he wrote his wife. He and Holcomb took partial shelter in an abandoned position. "We then tried to get reports. Two companies we never could get in touch with. [Egbert] Lloyd came in and reported he was holding some trenches near a mill with six men. Cates, with his trousers blown off, said he had sixteen men of various companies. . . . It was hot as a furnace, no water, and they had our range to a 'T.'"

Pinned Down

As the day wore on, the men in the open wilted in the heat. Denig wrote, "You could hear men calling for help in the wheat-fields. Their cries would get weaker and weaker and die out." The artillery and Maxim machine-gun fire was bad enough, but the Germans also enjoyed air superiority over the battlefield. Added Denig, "the dark-gray German planes with their sinister black crosses, looked like Death hovering above." Lt. John Thomason commented, "There's something about being machine-gunned from the air that gets a man's goat." Indeed, the U.S. Marines would not again be so totally vulnerable to enemy airpower until Pearl Harbor, Wake Island, and Guadalcanal in 1941–42.

In Hughes' battalion, Sgt. Jerry Thomas and another Marine took cover behind a heavy iron roller a French farmer had left in the wheat field. "About an hour and a half later, I looked up and there was still a lot going on," remembered Thomas. "They were dropping hand grenades out of airplanes on us. . . . What had caused us to be slaughtered was the fact that the Moroccan division, which was supposed to have come up on our right, was delayed. . . . There was nobody on our right except German machine guns. . . . Maybe at noon or a little after, I was able to get up and peek around. That's after the Moroccans came forward."

At 11:45 AM, Lee sent this message to Harbord from his PC in the Vierzy railroad station: "Reports indicate growing casualties, amounting heavy, say about 30 per cent. Seventy-eighth Company by runners say have only one platoon left. All are requesting reinforcements and M.G. and Chauchat ammunition. First Battalion reports no French troops on right, and are held up 300 yards in front of Tigny. Have in line from right, First, Third and Second Battalions; Reserves, Battalion Engineers, Headquarters Company and two companies Sixth Machine Gun Battalion. Have ordered line to dig in."

At 12:15 PM Lee sent a runner to Sibley asking, "Has the town of Tigny been taken by our troops? If you don't know find out. If you are stopped dig in." A half-hour later Sibley sent runners to his companies telling them: "Hold the line you have now—dig in—get in touch with [companies] on your right and left. Reinforcements coming."

But reinforcements were not coming, and at 1:15 PM Sibley reported to Lee that Tigny had not been taken.

Harbord evidently found Lee's 11:45 report of the failure of the 6th Regiment to reach the Soissons–Chateau-Thierry highway difficult to assimilate. Nearly two hours later, at 1:30 PM, Harbord answered glumly: "The Division Commander desires that you dig in and entrench your present position and hold it at all costs. No further advance is to be made for the present. He desires to congratulate your command upon its gallant conduct in the face of severe casualties."

The message merely confirmed a fact: the 6th Marines were already digging in and holding what they had. German artillery fire was heavy for the rest of the day. With the 6th Marines badly shot up and dangerously pinned down, the 2d Division would get no closer to Soissons. The mission changed to evacuating the survivors and the thousands of casualties, in many respects a more difficult task than the doomed assault itself. As Major Sibley would report to Lee much later in the day at 8:05 PM: "Situation worse than I had wished to believe."

After he felt it reasonably safe to move from his temporary shelter, Sergeant Thomas reported to the one officer he could find, Capt. Macon C. Overton, commander of the 76th Company, whom he found sitting in a ditch alongside a sunken road.

Overton told Thomas that he had to go back to report to Major Hughes, that he knew what was in front of him and what was left of his company but not what had happened to the rest of the battalion. As far as Overton knew, Thomas was the senior man remaining in 75th Company. He told Thomas to locate the rest of the company. Thomas went forward and slithered from foxhole to foxhole, finding about a hundred Marines, including thirty-three from his own company. Overton went back the several hundred meters to Hughes' PC. While there the PC was shelled and most of those present killed or wounded. Hughes was painfully injured. Overton grimly returned to Thomas's position and told him they were going to be relieved by the French at about midnight.

About two or three in the afternoon, Sergeant Gulberg, prostrate in the wheat field, was reached by his friend "Smiley," who himself had been hit a glancing blow in the forehead. Gulberg wrapped his arms around Smiley's neck, and together they hobbled back to a first aid station in a shell hole. A doctor there gave them first aid and sent them on to the regimental dressing station in a cave in Vierzy, which was jammed with wounded.

At 3:45 PM, Lee sent this message by runner to his battalion commanders: "The Division Commander directs us to dig in and hold our present line at all costs. No further advance will be made for the present. He congratulates the command on its gallant conduct in the face of severe casualties. Let me have a sketch of your position and disposition. Ammunition at crossroads 112 southeast of Vierzy. Lee"

"As twilight came, we sent out water parties for the relief of the wounded," Major Denig wrote home. "At nine o'clock we got a message congratulating us, and saying the Algerians would take over at midnight. We then began to collect our wounded."

Throughout the day the 5th Regiment had held the ground it had taken the previous day, harassed by enemy shelling and intermittent bombing and strafing from German aircraft circling lazily overhead. The Marines fired their rifles and machine guns against the German aircraft with no noticeable effect. At 2 PM, Major Keyser received orders to report with his 2d Battalion once again to the 9th Infantry, but before he could execute the order it was canceled and his battalion put into the line to the right of the 6th Regiment.

At 4 PM, Harbord ordered Major Turrill to take his battalion into the large tunnel at Vierzy, which gave him relief from the German shelling and bombing. At about the same time the 23d Company, 6th Machine Gun Battalion, gleefully reported shooting down an enemy plane. Not unexpectedly, every battalion on the front claimed the same kill.

Ebb Tide for the 6th Marines

At 6:40 PM Lee sent a message to Neville, his brigade commander, who was still chafing over being bypassed by Harbord in the battle. "Am enclosing two sketches of positions of First and Third Battalions and a statement of the C.O. Second," Lee reported. "It is impossible to move from one position to another without drawing all sorts of fire. Losses are placed by Battalion Commanders at from 40 to 50 per cent. Their appeals for doctors, ambulances and stretcher-bearers are pathetic. Cannot the ammunition trucks . . . be used to evacuate the 200 or more cases now in the Regimental D.S. [dressing station] under Doctor Boone?"

Lee was not exaggerating his losses. Of the 2,450 men of his regiment who made the attack, 1,300 were dead or wounded. Hughes' 1st Battalion had lost eleven officers, including Capt. John Kearns of the 95th Company. In Holcomb's 2d Battalion, only three officers remained. Sibley's 3d Battalion had started off that morning with thirty-six officers and 850 men. At the end of the day Sibley's effective strength was sixteen officers and 385 men.

At 8:05 PM, Sibley summed up the day in a message to Lee that said in part: "Will continue holding line until we can be reenforced or relieved. . . . In front lines canteens are practically all empty and very few remaining rations. Can water and rations be sent to us or a relief sent? We have no flares—pyrotechnics or flare pistols. Have no hand grenades. . . . Many of their [sic] Chauchats out of action because of loss of men."

By then the shelling had diminished and the ambulances and trucks started reaching Vierzy. About an hour and a half later Sergeant Gulberg was loaded into the back of a Packard truck. There was a thin layer of straw on the floor of the truck bed, on which the wounded were packed in rows.

Gulberg's medical evacuation, rough as it was, went smoother than most. German artillery fire prevented most ambulances from using the road leading to the regimental dressing station in the Vierzy ravine. The surgeons and corpsmen, exhausted and frustrated, commandeered unloaded ammunition trucks to convey the worst casualties to a distant field hospital. One battalion surgeon recorded this ordeal in his log book: "Packed closely to conserve precious space on the hard floors of heavy trucks, load after load of critically injured men left the mouth of the cave. . . . Passing through poisonous gas and over shell-torn roads undergoing terrific bombardment, these trucks, with their groaning and screaming cargoes bouncing around, rushed to . . . reach possible safety many kilometers away. . . . Many died en route."

At 8:30 PM Sibley received a message, dispatched an hour earlier by the 6th Regiment headquarters, with the welcome news that he was to send back guides to bring forward a French battalion. The regimental staff officer who drafted the message ended with an unnecessary reminder, "Bring in all wounded when relieved."

Samuel W. Meek Jr. had gone to Yale with Johnny Overton; both were members of the Class of '17; both were from Nashville. Now Meek was a second lieutenant in the 82d Company in Sibley's 3d Battalion. Hearing that Johnny had been killed, Sam started out across the battlefield to find his body. He found it in a wheat field and buried it, reporting, "He lies about 2,000 yards from Vierzy. His grave is marked by his identification tag on a stick in the ground."[5]

In Hughes' 1st Battalion sector, the French came in at midnight, according to Sergeant Thomas' memory. By then he was the apparent commander of the 75th Company. "I got my 33 men. I went back to battalion headquarters. We made stretchers out of blankets wrapped around rifles, and we carried the wounded out. Later we may have found another 35 or 40 men at different places, but my company lost over 50 per cent. . . . We really took a shellacking."

In Holcomb's 2d Battalion, it was much the same: "So we stayed there that night and a bunch of Frenchmen, I think Moroccans, I'm not sure, came in and relieved us," said Cates. "We lost approximately, I would say, two-thirds of the battalion in that attack."

Pvt. James Hatcher and other survivors of the 84th Company struggled back through the wheat carrying a Marine wounded in both legs on an improvised litter. "A short distance after passing the front line we met Lieutenant-Colonel Sibley standing alone in the wheat waiting for the last of his boys to pass."

Private Brannon of the 80th Company remembered, "After midnight a force of Algerian troops came to relieve us, and gathering as many of our wounded as we could carry, we started back." The men had to cover a lot of ground within range of German artillery, still blazing away sixteen hours after the assault began. Most of the men had gone without food for four days. "Late in the evening of the 20th," Brannon said, "we survivors got a meal of slum gullion."[6]

A Costly Victory

The French 58th Colonial Division completed the relief by 4 AM on the morning of July 20. The 2d Division was to move back to its starting position in the Forêt de Retz where it would go into bivouac. Harbord and his chief of staff, Col. Preston Brown, stood by the side of the road and watched the two depleted brigades pass.

"Battalions of only a couple of hundred men, companies of twenty-five or thirty, swinging by in the gray dawn, only a remnant, but a victorious remnant, thank God," wrote Harbord in his diary. By Sergeant Paradis' count, forty-nine men marched back of the 196 Marines of the 80th Company who had gone into the attack the previous morning. Five more, who had been pinned down by the Germans, came in the following morning.

From midnight until well after dawn on July 20, the Marines and doughboys marched in a steady stream past the division headquarters toward the rear. After the march past, Harbord moved his headquarters to Vivieres.

The truck carrying Sergeant Gulberg took all night to thread its way back through the Villers-Cotterets forest. At seven in the morning it reached a French field hospital. "The hospital building was full and so was the yard," remembered Gulberg. "The doctors were busy giving anti-tetanus injections, and the Red Cross was giving out coffee, tea, cakes and cigarettes. . . . About three in the afternoon they began tagging us. Those not too seriously wounded were marked 'Evacuate' and the serious cases were marked, 'Operate here.'" Gulberg was marked "Operate here."

By late afternoon practically all the division, with the exception of the artillery, had gone into bivouac in the woods near La Verte Feuille Farm. The 6th Regiment went into bivouac near Translon Farm. The intense shellfire had weakened the trees, and there was a high wind; one Marine was killed and two seriously injured by falling branches. The Germans further treated the regiment to a shelling with long-range Austrian 130-mm guns. Lee sent a motorcycle courier to brigade headquarters asking for a more favorable resting place a little farther to the rear.

The 5th Regiment had also marched back in the early morning hours, back into the Forêt de Retz, about one kilometer back of the jump-off point it had crossed two days before. At first count, the 5th Regiment had lost forty-four men dead, 360 wounded, and thirty-four missing. This number grew as returns came in.

The rolling kitchens—mule-drawn four-wheeled carts with wood-burning stoves—were waiting. On the morning of the twentieth, the 45th Company reached its kitchens and had hot cakes, syrup, and coffee, its first hot food since the sixteenth.

"I have never seen anything look so good," said 2d Lt. Merwin Silverthorn, the junior platoon commander.

Harbord ordered Neville to move his brigade to the woods south of Taillefontaine. For those Marines who still had them, two shelter halves buttoned together made an acceptable pup tent. Considerably more comfortably, Neville set up his headquarters in the village itself.

Next day, on July 21, Harbord reported to Major General Bullard's III Corps headquarters. Bullard informed him that he had telegraphed General Pershing that both the 1st and 2d divisions had done well but that the 2d had done exceptionally well. That evening General Pershing came by the 2d Division headquarters and told Harbord, "It appears I have to congratulate you every time I see you."

With these praises singing in his head, Harbord issued an effusive general order: "It is with keen pride that the Division Commander transmits to the command the congratulations and affectionate personal greetings of General Pershing, who visited the Division Headquarters last night. . . . You advanced over six miles, captured over three thousand prisoners, eleven batteries of artillery, over a hundred machine guns, minnenwerfers [sic], and supplies. . . . The story of your achievements will be told in millions of homes in all Allied lands tonight."

Sergeant Gulberg awoke in the field hospital on the morning of the twenty-first when a French nurse came in with bread, cheese, and a cup of wine. He was placed once again in a truck. This took him to a railroad station, where he was placed on one of the new American hospital trains.

"Oh, what a relief to ride in a real train once more," wrote Gulberg. "These cars were fitted up like Pullmans, with upper bunks for litter cases, and seats for the walking cases. We stopped several times en route and were fed royally by the Red Cross, who were stationed at all the fair sized railroad stations."

Gulberg's destination was Base Hospital no. 27 at Angers. On clean white sheets and after a good breakfast he decided that it was not such a bad war after all.

"He who gets into a hospital, providing he isn't hit too hard, is considered a lucky guy," said Gulberg.

The Germans bombed both the brigade and division headquarters during the night of July 21, probably to the secret satisfaction of the Marines sleeping in the woods, but caused no casualties.

By the twenty-second, the count of prisoners taken in the two days of fighting had reached sixty-six officers and 2,810 enlisted Germans. These were the able-bodied ones. The number of wounded prisoners evacuated through the medical chain was unknown. Pershing, Degoutte, and Petain all hastened to send flowery compliments to the division.

Soissons in Perspective

The experiences of the two Marine regiments at Soissons had been quite different. The 5th Marines had pursued a surprised and demoralized enemy. The 6th Marines had encountered a stubborn and well-prepared defense, a situation that, in the words of an early historian of the Corps, led to "the hopeless and bitter experience of trying to overcome machines with their bare bodies."

In its two-day battle the Marine brigade had lost at least two thousand killed and wounded, with two-thirds of the loss in the 6th Marines.[7]

All told, the Marines sustained about six thousand casualties at Belleau Wood and Soissons. The combined losses over a six-week period meant that a decidedly different 4th Brigade would have to pick up the baton for the remainder of the war. Private Hatcher's company discovered this somber reality marching back through the forest after Soissons. "Someone started singing the old marching song 'Hail, Hail the Gang's All Here,'" he wrote. "As usual the column joined in the song but after a few words the singing died away and the little column marched along in silence. Those few words had brought home all too plainly the fact that the 'gang' was not 'all here.'"

There were those who would say that the attack of XX Corps south of Soissons was the spearhead that began the general retreat of the Germans and moved the war toward its end. Said Pershing in his *Final Report*, "Due to the magnificent dash and power displayed in the field of Soissons by our 1st and 2d Division, the tide of war was definitely turned in favor of the Allies."

Well after the war, Harbord, in his *The American Army in France* (1936), quoted German chancellor Georg von Hertling regarding that day in May 1918, "On the 18th even the most optimistic among us understood that all was lost."

Belleau Wood was significant, a touchstone battle for the Marines because it stopped the German threat to Paris and showed that the new American outfits could fight. Soissons was decisive. The short, violent battle enabled the Allies to regain the initiative, which they never again lost, and forced the Germans to begin their long, dogged retreat to the Meuse. The Marine Brigade at Soissons represented a mere portion of the 275,000 American troops attacking German positions during the Aisne-Marne offensive, but in their gritty determination and hell-for-leather spirit in the thickets and wheat fields east of the Forêt de Retz the Marines upheld their newly acquired reputation as "storm troops."

Harbord received orders on the twenty-third to move his division to the vicinity of Nanteuil-le-Haudouin, virtually the same location it had left one long week earlier. About two thousand replacements were absorbed into the brigade.

On July 30, from the 96th Company's bivouac at Chavigny, Cates wrote his mother and sister:

Again I am the company commander of the 96th as Capt. Woodsworth, Lieuts. Robertson, Duane, and Fritz were all wounded. I received two very slight wounds—a machine gun bullet went thru my roll and coat and stuck in my shoulder—just did break the skin. . . . The other wound was just above my knee—a shell exploded real close and a big slab of shrapnel cut my trousers and made a gash about two inches long but not enough to stop me. . . . We had to go thru a heavy barrage and machine gun fire, and we lost quite a few men, but those that did get by made the Huns run like rabbits—they were more than willing to stick up their mitts and yell *Kamerad!*

CHAPTER ELEVEN

Marbache and St. Mihiel

Midsummer in France brought promises of an abundant harvest and revived hopes for an Allied victory in the long, stalemated war.[1] John Lejeune, en route to take command of the 4th Brigade, drove to Nanteuil-le-Haudouin on July 25 and reported for duty to General Harbord. After dinner with Col. Harry Lee at the 6th Regiment's headquarters mess, he went on to 4th Brigade headquarters. Here he spent the evening with his old friend, Col. Buck Neville, and next morning, the twenty-sixth, took command of the Marine brigade, visiting all its battalions. His long-sought command of the brigade, however, would last only seventy-two hours.

While at lunch on the twenty-seventh, Harbord was interrupted by a phone call summoning him to Chaumont to see Pershing. He was on the road in fifteen minutes for what would be a five-hour motor trip. Pershing saw him in his summer quarters, the beautiful chateau Val des Escoliers. Pershing, Harbord learned, was assigning him to command of the troubled Services of Supply.

Harbord did not get back to his own headquarters until midnight. Early the next morning, a Sunday, he sent for Lejeune and told him that as senior brigadier he would have temporary command of the division. But, warned Harbord, if he wished to retain command, it would be necessary that he be promoted to major general. Lejeune replied that the new Naval Appropriations Bill did authorize two major generals for the Marine Corps and that before leaving Washington he had been reliably informed that one of those appointments would be his. Harbord advised him to see what he could do to hurry up the process.

Lejeune did not know Vice Adm. William S. Sims, commander of U.S. Naval Forces Operating in European Waters, but with Harbord's help he drafted to the Navy Department a cable that he hoped Sims would release. He sent it off by motorcycle to Paris for his friend Admiral Wilson to dispatch to the "London Flagship," as Sims liked to call his headquarters. In the same packet went a letter to Col. Robert Dunlap, now a planner on Sims' staff, asking him to bring the message to Sims' attention.

Lejeune Takes Command of the 2d Division

It had been Harbord's custom to entertain, when circumstances permitted, his colonels and brigadier generals at Sunday luncheons. Such a luncheon had already been scheduled, and it became a departure ceremony, with music by the 23d Infantry band. Harbord left with a feeling of satisfaction. Before Soissons, he believed, the 2d Division had been a loose aggregation of fighting units—the 3d and 4th brigades of Infantry and the 2d Field Artillery Brigade—but now he considered it a united division. Harbord took with him to Tours, which would be his new headquarters, his own personal staff, which included his Marine aide, Maj. Fielding Robinson, his Marine orderly, his Marine mess boy, and his Marine chauffeur.

John Lejeune relieved Harbord in command of the 2d Division on July 29, 1918. He was not the first Marine to command an army division—Brig. Gen. Charles Doyen had commanded the same outfit briefly the previous year. But Lejeune became the first Marine to lead an army division in major combat, and he would so lead it throughout the remainder of the war. General Pershing's decision to entrust Lejeune with a division of regulars at the start of the American First Army's initial offensive reflected the respect many army officers had for Lejeune's strength of character.

Lejeune inherited from Harbord the very capable Col. Preston Brown, USA, as chief of staff. Brig. Gen. Hanson E. Ely, USA, still commanded the 3d Brigade of Infantry, and Brig. Gen. Albert J. Bowley, USA, continued in command of the 2d Artillery Brigade. Colonel Neville resumed command of the Marine brigade. Pete Ellis, now a lieutenant colonel, took over as brigade adjutant. He would direct the brigade's staff work and do so brilliantly.

Lt. Col. Fritz Wise had returned to command of the 2d Battalion, 5th Regiment, on July 21, taking over from Maj. Ralph Keyser. Maj. Frederick Barker came back to the brigade on July 28 from his stint as assistant provost marshal in Paris and was given command of the 1st Battalion, 6th Marines, in relief of "Johnny the Hard" Hughes. Major Hughes' cumulative combat injuries had caught up with him. Still nursing a bullet wound in his leg from prewar fighting in the Dominican Republic, hampered by the effects of mustard gas in his lungs from Belleau Wood and of bones broken during the shelling of his forward command post at

Soissons, Hughes would spend the rest of the war in a French hospital.[2] Somewhat later Lt. Col. Thomas Holcomb reluctantly gave up command of the 2d Battalion, 6th Marines. Maj. Robert Denig, who was to succeed him, had been loaned to the 9th Infantry to take over its 3d Battalion. Command of Holcomb's battalion went to Maj. Ernest C. "Bolo" Williams, who arrived with something of a mixed reputation.

Williams, a rough-edged man and a hard drinker, had a Medal of Honor from the occupation of Santo Domingo. In November 1916 he had stormed with twelve Marines the *fortaleza* at San Francisco de Macoris, defended by from forty to a hundred (depending upon who was counting) Dominican rebels. He had come to France in June with the 3d Replacement Battalion and, after a sojourn for indoctrination at the army's I Corps School, had arrived at the brigade on the first day of August. Command of the 2d Battalion, 6th Regiment, came a few days later.

On July 29, the day Lejeune assumed command, he received orders to move his division to an undisclosed destination two days away. An advance detachment was to go to Meaux, where details would be provided.

Lejeune went himself in his Cadillac, first to Meaux, where he was told to report to St. Dizier for further instructions. Instead, on his own volition, he went to Chaumont to thank Pershing for the command of the division and, incidentally, to learn its destination. He learned that his division was being concentrated at Nancy for a period of training to absorb new replacements. Next day he drove on to Nancy.

Roosevelt Visits "His" Marines

Lejeune found Nancy to be a miniature Paris. Billeting for both officers and men was more comfortable than anything they had previously experienced. A highlight of the short stay at Nancy was a visit by Assistant Secretary of the Navy Franklin Roosevelt. With great things happening in France, Roosevelt had badgered Daniels for permission to go to Europe to help Admiral Sims with the "business end" of things. "Uncle Joe" Daniels was becoming increasingly distrustful of FDR's personal loyalty, but finally, on July 1, he gave him permission to go.

FDR boarded the new destroyer USS *Dyer* in New York on July 9. Accompanying him was his chief of staff, Capt. Edward McCawley Jr., USN, and his Marine orderly, Sgt. W. W. Stratton. The rest of his party would follow on the British transport *Olympia*. For the voyage FDR adopted a quasi-uniform of flannel shirt, leather coat, and khaki riding breeches.

The *Dyer* eased through the narrow entrance into Portsmouth on July 21. Admiral Sims met FDR on the pier. They motored in a Rolls Royce to London, where FDR was put up in a magnificent suite at the Ritz as a guest of the Admiralty. Roosevelt learned about Soissons and wrote home, "One of my Marine Regiments has lost 1200 and another 800 men."

On July 29, King George V received Roosevelt at Buckingham Palace. FDR thought the king had a nice smile. That evening, at dinner at Gray's Inn, he met Winston Churchill, then the minister of munitions, for the first time and found him rather overbearing. Next day there was a call on the prime minister, David Lloyd George, and dinner that evening at the House of Commons, where the foreign secretary, Arthur Balfour, told him that everyone knew that it was the U.S. Marines who had stopped the Germans at Chateau-Thierry. The British wanted him to go to Italy to press for a unified naval command in the Mediterranean. He found time to do some shopping, discovering that his favorite silk pajamas had gone up in price from thirty to sixty shillings.

Roosevelt set out from Dover on July 31 in a British destroyer for Dunkirk. French limousines whisked him and his party to Paris. He stopped on the way to change his destroyer costume to leather puttees and a gray tweed jacket. In Paris there were wonderful rooms in the Hotel Crillon and successive meetings with Marshal Joffre, President Poincare, and Premier Clemenceau, with time in the evening for the Folies Bergères.

Roosevelt and his party finally left for the front on August 4. FDR insisted on walking part way into Belleau Wood, where he saw the debris of war. Next day he visited the Marine brigade, inspecting a battalion of the 5th Marines in a village near Nancy. It was easy to tell the replacements, in their forest-green uniforms, from the veterans, in their army olive drab. It disturbed him that "his" Marines were for the most part indistinguishable from army troops. General Lejeune suggested that the Marine eagle-globe-and-anchor emblem could be worn on the "choke" collars of their uniform coats. FDR immediately granted Lejeune authority to do so.

Lejeune gave Roosevelt a dinner, attended by his brigadiers and senior colonels, at the Café de Paris in Nancy. Roosevelt remained overnight in Lejeune's headquarters, going on the next day to see Verdun.

The dinner at the Café de Paris also celebrated Lejeune's promotion to major general. Two days earlier a message had arrived from the War Department informing Lejeune that President Wilson had approved his promotion, effective immediately. A parallel message confirmed the promotion of Neville to brigadier general. Logan Feland was promoted to colonel and stayed in command of the 5th Regiment.

Into the Lines at Marbache

Both the 1st and 2d divisions had been assigned to the French Eighth Army. Tactical control rested with the French XXXII Corps.

On August 4, General Gerard, the Eighth Army commander, met with the corps and division commanders at 2d Division headquarters. He acknowledged that the 1st and 2d divisions needed rest and recuperation after their strenuous efforts but declared that it was now necessary to relieve two French divisions on the line in front of them. He promised that the stay in the line would be brief.

Major General Passaga, commanding the XXXII Corps and described by Leje-une as "a noble old Roman," had three divisions on line. The 2d Division would be on the right, relieving the French 64th Division.

By the following morning the 2d Division was on the march again, destination the Marbache sector, named for the dismal little town of Marbache. The sector, with a frontage of about twelve kilometers, was on the south face of the St. Mihiel salient. The front here was very quiet, and the subsectors were both broad and deep. Rather than a continuous line there was a chain of small combat groups, roughly arranged into two belts. Marbache lay six kilometers to the rear. The relief of the 64th Division began the night of August 5/6.

The Moselle River ran through the Marbache sector. Lejeune assigned the 4th Brigade the left half of the sector, generally lying in the valley of the Moselle. The brigade line extended about 3.2 kilometers east and west of a point just north of Pont-à-Mousson, the 5th Marines on the east bank of the river, the 6th Marines on the west. Connecting the two regiments was a heavily camouflaged stone bridge at Pont-à-Mousson. The French said the Germans had not blown up the bridge because they expected to use it some day.

Neville placed the 2d Battalion of each regiment in the frontline trenches. As usual, machine-gun companies were attached to each infantry battalion. From the high ground to the rear, Marines with field glasses could see the spires of Metz, the old Roman stronghold, twenty-four kilometers away across the Lorraine countryside.

The relieving units, as was always done, moved into the lines at night. To pre-serve secrecy further, French telephone operators stayed at their posts. No talking in English on the telephones was permitted, and in particular, use of the word "American," or *"Americain,"* was strictly prohibited.

Wise's 2d Battalion, 5th Regiment, after a two-day foot march, entered the lines at Pont-à-Mousson the night of August 7, relieving the French 340th Infan-try. Wise took a house in the middle of the town for his battalion headquarters. Although the German lines were only a few kilometers away, the town had not been heavily shelled. There had been no real fighting there since 1915. On the morning following the relief, Wise walked his front line. He did not like the look of the barbed wire. It was old and rusty, and half of it was down. He sent out patrols that night to test the wire.

Some of the less seriously wounded casualties from Soissons returned to the 4th Brigade at Marbache. Attendants at the Nantes hospital had syringed blood clots out of Lt. Graves Erskine's ears, restoring his hearing. After a week or so rest he rejoined the 2d Battalion, 6th Marines, and once again had the 2d Platoon, 79th Company. He learned that Holcomb was now the regimental "exec" and that "Bull" (which is what the new Marines made out of "Bolo") Williams had the battalion.

Three companies of the Williams' battalion relieved the French in the front lines west of the river at Pont-à-Mousson. The 80th Company, Sergeant Paradis' old outfit, was held in reserve about a quarter of mile to the rear in an old factory building. Paradis himself was still at battalion headquarters as a runner. He disliked his new battalion commander intensely, considering him a drunk. Williams on the two-day march had ridden his horse at a pace that in the heat had caused many of the marchers to fall out.

Williams set up his battalion headquarters in an old chateau about two hundred meters behind the frontline trenches. The chateau had a beautiful garden laden with ripened vegetables and fruit. Paradis and the other enlisted men of the headquarters feasted on fried potato pancakes, big blue gooseberries, red and black currants, and dead-ripe yellow plums.

General Passaga offered a prize of two hundred francs for each German prisoner taken. He warned that the Germans invariably raided a particular section of the front within a few days of a new division taking over the sector. The raid was a kind of graduation exercise for "storm troops" being trained at Metz. The Germans did precisely what Passaga predicted.[3]

About 2 AM on August 9, Wise's wire party came back through the lines to report that a large column of Germans was approaching. To blow gaps in the wire, the Germans carried "Bangalore torpedoes"—long lead pipes filled with explosive. One of these exploded prematurely, killing or wounding several of the Germans. This commotion set off machine-gun and artillery fire on both sides that went on for about an hour. The German patrol leader called down a box barrage, some rounds of which hit his own men. One Marine was killed and seven wounded. A storehouse holding grenades and pyrotechnics in the 18th Company's area blew up. After the barrage stopped, 2d Battalion sent out a patrol that brought in two prisoners, one badly wounded by the explosion of the lead pipe.

Wise slept through it all. His adjutant finally got him up at about daybreak, and he went forward to see what had happened. The wounded German died. The unwounded prisoner said under interrogation that there had been about 125 Germans in the raiding party.

General Passaga was elated. He came to the front immediately to deliver the prize money. He told Wise how pleased he was and gave him a whiskery kiss on both cheeks. He presented Wise with four hundred francs, two hundred for each prisoner, including the one who died, and there were promises of medals. The money went into the companies' mess fund.

Sergeant Paradis was standing watch on a wooden platform high in a pine tree at the 2d Battalion, 6th Regiment's PC, when the raid came against the 5th Marines across the river. He had a good view of the pyrotechnics. A scout from the battalion intelligence section was caught out between the lines during the barrage. He waited until morning to come back in, bringing with him a cup of honey he had extracted from a beehive. Strained through a piece of window curtain to get out the dirt, it went well with the potato pancakes.

Lejeune took command of the Marbache sector at 8 AM on August 9. This time the now battle-wise Marines allowed a quiet sector to remain quiet. The only combat other than the German raiding party's mishaps on the ninth amounted to desultory artillery exchanges and active patrolling. Twenty-five percent of the Marines in the reserve battalions were allowed liberty in Nancy. Meanwhile, the veterans taught the new men the niceties of trench warfare, such as the making of "trench doughnuts" by frying hardtack or bread in bacon grease in half of a mess tin over a flame of burning candle wax and sprinkling the hot delicacy with sugar. Hand grenades thrown into the river would bring stunned fish to the surface, so there were some fine fish dinners.

"It was a *bon* sector in every sense of the word," said Paradis, who before the war had been an inspector with the Detroit Gas Company, "We even had electric lights in the building."

When not on duty, the Marines spent their time swimming in the Moselle, eating, writing home, playing cards, shooting craps, and "reading" shirts and underclothing for lice. The wingless, parasitic little insects seemed to congregate the most along the seams, under the arms, and around the neckband. Bets were made on who could pick off the most "cooties." A Philadelphia Irishman named Burke nearly always won the bet.

Julius Turrill was promoted to lieutenant colonel and became second in command of the 5th Marines under Col. Logan Feland. Capt. Raymond F. Dirksen took temporary command of the 1st Battalion, 5th Regiment, until being relieved by Lt. Col. Arthur J. Leary on August 24.

A flurry of congressmen making up the House Committee on Naval Affairs visited Lejeune at Marbache. Of incomparably greater interest to the troops, Elsie Janis, the celebrated entertainer, stopped by to do a show. Elsie was a musical comedy star of considerable renown on Broadway and in London. Billed as "The Sweetheart of the AEF," she was the first popular American star to entertain U.S. troops close to the front lines. Closely chaperoned by her mother, she sang, she danced, she acted, she told stories, and she closed by doing a succession of handsprings.

Following treatment for his wounds sustained at Belleau Wood in Paris, 1st Lt. Lemuel Shepherd was sent to a convalescent hospital at Biarritz. Discharged in August, he returned to the 5th Marines to rejoin the 55th Company.

Training New Replacements

The quiet spell in the Marbache sector lasted only ten days. A telegram received by Lejeune from IV Corps two days after he moved into Marbache informed him that the 82d Division would relieve his 2d Division commencing August 15.

On the night of August 17/18, Wise's 2d Battalion, 5th Regiment, was relieved by a battalion of the 327th Infantry and marched to the Bois de l'Eveque. The march completed Wise's command of the 2d Battalion. Maj. Harold L. Parsons relieved him the next day.

Wise learned that he had been a "bird" colonel since the first of July. There was already a sufficiency of colonels in the Marine brigade, and he was ordered to the army's 4th Division. Maj. Gen. John L. Hines, who would live to be a hundred years old, was Wise's new division commander. He gave Wise the 59th Infantry Regiment. Wise found his regiment in the same Montgirmont–Les Esparges sector where his Marine battalion had served in the spring.

By August 19 the 2d Division had moved back to a training area made available by the French, centered on Colombey-les-Belles and the Bois de l'Eveque, south of Toul and Nancy. On leaving the line the 2d Division passed from the French Eighth Army to the new American First Army, headquartered at Neauchateau and under Pershing's personal command.

A replacement battalion of a thousand Marines was waiting for the Marine brigade, but even with this reinforcement Buck Neville found himself short some 2,500 men. AEF headquarters offered Lejeune army replacements to fill out his ranks. Lejeune believed this would be disastrous to morale and efficiency. He wrote his friend Harbord asking that all Marines presently serving with the Service of Supply be culled out and sent to the brigade. Harbord responded with alacrity and soon, in Lejeune's words, "every variety of Marine came home!" This brought the brigade up almost to strength.

A period of intensive training followed. Each battalion had full use of the firing ranges before returning to its regimental area. A division-sized attack simulation topped off the training.

About this time the division adopted the star-and-Indian-head insignia, working out a logical scheme wherein each regiment, battalion, and separate detachment had a color-coded background for the profiled Indian. The troops began calling their division commander, Lejeune, the "Old Indian."

The Bois de l'Eveque boasted a good-sized maneuver ground. Lejeune arranged for a parade and review—with detachments from all division units, some five thousand troops, on the field—for ten o'clock on Sunday, August 25. There was a certain apprehension that so many troops drawn up in close formation on an open field might attract inquisitive German aircraft. Extra antiaircraft precautions were taken. Maj. Gens. Hunter Liggett and John T. Dickman, commanders of the I and IV Corps, respectively, were the reviewing officers. Some seventy-five personal decorations were awarded, a mix of Distinguished Service Crosses, Medailles Militaires, and Croix de Guerre, with General Liggett, as Pershing's designated representative, doing the pinning. Col. Preston Brown was promoted to brigadier general but would stay with the division for the time being as Lejeune's chief of staff.

It was a clear bright day, and a German airplane came overhead. The pilot circled down to take a closer look. Puffs of white smoke from bursting antiaircraft shells blossomed around the plane. Suddenly it crumpled and crashed a mile away. Lejeune took the downed airplane as a good omen. Orders for the march to the front came the next day.

St. Mihiel

Once again the great armies began positioning themselves for a new campaign along the western front. Long convoys of troop-laden camions and horse-drawn artillery clogged the roads. Reconnaissance aircraft banked and wheeled over the German salients.

On August 27 General Pershing assigned the 2d Division to the American I Corps, commanded by Lejeune's friend, Maj. Gen. Hunter Liggett.

The American First Army was going into the line opposite the St. Mihiel salient, between the French Second and Eighth armies. To it were assigned three American and one French corps, for a total of fifteen American divisions and four French divisions. Two American corps would attack the south face of the salient and one corps the west face, for an active front of about eighty kilometers. The movement of so many divisions inevitably attracted the attention of the Germans. The salient was held by army Detachment C, commanded by General von Fuchs, a total of about twelve divisions organized into three corps.

The Marines had reason to remember the St. Mihiel salient from their baptism in trench warfare in the spring of 1918 in the Toulon sector, south of Verdun.

By the end of August the whole German line was falling back. The Germans had already pulled out of the Marne salient, and on the rest of the western front British and French attacks were making progress. The German high command appeared to be preparing for a final stand along the Antwerp–Meuse line, the last line in front of the border. On the German right flank, essentially the British front, some ninety-six kilometers separated the present front lines from the final line, and the successive defensive lines through which the Germans would fall back were well separated. To the southeast, on the German left flank, the distance to the rear was scarcely twenty-four kilometers and the defense lines were close together. Two railway systems served the German front. The one in the north ran through Liege, the one in the south through Luxembourg and Metz. A lateral railroad connecting these two systems ran through Sedan and Mezieres. If this lateral link could be broken, the German armies would be cut in two.

Ferdinand Foch, newly promoted to the proud title of "marshal," visited General Pershing on August 30, 1918. The main offensive, as outlined by the marshal, would drive in the general direction of Mezieres, the key point of German lateral communications, and would consist of two attacks. The first attack, to be delivered as soon as possible by the French Second Army reinforced by four to six American divisions, would be between the Meuse River and the Argonne Forest. The second attack, to be launched a few days after the first, would be from the Argonne, with an American army on the right astride the Aisne River and the French Fourth Army on the left.

Pershing concurred in general but suggested certain changes. He did not like the proposed scattering of American troops. He wanted the offensive between the

Meuse and Argonne to be totally American, with the French taking the front west of the Argonne. Foch demurred: so large an American army would be deficient in artillery, aircraft, and services of all kinds, which would have to be supplied by the French. Pershing politely suggested that the imbalance of arms in the AEF was a consequence of British and French insistence that American infantry be brought to France at the cost of everything else. Pershing also reminded Foch that the planning by his headquarters, temporarily interrupted by the German spring and summer offensives, had been focused on the prospect of a Lorraine offensive leading into Germany's vital areas, an approach tried by the French in 1914 and abandoned thereafter. Now neither the British nor the French had the men for such operations. All American supply and transportation plans had been predicated on the premise that the American portion of the western front would eventually extend from the Meuse to the Swiss border.

Foch yielded to Pershing's arguments, and on September 2 Petain and Pershing met at Foch's headquarters to come to final decisions. In these discussions, St. Mihiel was designated as "Operation A," the Meuse–Argonne as "Operation B." The attacks of the French Fourth and Fifth armies to the left or west of these were "Operation C" and "Operation D," respectively. All four operations would come under the direction of Petain as general commanding the Armies of the North and Northeast. Pershing accepted the decision that St. Mihiel would be limited in scope and only a preliminary to the main offensive.

The German high command knew the offensive against St. Mihiel was coming and had debated the advisability of withdrawing from the salient to what it called the Michel position, a part of the so-called Hindenburg Line. It decided to hold but did reposition its forces for a more elastic defense.

Field Orders

First Army issued its field orders for the St. Mihiel offensive on September 7. Pershing's plan was for the I and IV corps to make the main attack going north from a line running west from Pont-à-Mousson, while the V Corps attacked southeast against the western face of the salient. The French II Colonial Corps would essentially hold at the apex of the salient outside St. Mihiel itself. This giant converging attack would "pinch off" the salient. The attack, planned in minute detail, would begin with a four-hour bombardment of great ferocity. Liggett's I Corps was on the extreme right of the American line. Its neighbor to the east was the French Eighth Army. To the left, or west, was the U.S. IV Corps.

Liggett issued I Corps' field orders on September 8. From left to right, his divisions were the 2d, 5th, 90th, and 82d. The corps in its attack would pivot on the 90th Division and advance toward Thiaucourt. The 2d Division was given the mission of taking Thiaucourt itself and a collateral mission of helping IV Corps, on its left, by reducing the Bois d'Euvezin and the Bois du Beau Vallon. (The map

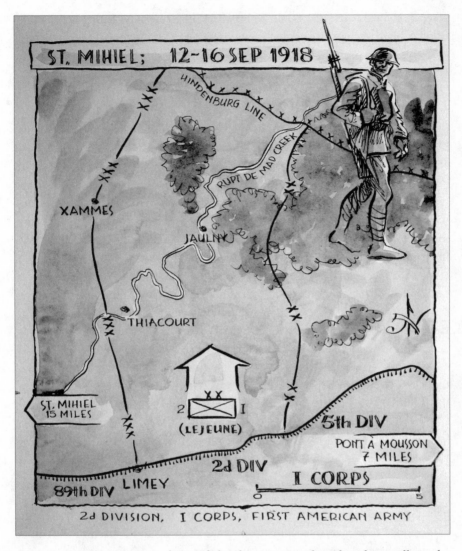

showed that the terrain in front of the division was dotted with woodlots, the familiar *"bois,"* bringing chilling memories, no doubt, of Belleau Wood, fought three months earlier.)

The 2d Division was to attack on a 2.4-kilometer front, bounded by Remenau-ville on the east and Limey on the west, at the start and widening out to about 3.2 kilometers. The ground was rolling and partially wooded. Thiaucourt, the major objective, was about 6.4 kilometers distant.

Lejeune submitted his tentative plan of attack to Liggett later on the eighth. Final orders were issued on the tenth. First Army had set the time of attack at 5 AM, September 12. In the 2d Division zone of action, the first phase line for the first day was at the Bois de Heiche, about at the German divisional reserve line. The second phase line for the first day would be between Thiaucourt and Jaulny, crossing the Rupt de Mad, a minor stream that went slantwise across the zone. The second day's objective was to push the left of the line up to Xammes and continue forward to the Hindenburg Line from Rembercourt to Charey.

Approaching Zero Hour

John Lejeune's 2d Division began its march to the front on September 1, staging through Francheville, about sixteen kilometers south of Limey. General Liggett already had his 82d and 90th divisions in line. Marching, as usual, was at night, with billeting in woods by day. All troops were in their assembly positions to the rear of the lines at Limey by the fifth. Here they received very complete orders, maps, and intelligence data for St. Mihiel, a welcome improvement over the last-minute confusion that had prevailed at Belleau Wood and Soissons. General Pershing paid them a visit on the morning of the seventh.

As the leftmost division of I Corps, the 2d Division would be in the center of main attack. Its neighbor across the corps boundary would be the 89th Division of the IV Corps. The 2d Division, somewhat overstrength at 1,030 officers and about twenty-six thousand enlisted, began to move into the lines on the following day, September 8, wedging its way between the 89th and 90th divisions.

On the German side of the line, the 77th Reserve Division (General Adams) of the "Gorz Group," or 57th Provisional Corps (General von Hartz), held the front, the regiments, west to east, being the 257th, 419th, and 232d. The 77th Division, in addition to the general support provided by corps and army artillery in the region, had its own nine batteries of light artillery and eight batteries of heavy artillery. However, it was weak in infantry, with only about five hundred effectives in each of its battalions.

Liggett reinforced Lejeune for the offensive by the attachment of forty-five light tanks and eighteen medium tanks. The medium tanks were to breach the barbed-wire entanglements while the light tanks engaged the machine-gun nests, a formula that had worked quite well at Soissons.

Lejeune issued his completed attack order on September 10. The division would attack in a well-practiced formation: column of brigades, with regiments abreast and battalions in column. Robert E. Lee and Ulysses S. Grant would have found this formation familiar, particularly Grant. The 3d Infantry Brigade would lead the assault, the 23d and 9th infantry abreast, with their battalions in column. The 4th Marine Brigade would follow, the 6th Marines on the left behind the 23d Infantry and the 5th Marines on the right, on the heels of the 9th Infantry. Lejeune ordered Neville to assign one battalion of Marines temporarily to the 3d Brigade to relieve the outpost line. Neville assigned this mission to the 2d Battalion, 5th Marines, now commanded by Maj. Robert E. Messersmith.

The dark-haired, youthful-appearing Messersmith was a veteran of all the brigade's actions. Born in Berks County, Pennsylvania, in 1885, he had been briefly a cadet in the Revenue Cutter Service (which was to merge with the Lifesaving Service in 1915 to form the Coast Guard) before being commissioned in the Marine Corps in 1909. His service had been the usual mix of barracks duty, sea duty, and expeditionary service that had taken him to Cuba, Panama, and Nicaragua, the last including the fighting at Coyotepe and Barranca. He had arrived as a captain in Quantico in July 1917, in time to take command of the 78th Company, 2d Battalion, 6th Marines. Commanding that company at Belleau Wood, he had been gassed in action. After a month of hospitalization and convalescence he had come back to the brigade in time to lead his company at Soissons. Near Vierzy he was wounded to the rear of his left ear seriously enough to cause another month's hospitalization. He returned to the 6th Regiment while the brigade was in the Marbache sector and was transferred on August 19 to the 5th Regiment as second in command of the 2d Battalion. A promotion to major followed days later, and on September 11 he assumed command of the battalion. His future, if he could survive, seemed bright.

Major Messersmith's last-minute assumption of command meant that five of Neville's six infantry battalion commanders would be leading troops in combat at that level for the first time at St. Mihiel. Berton Sibley, still commanding the 3d Battalion, 6th Regiment, represented the senior surviving troop commander from Belleau Wood and Soissons.

A trickle of "Old Corps" veterans wounded in the opening round at Belleau Wood returned from convalescence just in time for the St. Mihiel campaign. Marine gunner James Gallivan, carrying a cane—for use and not just for show—returned to duty with the 2d Battalion, 5th Marines, on September 10. After being hit at Les Mares Farm he had been evacuated to Base Hospital no. 34 and then, on July 28, had been sent on to the convalescent camp at Blois. Here he had passed the time teaching the niceties of guarding German prisoners to newly arrived soldiers. He found his longtime friend and nemesis Wise gone from the battalion, but Messersmith was an old acquaintance.

With some justification the younger survivors of Belleau Wood and Soissons began to consider themselves "Old Corps" veterans in their own right. Displaying more patience than scorn, they had helped train the hundreds of replacements who had joined the brigade at Colombey-les-Belles. Pvt. 1st Class James Hatcher of the 84th Company tried to set a strong example to the replacements waiting in the trenches to begin the assault on Thiaucourt. A cold rain "made bad matters worse," he wrote. "We were soaked to the skin and half frozen as the first streaks of light began to break through . . . but that was the zero hour and so 'over we went.'"

When the 96th Company went into the line at St. Mihiel, Lt. Clifton Cates was left behind. Orders had been received to leave 20 percent of the officers and men in the rear as a nucleus for rebuilding the companies if casualties were heavy. Capt. Wethered Woodworth, having returned to duty from his Soissons wound, decided the men who had done the most fighting would be the ones left behind.

The German 77th Reserve Division in front of the 2d Division had been in position for a number of weeks. Its leading edge was a line thinly held by two battalions of the 419th Infantry.

"The intelligence maps of the Boche lines were wonderful," wrote Maj. Tony Waller, still commanding the brigade's 6th Machine Gun Battalion. "We knew the location of every P.C., dressing station, tank trap, dump, machine gun position, artillery position, etc.; how he made his relief and by what routes; therefore, we could estimate how he would retreat."

Each attacking battalion was to advance on a two-company front with a machine-gun company attached and two companies in support. The Stokes mortars and 37-mm guns from regimental headquarters would move with the lead battalions.

The 9th Infantry, on the right, led off with its 3d Battalion, now commanded by Maj. Robert Denig of the Marines. Feland's 5th Marines was to follow the 9th in column of battalions: 3d Battalion (Shearer) and 1st Battalion (O'Leary) and, finally, 2d Battalion (Messersmith) falling in as the advance passed through the outpost line.

The 23d Infantry, with the 1st Battalion, 6th Marines (Barker), attached, was to attack on the left. Barker's mission was to maintain contact with the 89th Division across the I/IV Corps boundary. Lee's 6th Regiment would follow the 23d, with the 3d Battalion (Sibley) in front and 2d Battalion (Williams) in support.

A machine-gun barrage would be fired by the 4th and 6th machine gun battalions, after which the machine-gun battalions would revert to their respective brigades. Engineer detachments had been parceled out to artillery and leading infantry battalions. Eighteen aircraft and two balloons had been assigned the division. The 3d Brigade would have attached a gas and flame company, in addition to the company of medium tanks and two companies of light tanks. The 4th Brigade, following along behind, had a company of light tanks attached. The division's artillery brigade had been reinforced up to a total of thirty batteries of 75-mm guns, three batteries of 105-mm howitzers, fifteen batteries of 155-mm howitzers, four batteries of 120-mm guns, and three batteries of long-range 155-mm guns. The heavy batteries would fire a four-hour preparation. At five o'clock the light batteries would begin a rolling barrage, moving the impact forward one hundred meters every four minutes to the first phase line, which was to be reached in a little more than three hours. Beyond the first phase line a standing barrage would be fired until eleven o'clock.

On the night before the assault the machine-gun companies, moving to the front by mule cart, took over prepared battery positions for the barrage, each company manning three batteries of four guns each. The machine guns were to open with overhead fire at H-hour and continue until the infantry entered the danger zone of their fire. Then they were to pack up, and the companies were to join up with their assigned infantry battalions.

H-hour was 5 AM, Thursday morning, September 12, 1918. It promised to be quite a morning. The overnight rain continued.

Over the Top at St. Mihiel

The Germans knew they were coming. The concentration of troops had been observed, and there were reports, sent through Switzerland, from secret agents. On September 7 General von Fuchs briefly contemplated the possibility of a spoiling attack to the south to break up the American concentrations but decided such an attack was infeasible. Instead he sought approval of Imperial Headquarters for a deliberate withdrawal. That was approved, with the caveat that the outpost line be held as long as possible. Accordingly, von Fuchs planned to deepen his outpost line but to draw his main line of resistance back to the artillery protective line. These dispositions were to be completed by 3 AM on the twelfth.

Major Nauman, commanding the 419th Infantry, issued oral orders to his battalions at about 6:30 PM on the eleventh. His outposts, well supplied with machine guns, would stay in place. He would thicken their line by having his 2d and 3d battalions, each reinforced by one company from his reserve battalion, move to the forward edge of the woods, which was well protected with wire. This would leave his reserve battalion with just its machine-gun company and one rifle company. The machine-gun company was given supporting-fire missions. The rifle company would be Nauman's meager regimental reserve.

Nauman's battalions were in motion deepening the outpost line when the thunderous American artillery preparation came down on them at 1 AM on the twelfth. It was raining heavily. Artillery preparations always seemed to bring on rain. Nauman's frontline battalions seemed to dissolve into nothingness. Only a few stragglers got back to him, and on the following day he could collect only about three hundred of his men.

Waller's 6th Machine Gun Battalion fired its part of the initial barrage, its overhead fires going on for forty or fifty minutes. Each company expended about fifteen thousand rounds, firing at a rate of one strip of twenty-five rounds per minute so the guns would not overheat.

For the jump-off, the 3d Brigade was in an old trench position north of the Limey–Pont-à-Mousson road. The 4th Brigade was south of the road, also in old trenches. The German counterbarrage was ineffectual. The lead companies moved out in four waves at fifty-yard intervals. The first two waves were lines of skirmishers spaced at five-to-ten-yard intervals between men. The remaining waves were lines of sections in column, followed by machine guns, mortars, and 1-pounders. Support companies followed at two hundred meters, support battalions at five hundred meters.

The Germans were far from at their best that morning. Barbed wire and torn-up ground caused the Americans more delays than enemy fire. The advance went through the main line of resistance and reached the first phase line at about ten o'clock, an hour ahead of schedule.

Further advance had to await the lifting of the standing barrage at 11 AM. From here forward was the territory of the 257th Reserve Infantry (Lieutenant Colonel Hann). Hann's regiment was swept away. He attempted to make a stand on a ridge south of Thiaucourt but could not collect enough men, so he went on back through Xammes to the Michel position, his regiment down to 250 men.

After the standing barrage lifted, the doughboys of the 23d Infantry went through Thiaucourt just before noon and moved on to establish a defensive line about 1,500 meters to the north of the town. The 23d then pushed patrols on to Jaulny and Xammes. The 9th Infantry was equally successful. In fact, the 3d Brigade regulars assaulted so effectively that by 1 PM they had seized all of the division's objectives for the day without any need to commit the Marine brigade. Barker's battalion was released from the 23d's control and rejoined the 6th Regiment near Thiaucourt.

General von Hartz had two divisions, the 31st and the 123d Saxon, in corps reserve. At dawn he had started them forward to be in position for a counterattack. The attack of the Saxons hit the U.S. 5th Division on the 2d Division's right. The 31st came at the 2d Division on both sides of Jaulny but did poorly. By noon von Fuchs knew that the Gorz Group was finished, and he ordered a general retirement to be covered by the Mihiel Group, or XII Reserve Corps. One Marine machine-gun platoon commander with two guns caught a German column, about a hundred men, in enfilade and virtually annihilated it.

The American advance paused to allow its artillery to displace forward. Only one good road ran from Regnieville to Thiaucourt, and it had to be used by both the 2d and 5th divisions. Major Williams' 2d Battalion, 6th Marines, received orders at 6:50 PM to move up on the left flank of the 23d Infantry.

The frontline battalions of the Mihiel Group stayed in position until dark and then withdrew. The night was generally quiet. The 2d Division's front line ran along a general east–west line north of Thiaucourt. When morning came the 31st Division was opposite the 2d Division in what the Germans still called the "Flirey sector," although Flirey was now eleven kilometers behind the American lines. When morning came the 23d Infantry occupied the villages of Xammes and Jaulny without difficulty.

Nothing much happened on the 2d Division front on the thirteenth, but early in the day strong detachments from the IV and V corps met at Vigneulles, effectively sealing off the salient. The moment itself proved anticlimactic, yet for generations to come the U.S. Army schools at Forts Benning and Leavenworth would teach the St. Mihiel operation as the classic example of "pinching" off a salient by attacking its shoulders.

The Marines Take the Lead

During the afternoon of September 13, Lejeune ordered the 4th Brigade to relieve the 3d. Neville's brigade moved up under cover of darkness, taking over from the doughboys, battalion by battalion. The 5th Marines relieved the 9th Infantry and the 6th Marines the 23d. Command of the sector passed at midnight, with brigade headquarters established at Thiaucourt.

In the early morning of the fourteenth, Neville ordered the 5th Marines to run an outpost line from the northern end of the Bois de Hailbat to the northeast corner of the Bois de la Montagne, and the 6th Marines in turn to outpost the line from the edge of the Bois de la Montagne to the northern edge of a wood lying between Xammes and Charey. This was followed in the afternoon by division ordering the brigade to send out strong patrols toward the general line Rembercourt–Charey to feel out the German main line of resistance. The 5th Marines accordingly sent out three patrols. Then at 4:30 PM division caused considerable confusion by ordering both the 5th and 6th regiments to send out two companies in a reconnaissance to begin at 5 PM.

In the 5th Marines' zone, the 45th Company, 3d Battalion, reconnoitered the Bois de Hailbat and the 47th Company the Bois de Rupt. The two companies spent the night in the woods, with the 47th Company maintaining contact with the 6th Marines on its left.

Things went less smoothly in the 6th Marines' zone. The 82d and 83d companies of Sibley's 3d Battalion had taken over the regiment's front lines during the day. At 5:40 PM the 3d Battalion was ordered to advance. This crosscut the orders Major Barker's 1st Battalion had received to send out two companies in deep reconnaissance. At 11:40 PM, Sibley reported he was rotating his assault and support companies, an intricate passage of lines in its own right. About this time the two companies from Barker's battalion passed through their position on their way to outposting the Bois de la Montagne.

The confusion could have had costly consequences, but no German counterattacks occurred, and by midnight Sibley's battalion was east of Xammes and astride the Thiaucourt–Clarey road and Barker's two companies held good positions within the Bois de la Montagne. In the morning Barker moved his remaining two companies forward into the woods.

To extend the line of Barker's battalion, Colonel Lee ordered Major Williams' 2d Battalion, 6th Marines, to reconnoiter the woods farther to the west, expecting to find them devoid of Germans. Instead, they ran into about forty Germans, who fled upon being fired on. The battalion sergeant major, German-born William Ulrich (later major, USMC), ran after them and in German persuaded them to surrender.

The battalion continued forward and next encountered entrenched Germans determined to fight it out. Williams attacked and got to the northern edge of the woods. A composite regiment made up of the remnants of the German 10th Division tried three or four halfhearted counterattacks but failed to budge the Marines.

The Germans executed a skillful retreat, pulling back to the Hindenburg Line under cover of their heavy artillery and dedicated pockets of Maxim machine gunners. Marine casualties mounted. Lt. Graves Erskine went down hard in one of the residual fights beyond the Rupt de Mad creek. A nearby Marine private carried the hard-luck Erskine to safety on his back.

When the fighting subsided, Lejeune ordered the 20 percent of each company that had been left behind to rebuild the roads leading across no-man's-land. One of the working parties was Cates and his fifty stay-behinds from the 96th Company. He found stone to fill the roadbeds in a ruined village. When he learned that Captain Woodworth had been shot through the chest, Cates begged Lieutenant Colonel Holcomb, the 6th Regiment's second in command, to send him forward to take over the company. Holcomb demurred for the moment.

The U.S. 78th Division began relieving Lejeune's 2d Division during the night of September 15/16. The 155th Brigade took over the front line from the 4th Brigade. The 309th Infantry relieved the 5th Marines and the 310th Infantry the 6th Marines. With command passed at 10 AM on the sixteenth, the 2d Division started its march to the Ansauville area, twenty-four kilometers to the rear.

The 2d Division at St. Mihiel had taken 118 guns and about 3,300 prisoners, most of them by the 3d Brigade on the first day. In western-front terms, casualties had been light. The division's own losses were 195 killed, 1,041 wounded, 23 gassed, and 292 missing, for a total of 1,552. Of these the Marine brigade lost 132 killed and dead of wounds, 574 wounded in action.

An Early Autumn

For the Marines, St. Mihiel was a subdued yet confusing battle in which they sustained over seven hundred casualties without the opportunity to make major contributions to the outcome. Most men in the ranks had to wait until they read the next edition of *Stars and Stripes* to learn they had been participants in a stirring American victory that had erased a major, four-year-old German salient and forced the *Boche* to retreat behind their vaunted Hindenburg Line.

For five days after coming out of the lines the 6th Regiment was bivouacked in a woods. It rained most of the time, and the weather was cold and miserable. Yet the secure bivouac had its endearing moments. Private Hatcher recalled his arrival at the site after an all-night march from Thiaucourt. "We found our rolling kitchens and a hot breakfast awaiting," he wrote. "After breakfast I lay down on the long grass in a small clearing to rest. Everything seemed very quiet and restful there."

Clifton Cates, expecting his captaincy momentarily and having finally convinced Holcomb to restore his Soissons command, once again had command of the 96th Company, with six new second lieutenants. Cates wrote to his sister on September 25 that while they were at the front a sentry had challenged a man who had forgotten the password—the sentry had him whistle the "Marines' Hymn" before he would let him pass.

At Ansauville, Lejeune's veteran chief of staff, Brig. Gen. Preston Brown, USA, was detached and his place taken by Col. James C. Rhea, USA. After the division was fully assembled it marched farther to the rear to Toul, where Lejeune opened his headquarters on September 21.

It was the week of the autumn equinox, and there was already a chill in the air. The frequent rains had increased the vulnerability of many men to the rapidly spreading Spanish influenza epidemic. Hundreds of Marines would be stricken in the coming weeks.

The war rolled on. Ahead of the brigade loomed something much tougher than the St. Mihiel salient.

CHAPTER TWELVE

Blanc Mont

Gen. Hunter Liggett, commander of the I Corps, told General Lejeune most confidentially after the battle at St. Mihiel that Foch and Petain planned a great offensive for the latter part of September between the Meuse and Suippes rivers by the American First Army and the French Fourth Army.[1] Liggett said that the 2d Division would be badly missed on D-day of the big attack.

Lejeune had no way of knowing it, but employment for the 2d Division was already planned for elsewhere. On September 16, Petain asked Pershing for three divisions for use in the Fourth Army attack. Pershing offered him two: the veteran 2d Division and the newly arrived 36th Division, which still lacked artillery, engineers, and most of its transport and service support.

After the successful affair in the St. Mihiel salient, the 4th Brigade had marched on September 20 to a rest area south of Toul. Three days later Lejeune received orders from First Army headquarters to move the division by rail to an unnamed destination about ten hours distant, the move to begin on September 25 and to be completed by the twenty-eighth.

Even as St. Mihiel was being fought, planning proceeded for the American First Army attack on the front lying between the Meuse River and the Argonne Forest. This, in concert with an attack by the French Fourth Army west of the Argonne, was aimed at driving the Germans back from the rail lines that converged near the town of Mezieres. If successful this operation would put in peril all German armies between the Argonne and the North Sea.

The American First and the French Fourth Army were to attack simultaneously

196

on September 26. The First Army was to have three corps headquarters, with nine divisions in the attack and six in reserve. The III Corps (Bullard) was on the Vesle, and the I Corps (Liggett) and V Corps (Cameron) were involved in St. Mihiel.

Lejeune left Toul early on the morning of the twenty-fifth and learned that his new division headquarters would be at Marie-sur-Marne, near Chalons. He found it an imposing stone chateau, which once had been occupied by King James II in his exile from England (and whose face looked out sternly from a portrait), but the chateau, historically significant though it might be, had no bathroom. The French billeting officer advised him that Gen. Henri Gouraud, commanding general of the French Fourth Army, wished to see him at his Chalons headquarters.

Lejeune reported to Gouraud as directed and found this celebrated hero of Gallipoli a tall, erect man with a heavy dark-brown beard and a face bronzed from years of African sun. He won Lejeune's immediate affection by pointing out that he too was a "marine," as indicated by his khaki uniform and anchor insignia of the Colonial Forces rather than the sky-blue uniform of the regular French army. One sleeve of his uniform was empty, and he walked with a pronounced limp from another wound.

Hanging on the wall of Gouraud's office was a relief map of the front occupied by the Fourth Army. Gouraud talked at considerable length of the great battle that was to begin on the following morning with the combined attack of the First American and Fourth French armies. Gouraud told Lejeune that the French had learned from sad experience that the high hills east of Rheims were impregnable. The plan was to outflank these positions. The Fifth Army would cooperate on the west; the Fourth Army would have to take the high ground north of Somme-Py. Gouraud did nothing to correct Lejeune's impression that the 2d Division was assigned to the Fourth Army. Lejeune left with the feeling that Gouraud had searched his soul and knew exactly what kind of man he was.

"We Can Take Blanc Mont Ridge"

News of the impending move had reached the Marine brigade on September 24. As usual, the move was a combination of rail, motor transport, and marching. The leading elements arrived at Chalons on the twenty-sixth.

On the afternoon of the twenty-seventh, a rumor disquieted Lejeune. His chief of staff reported that the French planned to divide the 2d Division into brigades, each the equivalent of a French division, and assign each to a French division, leaving the 2d Division headquarters with no tactical mission.

Lejeune asked for an immediate meeting with Gouraud. They again went into Gouraud's private office. Gouraud stood before his map and described the progress of the attack. On his left, a strong German line in the vicinity of Somme-Py had stopped the French. No attack had been made between the Suippes River and Rheims, because of the strongly fortified German positions in the high hills known as Les Monts. Gouraud's right wing had done somewhat better, but opposite Somme-Py was a curved ridgeline marked on the map as Le Massif du Blanc Mont, running northeast from the Suippes River to a point about four kilometers south of St. Etienne and then almost due east to Medeah Farm. Gouraud explained that the enemy's main line of resistance ran along this ridge. He placed his hand on that part of the ridge between Medeah Farm and Blanc Mont. If this ridge were taken and an advance made beyond it to St. Etienne-à-Arnes, the Germans would be forced to fall back to the line of the Aisne River, a distance of nearly thirty kilometers. He doubted, however, if his worn-out divisions, unless heavily reinforced, could take this position.

"General," responded Lejeune, rising to the bait, "if the 2d Division is kept together as a unit and is allowed to attack on a narrow front, I am confident that it can take Blanc Mont Ridge in a single assault."

Gouraud replied that he had no intention of dividing Lejeune's command, that in fact the 2d Division was not as yet attached to his army but was being held in the reserve of the Group of Armies of the Center at the disposition of Marshal Foch and General Petain. He would, he said, bring to Petain's attention what Lejeune had offered and ask Petain to assign the 2d Division to his Fourth Army.

Next morning Gouraud summoned Lejeune to his headquarters. He explained that General Petain had just left, adding that "[Petain] was greatly pleased and has issued instructions for the assignment of the 2d Division to the Fourth Army. You will receive orders this afternoon to begin the movement of the division toward the front."

"A Swift and Powerful Blow"

Movement orders arrived. The 2d Division was to proceed to the Souain–Suippes area, ten kilometers south of Somme-Py, where the French, with little success, were attacking the German line. The move, partly by camion and partly by marching, was to begin on the twenty-ninth and be completed by the next day. Neville set up his Marine brigade headquarters at Suippes. This put the brigade into position to reach the front lines in a single day's march. Twenty percent of each regiment was left behind on division orders, twice the cadre usually left behind previously and a grim portent of casualties to come.

"We entrained again, crowding into the '40 and 8,'" wrote Pvt. James Hatcher of the 84th Company, "and after many hours of crowding and quarreling over mashed toes and bruised ears, we reached Chalons. There we detrained and made another of those long marches, for which the American troops became famous, to an area in rear of the Champagne front, not far from the famous city of Rheims."

John W. Thomason's Keep On to the Left until You Meet the Moroccans and Go Forward *reflects the forced march through the forest by the 4th Marine Brigade to reach the line of departure for Soissons.* (Courtesy *Naval History*)

Lester G. Hornby's contemporary etching Charge on Wooded Machine Gun Nests near Soissons, July 1918 *portrays the open fields and thickets that made Soissons so costly for the Allied attackers.* (Marine Corps Art Collection)

Lt. John W. Overton, a former captain of the Yale track team, legendary middle-distance runner, and platoon commander in Maj. Thomas Holcomb's 2d Battalion, 6th Marines, died leading his men at Soissons. (From USMC recruiter's bulletin, May 1920, Reference Section, HD/MCU)

Lt. Clifton B. Cates, 96th Company, 6th Marines, displays a German "potato masher" grenade near Verdun. Cates thrived in western-front combat and later commanded a division at Iwo Jima, ultimately becoming the nineteenth commandant. (Courtesy *Naval History*)

Maj. Gen. John A. Lejeune shown midway through his postwar nine-year tour as comman-dant. Lejeune's inspiring leadership, visionary intellect, and political savvy made him one of the most influential Marines of the twentieth century. (USMC #521160, HD/MCU)

Marine, Mud, and Misery, *by Col. Charles Waterhouse, USMC (Ret.), reflects the ordeal of St. Mihiel, where the Marines sustained seven hundred casualties from German shrapnel and poison gas while experiencing the onset of the Spanish flu epidemic.* (Marine Corps Art Collection)

The 5th Marines at Champagne, *by John W. Thomason, who experienced what he sketched. The 5th Marines seized heavily fortified Blanc Mont in good order, only to sustain their worst losses of the war from waves of German counterattacks.*
(Marine Corps Art Collection)

Lester Hornby's At a Bridge near Romagne *portrays exhausted infantrymen pausing in their advance to the Argonne Forest to bind wounds and refill canteens. Hornby, at thirty-six, may have been as thirsty as the young men he sketched.*
(Marine Corps Art Collection)

The Last Night of the War, *by Frederick C. Yohn, portrays the 5th Marines' desperate struggle through enemy fire and the river itself to reach the German-held east bank of the Meuse the night of November 10/11, 1918.* (Courtesy Navy Art Collection, Naval Historical Center, Washington, D.C.)

A former Marine gunner, Capt. Charley Dunbeck was bayoneted and shot at Belleau Wood and shot again at Blanc Mont. Undaunted, he led the 2d Battalion, 5th Marines, across the Meuse on the final night of the war. (USMC #526563, HD/MCU)

Colonel Harry Lee, mounted, center, leads the 6th Marines past the reviewing stand as the 2d Division parades along New York's Fifth Avenue on August 8, 1919, upon their return from occupation duty in Germany. (National Archives 127-N-519458, HD/MCU)

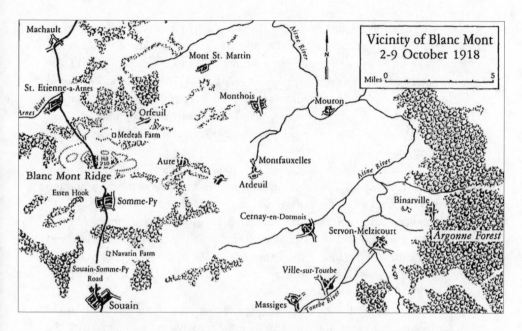

Lejeune opened his headquarters at Suippes on the morning of the thirtieth. He found it a dilapidated, desolate place, behind the German lines for four years and "shelled frequently and bombed often." His personal retinue cleaned up the filth of the windowless house he was to occupy.

Gen. Andre Naulin's XXI Corps—in whose ranks the Marines had fought at Belleau Wood—now held the approaches to Blanc Mont. The countryside was rolling, with some fairly steep slopes. Underlying the hills was a chalky limestone which, when the thin top soil was scraped or blasted clear by shellfire, showed as stark white patches. Scrub pine was about all that grew here. Five kilometers north of Somme-Py was Blanc Mont itself—the White Mountain—which got its name from the limestone.[2]

Opposite the XXI Corps was the German XII Corps, also known as the Py Group, under Gen. Krug von Nidda. The Germans had held Blanc Mont Ridge since September 1914. Battle after battle had been fought over its slopes, which were scarred and shell pocked, covered with tangled masses of rusting wire and a webwork of deep trenches and concrete fortifications.

General Gouraud assigned the 2d Division to XXI Corps on October 1. Naulin directed Lejeune to relieve the French 61st Division and a part of the 21st. Naulin issued a new order to the division at 5 PM that evening. Not only was the 2d Division to enter the front lines, but it was to attack on October 2. Lejeune asked that the attack be postponed until the 3d to allow the 4th Brigade a chance to do a daylight reconnaissance of its front and also to bring up all of the 2d Field Artillery Brigade. Naulin accepted the delay.

Seeking to motivate his men for what would surely prove to be a monumental task, Lejeune issued an order of the day on October 1 that said, rather grandiloquently, "Owing to its worldwide reputation for skill and valor, the Second Division was selected by the Commander-in-Chief of the Allied Armies as his special reserve, and has been held in readiness to strike a swift and powerful blow at the vital point of the enemy's line. The hour to move forward has now come, and I am confident that our Division will pierce the enemy's line, and once more gloriously defeat the enemy."

Pvt. 1st Class Hatcher remembered Lejeune's challenge: "[We] were selected from the entire Allied army by the commander-in-chief to storm the ridge and the heights beyond. . . . I knew that we were faced with a man-sized job."

The night of October 1/2 was clear and cold. Lejeune's headquarters at Suippes was both bombed and shelled. Lejeune took shelter in the caves of the village and found them jammed with soldiers and Marines. He did not stay long but went back to the doorway of his house and spent the balance of the night watching the stream of traffic—his division moving to the front.

The line occupied by the division began about one kilometer northeast of Somme-Py and ran to the southwest to its juncture with the boundary with the French XI Corps about two kilometers west by south of Somme-Py. The relief was effected the night of October 1/2, with the 4th Brigade taking over the entire division front of three kilometers. The 5th Marines occupied the right of the sector and the 6th Marines the left. All other things being equal, that is the way the brigade usually deployed, senior regiment on the right. The 3d Brigade was in a support position six kilometers to the rear, in the vicinity of Navarin Farm.

John Thomason quotes a French staff captain as saying:

> "All this terrain, as far as Rheims, is dominated by Blanc Mont Ridge yonder to the north. As long as the Boche holds Blanc Mont, he can throw his shells into Rheims; he can dominate the whole Champagne sector, as far as the Marne. Indeed, they say that the Kaiser watched from Blanc Mont the battle he launched here in July. And the Boche means to hang on there. So far, we have failed to dislodge him. I expect"—the Frenchman broke off and smiled gravely on the circle of American officers—"you will see some very hard fighting in the next few days, gentlemen."

"A Hideously Battle-Scarred Country"

Lejeune was to open his forward headquarters at 8 AM on October 2 in what had been the headquarters of the 61st Division, a collection of dugouts known as "PC Wagram" about one kilometer north of Souain on the Souain–Somme-Py road. Lejeune's staff car drove forward to Wagram through "a hideously battle-scarred country." The debris of battle was everywhere. As Lejeune described the scene in his *Reminiscences,*

The town of Souain was completely destroyed, and the whole area north of it gave full evidence of the fact that it had been continuously a battlefield for more than four years. It was the white chalk country, and not only was it a perfect maze of trenches and covered with a tangle of barbed wire, but the very soil was desiccated and pulverized. It had been shelled, and bombed and mined so frequently that it had lost all semblance of its former self. Not a tree was standing anywhere near Navarin Ferme, or elsewhere in its vicinity, nor was there even a brick on the site of the farm to show that buildings had once stood there. The debris of battle was still lying about—broken cannon and machine guns, rifles, bayonets, helmets, parts of uniforms, articles of military equipment, and partly buried horses; most gruesome of all, fragments of human bodies were often found. Arms and legs thrust out of the torn soil, and unrecognizable, long-buried human faces, thrown up to the surface of the ground by exploding shell, were frequently visible. The fearsome odors of the battlefield, too, were always present. P.C. Wagram was in the midst of the devastated area. It was not a home, but a horror.

The telephone system inherited from the 61st Division was virtually useless. Until the division could get in its own lines, communications forward of division would be by motorcycle and, forward of regiment, dependent on the age-old system of runners. Until they survived long enough to learn the way, runners tended to get confused or lost in the maze of trench lines.

The front taken over by the 2d Division, only partially secured by the French, consisted of four lines, known as the Krefeld, Prussian, Elbe, and Essen trenches. The right of the 2d Division line was in the Essen trench. West of Somme-Py the Germans still held the Essen trench where it bent around a strongly fortified hill. The Marines soon named the bend in the trench line the "Essen Hook."

The task for the 2d Division and the French 21st Division on the second of October was the cleaning up of the Essen and Elbe trenches. The French 170th Division on the right was already well forward, but the 21st Division, on the left, had not been able to take the Essen Hook and was dug in 130 meters south of Elbe trench.

First Lieutenant Cates took an overstrength 96th Company in at Blanc Mont— nine lieutenants and more than 250 men. They moved into the line, a trench the French had taken. "It was dark as pitch and the ditches were full of dead *boche* and Frenchmen."

Lt. Col. Harry Lee, commanding the 6th Marines, found that the Essen trench in front of his regiment was empty of Germans but controlled by fire coming from strongpoints to the west. He also learned that the 21st Division was undecided as to whether it would attack or not. "If they should attack, the 6th Regiment will act in conjunction with them and occupy the trenches as previously planned," reported Lee to Neville. Otherwise, he recommended that for the afternoon of October 2 the trench be patrolled but not occupied.

Attack Orders for October 3

While this limited attack was in progress, Lejeune, accompanied by his brigade commanders, visited the headquarters of the XXI Corps and met its commander, Gen. Andre Naulin, face to face for the first time. Gouraud arrived and joined the discussion. As it worked out, there would be a frontal attack by the 4th Brigade and an oblique attack by the 3d Brigade from the advanced position held by the French 170th Division. Lejeune returned to PC Wagram and called a conference of his brigade and regimental commanders to work out the details for the attack.

It was well that he did, because the XXI Corps attack order did not reach his headquarters until ten o'clock that night. It was in French and had to be translated. The objective for the 2d Division was the line extending along the road from Medeah Farm west to Blanc Mont Ridge, inclusive. The division order had to be written and then committed to the mimeograph machine. Finally, at about 3 AM, the motorcycle dispatch riders took the order off to the brigades.

Lt. Col. Pete Ellis, the brigade adjutant, had already written the 4th Brigade order, based on the conference held that afternoon. It was signed at 9:45 PM. The tone was almost laconic: "This Brigade will attack in column of Regiments, the 6th Regiment in 1st line and the 5th Regiment forming the 2nd line of support. . . . The Regiments will take the usual formation—column of battalions—each regiment with one battalion in 1st line, one in support, and one in reserve."

The German trench lines had not been completely cleaned up. The 6th Regiment went "over the top" that night in a local attack. Cates's 96th Company had fought its way the previous night into a communication trench in which were Germans at the other end and had stayed there all day. At 6 PM Cates received orders to take two platoons of his company against the Essen trench. He told the remaining two platoons to build up a base of fire against the German machine gunners, who were very thick on his left. He went over with the first platoon, followed by the second platoon at thirty paces. His Marines charged forward yelling a "regular Indian war hoop" that Cates was sure "put the fear of God into the *boche*."

Cates described the charge to his family: "They [the Germans] opened up with a few machine guns, and I saw about twelve grenades come flying over, but that was all; they ran like sheep. My men went at it on the dead run, as the trench was only three hundred yards away. In less than two minutes we had gained our objective, so I sent up a flare signaling to that effect. We had lost only about ten men wounded, and we soon had them cleared off the field."

The 6th Regiment took its share of the Essen trench with a loss of fifteen Marines. This put the division into its attack position for the next day. There remained the Essen Hook, about 275 meters to the left of the boundary separating the XXI and XI corps, a very strong position of machine-gun nests that the French had not been able to take.

"We spent another quiet day," remembered Don Paradis of the 80th Company concerning October 2. By now he was an acting gunnery sergeant (although he would not receive his warrant until December 9, 1918). "Even had hot chow brought in to us after dark the night of October 2d. There was quite an odor of dead bodies blowing across No-Man's-Land but I don't remember that it affected anyone's appetite."

The German high command had decided on a general retirement across the entire front, but it was going to be a fighting withdrawal designed to inflict maximum casualties on the Allies. A series of step-by-step withdrawals had been directed. Ground was not to be given up unless ordered, and any lost ground considered essential to the retreat would be retaken by counterattack.

Over the Top at Blanc Mont

Jump-off for the general attack on Blanc Mont was at 5:50 AM on October 3. Lee, busy occupying the Essen trench, did not receive the brigade order until 4:40 AM. Maj. "Bolo" Williams, commanding the 6th Regiment's lead battalion, would later say that he did not have a chance to read it until after he had taken his objective.

The 6th Regiment was to advance directly to the front from the positions it held. The 5th Regiment was to stand fast and then fall in behind, in support of the 6th Regiment. The 3d Brigade was to move through the zone of the French 170th Division and then pass through the lines of that division.

The division objective was a line four kilometers long connecting Medeah Farm with the Blanc Mont road. Each brigade deployed in a column of battalions, a formation Napoleon would have found familiar. Each brigade was to be supported by a battalion of French tanks. The battalion supporting the 4th Brigade had two companies of twelve tanks each. The 6th and 5th regiments were each assigned a company. The ground didn't favor the use of tanks, and nothing much would come of their presence.

The 2d Field Artillery Brigade had been reinforced with French batteries and other additions to a total of thirty light and eighteen heavy batteries. The artillery preparation was to last a short but violent five minutes. The 2d Division had learned the lesson of the shock value of a short, intensive preparation as opposed to a prolonged bombardment, which churned the earth but did little more than drive the enemy underground into bomb-proofs already prepared. The attack was then to follow a rolling barrage fired by the close-in 75-mm guns, rate of progress of one hundred meters every four minutes. The heavy 155-mm howitzers would continue to fire on Blanc Mont Ridge, and the longer-barreled guns would search out German positions to the rear.

The attack plan was deceptively simple. In execution, however, there would be complications. The two brigades were separated by more than a kilometer of broken ground and were to converge on Blanc Mont Ridge. This left a triangu-

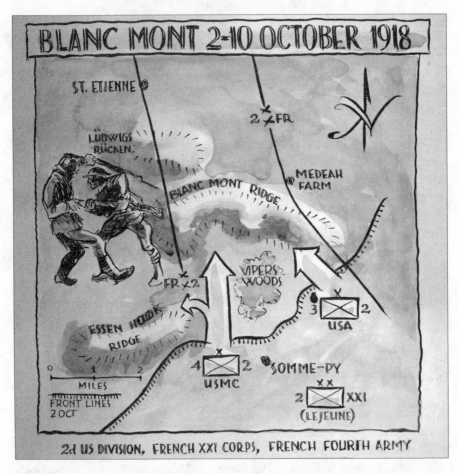

lar wedge of no-man's-land uncovered. This triangle (soon nicknamed "Vipers' Woods") was cleared out later, after the objective was taken.

The Marine brigade was attacking through the section of the line held by the 6th Marines. The 6th Marines would lead off on a front of about one and a half kilometers in a column of battalions. The 5th Marines, withdrawing from the Essen trench, would follow in support and would have the tasks of clearing out the triangle and protecting the flanks of the 6th Marines. The Marines had complete confidence in the 3d Brigade on their right but were dubious that the French 21st Division on their left would advance at all.

About ten o'clock, Gunnery Sergeant Paradis received orders that he would lead the 80th Company up a communications trench to the next line of trenches, which was supposed to be empty of Germans. He was then to turn left and proceed down the trench until he reached the French. The 96th Company would be on the 80th's right. Paradis moved out at about midnight and soon found out where the stench of dead bodies was coming from.

"There was one body in the communication trench, two in the main trench, one I did not see and stumbled over," wrote Paradis.

He heard the French company coming down the trench toward him. He and the French lieutenant fumbled with the passwords and finally made themselves understood to each other. It was 3 AM.

Buck Neville's brigade moved out on schedule. The 6th Regiment went into the main attack with the promise of special artillery fire to neutralize the Hook. Lejeune also ordered Neville to designate a battalion to watch the Hook. Bolo Williams' 2d Battalion led off, followed in turn by Fred Barker's 1st Battalion and the 3d Battalion, now commanded by Maj. George Shuler.

Shuler was one of the 5th Regiment's "originals" who had come over in June 1917. He had been regimental adjutant, which equated to operations officer at that time, of the 5th Marines at Belleau Wood and Soissons. Promoted to major, he had been transferred to the 6th Regiment and had relieved Maj. Berton Sibley in command of the battalion after St. Mihiel.

The 5th Marines, under Col. Logan Feland, had in column the 2d Battalion (Maj. Robert E. Messersmith), 3d Battalion (Maj. Henry L. Larsen), and 1st Battalion (Maj. George W. Hamilton). Both Hamilton and Larsen had performed ably under heavy fire as captains at Belleau Wood. Hamilton had led his company in the seizure of Hill 142 on the battle's first morning. Larsen, initially an assistant brigade adjutant under Maj. Holland Smith, had been Maj. Benjamin Berry's adjutant in the bloody assault on the wood itself, taking temporary command of the 3d Battalion, 5th Regiment, when Berry went down.

General Neville parceled out the two regimental machine-gun companies and the four companies of the 6th Machine Gun Battalion (still under Maj. Littleton W. T. Waller Jr.), one to each infantry battalion, as had become usual.

Some of the sergeants carried shotguns loaded with buckshot. There was a belief based on an angry exchange of diplomatic protests in September that if the Germans caught a man with a shotgun they would execute him on sight on the ground that such weapons, by causing unnecessary suffering, violated the laws of war. The U.S. Department of State responded through a neutral Swiss emissary that the German protest rang hollow, coming as it did from a nation that had introduced poison gas and flamethrowers to modern warfare, adding that any summary executions of American prisoners would be met by reprisals in kind. The Marines knew little and cared less about the dispute, but many NCOs favored the weapons—typically, militarized ("sawed off," in gangster parlance) Remington or Winchester 12-gauge pump guns fitted with slings and bayonet lugs—for close-in trench work.

The zone of action assigned to the Marine brigade was defended by the German 51st Reserve Division. Behind the 51st Division was the 200th Division. A battalion of the 235th Reserve Infantry Regiment, down in strength to about two hundred officers and men, held the German outpost line. The main line of resistance filled the trenches and concrete emplacements on Blanc Mont itself, about three kilometers to the rear of the outpost line.

The Germans, in response to the barrage, fired phosphorus shells.

"They burst like giant Fourth of July sparklers in the air showering down what looked like red-hot iron," remembered Paradis. "I led a section column of about 20 men; we were the extreme right of our company. When we reached our objective, which was the very center and top of Mont Blanc [*sic*] I was to connect with the 96th Company, Captain [*sic*] Cates, on our right. Blanc Mont was covered with scrub pines which reminded me very much of the jack pine country around Kalcaska, Michigan, where I grew up as a child."

A double rainbow arched overhead. Cates told the Marines of the 96th Company that it was an omen of good luck. Afterward, he wrote home: "At 5:55 AM we went over the top again. This time we had to go in four wave formation and had to go very slow, as we were following our creeping barrage which only moved forward at the rate of one hundred yards every four minutes. The regiment was in column of battalions and our battalion was the leading battalion with my company the company in front. . . . [W]e followed our barrage as close as possible without getting into it."

Principal initial resistance came from machine-guns nests from the front, from the right flank ("Vipers' Woods"), where the ground between the two brigades was not completely covered, and most particularly from the left flank, where the French had been stopped cold in front of the Essen Hook. But in general Marine losses were light in the advance, and they captured several hundred prisoners. The 6th Marines met more resistance as they reached the Somme-Py Woods. The support battalion came up on the lead battalion's right. The objective was taken by 8:30 AM, and the reserve battalion was given the task of mopping up. The 5th Regiment now turned its full attention to the exposed left flank.

Major Williams' 2d Battalion, 6th Marines, with all four companies on line and with the 81st Machine Gun Company attached, advanced rapidly at first, against nothing but occasional machine-gun fire. This increased to heavier fire coming in from the left flank. The Marines swept aside the right flank battalion of the 235th Regiment and got into the rear of the 200th Division, the frontline units of which continued to resist the advance of the French 21st Division.

The posts of command for the infantry and artillery brigades of the 200th Division were in dugouts on Blanc Mont. The infantry were the 2d Jager Brigade. The Jagers no longer wore the green uniforms worn earlier in the war, but they were still considered elite troops. Lieutenant Richert manned a division observation post on Blanc Mont. At 8:15 AM he reported to his division commander, somewhere to the rear in a presumably safer position, that the Jager regiments on the front lines were holding against the Americans.

Partly because of the flanking fire and also because of the lay of the land, Williams' 2d Battalion, 6th Marines, slid to the right as it went up the slope. The Jagers on its left were putting up a stubborn defense. Williams detailed Clifton Cates' 96th Company to face to the left as a flank guard. The gap separating the right of the 2d Battalion from the 3d Brigade widened. Major Barker's 1st Battalion, with the 6th Regiment's machine-gun company attached, went into it. Both battalions began to dig in. Major Shuler's 3d Battalion, with the 15th Machine Gun Company attached, followed in support behind Williams' 2d Battalion.

The Jager regiments were still holding off the French 21st Division, and each Marine battalion in turn as it went up the slope was enfiladed by machine-gun fire coming from the Essen Hook.

By 8:30 AM Williams' battalion had reached the main line of resistance and had taken a section of the Medeah Farm road, which ran along the ridge. The 3d Brigade took Medeah Farm itself by 8:40 AM without serious loss.

The headquarters of the 2d Jager Brigade pulled out of the Blanc Mont position; Lieutenant Richert remained. The German division commander put his reserves into motion, ordering a counterattack by the 149th Regiment, 213th Division. At that same time he called on XII Corps for reinforcements. He was sent a battalion of the 74th Regiment. By 9:20 AM the Americans were in the headquarters dugouts, and the telephone lines to the rear went out.

"We arrived at the top just as a bunch of German prisoners came out of a large dugout," remembered Gunnery Sergeant Paradis. "There were about 25, some looked to be not over 16 years old. They were so scared that their knees actually knocked together.... Later in the day I found a Luger and a Mauser pistol under a bunk, in this dugout.... I sold them for 250 francs when we came out of the lines."

Cates had a "showdown pistol duel" with one German officer. The German burst out of a dugout ten feet away. They both shot at the same instant. The German missed. Cates' bullet caught the German in the chest, tumbling him back into the dugout. Cates tossed in a grenade.

"You should have heard the rest of the damn rascals yell 'kamerad.'" Cates wrote home. "One of my runners got six more prisoners out of there."

The French battalion that was to have advanced on Cates's left had not kept up. Cates could see a German battalion filing into position to his rear. He directed four of the tanks to put down 1-pounder and 3-inch fire on them. That put an end to the German counterattack. Cates figured his company had taken about a hundred casualties. In turn: "We had taken over 250 prisoners besides worlds of stores, ammunition, 18 Austrian 88s. Each other company did just about as well. It was a grand day for the old 96th Co. We ran up against some of Germany's best troops in this attack. One bunch, the Prussian Guards, were the remains of the bunch we whipped at Bouresches and Belleau woods.... I believe the whole German army is disorganized and in a pitiful plight. It is truly a question of time until it is over. I expect peace within two weeks."

Two of the Medals of Honor awarded Marines in the First World War were earned that day, both by members of the 78th Company, 2d Battalion, 6th Regiment. At about 6:20 AM, Pvt. James Kelly, the advance having been impeded by a German machine gun that had escaped the barrage, charged forward, killed the gunner with a grenade, killed another crew member with his pistol, and marched the remaining eight members back through a curtain of bursting shells. Shortly thereafter, Cpl. John H. Pruitt single-handedly went against two German machine guns, killed two Germans, and captured the rest of the crews. A little later he pulled forty Germans out of a dugout and made them prisoners. Continuing at the front edge of the action, he was sniping at the retreating enemy when mortally wounded by shellfire.

As soon as it was broad daylight, Lejeune had gone to the high ground of Navarin Farm to watch the battle. It was a hazy morning, and visibility was poor. He could see little until Very pistol flares at between 8 and 9 AM signaled that the day's objectives had been taken. General Naulin, pessimistic at first, was now jubilant. Lejeune pointed out to him that XI Corps on the left flank had not crossed its jump-off line. Naulin nevertheless ordered Lejeune to press on. Lejeune demurred—to press on would create a narrow salient that would be an invitation to disaster. He said that if necessary he would appeal Naulin's order to Gouraud. A short while later a message from Naulin said to consider the order as never having been given. Lejeune replied that he was preparing to advance to a point about one kilometer southeast of St. Etienne.

With the entire left flank of the brigade open, Major Messersmith's 2d Battalion, 5th Marines, was brought up to extend the line to the southwest. Capt. DeWitt Peck was wounded this day, and Lt. Lemuel Shepherd found himself once again in command of the 55th Company, although his tenure would be brief. The Germans seemed to be preparing to attack that flank, so Colonel Feland echeloned Major Larsen's 3d Battalion, 5th Marines, to the left and rear of Messersmith's battalion.

Attacking the Essen Hook

The one still unemployed battalion, Maj. George Hamilton's 1st of the 5th, brought up the rear of the brigade. Feland ordered Hamilton to reduce the still-dangerous nest of machine guns in the Essen Hook. Hamilton sent the 17th Company, under Capt. Leroy P. Hunt, to take out the guns, the ones that had delivered flanking enfilade fire against each successive Marine formation crossing the line of departure. For Hunt, the mission involved wheeling ninety degrees to the west and entering the French 21st Division's zone of action.

Hamilton had chosen his assault commander well. The twenty-six-year-old Leroy Hunt had proven himself resilient and cool-headed under fire. Gassed at Belleau Wood and wounded at Soissons, Hunt had learned to coordinate under stress his platoon commanders' assaults with the fire of his supporting arms.

A covered trench line got the company to within about eight hundred meters of the Hook. Hunt brought a 37-mm gun and several heavy machine guns to bear on the offending German guns, knocking out several. Hunt then maneuvered to within three hundred meters of the position, covering it with machine-gun fire while two of his platoons came in from the north and south, a difficult double envelopment. The 17th Company captured the position, along with a hundred German prisoners. Hunt then handed over the position to the French and moved his company north to extend farther the left flank of the 5th Marines. But Hunt's tactical success proved short-lived. The French lost the Essen trench to a German counterattack within hours, and Maxim machine-gun fire would continue to harass the Marine flank.

"Our Left Is in the Air"

The Marines now had a foothold on Blanc Mont, but the western portion, in the zone of the 21st Division, was still held by the Germans. General Naulin, annoyed at the XI Corps' inability to take the Essen Hook, ordered his weary, just-relieved 170th Division to move to the west, behind the 2d Division, to cover the left flank. But he also cautioned that the Americans must not wait for the arrival of the 170th "before resuming the march." Other than that, Naulin thought the American performance splendid and asked the 2d Division to get off a renewed attack that afternoon.

By 2 PM on October 3 Lejeune had published an order pronouncing the morning's attack "a complete success," advising that the 21st Division had passed the Essen trench and that another French division was moving up in support of the 2d Division's left. Lejeune ordered his brigades to continue their advance to the northwest.

Lejeune's favorable report overlooked the division's increasingly exposed left flank. Severely pinned down, the French 21st Division had barely advanced at all. The farther north the 6th Marines attacked, the more vulnerable they became to German fire and counterattacks from the west. As the afternoon wore on, the Marine battalion commanders extended their lines farther and farther westward, groping like blind men for the nonexistent French right flank. At one point Major Williams warned, "The French have not come up, and our left is in the air."

Private Hatcher, advancing with Shuler's 3d Battalion, 6th Regiment, recalled: "The French on our left had failed to carry the enemy's first line positions in their front, and so the Germans were by that time sending in a heavy flanking fire against us from high ground to our left. . . . For the next mile the going was pretty bad."

Later that afternoon, General Naulin received a message: "Marshal Foch has just learned of the success of the XXI Corps, and of the American 2d Division, attached to it. He directs that this success be exploited to the limit. All must press forward at once, without hesitation. The breach is made; the enemy must not be given time to repair it."

Once again the French thought there might be an opportunity for a cavalry charge and breakthrough in the grand Napoleonic manner. The French 3d Cavalry Division was moved into position, and a liaison officer arrived at 2d Division headquarters. No occasion for its use would be found.

In the 3d Brigade's zone, the 23d Infantry passed through the 9th Infantry and pushed forward, with the 9th following in support. The doughboys of the 23d Infantry veered a little to the left of their designated axis of attack and advanced about two kilometers in the direction of St. Etienne.

In the 4th Brigade, Neville ordered the 5th Regiment to pass through the 6th and continue the advance in concert with the 3d Brigade to the right and the French on the left. The 5th made its passage of lines at 7:30 PM. German machine-gun fire opened up immediately from the front and flanks. The regiment pushed forward about a kilometer and a half and dug in for the night under heavy artillery and machine-gun fire. At nightfall the division held a salient about 1.6 kilometers wide at the base, 2.4 kilometers deep, and only 450 meters wide at its rather porous apex. The 5th Marines repelled two local counterattacks during the night. Neville sent two companies from the 6th Regiment forward to cover the 5th's left flank.

The 2d Division prepared to advance beyond St. Etienne, but it was out of the question, until the French came up on both flanks, to deepen the salient yet farther. Late in the evening the French 22d Division, which had been designated to relieve the stalled 21st Division, marched into the 2d Division's zone of action with plans to attack to the west in the morning.

Lejeune had reason to be proud of his division's work that day: an advance of five kilometers, seizure of part of Blanc Mont's previously unassailable slopes, and some two thousand prisoners taken. General Gouraud telephoned him to tell him of other advances that would soon wrest Rheims from the grip of the Germans.

Harry Lee had understood that only the eastern half of Blanc Mont was the 6th Regiment's responsibility. During the night a patched-together German reserve consisting of a dismounted cavalry regiment and several Bavarian units reoccupied the western portion of Blanc Mont and reinforced the lines in front of the 2d Division. To the left front the Germans had turned the town and cemetery of St. Etienne into a fortress.

A Fire Trap for the 5th Marines

The 5th Marines encountered this improvised fortress when it advanced early on the morning of October 4, the second day of the battle. The regiment passed through the 6th Marines in a column of battalions, Major Larsen's 3d Battalion leading the way. Larsen went about two kilometers without encountering any significant resistance (the German line was farther west) and reached the dangling flank of the 3d Brigade. His battalion was able to extend the 3d Brigade line about

1.5 kilometers to the west. Larsen paused briefly, then went forward again, but within a few hundred meters he found his battalion enfiladed from both flanks. He pulled back to a woods, reforming on a line with the 3d Brigade.

The other two battalions of the 5th had been following in support. All three battalions were now in precariously exposed positions, taking heavy artillery and machine-gun fire. The Germans had set a firetrap for the Marines, allowing Larsen's penetration, then opening fire from three sides, seeking to isolate and overwhelm the regiment. Poison-gas shells began exploding within the perimeter. Essentially, the regiment was desperately holding a thinly wooded ridgeline position 1.5 kilometers southeast of St. Etienne.

Major Messersmith's 2d Battalion tried to relieve the pressure on Larsen but took heavy casualties and had to give way in disorder. Maj. George Hamilton, showing the same personal bravery leading a battalion he had exhibited as a company commander at Hill 142, led his 3d Battalion into the melee, stopping the retrograde movement but paying a heavy price as German artillery and Maxim machine guns continued to rake the scrub pines. Then the Germans counterattacked, hitting the battalion hard on its left flank. Hamilton faced about with difficulty and stopped the counterattack but took more heavy losses.

The second day's fight for Blanc Mont had become a company commander's battle. Even the battalion commanders, the only senior officers engaged in the actual fighting, lost contact with some of their companies for hours at a time. Col. Logan Feland, struggling to make sense of the dire, fragmented reports drifting in from his besieged regiment, could do little to ease the crisis. Neither Neville nor Lejeune were near enough to the fighting to discern the critical turn of events. At one point, XXI Corps ordered that the advance be continued to Machault. Lejeune dutifully issued a division order to continue the attack but artfully inserted a condition that H-hour would be designated later.

The 5th Marines were experiencing their worst day of the war. Larsen fought off a another counterattack from the west during the afternoon, but that evening at about 7:30 PM several hundred Germans came at him from the southwest and rear, forcing him to face about again to beat off their attack. All four of Larsen's company commanders went down. So did Lt. Merwin Silverthorn, shot in the heel. Two Medal of Honor holders, Lt. Henry Hulbert (Samoa, 1899) and Sgt. Matej Kocak (Soissons), died in the fighting. "The 5th Regiment was so reduced in strength that it was no longer combat effective," concluded historian Ronald J. Brown in his 2001 history of the 5th Marines. "Captain Charley Dunbeck, once again in command of the 43d Company in Messersmith's 2d Battalion after being bayoneted and shot in both legs at Belleau Wood, was shot in the head and had to be dragged to safety."

The blame for such flaws would be argued, but overall, viewed from a higher level, the attack on Blanc Mont should be regarded as a great success. The deep penetration made by the 2d Division caused the German high command to hasten the withdrawal of troops from the hills east of Rheims to the line of the Arnes and the Suippes.

Violent as their counterattacks were, the Germans continued to fight essentially a delaying action. After the Allied successes of October 3, Crown Prince Wilhelm—who was not the fool that Western cartoonists made him out to be—ordered a withdrawal to the "fourth line of resistance," the western extension of the Brunhilde position in the Argonne, which here ran through St. Etienne.

The 200th Division, opposing the 2d Division, reported on October 4 that the total rifle strength of its three regiments was only five hundred, the artillery had lost nearly all its gunners and from 60 to 70 percent of its horses, the few remaining horses were worn out, a third of the guns were unserviceable, the division signals detachments had had losses of 25 percent, only two officers and forty men were left of the division engineers, and the cavalry squadron was totally dismounted.

Lejeune consulted with Neville that afternoon, the fourth of October, and decided that the most pressing problem was to capture the rest of Blanc Mont Ridge. Neville told Lee to launch his attack at daybreak, coordinating his advance with the adjacent French.

These arrangements had scarcely been made when Feland telephoned that his 5th Marines were not only under heavy artillery fire but also virtually ringed by machine guns, especially from its left rear. Naulin had joined Lejeune at PC Wagram, and Lejeune heatedly informed him that this fire was coming from a position reportedly taken by the French. Providentially, Gouraud arrived at Wagram and ordered Naulin to keep his 22d Division in place until released by Lejeune. Gouraud further smoothed ruffled feathers by commending the 2d Division and expressing regrets for its heavy casualties.

The two French generals departed. Lejeune's telephone rang incessantly with reports of counterattacks being beaten off by both the 3d and 4th brigades.

Major Shuler's 3d Battalion, 6th Regiment, had reconnoitered in force and determined the extent of the enemy's defenses, mostly machine-gun nests, on the western end of the ridge. Artillery was brought down on these defenses. Again, the French did not come up, and after considerable loss Shuler's attack was broken off, with further action postponed until the next day.

Even so, Shuler's attack shook the Germans. This part of the German line was held by the remnant of the 149th Infantry (Major Grundel) of the 213th Division, but serving under the orders of the 2d Jager Brigade. Grundel was nearly captured, his 3d Battalion was scattered, and his 2d Battalion was "lost" until the next afternoon.

Sergeant Gulberg's Odyssey

Sgt. Gus Gulberg, wounded at Soissons and hospitalized at Base Hospital no. 27 at Angers, had a second operation and was given an overdose of chloroform that nearly killed him. After four weeks in bed he started to get around on crutches. After three more weeks he was judged fit for duty and ordered back to the front.

Gulberg reached the regimental rear of the 6th Marines at Somme–Suippe on October 3. The next morning, with about fifty other Marines fresh from the hospital, he started forward by truck to rejoin his company. At Somme-Py an MP stopped the truck and turned it back. Gulberg found he had been pressed into the grave-digging business. Each man was given six crosses and a spade.

"We buried men from eleven PM until three AM," he wrote in his diary.

"An Exceptionally Fine Assault Division"

Marshal Foch informed Petain that same October 4 that the Fourth Army had done fairly well, but not as well as he expected. He characterized the third of October as "a battle which was not commanded, not pressed, not held together."

Naulin's XXI Corps received this chiding in the form of an injunction: "Marshal Foch orders strong pressure in the direction already assigned; everyone forward, without halt."

Lejeune received his copy of this message at 10:25 PM on the fourth, along with the attack order for the next day. The 2d Division would retain its place in line as the left-flank division of the corps.

During the night of October 4/5 the German XII Corps regrouped as best it could. The sturdy remnant of the 200th Division stayed in the line on the right. The 51st Reserve Division was on the left but was to withdraw its headquarters and turn over its regiments to the 213th and 17th divisions.

For October 5, the third day of the assault, Lejeune planned an advance in line of brigades with regiments in column. In the 4th Brigade, Lejeune ordered the decimated 5th Regiment to stand fast and the 6th Regiment to reorganize and then attack, conforming its advance to the movement of the French 22d Division, which was attacking across the front of the laggard 21st Division. The 6th Marines, in conjunction with the 22d Division, would clear Blanc Mont itself.

The attack jumped off at 6:15 AM behind a curtain of powerful artillery support.

In the 6th Marines' zone of action, Col. Harry Lee had ordered his 3d Battalion to attack the Germans' main position on Blanc Mont. Shuler's 3d Battalion, with the help of a battalion from the French 22d Division and some informal volunteers from the 170th Division, took by assault the remaining hard core of the defenses, capturing at least sixty-five machine guns and 205 prisoners. The attack against Blanc Mont was completed by 9 AM, the linkup with the 22d Division was solid, and the 2d Division was ready to take up the general advance.[3]

To the Marines' right, the 3d Brigade was held up all day in its assault of the Medeah Farm–Orfeuil position by the failure of the French 167th Division to advance. The 6th Regiment resumed the attack at 3 PM, pushing forward its left and holding back on its right so as to maintain contact with the 3d Brigade. The 2d Battalion (Williams) led off, followed by the 3d (Shuler) and 1st (Barker). With the situation on the left under control, the 6th Marines, with the 2d Battalion in the lead, swung to the right and passed through the lines of the 5th Marines outside St. Etienne. Fighting was severe all day. The lead battalion, under Williams, down to three hundred men, was attempting to cover a front of one or two kilometers. After going forward for a few hundred meters, Williams was stopped by a strong machine-gun nest. At 6 PM the advance stopped for the night, still well southeast of St. Etienne.

The Germans to the immediate front were the reduced-strength 149th and 368th infantry, both from the 213th Division (Maj. Gen. Baron von Hammerstein). The German Third Army summary of operations for October 5 reads in part:

> On October 5th the enemy again attacked the Py and Perthes Groups, west of the Aisne, after powerful artillery preparation. His attacks, made in great force, were broken up by the stubborn resistance of our infantry, well supported by the artillery.... The enemy's losses were heavy.... Captured papers describe the American 2d Division as an exceptionally fine assault division; they indicate that it was chosen for employment here for the reason that this is considered the decisive point in the enemy's offensive.

Late in the day Naulin told Lejeune that he was assigning the 71st Brigade, 36th Division, temporarily to the 2d Division. The brigade climbed down from its trucks at Suippes on the afternoon of October 5. Lejeune asked for the brigade at 6:10 PM; his request was promptly approved by Gouraud, at 6:35 PM. General Naulin, however, decreed that the 71st be given a day of rest before going into the line.

"The Germans Promptly Discovered Our Movement"

Lejeune now gave his attention to continuing the attack toward Machault. He moved his headquarters forward from PC Wagram to a new position in Somme-Py. He ordered a deliberate attack, with adequate artillery support, for the early morning of October 6. The whole of the narrow 4th Marine Brigade front was given over to Maj. George Shuler's 3d Battalion, 6th Regiment. The 2d Field Artillery Brigade bombarded the hill in front of the 6th Marines for an hour. The 3d Battalion, 6th Marines, and a battalion of the 23d Infantry then went forward behind a rolling barrage. The soldiers did not gain much ground, but the Marines found the flank of the German position and rolled it up. This advance of about one kilometer took the hill. Forty prisoners and a number of machine guns were taken in two hours of fighting.

As the 84th Company advanced through a patch of woods toward an abandoned trench, Pvt. James Hatcher's luck ran out. "The Germans promptly discovered our movement and shelled us heavily," he wrote. "Just as I started out into the open a fragment of a shell, which exploded only a few yards in front of me, struck me in the right leg and I stumbled to my knees. I saw our boys jump into the trenches as I limped back into the woods."[4]

The 3d Brigade picked up the momentum. Hard fighting, which ultimately brought in nearly all of the 23d Infantry and parts of the 9th, brought the advance to the St. Etienne–Orfeuil road. Numerous messages were received from the French that they had taken St. Etienne and wished to turn the town over to the Americans. These reports proved highly optimistic.

By now the 2d Division was about fought out. On the night of October 6/7 the 71st Brigade of the U.S. 36th Division took over the entire division front. Only the frontline units were relieved and the 71st Brigade functioned temporarily as a brigade of the 2d Division. The 142d Infantry took over the zone of the 4th Brigade of Marines front while the 141st moved into the lines of the 3d Brigade of Infantry. The 5th Marines and 23d Infantry went back to Blanc Mont Ridge; the 6th Marines and 9th Infantry stayed with the relieving units to give them a bit of practical instruction. The 5th and 6th machine gun battalions also stayed in place, and the 2d Division's 37-mm guns and Stokes mortars were turned over to the incoming regiments.

Phased Relief of the 2d Division

Lejeune met with Naulin the morning of October 7, the battle's fifth day. Naulin informed him that a general attack would take place at daybreak on the eighth. Lejeune told him that he was expecting too much of untried troops and urged that the 71st Brigade not go into the attack until it had a few days' seasoning. Naulin was insistent.

"Tomorrow," he said, "will be another great day for the XXI Corps!"

General Naulin then suggested to Lejeune that in the interim the 2d Division might advance its left beyond St. Etienne. Lejeune demurred: his own troops were exhausted, and the fresh 71st Brigade would not be fresh on the eighth if it first had to make a local attack. Naulin took it to Gouraud, who apparently told Naulin to let Lejeune have it his way.

Final orders for the attack came at 8:45 PM on the seventh. Lejeune gave the entire division front to the 71st Brigade, with the objective of taking the high ground three kilometers north of St. Etienne. The flanks of the 71st would be protected on the left by a battalion of the 4th Brigade and on the right by a battalion of the 3d Brigade. The 71st moved out with the 141st Infantry on the right and the 142d on the left, the regiments in column of battalions.

The Marine battalion on the 142d's left flank was Major Barker's 1st Battalion, 6th Marines, charged with maintaining contact with the French to the west and also with the taking of St. Etienne itself. The 76th Company, under veteran

Capt. Macon Overton, accompanied by a few French soldiers, plunged into the shell-wrecked town. The 75th Company came up on Overton's right.

Optimistic reports received from the 71st Brigade early in the day became less so as the day wore on. Late in the afternoon, the fresh German 159th Infantry of the 14th Reserve Division counterattacked. The green 142d Infantry was in no condition to stand against the veteran Germans. The regiment fell back. Barker held at St. Etienne and was joined by the 2d Battalion, 2d Engineers (Lieutenant Colonel Strong). The withdrawal of the 71st Brigade had left the 75th Company, on Overton's right, in a desperate situation. All the officers of the 75th Company were killed or wounded, but Sgt. Aralzaman C. Marsh took command and with a handful of men held the position.

Lejeune, hearing that the 142d was falling back, went forward to the headquarters of the 71st Brigade and ordered its commander to reorganize his scrambled units and prepare for a German counterattack. He also canceled the relief of the 3d and 4th brigades and ordered these weary Marines and soldiers back into the lines.

On this day Lemuel Shepherd received his third wound, when a 77-mm shell fragment tore up his leg, resulting in his evacuation for the balance of the war. "If ever there was a hell on earth it was up there," Shepherd wrote his family from a hospital. Violent counterattacks by the Germans continued throughout the night. The reconstituted line held.

There was no general attack on the ninth, simply small, patchwork advances to straighten the line and strengthen the connections between units. The French 7th Division was understood to be in a trench line about two to three kilometers north of St. Etienne, and General Naulin was very anxious for the Americans to connect with it. The 71st Brigade was ordered to do this, making a formal attack with artillery support, if necessary, but the green brigade was so disorganized that no serious effort to do so was made.

On their side of the line, the Germans were withdrawing, leaving just one regiment from each division as rear guards. As Gouraud had predicted, they were retreating to the Aisne, where they formed a new line on October 13.

The rest of the 36th Division was now coming up. This was a National Guard division. Capt. John Thomason of the 49th Company later remembered the National Guardsmen coming up on one side of the road, the Marines marching back on the other. The fresh, strong companies of guardsmen sang and joked as they pass the weary Marines. Thomason has one of his Marines say, "Yeh, we went up singin' too, once—good Lord, how long ago! . . . They won't sing when they come out . . . or any time after . . . in this war."[5]

Because the 36th was incomplete, the 2d Division had to turn over its transport and much other equipment to the guardsmen and leave its artillery and engineers in place. Command was to pass from Lejeune to Maj. Gen. W. R. Smith at ten o'clock on October 10. Before turning over command, Lejeune ordered vigorous patrolling by the 71st Brigade to clear up the situation to the front, particularly the matter of the trench system north of St. Etienne. The 72d Brigade moved into support and reserve positions, the 144th Infantry relieving the 4th Brigade of Marines and the 153d Infantry relieving the 3d Brigade of Infantry. The relieved 2d Division units assembled near Navarin Farm and marched to the vicinity of Suippes. Lejeune stayed on with the commander of the 36th Division for another day and then moved to his new headquarters, Camp Montpelier, near Chalons.

Major Shuler's 3d Battalion, 6th Marines, was the last Marine battalion to hold a position in the Champagne sector. He was down to fewer than three hundred men but had been reinforced with two companies of the always-willing 2d Engineers. He was not relieved until the night of October 10. On coming out of the lines, Shuler laconically reported: "We shot the tar out of the Boche."

Sergeant Gulberg rejoined the 75th Company as it came out of the line.

"I fell in line and marched with them to some French barracks a few miles from Suippe, where we billeted for four days," he wrote. "It wasn't the same old gang that I had left. There were many new faces, and only six of the old timers of the 2d Platoon were left."

The Legacy of Blanc Mont

Lejeune provided a thumbnail summary of the battle in a October 19 letter to Col. Charles G. Long, assistant commandant, in Washington. "The Marine Corps has just cause to feel proud of its brigade," he said, but he admitted, "There isn't much left of the original crowd."

The honor of seizing Blanc Mont and forcing the Germans from the Hindenburg Line came at a high cost for Lejeune's 2d Division. From the second of October to the tenth, the division lost forty-one officers and 685 men killed, 162 officers and about 3,500 wounded, and six officers and 579 missing, for a total of 209 officers and 4,764 men. The division had taken prisoner forty-eight officers and 1,915 men and had captured twenty-five guns and 332 machine guns.

The week of almost continuous fighting had cost the Marine Brigade, at best count, 494 killed or died of wounds and 1,864 wounded. Belleau Wood had been worse, but Blanc Mont cost the Marines more than Soissons. Officer casualties were particularly high. "I was the only officer left in my company," Lieutenant Shepherd wrote home. The fourth of October, the day the 5th Marines took such a pounding, proved the costliest single day of the war for the brigade.

Capt. John Thomason, commanding the 49th Company in the 1st Battalion, 5th Marines, received the full allotment of 234 rations to feed his original, full-sized company on October 6, but by then he had less than half a platoon on hand to divide the spoils. "We were shot to pieces in the Champagne Sector," he admitted.

...ench army again cited the 5th and 6th Marines, the third citation ...wo such citations entitled the receiving unit to wear the *fourragere* (or ... er cord) in the red-and-green colors of the Croix de Guerre. The 6th Machine Gun Battalion had also met this requirement.[6] About two thousand Croix de Guerre were passed out to members of the 2d Division for Blanc Mont, and Lejeune himself was named a commander of the French Legion of Honor.

CHAPTER THIRTEEN

The Meuse-Argonne Campaign

The Marine brigade went into camp at Chalons after Blanc Mont.[1] Replacements from the 1st Marine Training Regiment at Quantico filled the depleted ranks once again.

The pace of the war accelerated dramatically. All of the Allied armies were on the offensive in a great converging attack: the British toward Cambrai; the French, east and west of Rheims, toward the Aisne; and the Americans, in what they called the Meuse-Argonne offensive, toward Sedan and Mezieres.

By the middle of October the American First Army numbered more than a million men and held a front that stretched nearly 130 kilometers. To ease his difficult span of control, Pershing reorganized the First Army into a First and Second army, giving command of the First, with an eighty-kilometer front, to Maj. Gen. Hunter Liggett, and of the Second, with a forty-eight-kilometer front, to Maj. Gen. Robert L. Bullard. As army group commander, Pershing established his advanced headquarters at Ligny-en-Barrois.

Lejeune visited the American First Army headquarters at Souilly on October 23, hoping to have his division rejoin the AEF in time for what seemed to be the war's final campaign. He met with Brig. Gen. Hugh Drum, the chief of staff, and learned that the 2d Division was in fact being reassigned from the French Fourth Army to the First Army. Drum told him that the 2d Division would be assigned to V Corps to be the point of the wedge for a great attack that was to break through the center of the German army.

The Meuse-Argonne, quite the largest battle in which Americans had ever taken part, had begun on September 26 and, by the time the Marines joined into it, had gone through two phases. The first assault had pushed the Germans back about ten kilometers. Then German resistance had stiffened. During the last days of September and throughout October the offensive had been characterized by short advances gaining limited objectives. On the eastern half of Pershing's front, half of the German Kriemhilde Stellung—a portion of what the Allies called the "Hindenburg Line"—had been taken. On the western half, the Germans were still firmly in place.

Half of the First Army had already crossed the Meuse, east of Sivry-sur-Meuse. North of Sivry the river made a sharp bend to the west. The front here lay along the riverbank. On the opposing side the Freya Stellung lay along the Barricourt Ridge, which came down from the northeast to the Meuse. The next step had to be an attack against the portion of the Kriemhilde Stellung still held by the Germans. This could open the way for a further crossing of the Meuse in the vicinity of Dun-sur-Meuse, about ten kilometers below Stenay.

On October 25 and 26 Lejeune's two brigades made night marches by muddy side roads to an assembly area in a woods near Exermont. Lejeune moved his headquarters to Charpentry, on the eastern edge of the Argonne Forest, on the twenty-seventh.

"Charpentry, the new capital city of the Second Division, was a sight to behold," wrote Lejeune. "It was situated in a . . . sea of mud. It was a ruined town, having been a target for German artillery since the day it was wrested from German hands by the Americans. . . . Division headquarters occupied a two-story building. It was nearly a complete wreck, and promised to fall down as soon as hit again."

Major General Summerall

Lejeune drove to V Corps headquarters at Chepy, five kilometers southwest, to report to Maj. Gen. Charles P. Summerall, who had taken command of the corps two weeks earlier. Summerall was the son of a long line of Florida preachers, and he might have been one himself had it not been for the impoverishment of his family by the Civil War. This made it expedient for him (Lejeune, Annapolis '88, was a like case) to go to West Point, where he graduated in 1892, twentieth in a class of sixty-two. He went into artillery and was a junior officer in Reilly's Battery, which supported the Marines in the relief of Peking in the 1900 Boxer Rebellion. His churchly background gave him the habit of delivering little homilies on every possible occasion.

General Summerall had made his reputation as an artillery brigade commander at Cantigny. Allied artillery doctrine, hammered out in trench warfare, was that the number of guns should be proportioned to the lineal frontage to be attacked or held. In 1917, experienced British and French artillerists listened in amusement to the newly arrived American gunner who preached that guns should be allotted not per linear front but to the number of infantry in action. In the spring of 1918, Summerall, commanding the 1st Artillery Brigade, 1st Division, at Toul and Cantigny, had the chance to test his new techniques, aimed at putting gunfire where the infantry wanted it. He was credited with perfecting the "creeping" or "rolling" barrage, or at least teaching American troops its uses, and facilitating call fires with better wire communications. After Cantigny he moved up to command of the 1st Division. He fought it well at St. Mihiel and at Soissons, where his guns virtually destroyed the Prinz Eitel Friedrich Division of Prussian Guards. Command of V Corps was his reward.

Summerall was also an ambitious, driving man. He told Lejeune quite pointedly that he had found it necessary to relieve several frontline commanders from duty. He then went into the details of the corps' role in the big attack due to begin at dawn on November 1. The V Corps front extended westward from the Bois de Bantheville to St. Georges. On the right, the 89th Division had broken through the Kriemhilde Stellung. On the left, the 42d Division, the celebrated Rainbow Division, was still in front of the Kriemhilde. Momentarily both the 1st and 2d divisions were in reserve. The 2d and 89th divisions would now move into the assault. The 2d Division would relieve the 42d, smash through the Kriemhilde, and go ahead, with the 89th Division on its right and the 80th Division of the I Corps on its left, against the Freya Stellung on Barricourt Ridge. On D-day, Summerall expected the 2d Division to advance nine kilometers, taking the fortified towns of Landres et St. Georges, St. Georges, Landreville, Chennery, and Bayonville, also the Bois des Hazois, the Bois l'Epasse, and finally, the Heights of Barricourt

At a second conference, Summerall promised Lejeune an enormous concentration of artillery. Because of the importance of the attack the 2d Division's own artillery would be reinforced with the fires of the artillery brigades of the 1st and 42d divisions, as well as all available corps and army artillery, a total of more than three hundred guns. Summerall then asked for assurances that the first day's objectives would be taken. Lejeune told him that he had every confidence that his division could take the day's final objective, the Heights of Barricourt, if an adjacent division could protect at least one of his flanks. Maj. Gen. William M. Wright, commanding the 89th Division, said his troops would stay abreast of the 2d Division.

"The Point of the Wedge"

John Lejeune called a conference of his brigade and regimental commanders and proceeded with detailed planning. The division would go forward from shell-cratered Sommerance in column of brigades on a front of slightly over two kilometers, advancing north by northwest toward the Barricourt Heights. The 4th Brigade would lead off on the first day, with the 3d Brigade to pass through and take over on order. For the jump-off, the 23d Infantry would be attached to the Marine brigade and would go in on the right against the Bois l'Epasse. Once the wood was taken, the 23d would revert to the 3d Brigade and the 4th Brigade would take over the whole division front.

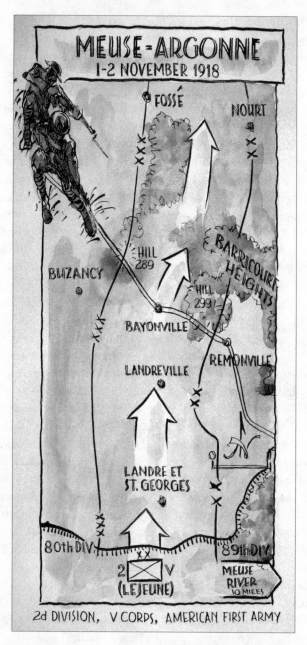

MEUSE-ARGONNE
1-2 NOVEMBER 1918

FOSSÉ

NOURT

BARRICOURT HEIGHTS

HILL 289

HILL 299

BUZANCY

BAYONVILLE

REMONVILLE

LANDREVILLE

LANDRE ET ST. GEORGES

80th DIV.

89th DIV.

2 V (LEJEUNE)

MEUSE RIVER 10 MILES

2d DIVISION, V CORPS, AMERICAN FIRST ARMY

The three artillery brigades—the most experienced American field artillery in France—would fire a preparation of two hours, then a standing barrage of ten minutes, and then would roll forward at the rate of a hundred meters every four minutes on favorable ground, every eight minutes on rough ground.

Machine-gun barrages, as usual, would provide close-in fires. All the machine guns in the 2d Division, except for two companies, were gathered for the preparatory fires, some 255 weapons. The Marine machine gunners were as good as any in the American army, but they envied their counterparts of the 89th Division their water-cooled Vickers machine guns, which weighed about twenty-five pounds less than, and could deliver five times the volume of fire of, the French Hotchkiss guns with which the Marines still fought.

Another new weapon caught the immediate interest of the Marines. In late October the first few Browning automatic rifles reached the Marine Brigade, where they were immediately test-fired and found to be decidedly better than the clumsy, heavier Chauchats. For the Leathernecks this was the advent of the legendary "BAR," which would remain a Marine favorite for forty years. The M1918 BAR handled easily, fired dependably, and, in the proper hands, could hit distant targets as well as a rifle. The BAR, chambered for a .30-06 cartridge and fed from a twenty-round box magazine, weighed sixteen pounds unloaded and could fire up to five hundred rounds per minute. For the Marines preparing to attack the Heights of Barricourt, there were hardly enough of the new BARs to equip a platoon, much less a brigade. Adjoining army troops quickly learned to safeguard their own new BARs from covetous Leathernecks with larceny ("midnight requisitions") on their minds.

The division was close to full strength. The latest replacements filtered down to their assigned companies, and a number of wounded veterans returned for this final push, including the irrepressible Capt. Charley Dunbeck, to whom Neville awarded command of the 2d Battalion, 5th Marines. Special troops attached for the attack included a company from the 1st Gas Regiment, a company of fifteen light tanks, a squadron and a half of aircraft, and a balloon company—all American units, except for a few French aircraft.

Summerall, accompanied by Lejeune, visited each of the twelve infantry battalions of the two brigades and gave repeated rousing exhortations to take the Heights of Barricourt, which would force the Germans to retreat behind the Meuse—in Lejeune's words, "Four hours of tramping through the mud and making speeches in the open air." Summerall hardly endeared himself to the troop commanders by threatening to relieve every field-grade officer if the Marine Brigade failed to achieve the objective. Before driving away, Summerall said once again to Lejeune that he had been compelled to relieve a number of officers for failure to carry out orders and that he would continue to do so. Lejeune quietly assured him that the officers of the 2d Division would carry out their orders.

The 2d Division began its movement into the lines on the night of October 30/31, relieving the support and reserve battalions of the 42d Division, a brigade of which was commanded by Brig. Gen. Douglas MacArthur, already famous for his flamboyant leadership. Command of the sector passed to Lejeune at noon on the 31st, and he opened his division headquarters at Exermont at 4 PM.

Of Exermont, Lejeune wrote to his wife that night, "It is a filthy hole. I have my room and our offices in an old peasant's house, and my room adjoins the stable which is under the same roof; my nearest neighbors are two mules in the stable."

German Delaying Tactics

Germany now stood alone. One by one the Allies had forced Bulgaria, Turkey, and Austro-Hungary out of the war. General Ludendorff had resigned on October 27. The German navy mutinied two days later. By this time all but a few diehards in the German army knew that the war was lost. But the high command, perhaps already planning the next war, was determined that the German withdrawal would cost the Allies heavily. Preliminary plans were to drop back to the Antwerp–Meuse line, which would mean a retreat on the American front of about forty kilometers to the east bank of the Meuse.

Opposite the American First Army was the German Fifth Army, commanded by the Marines' old adversary, General von der Marwitz.

Immediately opposite the U.S. 42d Division was the German 41st Division, the leftmost division of the Argonne Group. On its right was the 15th Bavarian Division, which the Marines had met at Blanc Mont. To its left was the 88th Division of the Meuse West Group.

As it happened, the German 52d Division was relieving the 41st Division at the same time Lejeune's 2d Division was relieving the 42d. By the morning of November 1, all three regiments of the 52d were in position, but the 41st Division lingered in the area. Average strength of the German regiments was eight hundred men, conventionally organized into three battalions, each with three rifle companies and a machine-gun company. By autumn of 1918, German regiments equated in strength to American battalions, German battalions to American companies, and German companies to American platoons.

The Germans knew a big American attack was brewing. As Gen. Max von Gallwitz, commanding the parent army group, later wrote: "We continuously detected additional new divisional insignia. As for the west bank of the Meuse, we discovered there [were] more than six divisions, as originally reported. That famous American crack unit, the 2d Division, withdrew from opposite Army Unit C and was now reported to be near Montfaucon."[2]

The German line in front of the 2d Division was held by a single battalion stretched out across a hill south of Landres et St. Georges, its position organized, in German fashion, in considerable depth, with strongpoints rather than a continuous line. Elements from both the 41st and 52d divisions defended St. Georges itself.

German artillery remained the most potent element of the defense. Col. Georg "Breakthrough Miller" Bruchmuller—whose guns had taken such a toll of Marines at Belleau Wood—had arrived on October 26 to be the chief of artillery for the German Fifth Army. Aware of the pending American assault, Bruchmuller ordered a preemptive bombardment against reverse-slope ravines and other likely assembly areas, saturating both sides of Sommerance with high-explosive and poison-gas shells. The barrage hit the 1st Battalion, 6th Marines, hard. Newly commissioned 2d Lt. Jerry Thomas had just rejoined the 75th Company as a platoon commander.

An exploding mustard-gas shell knocked him out of action before he could lead his first assault.

Dawn of Another D-day

The first of November broke cold and cloudy, with heavy fog in the morning. Lejeune was up before 2 AM to assure himself that his troops were in their jump-off positions and that the artillery and machine guns were in readiness for the bombardment that was to begin at 3:30 AM. He walked out onto a high ridge to watch the shellfire.

The artillery preparation was so thorough, recalled newly arrived Maj. Clyde Metcalf, "that scarcely a square foot of ground in the enemy's front line area was left unturned by bursting shells." The thirty-two-year-old Metcalf was an Illinois native, a one-time instructor of German at the University of Arkansas and a future historian of the Corps.

Colonel Bruchmuller's artillery batteries returned fire bravely, raking the presumed line of departure for the Americans. The 1st Battalion, 6th Marines, again took casualties, losing a hundred men even before H-hour. To the right, the 5th Marines also suffered while waiting. Pvt. Elton Mackin of the 49th Company grimaced at the enemy fire: "The barrage . . . came crashing back among us. . . . No walk-away this. . . . Here was strong resistance."

The American artillery fire gradually smothered Bruchmuller's gunners. Ten minutes before H-hour a standing barrage crashed down like a curtain two hundred meters in front of the German line. Lejeune's machine guns began their overhead fire. Lejeune was confident that his doughboys and Marines had learned to "lean on" the rolling barrage even if it meant suffering a few casualties from short rounds. On schedule, the three regiments crossed the jump-off line at 5:30 AM.

On the right flank, the 23d Infantry, with two battalions in the assault, moved out briskly, maintaining a disciplined pace and measured intervals. The soldiers took Landres et St. Georges and cleaned out the Bois de Hazois and the Bois l'Epasse in short order, then pulled aside to join the 9th Infantry in support of the 4th Brigade.

On learning that the 23d Infantry had taken its objectives on schedule, Lejeune went forward to establish an advance headquarters at Landres et St. Georges. En route he stopped at Sommerance, the PC of the 6th Marines, and met with Col. Harry Lee and Lt. Col. Thomas Holcomb, the regiment's second in command. Breakfast was being served at the regimental headquarters. Lejeune broke out his mess kit and somewhat self-consciously joined the chow line for a breakfast of bacon, beans, biscuit, and coffee before driving on to Landres et St. Georges.

In the 4th Brigade attack, the 5th Marines, the senior regiment, was on the right, as was the usual practice, and the 6th Marines on the left. The battalions of both regiments were in column. The brigade's first objective was an east–west line about four hundred meters short of Landreville.

Both regiments were in column of battalions, with a nine-hundred-meter interval between battalions. Maj. George Hamilton's 1st Battalion led in the 5th Marines zone, followed by Capt. Charley Dunbeck's 2d Battalion and Maj. Henry Larsen's 3d Battalion.

In the 6th Marines zone, Maj. Frederick Barker's 1st Battalion was in the assault, followed by Maj. George Shuler's 3d Battalion and Maj. Ernest "Bolo" Williams' 2d Battalion. After the initial barrage, each battalion had a machine-gun company attached to it for the advance, either the regimental machine-gun company or a company from the 6th Machine Gun Battalion, now commanded by newly promoted Maj. Matthew H. Kingman. Kingman, twice decorated for valor at Belleau Wood, had relieved Maj. Tony Waller, reassigned as division machine-gun officer.

Attacking the Heights of Barricourt

The attack went like clockwork. The Marines had indeed learned to stay close behind the creeping artillery barrage. The two small villages that stood in their way were virtually demolished by the artillery fire. Heavy belts of barbed wire caused momentary pauses. German gunners stood their ground until their guns were overrun.

Hamilton's battalion soon outflanked Landres and the ridge south of the village, reaching without difficulty its objective a few hundred meters south of Landreville. Barker's battalion met heavy machine-gun fire coming out of a small wood south of St. Georges.

Capt. Macon Overton, regarded by many in the 4th Brigade as "one of the most gallant young officers of the Marine Corps," led his 76th Company against the machine guns. The seemingly indestructible twenty-eight-year-old former All-Marine shortstop had commanded the company since Belleau Wood. He had become one of a handful of exceptional company commanders like Charley Dunbeck, George Hamilton, or the late Lester Wass who seemed to thrive on the chaos of close combat. Overton had already led his men in silencing five German machine-gun nests this morning. He was guiding a tank in its attack against a sixth machine-gun nest when a Maxim bullet killed him.[3]

Overton's final act of leadership helped Barker reach his objective, a small stream running east from the village of Imecourt, adjoining the Bois l'Epasse.

Major Barker was one of the veterans. He had come to France in the first convoy in June 1917 as a captain and commander of the 47th Company, 5th Regiment. In September, with a temporary promotion to major he had gone to Paris as an assistant provost marshal. Perhaps embarrassed at his good fortune to be working in Paris during Belleau Wood and Soissons, he rejoined the brigade in late July 1918 determined to make up for lost time, energetically commanding the 1st Battalion, 6th Regiment, at St. Mihiel and Blanc Mont.

As the 23d Infantry paused to rejoin the 3d Brigade, the Marines extended to the right to take over the entire division front. The remainder of the attack was to be made in column of brigades, with the 3d Brigade following the 4th. The artillery barrage was to roll forward and then stand just beyond each successive objective. This would give the battalions second in column time to move through the lead battalions and continue the attack in leapfrog fashion.

The 18th Company, 5th Marines, still led by Capt. LeRoy P. Hunt, had the mission of maintaining contact with the 89th Division on the right. On the left a provisional battalion consisting of the 95th Company, 6th Marines; Company G, 319th Infantry, 80th Division; and two machine-gun platoons had been put together under Maj. George C. Stowell and given the more difficult mission of connecting the 80th Division of I Corps and the 2d Division of V Corps.

Stowell had come to France in the fall of 1917 as a captain and commander of the 76th Company. He had commanded the company for the first week of Belleau Wood, when, for some reason now forgotten, he had been plucked out of that command and sent back to the 2d Replacement Battalion. He came back to the 6th Marines in early September and commanded the 75th Company at St. Mihiel and Blanc Mont. Now, with a temporary promotion to major, he was in command of what was called the "Liaison Battalion between 1st and 5th Corps."

The 80th Division had made little progress, leaving Stowell's provisional battalion to protect the open left flank on their own. Stowell and his pickup command attacked the village of Imecourt and captured its garrison of 150 Germans, then slid west into the 80th Division's zone of action, keeping abreast of Lejeune's advance.

The 4th Brigade now had the entire division front. At about 8 AM, Dunbeck's 2d Battalion, 5th Marines, and Shuler's 3d Battalion, 6th Marines, moved through the front lines and took up the assault. Dunbeck's battalion swept into the village of Landreville, where the Germans made the mistake of firing machine guns at them from windows. That nuisance taken care of, the Marines accepted the surrender of a hundred Germans, arms raised.

More serious was a German second line, a portion of the Freya Stellung, that ran generally east and west through Bayonville. Key to the position was tree-covered Hill 299, concealing a number of machine guns and some artillery. Dunbeck's battalion took the hill and reached its objective, about 450 meters north of Bayonville, by noon.

Captain Dunbeck insisted that his name was "Charley," not Charles, and that he had been named for a favorite horse on his father's stock farm in Lucasville, Ohio. Dunbeck, who had enlisted in 1903, had come to France with the 5th Regiment in that first convoy in June 1917 as a newly made marine gunner. Promoted to captain, he was wounded in both legs at Belleau Wood, but came back in July to command the 43d Company at Soissons, St. Mihiel, and Blanc Mont, where he was again wounded.[4]

Shuler's 3d Battalion, 6th Marines, met little resistance until it reached the villages of Chennery and Bayonville. These were taken with the aid of tanks. Again, about a hundred Germans, along with assorted machine guns and artillery pieces, surrendered.

About noon, the third echelon—"Heavy Hank" Larsen's 3d Battalion, 5th Marines, and "Bolo" Williams' 2d Battalion, 6th Marines—passed through the lines and began the final phase of the day's attack. By then all organized resistance had been overrun and the only remaining fight was from small isolated pockets of Germans. Larsen's battalion reached its objective, a line about one kilometer southwest of Barricourt, shortly after 2 PM.

Major Larsen, a second-generation Norwegian, had come into the Marine Corps as a second lieutenant in 1913 and was another of those in the 5th Marines who had come across in the first convoy. He had been second in command of the 3d Battalion at Belleau Wood, Soissons, and St. Mihiel, moving up to command, although still a captain, at Blanc Mont.

Bolo Williams reached his objective, the southern edge of the Bois de la Folie, about an hour later. One of his company commanders, Clifton Cates, said of Williams, "He had all the courage in the world but I wouldn't say he was the brainiest or friendliest man in the world."

By now the division had captured several batteries of artillery and had 1,700 prisoners and many cannon in the bag. The German prisoners were put to work carrying the wounded back to the dressing stations, four prisoners to a stretcher. The burial parties, attended by chaplains, followed behind the advancing troops.

General von der Marwitz began moving forward his reserves soon after the attack began. His 31st Division was already well forward. The 115th and 236th divisions, farther to the rear, were ordered to move up. Von der Marwitz hoped to hold the Freya Stellung between Champigneulle and Bayonville long enough to make an orderly withdrawal to the Meuse. This proved impossible. After the 2d Division broke through the Freya position and entered the Bois de la Folie, von der Marwitz ordered a new line, Buzancy to Bois de la Folie, formed to tie in with the still firm portion of the Freya Stellung to the east. By nightfall on the first, the 15th Bavarian was north of Sivry-les-Buzancy, its left flank bending back and connecting with the 52d Division on the ridge between Buzancy and the Bois de la Folie.

The U.S. 89th Division fought its way abreast the 2d on the right, but Lejeune's left flank remained open. A few independent-minded soldiers from the 80th Division caught up with Stowell's mixed battalion and were added to the defense for the night. To Stowell's rear, the bend in the line near Sivry further exposed the left flank of the 2d Division. Lejeune had Neville send the rearmost battalions of the 6th Marines across the division boundary into the I Corps zone to clear out the woods between Sivry and the Fontaine des Parades. Some hours after dark the Marines made contact with a battalion of the 80th Division.

The frontline battalions sent out patrols, and the brigade braced itself for an expected German counterattack. The left flank was still most vulnerable. The best the Germans could do was to form an outpost line, made up of the remnants of several divisions, north of Buzancy and in front of the Marine brigade.

Approaching the Meuse

For all his threats to relieve the Marine commanders if they faltered, Major General Summerall was unsparing in his praise for their performance on November 1, signaling Lejeune: "Your brilliant advance . . . destroyed the last stronghold in the Hindenburg Line."

At 8 PM Lejeune received Summerall's orders for the next day's advance. The division was to push forward to the Fosse–Nouart line at daylight. An hour later Summerall sent a modification: in addition to advancing to the Fosse–Nouart line, the division was to take the town of Buzancy, which lay in the 80th Division's sector. This would cause the division to attack in two directions: north toward Fosse–Nouart and west against Buzancy. Lejeune protested to Summerall that as of 10 PM his left flank was still in the air. He argued that if he was to attack to the west, the 89th should extend to the left to take over a portion of his front. Summerall acceded, the 89th Division's reserve began the march, and the 4th Brigade faced ninety degrees to the left.

These adjustments took time. Summerall grew impatient. Fortunately for Lejeune, a protest came from I Corps that an attack across its front would surely cause a mix-up. About 4 AM Summerall called off the attack, and for the 2d Division the "battle for Buzancy" had ended. By then it was too late to reform the 4th Brigade to attack north, so Lejeune ordered the 3d Brigade to relieve the 4th Brigade and continue the attack.

Fighting throughout the night, the 80th Division came up on the left flank in strength by the morning of the second, and Stowell was able to take his battalion back into the 2d Division's zone of action. During the day, the Marine brigade rested, except for Williams' battalion, which pushed forward patrols into the Bois de la Folie until stopped by the German outpost line.

Now the Spanish influenza began to extract greater losses than German fire. Major Barker, commanding the 1st Battalion, 6th Marines, came down sick and was hospitalized with a combination of flu and residual mustard gas in his lungs. Maj. Maurice Berry, recovering from his shattered arm suffered at Belleau Wood, relieved Barker momentarily. Maj. George Stowell, relieved of his boundary liaison duties, took command from Berry and led the 1st Battalion, 6th Marines, the balance of the war.

The Germans were in worse shape. Only fragments of the 52d Division remained in the Bois de la Folie. The skeleton 115th Division relieved these survivors on the night of November 2/3. On the 115th's left the 88th Division was still in the lines but reduced by now to a hodgepodge of mixed units, known by the names of their commanders, including the remnants of the 41st Division, shriveled down to a composite regiment. Its strength on October 31 had been 2,300 rifles. What it was now, no one knew. On the right of the 115th, the 31st Division, which the Marines had met briefly at Thiaucourt, was beginning the relief of the 15th Bavarian. To the rear, in its assembly area, the 52d Division could muster an infantry strength of only thirty-five officers and 242 men.

The Germans had decided to withdraw behind the Meuse as soon as possible. Von der Marwitz pulled the headquarters of Fifth Army back to Virton.

Lejeune ordered the third Infantry Brigade to move up in line of regiments to the Fosse–Nouart line on the third. The 23d Infantry, already in the Bois de la Folie, took the road to Fosse in a well-executed night march. The 9th Infantry moved north from Bayonville toward Nouart, brushing aside German rear guards. The doughboys reached the southern edge of the Bois de Belval by noon. The Marines followed in trace.

It was by now quite clear to the Germans at the highest levels of command that they must withdraw to their final position, the Antwerp–Meuse line. At 8 PM on November third von der Marwitz received orders for the Fifth Army to fall back behind the Meuse.

On November fourth the 3d Brigade pushed on forward, advancing eleven kilometers in two days. That night Lejeune, who had moved his headquarters forward to Fosse, ordered the 4th Brigade to go in on the right of the 3d Brigade and connect with the 89th Division. The 5th Marines, led by Dunbeck's 2d Battalion, went into the front lines.

The 236th Division was now in front of the 2d Division, covering the German withdrawal across the Meuse. Pushing back the 236th was primarily the job of the 3d Brigade. On the right the 5th Marines helped the 89th Division clear the Germans out of Forêt de Jaulny and went on to reach the Meuse at Pouilly on November 5.

The Americans were outrunning their support. The traffic jams and congestion in the rear were unbelievable. It was difficult getting ammunition and rations forward and equally difficult getting the wounded back. Pvt. Carl Brannen, 6th Marines, recalled, "The men were nearly all affected with dysentery from the scanty, unfit food and polluted water. . . . We were all weak and exhausted." A freezing rain added to the misery. Pvt. Elton Mackin, 5th Marines, wrote of his personal exhaustion, "Always, always, we faced another hill."

One Marine who took the logistics problems seriously was the salty 2d Lt. James Gallivan of the 2d Battalion, 5th Marines. Still a bit gimpy from his Belleau Wood wound, the old veteran surpassed himself in delivering hot food and coffee to the infantry companies. After so many months of enduring Lt. Col. Fritz Wise's heavy-handed sarcasm, Gallivan enjoyed working for Capt. Charley Dunbeck, a former marine gunner like himself. For his part, Dunbeck recognized a to\ done well, citing Gallivan's "coolness, bravery, and devotion to duty by lead\ party carrying food to the troops in [the] front line through an extremely heavy artillery bombardment."[5]

During night of November 5/6 the 236th Division withdrew across the river. Next day the 9th and 23d infantry moved up to the left of the 4th Brigade and the near bank of the Meuse belonged to the 2d Division. It came as no surprise to the Marines that the Germans had destroyed all bridges across the Meuse in their skillful retreat.

Rumors and Scuttlebutt

General Liggett ordered the First Army to press northward. General Summerall saw, to his chagrin, that the III Corps already had a foothold on the east bank of the Meuse, while his own V Corps was still on the west bank.

On November 6, Summerall ordered the 89th division to take over the defense of the river line. The 89th extended to the left as far as Pouilly.

Campaign planning lagged behind the quickening operational tempo. That afternoon Summerall ordered Lejeune to prepare to march on Sedan, the site of the 1870 French defeat in the Franco-Prussian War. Lejeune directed Buck Neville to prepare the 4th Brigade for the long march, while the 3d Brigade, still in position along the Meuse, took over the portion of the line vacated by the Marines. No sooner had the relief been made than the orders to march on Sedan were canceled.

On November 7, Summerall ordered the 2d and 89th divisions to prepare for a crossing of the Meuse River on a D-day and H-hour to be announced. The 4th Brigade edged forward from La Forge Farm to go into bivouac along the Beaumont–Sommauthe road, eight kilometers southwest of the river. A rumor rippled through the ranks that the Germans had sent a delegation through the lines seeking an armistice.

A Bloody Bridgehead

The last four days of the war featured chaotic, arguably senseless fighting as the antagonists sought to seize or deny final penetrations before the Armistice. Upstream from Sedan, the U.S. V Corps hastened to execute a forced crossing of the Meuse in strength.

The men in the ranks viewed the frenetic river-crossing preparations with despair. For the previous six weeks they had striven mightily to drive the Germans across the Meuse. They had finally done so. Exhausted, sick with influenza, and keenly aware that an armistice was finally at hand, they were averse to this perceived suicide mission to seize one final slice of enemy-held territory. The east bank of the river was not even Germany—it was still France. There was no honor in becoming the last man killed in the Great War for this dubious objective.

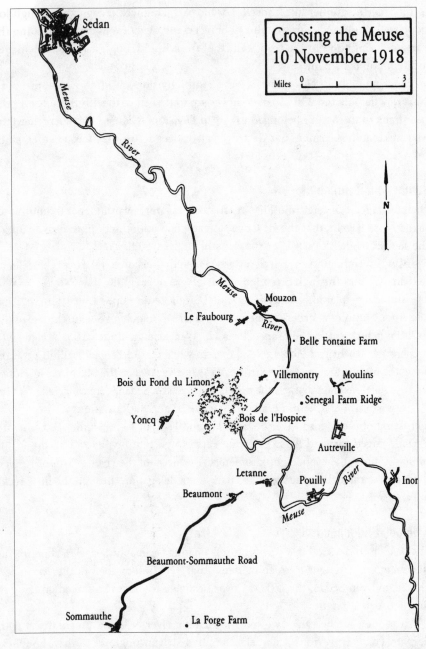

On the eighth General Summerall designated two crossing sites: Mouzon and Letanne, a section of the north-flowing Meuse distinguished by a series of great, looping bends. The 9th Infantry slipped a patrol across the river, which encountered no Germans but was advised by the French inhabitants that the *Boche* were all around.

Summerall fixed November 9 as D-day, but on that day Lejeune learned that all the pontoon bridges had been allocated to the 89th Division and that his 2d Engineers would have to fabricate four floating footbridges in sections at Beaumont and Yoncq for the 2d Division.

Lejeune planned for two, simultaneous crossings. The 4th Brigade would cross with the 3d Brigade in support. The 2d Engineers would bring their fabricated bridges down to the river in sections to be installed after dark. It turned out that they could not be ready in time, so Lejeune asked for a delay until the night of November 10/11, risking the wrath of an already impatient Summerall. Lejeune ordered Neville to assemble both regiments in the Bois du Fond du Limon, about halfway between the two crossing points.

General Summerall held a meeting on the evening of November 9 of the commanding generals and chiefs of staff of the 2d and 89th divisions and held forth on the subject of river crossings. Lejeune stated that it was obvious that the east bank of the Meuse was strongly held and recommended that the 90th Division, which was already across the river to the south, drive north to clear the front of the 89th Division, which could then cross against no opposition, and repeat the maneuver, clearing the east bank where it faced the 2d Division. The 2d Division would then drive north and clear the crossing site of the 77th Division. Summerall told him he would take the plan under advisement, but when Lejeune returned to his headquarters he learned that it had not been approved and that the simultaneous crossing of the 2d and 89th divisions would proceed on the night of November 10/11.

To carry out these orders, Lejeune planned for two battalions of the 5th Marines and a battalion from the 89th Division to cross at Letanne and two battalions of the 6th Marines and a battalion from the 5th Marines to cross north of Le Faubourg, near Mouzon. The 2d Field Artillery Brigade would bombard the opposite bank, and the machine-gun companies would cover the crossing with overhead fire.

Two footbridges were to go across north of Mouzon and two near La Sartelle Farm, north of Letanne. The two companies of engineers who were to put across the bridges were to be assisted by two rifle companies from the 9th Infantry. The main crossing, to be made by the 6th Marines, reinforced with the 5th Marines' 3d Battalion (Larsen), was to be at Mouzon. The crossing at Letanne, to be made by the 5th Marines, reinforced with a battalion from the 89th, was considered secondary, to be made mainly as a link with the main body of the 89th Division, which would be crossing at Inor.

All battalions had machine-gun companies attached. The assault battalions were to cross rapidly and seize the heights above the riverbank. The artillery would fire a curtain of shells that would move gradually, point to point, from the river.

The 6th Marines, in the main attack, was to take the ridge north of Mouzon. All three battalions of the 6th Marines would be used. One change took place: Maj. Clyde Metcalf relieved Bolo Williams in command of the 2d Battalion, 6th Marines.

Col. Logan Feland chose Maj. George Hamilton to lead the two battalions of the 5th Marines across near Letanne. Capt. Charley Dunbeck's 2d Battalion, 5th Marines, would cross the river, with the 1st Battalion, led by Capt. LeRoy Hunt in Hamilton's temporary absence, in support and the battalion from the 89th Division in reserve but remaining in the woods on the west bank of the river until needed.

The Germans had not fortified their side of the river. Mouzon was the boundary point between the Third Army of the Crown Prince's army group and von der Marwitz's Fifth Army. The 31st Division, its strength a meager 850 men and twenty-five machine guns, extended from Mouzon east to Alma Farm. The 352d Regiment, 88th Division—380 men and eleven machine guns—held the line from Alma Farm to Letanne. To the rear in reserve were two provisional regiments. One, with all the infantry that could be found from the 52d Division, was at Vigneron Farm. The other, what was left of the 236th Division, was between Autreville and Moulins. Together they probably did not total more than a thousand men. The 29th Machine Gun Battalion had one company on the riverbank and one in reserve. Colonel Bruchmuller's artillery was still strong, and there were still German aircraft in the sky.

Elton Mackin described his experience at the onset of the last night of the war as "sprawling on the muddy shore, peering at a wall of river mist and fearsome noises."

It was already dark in the Bois du Fond du Limon on the evening of November 10—the 143d birthday of the Marine Corps—when the battalion commanders of the 6th Marines received their orders for the main attack against Mouzon. Majors Barker, Metcalf, and Shuler had little time to coordinate. There was confusion over the time of the attack. The artillery, which was to fire a preparation an hour long, began its fires before the battalions even left the wood. Most of the preparatory fire had petered out before they reached the river.

The 2d Engineers formed a chain of men to act as guides from the woods to the crossing site. Two floating "footbridges" (actually a series of floating drums supporting an uneven line of duckboards—described by one Marine as "like a railway track turned upside down") were ready to be thrown across the river. The engineers carried the sections to the river. They were to be lashed end to end and floated across. It was an inky dark night accentuated with a heavy fog. Soon a freezing rain would lash the river valley.

The Germans spotted the bridging effort and brought down heavy artillery and machine-gun fire. Dawn came. The bridges for the 6th Marines crossing were still not in position. Realizing that the Mouzon crossing had died stillborn, the battalion commanders agreed on their own to pull back from their exposed positions. The battalions countermarched back into the Bois du Fond du Limon. Here they were overjoyed to learn that the Armistice had been signed, to be effective at 11 AM.

Things went differently for the 5th Marines at Letanne. Maj. George Hamilton, commanding the crossing force, planned for an hour's artillery preparation and

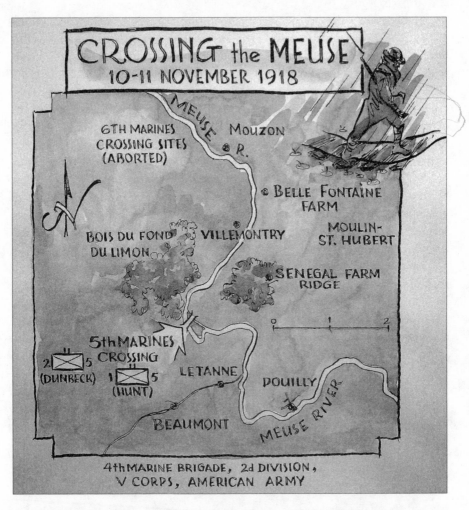

CROSSING the MEUSE
10-11 NOVEMBER 1918

6TH MARINES
CROSSING SITES
(ABORTED)

MEUSE R.   Mouzon

BELLE FONTAINE
FARM

MOULIN-
ST. HUBERT

BOIS DU FOND
DU LIMON   VILLEMONTRY

SENEGAL FARM
RIDGE

5th MARINES
CROSSING

2 5
(DUNBECK)   1 5
(HUNT)   LETANNE   POUILLY   MEUSE RIVER

BEAUMONT   MEUSE RIVER

4th MARINE BRIGADE, 2d DIVISION,
V CORPS, AMERICAN ARMY

then for Capt. Charley Dunbeck's 2d Battalion and the battalion from the 89th Division to cross simultaneously, each using one bridge. The 1st Battalion, under temporary command of Capt. LeRoy Hunt, would follow in support.

Dunbeck wrote out his orders to his company commanders at 5:30 PM on sheets torn from a German officer's field notebook. He held out the 55th Company as his battalion reserve. His orders to 1st Lt. Sydney Thayer, then in momentary command of the company, read in part as follows:

Your mission is to *screen the bridge* while other units pass over.
After all units have passed over, you will send one (1) platoon to Belle Font Farm [*sic*],
seize the place and connect with 6th Marines, who are operating north of Belle Font Farm [*sic*].
One platoon will remain at bridge as *bridge guard*.

The engineers shoved the ungainly footbridges across. The Germans immediately brought machine-gun and artillery fire to bear, knocking out one of the
bridges. The battalion from the 89th had not yet arrived. Hamilton decided to cross
on the one bridge with Hunt's 1st Battalion, followed by Dunbeck's 2d Battalion.
German artillery hit his Marines as they approached the bridge, causing many
casualties. Capt. John Thomason would later describe "the line of dead engineers
on the path between the heights of the Meuse near Pouilly and the place where the
bridge was that last night of the war." Maxim machine-gun fire swept the shaky
bridge. Many men drowned. The 1st Battalion worked its way across between the
hours of 9:30 and 10:30 PM. Those who got across were further struck as they clam-
bered up the bank by the fires from a strong machine-gun position. Fewer than
one hundred Marines from the 1st Battalion could be assembled before daylight.
Major Hamilton reported by message at 6:50 AM that he had organized them into
a single company.

Dunbeck's Marines watched the bloody assault in horror, waiting their turn on
the same footbridge. Many seemed reluctant. In a simple act of raw leadership, Charley Dunbeck said to them, "I am going across that river, and I expect you to go with
me." They did. Dunbeck led off with his headquarters, part of the 55th Company,
and a section of machine guns. One of Dunbeck's officers fell off the bridge and
yelled, "Save me, Captain! I can't swim!" Dunbeck pulled the floundering officer to
his feet and told him to wade—the water near the bank was only waist deep.

Dunbeck expected Capt. Samuel C. Cumming with the 51st Company to
follow his advance elements across the river, but German shells cut the bridge.
Repairing the flimsy, jury-rigged span took the engineers two hours of extremely
hazardous work. As the hours passed, Cumming assumed command of the second echelon, fretful that the battalion had become irrevocably split. As Cumming
remembered:

> It was 11 o'clock at night and raining and sleeting. Those of us in the rear were
> able to get back to the west bank of the river and waited for engineers to come
> and repair the bridge, so we could cross. On arriving on the east bank I found
> Capt Dunbeck had turned up river where there was heavy fighting, instead of
> down the river where we were ordered to form a bridgehead for the 6th Regi-
> ment crossing. I knew he had, in the confusion, taken the wrong turn. I there-
> fore turned down the river to where he was supposed to form a head. I had with
> me three and one-half companies of infantry and one machine-gun platoon.

Heavy shelling by the Germans continued. Cumming placed Capt. Hardin
Massie at the head of the column with the remnants of First Lieutenant Thayer's
55th Company and the machine guns, followed with Capt. Gilder Jackson's 43d
Company and Cumming's own 51st Company. Cumming, with the help of two
Marines, took out a German machine gun, shooting the gunner through the head

with his pistol while his two Marines bayoneted the other two members of the crew. He reached the point on the river where the 6th Marines were supposed to cross and set up a defensive position along the towpath with about two hundred Marines. Captain Massie was his only surviving officer.

Dunbeck meanwhile had moved his bobtailed battalion, something less than a company, up on Hamilton's left and had pushed patrols out toward Belle Fontaine Farm, where he expected to connect with the Mouzon force.[6]

The battalion from the 89th Division crossed some time after midnight and by daybreak had come up on Hamilton's right with some three hundred effectives. The 89th Division itself had crossed near Pouilly and was working northward.

Three machine-gun companies—the 8th, 23d, and 81st—were to have accompanied the infantry battalions. The 81st did not make it across; its bridge was shot away. The 23d Company, with just five guns left, covered the engineers as they put one of the bridges in place but only managed to get one gun across. The 8th Company (which could claim to be the most veteran of machine-gun companies, having come across with the 5th Marines) did get across and managed a final gun duel with the Maxims at a range of a hundred meters.

At brigade headquarters, Neville knew by sometime after midnight that the Mouzon crossing had failed and that he had two weakened battalions across the Meuse, with a third following. He asked Lejeune for another battalion. Lejeune sent him the 1st Battalion, 9th Infantry, to be held in support.

Armistice

When gray daylight appeared on November 11, Captain Cumming could see no sign of the 6th Marines. He asked for a volunteer to swim the river to see what had happened to the missing regiment. The swimmer started at about 7:30 AM and was two-thirds of the way across when German fire killed him. Cumming waited until 10 AM and then called for another volunteer. He picked one who said that he could swim the distance under water. The Germans did not see him until he reached the opposite bank. He dodged into some bushes, and Cumming knew he would get through.

Lejeune afterward said that the night of this last battle of the war was the most trying night he had ever experienced. It weighed heavily on him that in all probability the Armistice was about to be signed. At 6:05 AM on the eleventh he received a radio message:

Marshal Foch to the Commanders-in-Chief:
1. Hostilities will be stopped on the entire front beginning at 11 o'clock, November 11 (French hour).
2. The Allied troops will not go beyond the line reached at that hour on that date until further orders.

(Signed) Marshal Foch
5:45 AM

Was it a hoax?

Lejeune called the chief of staff of V Corps to verify the message. The chief of staff stiffly told him to ignore any word of an armistice unless it came to him officially from V Corps. Not until 8:45 did V Corps confirm the message. Lejeune repeated the order to his brigade commanders and then personally directed Colonel Feland to expedite getting the message to Major Hamilton and Captain Dunbeck.

At 8:35 AM news reached Buck Neville that the Armistice had been signed and that hostilities would cease at 11 AM. He informed his regimental commanders, hoping that they in turn could get the word through to the battalions fighting on the east bank. Only too aware that an armistice was not peace, he thought it obvious that the best possible defensive line had to be occupied. Lejeune or Neville, or possibly Feland—it is not clear which—determined that this should be Senegal Farm Ridge as occupied by the 1st Battalion, with the 2d Battalion extending the line along the highway to Belle Fontaine Farm. Local commanders recalled patrols that had pushed forward as far as Moulins.

During the last two hours before the Armistice, the Germans intensified their artillery fire. A few minutes before 11 AM there were tremendous bursts of fire from both sides—and then silence. "Silence laid a pall on everything," recalled Private Mackin. Reported the *New York Times,* "In a twinkling of the eye four years of killing and massacre stopped as if God had swept his omnipotent finger across the scene of world carnage and cried, 'Enough!'"

It took a bit longer than "a twinkling" for news of the Armistice to reach the Marines east of the river. In the morning Hamilton's 1st Battalion moved out in support of the battalion from the 89th, which was paralleling Dunbeck's 2d Battalion in its advance. Captain Hunt, leading what was left of his 18th Company, was about a mile from the river and approaching Moulins when word of the Armistice reached him at about 11:45 AM.

The last German order on this front was issued at 10:50 AM, when the 174th Infantry was directed by its brigade commander to send its reserve battalion up to the 166th Infantry on the left to block the American advance. The order was not carried out.

A German battalion commander facing the 2d Division reported: "At 11:15 hostilities cease. Not a shot is fired. Among our men [a] quiet, depressed mood, and quiet joy, while among the enemy there is loud manifestation of joy over the armistice."

Cumming and his Marines on the east bank at Mouzon were still isolated. As Cumming, who would retire as a major general, later remembered:

Whenever we saw any Germans we fired on them and this continued until about 2:15 in the afternoon of November 11th.

I noticed the Germans were not returning our fire and suddenly all along the main highway fronting us, there appeared above the embankment German rifles with flags and white handkerchiefs waving. I ordered my men not to fire and we waited to see what they were going to do.

Suddenly two Germans appeared and started walking toward our lines. When they got half-way I saw one of them undo his pistol belt and throw it to one side. I, therefore, called for a volunteer who could speak German to accompany me, and approached the German who was a captain. Speaking in German, he said he knew he had us surrounded and that we had no communication with the main body of our forces so he was informing us that an armistice had been signed that morning between the German high command and the Allied command. All firing should have stopped at 11 AM. I had continued to fire on his troops causing some casualties. He requested that I take his word about the armistice and cease firing on his troops. I informed him that I had heard of a possibility of an armistice and, on returning to my lines, would inform my men that it was an accomplished fact and we would observe the armistice. I picked up my pistol, which I had thrown to one side, he picked up his, and we both returned to our lines.

A few minutes later Germans came swarming over the embankment waving bottles of brandy. Drinks were quickly traded for American cigarettes. "One would have thought they were long-lost brothers," remembered Cumming. Not until a half-hour later did a Marine runner reach him with official word of the Armistice.

As Lejeune wrote later in an order published to the 2d Division:

On the night of November 10th, heroic deeds were done by heroic men. In the face of a heavy artillery and withering machine gun fire, the Second Engineers threw two footbridges across the Meuse and the First and Second Battalions of the Fifth Marines crossed resolutely and unflinchingly to the east bank and carried out their mission.

The frontline Marines were wet, chilled to the bone, and exhausted. Only gradually did it sink in that the war was over. The men gathered in small groups and built bonfires. They began to talk and sing songs. That night there was a display of pyrotechnics as weapons were fired into the air all along the line. Under the elation, though, there was an edge of bitterness. If it had been known that the war was to end, why had they been ordered to attack across the Meuse? The two battalions of the 5th Marines had suffered a seemingly unnecessary thirty-one killed and 148 wounded in the night crossing, plus more than seventy-five missing and presumed drowned. Total brigade losses since November 1 had been 323 killed, 1,109 wounded.

Some were quick to lay the blame at General Summerall's feet, but as Lejeune makes clear in his *Reminiscences,* the orders had come down from the top. Foch on November 9 had sent a telegram to the commanders of each of the Allied armies:

The enemy, disorganized by our repeated attacks, retreats along the entire front. It is important to coordinate and expedite our movements. I appeal to the energy and the initiative of the Commanders-in-Chief and of their Armies to make decisive the results obtained.

Pershing had ordered his First and Second armies to press forward. The First Army ordered the V Corps to press forward, and so it was that Pershing was able to report:

The Fifth Corps in the First Army forced a crossing of the Meuse east of Beaumont, and gained the commanding heights within the reentrant of the river, thus completing our control of the Meuse River line.

Lt. Jerry Thomas went "AWOL" from his hospital bed while still recovering from his mustard-gas immersion of October 31, but he did not catch up with his 75th Company in its Bois du Fond du Limon bivouac until noon on November 11. The reunion was bittersweet. Although more than seven hundred men had served in the company since June, only six men, including Thomas, remained of the pre–Belleau Wood roster.

And what were Lejeune's private thoughts? On the night of November 11 he wrote to his wife, "Last night we fought our last battle. . . . To me it was pitiful for men to go to their death on the evening of peace."

CHAPTER FOURTEEN

The Watch on the Rhine

A n hour before the Armistice went into effect, 2d Division issued Field Order 62, which warned: "The enemy will be kept under close observation and the troops will be held in constant readiness for immediate action. . . . Fraternizing will be absolutely prohibited. The present status is one of a temporary cessation of hostilities and is not that of peace."[1]

The German General Staff continued to function with most of its old efficiency; the Germans began to withdraw at once, some divisions moving on November 11.

The Allies started a bit slower. On the thirteenth the U.S. 77th Division relieved the 2d Division along the Meuse. The relief took place on the fourteenth in broad daylight, a new experience for Lejeune's troops. Two days later the division, now assigned to III Corps, assembled near Pouilly, where it would cross the Meuse. The 2d Division was badly used up. Much of its equipment was run down. Uniforms were in tatters.

Plans had been drafted before the Armistice for the organization of the Third Army, under Maj. Gen. Joseph T. Dickman, USA, as the American Army of Occupation. The Third Army would number more than 200,000 men. The divisions making up its lead echelon considered themselves the best fighting divisions in the AEF—if not the world—and they probably were, at that time.

General Dickman, West Point 1881, was, at sixty-one, three years older than Pershing. A cavalryman and an old Indian fighter, he had campaigned in Cuba, the Philippines, and the Boxer Rebellion and in 1905 had compiled the first edition of *Field Service Regulations,* modeled after German army regulations. He had impressed Pershing with his handling of the 3d Division at Chateau-Thierry

241

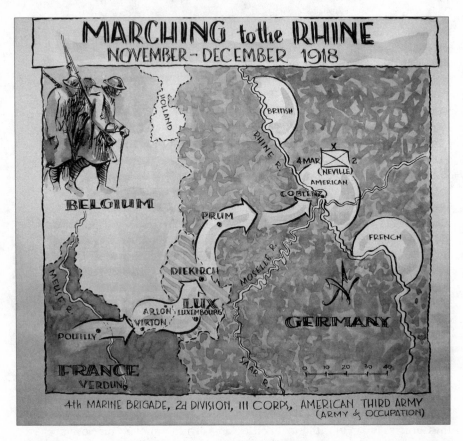

MARCHING to the RHINE
NOVEMBER - DECEMBER 1918

4th MARINE BRIGADE, 2d DIVISION, III CORPS, AMERICAN THIRD ARMY
(ARMY of OCCUPATION)

and had done well with the IV Corps at St. Mihiel and the I Corps in the Meuse-Argonne. Now quite portly, he was still a cavalryman at heart. Before going into Germany, Dickman had an audience with Marshal Foch, who pressed the point that the Germans should be held down firmly. Dickman did not agree. It was not the American way, he thought, to treat a defeated people harshly.

Maude Radford Warren, a writer for the *Saturday Evening Post* and one of the few civilians to accompany the march of the Third Army into Germany, observed graphically and symmetrically, if not quite accurately: "The Third Army would have radiating from it, like spokes from a hub, three corps. . . . It was a stupendous task to move close to half a million men over strange country along many unknown roads, and feed and clothe and warm them, and keep them out of danger and out of mischief."

The six lead U.S. divisions were actually organized into two corps. The III Corps, commanded by Maj. Gen. John L. Hines, USA, put the 2d Division into the good company of the 1st and 32d divisions. Hines, fifty years old and West Point 1891, had campaigned in Cuba and the Philippines, and he had been with Pershing in Mexico. Tall, lean, square jawed, and with a clipped mustache, he was cast in much the same mold as Pershing. Since coming to France he had commanded in succession the 16th Infantry, a brigade of the 1st Division, the 4th Division, and now the III Corps.

Marshal Foch set the time for crossing the armistice line for the whole front, from Switzerland to the sea, at 5 AM on Sunday, November 17. The 2d Division was to march to the German border, nearly a hundred kilometers from the Meuse to the Sure, in six marching days, with one day of rest.

The division had time to issue a certain amount of new equipment. The machine-gun companies of the 4th Marine Brigade traded their worn-out Hotchkiss guns for superb new Browning M1917 water-cooled weapons. Sufficient numbers of the already popular Browning automatic rifles arrived to replace the last cantankerous Chauchats. The Marines oiled their sleek new weapons, lamenting that they had not received them in quantity six months earlier.

Marching to Germany

The 2d Division began its march to Germany in two columns. The 4th Marine Brigade, with its supporting artillery, took the northern route. Lejeune spent the seventeenth on the road, watching his division march past: "Each infantryman carried his field kit and clothing roll, and in addition a belt and two bandoliers of ammunition, rifle or Browning automatic, steel helmet, gas mask, overcoat, etc., a total of seventy-five or eighty pounds. The men were still below par physically, and many suffered from sore and blistered feet caused by the English shoes which had been issued to them after the Armistice." The hated British shoes had hobnails in their soles and steel horseshoes in the heels; they were "as stiff as a board." The division stretched for forty-eight kilometers—two days' march—along the road.

The first day took the brigade across the Meuse, the river that had proved so costly to reach and cross. Just ahead was the retiring German army. Schedules were arranged in such a way that the American advance guard would not catch up with the German rear guard. The Germans were not entirely trusted. The Americans used advance guards on the march and outposts during the halts.

The second day brought them into Belgium and its ruined villages. There was a whole new set of place names. They moved through Virton and Arlon. The liberated Belgians were ecstatic: *"Vive nos liberateurs!"* Correspondent Maude Warren reported that as the Americans marched through flag-decked Belgian towns, the crying, laughing Belgians reached out to caress them as they passed.

The march then went through quiet and peaceful Luxembourg and the towns of Brouch, Mersch, and Larochette; the last they learned was also called Fels, the Luxembourgers being equally at home in their use of French and German. The Luxembourgers were cordial if not wildly enthusiastic. As Warren saw it: "The people of Luxembourg were used to having German soldiers march through their little towns. Unlike the Belgians they watched the Americans without enthusiasm, faces inanimate and somewhat fearful."

Captain Cates wrote home on November 27 from Luxembourg. Of the Meuse-Argonne he said: "We had gone thru the worst fight of our lives. It was not the fighting, but it was the cold, rainy, muddy weather. It rained every day and was bitter cold. We were drenched to the skin and our blankets were soaked. . . . I went in with a company of 250 and I came out with less than 50. Only one was killed and twenty-eight wounded; the others were sent back sick."

The men of the 2d Division, at this point, were far from parade-ground soldiers. On November 22, Brig. Gen. Malin Craig, Dickman's chief of staff, sent a message to General Hines calling the 2d Division "an eyesore." Hines' chief of staff moved the message to Lejeune by endorsement, "For his information and guidance." Lejeune did not take kindly to the criticism of his soldiers and Marines. By return endorsement he demanded that the "eyesore" statement be withdrawn: "The 2nd Division has fought, marched, moved by rail or camion, and bivouacked in the woods continuously since March 15, last. It has fought five pitched battles, always defeating the enemy, and has rendered service of incalculable value to the allied cause . . . in explanation of the present appearance of the Division, that it left the battlefield for this march without being refitted with clothing or equipment, and that practically all the men are now wearing the same uniforms that they wore in the battles in the Champagne district and in the recent American offensive."

Lejeune's alleged ragamuffins reached the German frontier at Diekirch on the banks of the Sure on November 23. Here the 2d Division halted, by prearrangement, until December 1, the day set for the crossing into Germany. Fresh army uniforms were issued. The new clothing and equipment helped, but the troops still hated their English-made shoes.

The twenty-eighth of November was Thanksgiving, and it was duly observed. There was a holiday menu of sorts, cooks sweating over the rolling kitchens, second helpings encouraged. Lejeune convened an awards formation at division headquarters and issued a number of Distinguished Service Crosses.

On the first of December, on schedule, the 2d Division, with the Marine brigade on the left, French troops on the division's left, other American troops on the division's right, crossed into Germany.

Maude Warren described the entry into Germany this way: "A sudden sweep over a cobbled street, the crossing of a bridge with a statue on the left, and we were in Germany. Prosperous fields, a few isolated houses from which no faces looked, and then a long village that contrived to look clean in spite of the manure piles here and there before the houses. Standing in the street, well out of the range of splashing mud, were German civilians, men women, and children, not in the least starved looking, all staring fixedly at the Americans. . . . All the people stared—some curious, some lowering, some hostile, some merely impassive."

The troops marched with colors, standards, and guidons proudly flying. This was a triumphant army. The division was now in hilly, almost mountainous, country. There were more strange place names: Mettendorf, Rittsersdorf, Prum, Gerolstein, Nohn, and Adenau. The rain had begun again. The roads were slippery and the grades difficult to negotiate.

Maude Warren reported with undisguised euphoria: "To an onlooker every mile of the march was picturesque. Those many, many men in khaki almost seemed as if they were converging from all the roads of the world."

The Marines marched through the German towns, flags flying, bands playing. The Germans stood on the sidewalks and watched silently. The indestructible John Thomason was still with the 49th Company. He tells about the march into Germany in a chapter in *Fix Bayonets* entitled "The Rhine." Thomason puts himself in the mind of the major commanding the 1st Battalion, 5th Regiment. The major, on horseback, looks back along the road at his battalion. His thoughts, as Thomason imagines them, go like this:

> The battalion, he reflected, was up to strength again. It hadn't been this large since it went to Blanc Mont, the end of September. He shut his eyes on that thought—a hundred and thirty men that came out, where a thousand went in—then replacements, and, after the Armistice, more replacements. Perhaps the quality was running down a little. The new chaps didn't seem as tall and broad as the old men, the tall, sunburnt leathernecks that went up the road from Meaux, toward Chateau-Thierry, in the spring. Odd, just six months since the spring.

But, as Thomason writes:

> There were very few men in the column who remembered the hike to Verdun, in the early spring of 1918; in one company eight, in another eleven; in the whole battalion the barest handful. It had been a long road. The first way-station was the Bois de Belleau; a lot of people stopped there, and were there yet. And there were more, comfortably rotting in the Forêt de Retz, south of Soissons. And more yet, well dead around Blanc Mont. And a vast drift of them back in hospitals. Men walked silent, remembering the old dead. . . . Twelve hundred men hiking to the Rhine, and how many ghosts.

The division entered the valley of the Ahr, leading to the Rhine. Until now there had been parallel roads, but in the Ahr Valley there was only a single river road, shut in by the steep hills. The German country people were reserved but not hostile. Some Marines felt more at home with them than they had with the French. On December 7 the advance guard reached the Rhine at Zinnzig. Lejeune opened his headquarters at Ahrweiler. The Marines walked up the river a short distance and found billeting in the houses on the west bank, their blistered feet reflecting the effects of the 160-kilometer march in their hobnailed English boots.

The Allied armies of occupation planned to cross the Rhine simultaneously on December 13 and establish three great bridgeheads centered on Mainz, Coblenz, and Cologne. From each of these cities a semicircle with a radius of thirty kilometers had been drawn. A neutral zone of ten kilometers extended outside each semicircle. The British would be at Cologne, the French at Mainz, and the French and Americans would share the Coblenz bridgehead. The semicircle drawn at Coblenz had the point of the compass at the Pfaffendorf Bridge. A French corps would garrison one third of the Coblenz semicircle; the U.S. Third Corps would garrison the remainder.

The 2d Division marched on to the extreme northwestern portion of the Coblenz semicircle and took responsibility for the river sector of the bridgehead on that flank. In the center was the 32d Division and on the right flank the 1st Division—the "Big Red One."[2] The 4th Brigade, with headquarters at Niederbieber, occupied the northern portion of the divisional area and took responsibility for the outpost line.

Watchful Waiting

Lt. Lem Shepherd was released from the hospital in mid-December and given the option of returning to the States or rejoining the 5th Marines. He chose to rejoin his regiment. On the way he stopped at the paymaster's in Paris and learned that he had been promoted to captain. He took command of the 55th Company in a small German town several kilometers west of Coblenz.

Col. Fritz Wise's 59th Infantry, 4th Division, was stationed on the Moselle about sixty-five kilometers from the Marine brigade. As full of himself as ever, the day after Christmas Wise drove over for a visit with the Marines. He found his old friend, Col. Logan Feland, still in command of the 5th Marines and Charley Dunbeck, still a captain, in command of his old outfit, the 2d Battalion. Dunbeck told him that only 143 of the "originals" were left.

Before leaving, Wise bumped into a familiar figure limping along through the gathering gloom of night and the fall of a light snow. It was James Gallivan, promoted on December 26 from Marine gunner to second lieutenant, U.S. Marine Corps Reserve, although few old salts considered it a promotion to go from exalted Marine gunner to temporary second lieutenant. Gallivan now had the Croix de Guerre and three citations that would later be transmuted into Silver Stars. One was for Belleau Wood. The second, recommended by Lejeune, was for Blanc Mont. The third, also recommended by Lejeune, was for the Meuse-Argonne, from November 1 to 11.

The assistant secretary of the navy, young Franklin D. Roosevelt, on January 2 sailed again for Europe, this time with his wife, Eleanor. The Roosevelts stayed at the Ritz in Paris and on January 18 drove to Boulogne to take a channel steamer to England. En route they stopped at Belleau Wood. The few bare sticks of what had once been trees gave Eleanor a ghastly feeling.

Eleanor came down sick with pleurisy, and FDR left her in London on January 31 to tour Belgium and then go on to Germany to visit the Marine brigade. He crossed the channel in the destroyer USS *Farnell,* whose captain was Lt. Cdr. William F. Halsey. There were still floating mines, and that made the crossing exciting. In Brussels he had lunch with King Albert. He then moved on into the Rhineland, expecting to see the Stars and Stripes floating over the great fortress Ehrenbreitstein. He was furious to find that it was not being flown, out of consideration of German sensibilities. Later, when he got back to Paris, he brought the matter to Pershing's attention. Pershing promised that it would be flying within the hour. According to FDR at least, the flag did not come down again until the last American left Germany.

After inspecting the Marine brigade on the bank of the Rhine, FDR told the Marines that they were especially privileged to be serving in Germany. He patted the pocket of his jacket, saying that it held his steamship tickets home but that he would be happy to trade the tickets for a Marine uniform. A private in the ranks shouted, "I'll swap you." As a souvenir of his visit the Marines gave him a Spandau light machine gun captured the last night of the war.[3]

In February 1919, Captain Woodworth and Lieutenants Cates and Vandoren, all of the 2d Battalion, 6th Regiment, had their turn at fourteen days' leave in London. "We expect to have a large and elegant time—we're routed through Paris," Lucian Vandoren wrote his mother. From Paris they went to Calais and there took a channel steamer to Folkestone. In London, digging deep in their pockets, they came up with thirty-seven shillings a day for a suite at the Hyde Park Hotel in Knightsbridge—"two bed-rooms, sitting room with hearth fire and bath—all beautifully appointed!"

On one big evening they went to the Paladium ("one of the Music Halls here") and afterward went to Murray's Club to dance and then on to Rector's, where there was more dancing and a late supper. On other days there were visits to the Pall Mall, Hyde Park, Regents Street, and the American Officers Club, which was "located in Lord 'Something or Other's' home and is perfectly exquisite." Vandoren had a pair of boots made "by the chap who does the same thing for the Prince of Wales." Having enjoyed Elsie Janis when she performed near Verdun the prior year, the Marines made a point of seeing her sing in the musical *Hello America* ("a darn good show"). Cates and Vandoren went alone to *Going Up,* another American musical, and afterward gave a supper party at the Hyde Park for two of the showgirls.

Back along the Rhine, large-scale field training had begun, reflecting Pershing's emphasis on open warfare. Trenches were a thing of the past. There were new *Infantry Drill Regulations* to be learned and taught. Target ranges were set up, and much firing was done both by the infantry and the artillery. Training crossed over into recreation, and there were many competitions, including an AEF rifle championship, involving twelve divisions, fired at Le Mans in May. The 2d Division team shot the highest aggregate score.

John Thomason, with a promotion to a captain, left the 49th Company to take command of the 17th Company, a sister company in the 1st Battalion, 5th Marines. He would stay a captain for many years to come.[4]

Most of the troops wanted to go home. A rumor had spread that General Pershing had decided to keep an army of occupation in Germany made up of regular divisions, of which the 2d Division was one. There was some unrest. A darker rumor circulated that the movement home would be in reverse order: first troops over would be the last to return.

Commanders sought to maintain troop morale by means of athletics, amateur theatrical shows, professional entertainments, and educational programs. The educational system peaked in an "AEF University" in far-off Beaune on the Côte d'Or. There was a liberal leave policy. Regular leave trains shuttled back and forth to pleasure spots. A 2d Division Association was formed, and the publication of the newspaper *Indian Head* began.

In April, the 32d Division, the right-hand neighbor of the 2d, left for home and demobilization. Boundaries were shifted, accommodating the three-division corps area to two. The 1st Division stayed on the right (the old rules of seniority continued to apply) and the 2d Division on the left.

Disagreements between the French and the Americans on the treatment of the Germans continued. The French accused Major General Dickman, quite unfairly, of being pro-German. At the end of April 1919, Maj. Gen. Hunter Liggett relieved him.

On the 30th of May, Captain Vandoren took the 80th Company and the 5th Regiment's band to Beaumont, "scene of our last scrap before the Armistice," for the dedication of the American Cemetery. "'Black Jack' [Pershing] and much other 'rank' was on hand," Vandoren wrote his mother. He could also tell her that he had received his third Croix de Guerre.

Secretary of the Navy Josephus Daniels was the main speaker for the dedication of the cemetery. After the speeches the 80th Company fired a salute over the rows upon rows of the dead, and a bugler played "Taps." After dinner the Marines were allowed to search the cemetery for the graves of their comrades.

The 80th Company marched out of the town to the tap of the drums of the regimental band, accompanied by the cheers of the townspeople and of a contingent of "colored" American soldiers. GySgt. Donald Paradis remembered "why the colored boys were there. It was they who had picked up the bodies of our comrades in their shallow graves all over the battlefields, then reburied them in neat rows each with a headstone and white cross, with their names, ranks, and companies on it. The most of us could remember the awful stench of the unburied dead on the battlefields and well knew the distasteful task they had performed."

A Fragile Peace

The Marines followed the peace negotiations going on in Paris for signs of German intransigence. If hostilities were resumed, it was planned that the 1st and 2d divisions would go forward, side by side, while other divisions still in France crossed the Rhine at and below Coblenz.

In May the Germans at Paris flatly refused the demands of the Allies. The U.S. III Corps on June 17 began to concentrate for an advance. The 2d Division formed to move forward in two columns, the 3d Brigade with the 15th Field Artillery on the right, the 4th Brigade and 12th Artillery on the left. The French 2d Cavalry Division took over the outpost line. This show of force may have affected the deliberations in Paris. A week later the Germans agreed to the treaty as drafted. The treaty was signed on June 28, and the Army of Occupation returned to its billets.

Five days later Lejeune received orders transferring the 2d Division from the Third Army to the Services of Supply for transportation home. The last field order of the division, issued July 12, 1919, began with the familiar phrase, "The 2d Division moves to a new area."

On July 15 the division began its move to Brest for return to the United States. Twenty-six trains, two on July 15 and four each day thereafter, were provided for the move. The last contingent arrived at Brig. Gen. Smedley Butler's Camp Pontanezen, Brest, on July 23. Embarkation on ships bound for home began the same day.

Homecoming

On the twelfth of August 1919, shortly after the 4th Marine Brigade debarked in New York, Secretary of War Newton Baker sent a congratulatory letter to Navy Secretary Josephus Daniels. Baker hailed the Marine Brigade's "unconquerable tenacity and dauntless courage" while under the control of the War Department, and he officially detached the Marines from the army and restored them to the control of the Navy Department. Baker concluded by saying, "Throughout this long contest the Marines, both by their valor and their tragic losses, heroically sustained, added an imperishable chapter to the history of America's participation in the World War."

Franklin D. Roosevelt responded on behalf of Daniels, thanking Baker for his compliments about the Marines and adding, "It is with very pardonable pride that we welcome them back to the Navy."

The war had pulled the Marine Corps in two directions—ashore with the army, seaward with the navy. In his annual report to the secretary of the navy, dated October 10, 1918, Major General Commandant George Barnett said, "It was believed to be essential that the Marine Corps do its full part in this war, and for that reason I feel it was absolutely necessary that the Marines should join the army on the western front, taking care, however, that this should not at any time interfere with the filling of all naval requirements."

In reality, Barnett had some fences to mend with both the army and the navy. Most critically, it was past time for him to lead the Corps into an authentic twentieth-century mission, one that would preserve the Corps' naval roots and avoid duplicating the army's role.

On balance, George Barnett had proven to be an effective wartime commandant. He successfully mobilized congressional support for the Corps' unprecedented expansion, managed the vastly enlarged recruiting and training effort, wedged a large brigade into the AEF, maintained the Corps' vaunted "First to Fight" claim, deployed newly created aviation forces to the Azores and France, delivered a second brigade to the theater of war, and maintained the Advance Base Force at full strength throughout the conflict. On the other hand, he failed to convince the Wilson administration and General Pershing to accept a full-blown Marine division in the AEF, provided only halfhearted support for the deployment of Marine aviation, gradually lost the confidence of Secretary Daniels, and never overcame the enmity of the Butler family.

For months Barnett dreamed of leaving quarrelsome Washington for a grand tour of all Marine units in the field in France. The opportunity came in late September 1918, when he and Maj. Gen. Charles L. McCawley, quartermaster of the Corps, sailed from New York on the USS *Leviathan*. Their timing seemed apt. The 4th Brigade had just completed the costly Blanc Mont assault and was replenishing its ranks at Chalons in preparation for the Meuse-Argonne offensive. But Barnett was stricken by the influenza epidemic and never made it to the front. The Armistice had occurred by the time he recovered, and the 4th Brigade was in Germany, preparing to cross the Rhine. Barnett, crestfallen, sailed home, leaving the role of distinguished Washington visitor to Assistant Navy Secretary Roosevelt.

Barnett returned to knotty problems concerning demobilization. Voluntary enlistments had been suspended at the end of the summer of 1918, and the Marine Corps for the closing months of the war received draftees from the Selective Service. Col. Albert Sydney McLemore, the Marines' recruiting and publicity mastermind, watched sadly while his carefully oiled recruiting machine was dismantled.

At the end of 1918, however, Secretary Daniels authorized the resumption of voluntary recruiting. Colonel McLemore wrote out a three-page plan, dated January 14, 1919, for the approval of General Barnett. McLemore reported that recruits were coming at the rate of about twenty a day, while discharges were being granted at about two hundred a day. At this rate, McLemore estimated, "by January 1, 1920 all reservists, selectives [draftees], and duration-of-the-war men, approximately 50,000 all told, will have left the Marine Corps."

In his memorandum, McLemore looked back at the success of the Publicity Bureau: "It has been proved indisputably that applicants come into Marine Corps Recruiting Stations in direct proportion to the publicity propaganda employed. . . . [Few people] know what the Marine Corps is; that it has a separate uniform . . .

a glorious history, and noble traditions. Marine Corps publicity is purely educational. Only facts are used, but an effort is made to dress them attractively."[5]

Final Parades

James Gallivan, the oldest second lieutenant in the Marine Corps, was one of those who came home in the SS *George Washington,* arriving in Hoboken on August 3, 1919—two years and six weeks after the departure of the 5th Marines from New York amid a sea of well-wishers—a lifetime ago, it seemed.

The balance of the 2d Division returned to New York in increments in early August. The last contingent arrived on the eighth of the month, just in time to join the division's homecoming parade, held that afternoon. The division assembled at Washington Square and marched up Fifth Avenue to 110th Street. General Lejeune, his staff, and his commanders reviewed the marching formations at 110th Street.

Then the division began to break up, as individuals and units went their separate ways. The Leathernecks said affectionate goodbyes to the army infantry, artillerymen, and engineers with whom they had shared so much. The Marine brigade headed for Quantico.

On August 12 the brigade stopped in Washington for a march past the White House. After that last review, President Woodrow Wilson wrote General Barnett a brief note: "The whole nation has reason to be proud of them."

The brigade demobilized at Quantico on the day following the White House review. Most of the men went home, taking with them their tin hats and gas masks as authorized souvenirs. They came back to a changed America. People seemed more cynical, urbane, and self-absorbed. Many women in their families—sisters, girl friends, wives, and even mothers—had joined the workforce. Not all would return willingly to the kitchen and washday on Mondays. Arguments raged for and against "women's suffrage," the constitutional right of women to vote. A wave of temperance threatened to bring about Prohibition. American industry had been busy retooling for the pent-up peacetime market since the Armistice. Pay that had been allowed to accumulate "on the books" now bought much less than it would have in 1917. The cost of a pair of Florsheim shoes now began at ten dollars, according to advertisements in the *Saturday Evening Post.* The war had made the wearing of wristwatches common and fashionable. The Elgin Watch Company celebrated victory with three new models: a "Foch" style, with a round luminous dial much like the kind worn most frequently in the trenches, for $18.50; a "Pershing" for twenty-one dollars; and a "Kitchener" for twenty. Fountain pens were now common. A Tempoint fountain pen ("A Tempoint That Writes Like You") made by the Wahl Company, the same people who produced the famous Eversharp pencil, was available for $2.50 with a choice of twenty-six different gold-tipped nibs. The automobile business boomed. By early 1919, Oakland Motor Car Company offered a "Sensible Six" (touring car or roadster $1,075, sedan or coupe $1,650). A Ford

Model T, of which more than fifteen million would be eventually produced, could be had for half that. Among other popular makes were the Franklin, Dodge, Dort, Willy-Overland, and Hudson, the last with a seven-passenger super-six phaeton for $2,200.

What Price Glory?

At Quantico, Lt. James Gallivan's old Belleau Wood leg wound grew worse. He turned himself into sickbay and was found physically unfit for service. He appeared before the Marine Retiring Board on September 9, 1919. With President Wilson's approval, Gallivan retired three months later, ending twenty-five colorful years of service as an indisputable member of "The Old Breed."[6]

Capt. John Thomason was one of those who decided to stay on in the Marine Corps. He went from Quantico to Cuba. After two years' duty in Cuba he was assigned to the Naval Ammunition Depot at Dover, New Jersey, which brought him close to New York, where he resumed his old friendship with Laurence Stallings.

After being wounded in Belleau Wood, Stallings had been treated in a series of French hospitals for almost a year, coming home as a captain in February 1919. There followed more time spent in the naval hospital in Brooklyn, and in 1922 surgeons at Walter Reed amputated his leg. He then went to work for the *New York World*. He and another *World* writer, Maxwell Anderson, wrote the play *What Price Glory?*

The play opened in New York at the Plymouth Theater on September 5, 1924. The protagonists were quintessential veteran Marines: Captain Flagg and First Sergeant Quirt. Like many of the real-life company commanders, Flagg—Louis Wolheim played him in the first production, though later, in the film version, Victor McLaglen would make the role his own—had risen from the ranks. The actor William Boyd, later better known as "Hopalong" Cassidy, played First Sergeant Quirt. In the film version, Edmund Lowe would play the part.

In an opening scene, a wartime recruit asks an old-timer where he came from. Says the old-timer: "Me? I've been to China, Cuba, the Philippines, San Francisco, Buenos Ayres [*sic*], Cape Town, Madagascar . . . wait a minute—Indiana, San Domingo, Tripoli, and Blackwell's Island."

The authors do not fix the exact time or place of the play or the precise unit. We learn, hazily, that the brigade is fighting for a town, up a road that has been one long shell hole since May, held half by the Marines, half by the Germans. It sounds very much like Bouresches.

The play established Stallings as one of the brilliant young writers coming out of the First World War, along with figures like Alexander Woolcott and Ernest Hemingway. Stark Young, the drama critic of the *New York Times*, thought the play superb: "'What Price Glory' is something you can put your teeth into," he wrote in a September 6, 1924, review.

Stallings, of course, knew of Thomason's sketches. He took Thomason to meet the editors of *Scribner's Magazine,* including the legendary Maxwell Perkins. They were impressed, and Thomason contracted to write and illustrate a series of stories. These five pieces, all written from the perspective of the second in command of the 49th Company, were the original content of the first edition of *Fix Bayonets!,* published by Charles Scribner's Sons in 1925. Thomason was launched as a successful writer. More Laurence Stallings plays also followed. A Stallings short story, "The Big Parade," would be made into an epic motion picture starring John Gilbert.[7]

Thomason and Stallings shared the conviction that the German army had not been sufficiently beaten and that some time the war would have to be fought again. They made a pilgrimage together back to France, including a somber visit to Belleau Wood.[8]

Capt. Lemuel Shepherd, on the voyage home in August 1919, was asked if he would like to make a relief map of Belleau Wood. He jumped at the chance. There was barely time for a weekend with his parents in Norfolk before he returned to France with a small survey party. Field work took three months. Making the map took another six months. Then it was placed in the Smithsonian Institution, where it would be displayed for many years. A Marine who had lost an arm at Belleau Wood was assigned there to describe the battle to visitors.[9]

The ground between the hallowed wood and the village of Belleau became one of five American national cemeteries in France. The entire wood was purchased by Mrs. James Carroll Fraser and subsequently passed to the jurisdiction of the American Battle Monuments Commission. It continues to be one of the battlefields and cemeteries most visited by Americans touring France.

Epilogue

orld War I devastated Europe as cruelly as the fourteenth-century
Black Plague.[1] The conflict also wreaked drastic changes on the societ-
ies, governments, and military establishments of the major combatants.
Nearly ten million men in arms died, and twenty million were wounded. The war
killed more than six million civilians. The Spanish influenza pandemic of 1918–19
claimed an additional fifty to a hundred million lives worldwide.

Against this horrific background, the greatest tragedy occurred at the peace
conference at Versailles, when the diplomats of the great powers failed to establish a just and lasting peace, leaving the door open for the even greater slaughters
to come in World War II. As British prime minister Lloyd George predicted at
Versailles, "We shall have to fight another war all over again in 25 years." He was
optimistic. The unsettled business erupted in twenty years.

The United States sustained about 50,000 deaths and 230,000 wounded of the
4.3 million people mobilized in 1917–18. The slow process of demobilizing and
reconfiguring the armed forces dominated the War and Navy departments and
each armed-service headquarters for more than a year after the Armistice.

The Marines have rarely fared well in postwar downsizing and cost-effective-
ness analyses, and the Corps—notwithstanding its combat record—faced tough
questions about its future utility to the nation. It did not help that the Marines had
done little to resolve their interminable search for a unique and useful twentieth-
century mission. Nor did they receive much support from their erstwhile com-
panions in the army or the navy. The army would not soon forget the Marines'
chest-beating boasts ("First to Fight!") or their exclusive publicity windfall resulting from Floyd Gibbons' dispatch from Belleau Wood. The navy grew impatient
with the Marines' lingering fascination with service ashore as a duplicate army
instead of their traditional service with the fleet. Finding a new naval mission and
attaining the capabilities for its execution would demand all the vision and leadership John Lejeune could muster in his forthcoming eight-year tenure as major gen-

eral commandant—and even that would not suffice. Defining the primary mission of the Marines as amphibious assault troops and creating the Fleet Marine Force as a major component of the fleet commander would fall to a future commandant, Maj. Gen. John H. Russell, fifteen years after the Armistice.

Marine aviation, in particular, faced a challenge from service and congressional budget cutters who questioned the need for a third air force. The tireless Marine aviation pioneer Maj. Alfred Cunningham pled his case before the General Board of the Navy in 1919, claiming, "The only excuse for aviation in any service is its usefulness in assisting the troops on the ground," an apt prediction for the Marines but a still unproven tactical concept. The board expressed interest, but Cunningham watched in dismay as the numbers of Marine aviators dropped from a wartime high of 282 pilots to 43 by 1921.

Some 32,000 Marines had served in France. There had been 11,366 casualties, of whom 2,459 were killed or were forever missing in action. Poison gas had killed or incapacitated nearly 1,000 of them. Although the 2d Division captured some 12,000 German soldiers, only 25 Marines were taken prisoner. ("Surrendering wasn't popular," said Col. Albertus Catlin.)

The German army that faced the Leathernecks from June until November 1918 may have represented a shadow of its glory years of 1914–15, but the gray-clad infantry, machine-gunners, and artillerymen defending Belleau Wood, Soissons, Mont Blanc, and the Meuse highlands still constituted the most lethally efficient foe the Marines had ever fought. Time and again the Germans exacted a deadly cost for Marine assaults through the wheat fields and shattered forests of the western front. As Capt. John Thomason reflected in 1928, "The butcher's bill of the American 2d Division will compare cruelly and honorably, for the five months it was engaged, with that of any division in any Army in the war. The casualties of the Marine Brigade were nearer two hundred than one hundred percent."

Man for man, the Marines fought exceptionally well against the German veterans. Blessed with good leaders at the company and battalion levels and superbly supported by the 6th Machine Gun Battalion, the Marines learned how to make the most of field artillery, tanks, and aircraft. The real strength of the Marine brigade lay in its NCOs, both the vaunted "Old Breed" professionals and the many newcomers, who had risen rapidly through the ranks. Many of the best NCOs, like Gerald Thomas, earned battlefield commissions, survived the postwar downsizing, and led the Corps with distinction in subsequent wars.

The garlands won by the Marines should not in any sense diminish the combat proficiency of many army units, notably the Leathernecks' friendly rivals within the 2d Division, the tough and feisty 9th and 23d infantry regiments.

Yet there were certain characteristics that distinguished the Marine brigade from other Allied units, among them a special emphasis on training, discipline, marksmanship, leadership, and esprit. In view of the Marines' traditional insistence that new recruits honor the combat performance of their forbears, it is possible that the institutional memories of Belleau Wood, Soissons, and Mont Blanc were to influence the latter-day assaults of another generation of Leathernecks who crossed the reef on D-day at Tarawa or assaulted Okinawa's Sugarloaf Hill and Kunishi Ridge.

Nor should it come as a surprise that the senior combat leadership of the Marines in their back-to-back amphibious assaults on Iwo Jima and Okinawa in 1945 came almost exclusively from veterans of World War I. Lt. Gen. Holland M. Smith commanded all expeditionary troops at Iwo Jima. Graves B. Erskine, Clifton B. Cates, and Keller E. Rockey, as major generals, commanded the three divisions. Five days after the end of organized resistance at Iwo Jima, Maj. Gen. Roy S. Geiger's III Amphibious Corps landed on Okinawa. Two major generals, Lemuel C. Shepherd and Pedro A. del Valle, commanded the two Marine divisions. (Del Valle had commanded the Marine detachment on the battleship *Texas* with the British Grand Fleet in the North Sea in 1918). Maj. Gen. Francis P. Mulcahy, like Geiger a veteran of the Northern Bombing Group in France, commanded the Tenth Army's Tactical Air Force during its epic battle with Japanese kamikazes at Okinawa.

The Marines entered World War I as a small force of seagoing light infantry whose forte had mainly been in the "small wars"—low-intensity littoral conflicts that lent themselves to quick resolution by an intervening landing force from the fleet. Their performance on the western front—especially at Belleau Wood—revealed a much greater military usefulness. At a high cost of life and limb, the Marines proved themselves to be a strategically important fighting force whose readiness, combined with the mobility of the fleet, offered the potential for an enhanced role in national security.

John Thomason concludes that the Marine Brigade was unique because "all its opportunities were conspicuous. It came upon the front at critical times. Great events hinged upon its attacks. Much of that was chance. . . . But there was nothing of luck—there was cold, hard discipline, and much war-wisdom, learned under the guns, and sheer, clean skill, in the fighting which made these opportunities good."

There are those who study Marine history who believe that the three "touchstone battles" of the Corps are Belleau Wood, Iwo Jima, and the Chosin Reservoir. Leathernecks of all stripes may dispute the selections, but it is quite certain that no battle ever had such a dynamic effect on the Corps as Belleau Wood. Beyond doubt, the Corps would never be the same after June 1918.

Appendix

Pharmacist's Mate First Class John H. Balch, USN: 6th Marines, Soissons, July 19, 1918, and Blanc Mont Ridge, October 5, 1918.

Lieutenant (Medical Corps) Joel T. Boone, USN: 6th Marines, Soissons, July 19, 1918.

Sergeant Louis Cukela, USMC*: 66th Company, 5th Marines, Soissons, July 18, 1918.

Hospital Apprentice First Class David E. Hayden, USN: 6th Marines, Thiaucourt (St. Mihiel), September 15, 1918.

Gunnery Sergeant Charles F. Hoffman, USMC (name used during WWI by Ernest A. Janson)*: 49th Company, 5th Marines, Hill 142, Belleau Wood, June 6, 1918.

Private John J. Kelly, USMC*: 78th Company, 6th Marines, Blanc Mont Ridge, October 3, 1918.

Sergeant Matej Kocak, USMC*: 66th Company, 5th Marines, Soissons, July 18, 1918.

Lieutenant Commander (Dental Corps) Alexander G. Lyle, USN: 5th Marines, near Verdun, April 23, 1918.

Lieutenant (j.g.) (Dental Corps) Weedon E. Osborne, USN: 5th Marines, near Bouresches, Belleau Wood, June 6, 1918. Killed in action.

Lieutenant (Medical Corps) Orlando H. Petty, USN: 5th Marines, Belleau Wood, June 11, 1918.

Corporal John H. Pruitt, USMC*: 78th Company, 6th Marines, Blanc Mont Ridge, October 3, 1918. Killed in action.

Gunnery Sergeant Robert G. Robinson, USMC: Squadron C, 1st Marine Aviation Force, near Pittham, Belgium, October 14, 1918.

Gunnery Sergeant Fred W. Stockham, USMC**: 96th Company, 6th Marines, Belleau Wood, June 13–14, 1918. Died (poison gas) as a result of the action.

Second Lieutenant Ralph Talbot, USMC: Squadron C, 1st Marine Aviation Force, October 8 and 14, 1918, near Pittham, Belgium.

---

* Awarded both the Navy and Army versions of the Medal of Honor for the same action.
** Awarded the Army version of the Medal of Honor.

Notes

Prologue: Les Mares Farm, Northern France, June 3, 1918

1. Unless otherwise noted, the material in the prologue is derived from: Robert B. Asprey, *At Belleau Wood* (New York: G. P. Putnam's Sons, 1965); Brig. Gen. Albertus W. Catlin, *With the Help of God and a Few Marines* (Garden City, N.Y.: Doubleday, Page, 1919); Maj. Edwin N. McClellan, "Operations of the Fourth Brigade of Marines in the Aisne Defensive," *Marine Corps Gazette,* June 1921; Brig. Gen. Edwin H. Simmons, "An Appreciation of Gen. Lemuel C. Shepherd, Jr., VMI '17," Distinguished Lecture, Virginia Military Institute, Lexington, Virginia, October 22, 1986, and "Remembering General Shepherd," *Fortitudine,* Fall 1990; Col. Dick Camp, USMC (Ret.), *Leatherneck Legends: Conversations with the Marine Corps' Old Breed* (St. Paul, Minn.: Zenith, 2006).

Chapter 1: "The War to End All Wars"

1. Unless otherwise noted, the material in this chapter is derived from: *The Annals of America,* vol. 14, *1916–1928, World War and Prosperity* (Chicago: Encyclopedia Britannica, 1976); Josephus Daniels, *The Wilson Era: Years of Peace, 1910–1917* (Chapel Hill: University of North Carolina Press, 1944), *The Wilson Era: Years of War and After, 1917–1923* (Chapel Hill: University of North Carolina Press, 1946), and *The Cabinet Diaries of Josephus Daniels,* ed. E. David Cronon (Lincoln: University of Nebraska, 1963); John A. Lejeune, *The Reminiscences of a Marine* (Philadelphia: Dorrance, 1930); Col. Robert D. Heinl Jr., *Soldiers of the Sea: The United States Marine Corps, 1775–1962* (Annapolis, Md.: Naval Institute Press, 1962); Barbara W. Tuchman, *The Zimmermann Telegram* (New York: Viking, 1958); Geoffrey C. Ward, *A First-Class Temperament: The Emergence of Franklin Roosevelt* (New York: Harper and Row, 1989); Maj. Edward F. Wells, USMC (Ret.), "FDR and the Marines," *Fortitudine,* Fall 1981–Winter 1982; Kenneth S. Davis, *FDR: The Beckoning of Destiny, 1882–1928* (New York: G. P. Putnam's Sons, 1971); Franklin D. Roosevelt, "Trip to Haiti and Santo Domingo, 1917," FDR Group 10, FDR Library, Hyde Park, New York; Dirk Anthony Ballendorf, "A Shot Not Heard Round the World: The U.S. Marines and the Start of World War I on Guam," paper presented at the annual meeting of the Society for Military History, April 9–12, 1992, copy held in Reference Section, History Division [hereafter HD], Marine

Corps University, Quantico [hereafter MCU]; Brig. Gen. Edwin H. Simmons, USMC (Ret.), *The United States Marines: A History,* 3d ed. (Annapolis, Md.: Naval Institute Press, 1998), "An Appreciation of General Shepherd," and "Remembering General Shepherd"; Maj. Gen. George Barnett, "Soldier and Sailor, Too," unpublished memoir, bound copy, Reference Section, HD, MCU; Gen. John J. Pershing, *My Experiences in the World War* (New York: Frederick A. Stokes, 1931), vol. 1; Marshall Joseph J. C. Joffre, *The Personal Memoirs of Joffre,* trans. Col. T. Bentley Mott, 2 vols. (New York: Harper and Brothers, 1932); Lt. Col. Charles A. Fleming et al., *Quantico: Crossroads of the Marine Corps* (Washington, D.C.: History and Museums Division, Headquarters, Marine Corps [hereafter HQMC], 1978); Maj. John H. Johnstone, *A Brief History of the 1st Marines* (Washington, D.C.: Historical Branch, G-3 Division, HQMC, 1968); Capt. Robert J. Kane, *A Brief History of the 2d Marines* (Washington, D.C.: Historical Division, HQMC, 1970); Benis M. Frank, *A Brief History of the 3d Marines* (Washington, D.C.: Historical Branch, G-3 Division, HQMC, 1968); James S. Santelli, *A Brief History of the 4th Marines* (Washington, D.C.: Historical and Museums Division, HQMC, 1970); Maj. James M. Yingling, *A Brief History of the Fifth Marines* (Washington, D.C.: Historical Branch, G-3 Division, HQMC, 1963); Col. Frederic M. Wise and Meigs O. Frost, *A Marine Tells It to You* (New York: J. H. Sears, 1929); *Dictionary of American Fighting Ships,* vol. 7 (Washington, D.C.: Naval Historical Center, 1981); Steve Donoghue, "A Salty Second Lieutenant," unpublished manuscript, n.d., Lt. James Gallivan, biographic files, Reference Section, HD, MCU [hereafter Gallivan biographic file]; 2d Lt. Charles P. Cushing, USMCR, "When the Marines Shoved Off," *Recruiters' Bulletin,* July 1917.

2.   The full text of the telegram is found in Tuchman, *Zimmerman Telegram.*

3.   The authors are reluctant to claim any thing or person as being "first," "last," "unique," or "the only." Someone can always find the exception.

4.   The *Prinz Eitel Friedrich,* a big ship of 14,180 tons, had put into Norfolk for repairs in March 1915, failed to leave within the time allotted by international law, and had been interned. The *Kron Prinz Wilhelm* was even more of a prize. A passenger ship of 23,500 tons, she left New York in August 1914 to rendezvous with the cruiser *Karlsruhe* north of the Bahamas. At sea, the *Karlsruhe* hurriedly fitted her out with two 88-mm guns and a gun crew so as to convert her into an auxiliary cruiser. In the next seven months she took and sank fifteen British merchant ships and rammed another. Late in March 1915, low on coal, the *Kron Prinz Wilhelm* headed for the neutral port of Norfolk, accepting intern status. At the Philadelphia Navy Yard, in June 1917, a working party of U.S. Marines tore down "Berlin," the German sailors' village.

5.   Barnett indicates that this meeting took place some days before the declaration of war, but his memoirs are quite spongy and imprecise. One can only suppose that he was in an acute decline when he wrote them.

6.   Balfour, a former prime minister, had come out of retirement at the war's beginning to become the First Lord of the Admiralty and, later, foreign secretary. His visit to Washington at the head of the British mission in April 1917 impressed his American hosts, who invited him to speak to the House of Representatives.

7. General Simmons' 1986 Distinguished Lecture, Virginia Military Institute, Lexington, Virginia, and the similar article in *Fortitudine,* Fall 1990, were drawn from General Shepherd's oral history, his official biographical file, and many conversations with him over the years.

8. Shepherd always found the date, May 3, easy to remember, because on that date in 1863 Stonewall Jackson made his famous flank march at Chancellorsville and, noting that many of his commanders were from VMI, said, "The Virginia Military Institute will be heard from today."

9. "2,600 Marines to Go with Pershing: Doyen Heads Sea Soldiers; His Marines Fresh from Active Fighting in Haiti and Santo Domingo; Has Force of Picked Men," *New York Times,* Sunday, May 20, 1917, p. 1. General Lejeune did not include the sardonic additional stanza to the "Marines' Hymn" when he copyrighted the original verses in 1929.

Chapter 2: Fivefold Expansion

1. Unless otherwise noted, the material in this chapter is derived from: Lejeune, *Reminiscences;* Brig. Gen. S. L. A. Marshall, USAR (Ret.), *The American Heritage History of World War I* (New York: American Heritage, 1964); Jack Shulimson, "The First to Fight: Marine Corps Expansion, 1914–18," *Prologue* 8 (Spring 1976); U.S. Marine Corps, Reserve Officers of Public Affairs Unit 4-1, *The Marine Corps Reserve: A History* (Washington, D.C.: Division of Reserve, HQMC, 1966); Col. Albert Sidney McLemore, USMC, biographic files, Reference Section, HD, MCU [hereafter McLemore biographic file]; U.S. Marine Corps, *Marine Corps Recruiters' Bulletin* for November 1916 and April, May, June, and July 1917; U.S. Marine Corps, *Annual Report of the Major General Commandant to the Secretary of the Navy,* for Fiscal Years 1915, 1916, 1917, and 1918 [hereafter Major General Commandant, *Annual Report,* (year)]; Kemper F. Cowing, comp., *Dear Folks at Home (Letters from the Battlefield)* (Boston: Houghton Mifflin, 1919); Col. James E. Hatcher, AUS (Ret.), "A Memoir of Service in World War I as a Private, USMC," unpublished manuscript, n.d., Marine Corps Archives, Gray Research Center, Quantico; Simmons, *The Marines: A History;* Lt. Col. Charles H. Cureton, USMC, "Parade Blue, Battle Green," in *The Marines,* ed. Brig. Gen. Edwin H. Simmons, USMC (Ret.), and J. Robert Moskin (Quantico, Va.: Marine Corps Heritage Foundation, 1998); Sgt. Martin "Gus" Gulberg, *A War Diary* (Chicago: Drake, 1927); Bernard C. Nalty et al., "United States Marine Corps Ranks and Grades, 1775–1969" (Washington, D.C.: Historical and Museums Division, HQMC, 1970); Lowell Thomas, *Old Gimlet Eye: Adventures of Smedley D. Butler* (New York: Farrar and Rinehart, 1933); Catlin, *A Few Marines;* Fleming, *Quantico;* Maj. Gen. Harry Lee, biographic files, Reference Section, HD, MCU; Maj. Harold C. Snyder, "The Marine Officers' School," *Recruiters' Bulletin,* July 1917; Gen. Clifton B. Cates, biographic files, Reference Section, HD, MCU [hereafter Cates biographic file]; Cates interview, March 28, 1967, Oral History Collection, HD, MCU [hereafter Cates interview]; U.S. Army *Infantry Drill Regulations, United States Army, 1911, Corrected to April 15, 1917* (Washington, D.C.: Government Printing Office, 1917);

Gen. Graves B. Erskine, USMC, biographic files, HD, MCU, and oral history, 1975, HD, MCU [hereafter Erskine oral history]; Lt. Gen. Thomas Holcomb, biographic files, Reference Section, HD, MCU; Lt. Walter S. Poague, *Diary and Letters of a Marine Aviator* (Chicago: privately published, c. 1919, copy in Rare Books Collection, HD, MCU); Maj. L. W. T. Waller Jr., "Machine Guns of the Fourth Brigade," *Marine Corps Gazette,* March 1920; Lt. John W. Overton biographic file, Reference Section, HD, MCU [hereafter John Overton, biographic files]; Capt. Macon C. Overton, biographic files, Reference Section, HD, MCU [hereafter Macon Overton biographic file]; Lt. Col. Merrill L. Bartlett, USMC (Ret.), "The Spirited Saga of 'Johnny the Hard,'" *Naval History,* June 2007 [hereafter Bartlett, "Johnny the Hard"]; Maj. John A. Hughes, biographic files, Reference Section, HD, MCU [hereafter Hughes biographic file]; Capt. [*sic*] Bertron William Sibley, biographic files, Reference Section, HD, MCU [hereafter Sibley biographic file]; Lt. Col. Lemly memo to the Quartermaster, 14 January, 1918, copy in Col. William B. Lemly, USMC," biographic files, Reference Section, HD, MCU; Col. John W. Thomason, biographic files, Reference Section, HD, MCU [hereafter Thomason biographic file]; Col. Roger Willock, USMCR, *Lone Star Marine* (Princeton, N.J.: Roger Willock, 1961); Brig. Gen. Edwin H. Simmons, "Thomason's *Fix Bayonets*," Military Classics Seminar, 21 June 1994, personal papers, HD, MCU; Donald R. Morris, "Thomason U.S.M.C.," *American Heritage,* November 1993; Joan T. Brittain, *Lawrence* [sic] *Stallings* (Boston: Twayne, 1975).

2. In 1918 the warrant grade of "pay clerk" would be added.

3. The Marine Corps calculated that on November 11, 1918, with various allowances, the average annual private's pay was $868.

4. Ten years later Rowell would become the first Marine aviator to receive the Distinguished Flying Cross, for leading his squadron of deHaviland DH-4 biplanes in a glide-bombing attack to break the Sandinista siege of a Marine outpost at Ocotal, Nicaragua.

5. Edwin Denby rose to the rank of major in the Marines, then, returning to politics, replaced Josephus Daniels as secretary of the navy in the Warren Harding administration in 1921. He gained early fame when Marines were ordered to prevent a wave of mail robberies, proclaiming, "When our Corps goes in as guards over the mail, that mail must be delivered, or there must be a Marine dead at the post of duty." Three years later Denby resigned in disgrace for his complicity in the Teapot Dome oil leasing scandal.

6. However, the practice of designating "lance corporals" or "jawbone corporals" survived, and in 1959 the grade of "lance corporal" officially entered the enlisted hierarchy.

7. Some of this 1917 doctrine was still being taught to second lieutenants at Quantico as late as 1942.

8. The Quantico Hotel would be known to generations of Marine officers as the Waller Building, or Waller Hall. It was closed in 1968 because of structural failure and eventually torn down.

9. An undated copy of this letter from General Pershing to Maj. Gen. George Barnett is in the Barnett biographic files, Reference Section, HD, MCO. From the phrase

"for nearly six months" it can be deduced that the letter was written in late October or early November. It may well have been the spur to Barnett's sending Lieutenant Colonel Lemly to France.

Chapter 3: New Frontiers

1. Unless otherwise noted, the material in this chapter is derived from: Lt. Col. Jay M. Salladay, USMC, "The Occupation of the Virgin Islands of the United States of America," *Marine Corps Gazette,* September 1918; Major General Commandant, *Annual Report,* 1917; Lt. Col. Edward C. Johnson, *Marine Corps Aviation: The Early Years, 1912–1940,* ed. Graham A. Cosmas (Washington, D.C.: History and Museums Division, HQMC, 1977); John A. DeChant, *Devilbirds* (New York: Harper and Brothers; 1947); Lt. Col. Clyde H. Metcalf, USMC, *A History of the United States Marine Corps* (New York: G. P. Putnam's Sons, 1939); Lejeune, *Reminiscences;* Col. Roger Willock, USMCR (Ret.), *Unaccustomed to Fear: A Biography of the Late General Roy S. Geiger* (Princeton, N.J.: privately published, 1968; reprinted by the Marine Corps Association, 1983). Oral history interviews with Lt. Gen. Karl S. Day, USMCR (Ret.), August 15, 1969; Maj. Gen. Lawson M. H. Sanderson, USMC (Ret.), July 14, 1969; Maj. Gen. Ford O. Rogers, USMC (Ret.), December 3, 1970; and Gen. Christian F. Schilt, USMC (Ret.), November 17 and 21, 1969; all from Oral History Collection, HD, MCU. U.S. Marines, Public Affairs Unit 4-1, *Marine Corps Reserve History;* Poague, *Diary;* Maj. Alfred A. Cunningham, "Value of Aviation to the Marine Corps," *Marine Corps Gazette,* September 1920; U.S. Marine Corps, *Marine Flyer in France: The Diary of Captain Alfred A. Cunningham, November 1917–January 1918* (Washington, D.C.: History and Museums Division, HQMC, 1974); "Military History of Ralph Talbot, Late Second Lieutenant, Marine Corps, October 10, 1922," Talbot Collection PC 410, HD, MCU [hereafter Talbot Collection]; Maj. Edna Loftus Smith, *Marine Corps Reserve Aviation, 1916–1987* (Washington, D.C.: HQMC, 1959).

2. Apparently Lejeune was not much impressed by his orientation flight. He does not mention the flight, nor does he even mention Cunningham by name, in his *Reminiscences.*

3. The 1917 table of organization for an army division included for the first time an "aero unit" for artillery spotting.

4. Five years after World War I, 1st Lt. Ford Rogers flew his DH-4 a distance of 10,953 miles in 127 hours of air time to publicize the skills of Marine pilots and their enlisted mechanics.

Chapter 4: "Over There"

1. Unless otherwise noted, the material in this chapter is derived from: Pershing, *My Experiences in the World War;* Cowing, *Dear Folks at Home;* Metcalf, *History;* Wise and Frost, *A Marine Tells It to You;* Catlin, *A Few Marines;* Col. Oliver L. Spaulding, USA, and Col. John W. Wright, USA, *The Second Division, American Expeditionary Force, in France* (New York: Hillman, 1937); Gallivan biographic file; Simmons, "Appreciation of General Shepherd" and "Remembering General Shepherd"; Maj. Frederick A. Barker, USMC (Ret.), biographic files, Reference Section, HD, MCU [hereafter Barker biographic file]; U.S. Army, *United States Army in the*

World War, 1917–1919, vol. 3, *Training and Use of American Units with British and French* (Washington, D.C.: Historical Division, Department of the Army, 1948); McClellan, "Aisne Defensive"; Gulberg, *War Diary;* Hatcher, "Memoir of Service"; Col. William B. Lemly memo; Col. F. Brooke Nihart, USMC (Ret.), "Muskets to Missiles," in *The Marines,* edited by Brig. Gen. Edwin H. Simmons, USMC (Ret.), and J. Robert Moskin. Quantico, Va.: Marine Corps Heritage Foundation, 1998; Waller, "Machine Guns"; Lt. Col. George M. Chinn, *The Machine Gun: History, Evolution, and Development of Manual, Automatic, and Airborne Repeating Weapons* (Washington, D.C.: Bureau of Ordnance, Department of the Navy, 1951); Maj. Edward B. Cole, USMC, biographic files, Reference Section, HD, MCU [hereafter Cole biographic file]; Lejeune, *Reminiscences;* John Overton biographic file.

2. *Chasseur,* French for "hunter," was the French army designation for certain regiments of elite light infantry *(chasseurs à pied)* or specialized mountain troops *(chasseurs Alpins).*

3. Catlin, *A Few Marines* (pp. 20–23) identifies the letter writer only as "Dick," a private in the 6th Marines, writing his father in the winter of 1917–18 from "Somewhere in France."

4. Nissen huts, widely used by the British in World War II as well as World War I, were the forerunner of the familiar American Quonset hut of World War II.

5. Not until 1927 did the Marine Corps abandon the choke collar on its officer service uniforms and adopt the flat-lapel coat. The large quantity of enlisted green coats on hand delayed the introduction of the roll-collar coat for enlisted Marines until 1928.

6. The overseas cap, a simplified copy of a French forage cap, is enshrined in the caps worn by many veterans' organization—that is, the blue cap of the American Legion and the red cap of the Marine Corps League. It was cheap, it packed well, it fit under the trench helmet, and it was absolutely no good in the rain, of which there was a great deal in France. The Marines, depending upon their mood, called it variously their "go-to-Hell" cap or "piss-cutter."

7. Although Catlin claims this was said, such an effusive and potentially divisive statement does not seem in character for Pershing. Catlin may have gotten it from Harbord, who was at this time still Pershing's chief of staff. Harbord would not infrequently gild the language of his commander in chief.

Chapter 5: The Trenches of Verdun

1. Unless otherwise noted, the material in this chapter is derived from: Catlin, *A Few Marines;* Spaulding and Wright, *Second Division;* Metcalf, *History; Handbook of the German Army in War, April 1918* (London: Imperial War Museum; Nashville, Tenn.: Battery, 1996); Wise and Frost, *A Marine Tells It to You;* Waller, "Machine Guns"; Gulberg, *War Diary;* I. F. Haber, *The Poisonous Cloud: Chemical Warfare in the First World War* (Oxford, U.K.: Clarendon, 1986); Lt. Col. Ronald J. Brown, USMCR (Ret.), *A Few Good Men: The Fighting Fifth Marines* (Novato, Calif.: Presidio, 2001); Hatcher, "Memoir of Service"; Gen. Holland M. Smith and Percy Finch, *Coral and Brass* (New York: Charles Scribner's Sons, 1948); Norman V. Cooper, *A Fighting General: The Biography of Gen. Holland M. Smith* (Quantico, Va.: Marine Corps Association, 1987); Lt. Lucian H. Vandoren, letter to his father, May 19, 1918, personal papers, HD, MCU [hereafter Vandoren papers]; Thomason biographic file.

2. According to the German army handbook, command of a German corps or group called for a *general der Infanterie,* or sometimes a *general der Kavellerie* or *general der Artillerie.* The British or American equivalent would be lieutenant general. Command of an army called for a *generaloberst,* or colonel general, for which there is no British or American equivalent.

3. Splitting the French and British armies is exactly what the German army did so successfully in the battle for France in May 1940.

Chapter 6: "Retreat, Hell!"

1. Unless otherwise noted, the material in this chapter is derived from: U.S. Army, *United States Army in the World War, 1917–1919,* vol. 4, *Military Operations of the American Expeditionary Forces* (Washington, D.C.: Historical Division, Department of the Army, 1948); Spaulding and Wright, *Second Division;* McClellan, "Aisne Defensive"; Asprey, *At Belleau Wood;* Catlin, *A Few Marines;* Metcalf, *History;* Pershing, *My Experiences in the World War;* Wise and Frost, *A Marine Tells It to You;* Haber, *Poisonous Cloud;* Gen. Clifton B. Cates, letters to his family from the war in France, 1918, Personal Papers Collection, MCU [hereafter Cates letters]; Erskine oral history; Hatcher, "Memoir of Service"; Brig. Gen. Logan Feland, "'Retreat Hell!" *Marine Corps Gazette,* September 1921; Simmons, "Appreciation of General Shepherd" and "Remembering General Shepherd"; Camp, *Leatherneck Legends.*

2. According to Haber, in *Poisonous Cloud,* the French called their version of mustard gas "yperite" and began using it in the middle of the summer of 1918. British use came a month or so later. American artillery did not get it until the first of November.

3. The Germans would continue to hold the northern half of Chateau-Thierry until the Allied offensive of June 18 and 19 drove them back.

4. General Simmons' observations recorded during his tour of the battlefields, May 2000.

5. Feland, "Retreat Hell," an essay in the September 1921 *Marine Corps Gazette,* repeated an address he gave on June 30, 1921, at the Marine Barracks, Washington, D.C.

6. One of the claimants for the "Retreat Hell" remark was the 2d Battalion commander, the irrepressible Freddie Wise. Logan Feland, Wise's good friend and the regiment's second in command, supported Wise's claim, stating that Captains Corbin and Williams undoubtedly said pretty much the same thing, but "Colonel Wise had been in the Marine Corps 20 years longer and naturally knew more about 'cussing' than Captain Williams."

7. Catlin, *A Few Marines,* does not identify the wounded Marine from Toledo.

Chapter 7: Belleau Wood

1. Unless otherwise noted, the material in this chapter is derived from: Asprey, *At Belleau Wood;* Catlin, *A Few Marines;* Metcalf, *History;* Spaulding and Wright, *Second Division;* Brig. Gen. Edwin H. Simmons, USMC (Ret.), "The Great War Crucible," *Naval History,* December 2005; Floyd Gibbons, *"And They Thought We Wouldn't Fight"* (New York: George H. Doran, 1918); Maj. Gen. James G. Harbord,

USA, *The American Army in France, 1917–1919* (Boston: Little, Brown, 1936); Gen. Clifton B. Cates, *History of the 96th Company, 2d Battalion, 6th Regiment, United States Marines* (Washington, D.C.: HQMC, 1935); Cates letters; J. Michael Miller, "A Single Day of Combat for a Marine Corps Rifle Company," *Leatherneck,* November 2005; Gen. Alfred H. Noble, USMC (Ret.), biographic files, Reference Section, HD, MCU; Erskine oral history; Gulberg, *War Diary;* Cole biographic file; Waller, "Machine Guns"; Simmons, "Appreciation of General Shepherd" and "Remembering General Shepherd"; Hatcher, "Memoir of Service"; Ernst Otto, "The Battles for the Possession of Belleau Wood, June, 1918," U.S. Naval Institute *Proceedings,* November 1928; Lejeune, *Reminiscences;* Laurence Stallings, *The Doughboys: The Story of the AEF, 1917–1918* (New York: Harper and Row, 1963); Brittain, *Lawrence* [sic] *Stallings;* U.S. Navy, *The American Naval Planning Section, London* (Washington, D.C.: Government Printing Office, 1923); Cowing, *Dear Folks at Home.*

2.   Brigadier General Simmons' observation notes, tour of Belleau Wood, May 2000.

3.   The inspirational war cry is widely attributed to Dan Daly, the bantam-sized senior NCO, who wore two Medals of Honor (Peking 1900, Haiti 1915). Yet Daly served in the 6th Regiment and would have been part of Sibley's assault to the east rather than with Berry's battalion of the 5th Marines. Although Gibbons related the account, he had it at second hand and did not identify the sergeant ("An old gunnery sergeant . . . [whose] cheeks were bronzed by the wind and sun of the seven seas"). It is highly likely that Daly screamed those words, or words to that effect, at some time during a critical moment of the initial assaults on Belleau Wood. Other "Old Corps" NCOs, equally feisty and fearless, likely issued similar taunts to get their wavering troops back on their feet for the final charge. Whatever their exact provenance, the words attributed to Daly at Belleau Wood were inscribed in the granite walls of the central gallery of the National Museum of the Marine Corps in 2006.

4.   Lt. Alfred H. Noble commanded the 83d Company in every campaign from Belleau Wood through the Armistice, receiving the Navy Cross, Distinguished Service Cross, two Silver Stars, and two Croix de Guerre awards for his combat leadership. He would serve thirty-nine years as a Marine officer, retiring in 1956 as a four-star general. The 83d Company's good-luck mascot was a pet anteater that "enlisted" during the company's prewar service in Central America and was to survive the war on the western front.

5.   The Americans, lacking a suitable rifle grenade launcher for their Springfield "'03" rifles, adopted the French Viven Bessieres (VB) system, a cup-type *"tromblon"* attachment to the muzzle (resembling a small goblet) that allowed a standard bullet to pass through the grenade, generating enough gas to propel the explosive some two hundred yards forward.

6.   Maj. Edward Cole posthumously received the Distinguished Service Cross and the Navy Cross for his valor at Belleau Wood. In his honor the Navy launched the USS *Cole* (DD 155) on January 11, 1919.

7.   For his heroism at Belleau Wood, the twenty-one-year-old Shepherd received the Army Distinguished Service Cross, the Navy Cross, and the French Croix de Guerre.

8. As early as the time spent in the trenches south of Verdun, Marines had begun to tell each other that the Germans were calling them *"Teufelhunden."* After Belleau Wood this was widely repeated and became part of the Marine Corps lexicon. The German military historian Prof. Dr. Jürgen Rohwer, in response to a query as to the use of "Devil Dogs," replied: "I think the term *'Teufelhunde'* is not common for the German language. The other term: 'The American Marine fought like devils' is easy to believe. In German: *'Die amerikanichen Marine-Infanteristen kampften wie die Teufel.'* In the other German version it must read: *'Die Amerikanier kampften wie teuflische Hunde',* but this is not a normal expression." (Prof. Dr. Jürgen Rohrer, letter of March 11, 1993, to General Simmons, copy in Reference Section, HD, MCU.)

Chapter 8: "In Every Clime and Place"

1. Unless otherwise noted, the material in this chapter is derived from: Lejeune, *Reminiscences;* Col. Jon T. Hoffman, USMCR, *USMC: A Complete History* (Quantico, Va.: Hugh Lauter Levin Associates for the Marine Corps Association, 2002); Marshall, *History of World War I;* H. P. Willmott, *World War I* (New York: Dorling Kindersley, 2006); Maj. Edwin N. McClellan, USMC, *The United States Marine Corps in the World War* (Washington, D.C.: Historical Branch, G-3 Division, HQMC, 1968, reprint of 1920 edition); McClellan, "American Marines in the British Grand Fleet," *Marine Corps Gazette,* June 1922, and "American Marines in Siberia during the World War," *Marine Corps Gazette,* June 1920; Heinl, *Soldiers of the Sea;* Rear Adm. William S. Sims, USN, *The Victory at Sea* (Garden City, N.Y.: Doubleday, Page, 1920); Bernard Grun, *The Timetables of History: A Horizontal Linkage of People and Events* (New York: Simon and Schuster, 1975); Allan R. Millett, *Semper Fidelis: The History of the United States Marine Corps* (New York: Macmillan, 1980); Cowing, *Dear Folks at Home;* Johnson, *Marine Corps Aviation;* Brig. Gen. Edwin H. Simmons, "Marines over the Western Front," *Naval History,* June 2006; Alfred A. Cunningham papers, Personal Papers Collection, Marine Corps Archives, Gray Research Center, Quantico; Roger M. Emmons, *The First Aviation Force, 1917–18: Development and Deployment,* manuscript file copy, n.d., Reference Section, HD MCU; Willock, *Unaccustomed to Fear;* Lt. Gen. Karl S. Day and Maj. Gen. Ford O. Rogers, oral history interviews, Oral History Section, HD, MCU; Colgate W. Darden Jr., biographic files, Reference Section, HD, MCU; Talbot Collection.

2. The American-made DH-4 and British-made DH-9A were not greatly different. Both were single-engine, two-seat biplanes, with the superb 12-cylinder, 400-horsepower Liberty engine. With some modifications, the DH-4 remained in the Marine Corps inventory until 1930.

3. The Mitrailleuse was the world's first machine gun to be used in major combat. The wheeled, manually operated, 25-barrel weapon of 13-mm caliber saw action in the Franco-Prussian War of 1870–71. Although replaced by more modern and fully automatic heavy machine guns in World War I, "Mitrailleuse" remained a generic name for any automatic weapon that could be used as an antiaircraft gun.

4. Pritchard served in the Army Air Forces in World War II, retiring in the grade of colonel.

Chapter 9: Soissons: The First Day

1. Unless otherwise directed, the material in this chapter is derived from: Lejeune, *Reminiscences;* Edwin N. McClellan, "The Aisne-Marne Offensive," *Marine Corps Gazette,* March–June 1921; Cates letters; Maj. Gen. James G. Harbord, USA (Ret.), *Leaves from a War Diary* (New York: Dodd, Meade, 1925); Harbord, *The American Army in France* and "History of the Second Division," *U.S. Army Recruiting News,* November 20, 1929; Spaulding and Wright, *Second Division;* Gen. Gerald C. Thomas oral history interview, September 6, 1967, Oral History Collection, HD, MCU [hereafter Thomas oral history]; Brig. Gen. Edwin H. Simmons, USMC (Ret.), "The First Day at Soissons," *Fortitudine,* Summer 1993; John W. Thomason, *Fix Bayonets and Other Stories* (New York: Charles Scribner's Sons, 1925); Lt. Gen. Merwin H. Silverthorn, USMC (Ret.), oral history interview, 1969, Oral History Collection, HD, MCU [hereafter Silverthorn oral history]; Erskine oral history; Lt. George G. Strott, HC, USN (Ret.), *The Medical Department of the United States Navy with the Army and Marine Corps in France in World War I: Its Functions and Employment* (Washington, D.C.: Bureau of Medicine and Surgery, U.S. Navy Department, 1947); Cowing, *Dear Folks at Home;* Maj. Gen. Robert Blake, USMC (Ret.), oral history interview, 1968, Oral History Collection, HD, MCU [hereafter Blake oral history]; Waller, "Machine Guns"; Elton E. Mackin, *Suddenly We Didn't Want to Die* (Novato, Calif.: Presidio, 1993); GySgt. Donald V. Paradis, oral history interview, 1973, Oral History Collection, HD, MCU [hereafter Paradis oral history]; Hatcher, "Memoir of Service"; Brown, *A Few Good Men.*

2. The Marines, busy at Belleau Wood, had no part in the fourth German offensive of 1918, which was fought and brought to a halt by Allied armies in the Noyon–Montdidier sector during June 9–15.

Chapter 10: Soissons: The Second Day

1. Unless otherwise noted, the material in this chapter is derived from: Spaulding and Wright, *Second Division;* Metcalf, *History;* Waller, "Machine Guns"; Harbord, *Leaves from a War Diary* and *The American Army in France;* Brig. Gen. Edwin H. Simmons, USMC (Ret.), "The Second Day at Soissons," *Fortitudine,* Fall 1993; Col. Allan R. Millett, USMCR (Ret.), *In Many a Strife: General Gerald C. Thomas and the U.S. Marine Corps, 1917–1956* (Annapolis, Md.: Naval Institute Press, 1993); Thomas oral history; McClellan, "Aisne-Marne Offensive"; Sibley biographic file; Paradis oral history; Erskine oral history; Cates oral history, *96th Company,* and letters; Gulberg, *War Diary;* U.S. Marine Corps, Muster Roll, 82d Company, 6th Regiment, August 1918, Reference Section, HD, MCU; Silverthorn oral history; Strott, *Navy Medical Department;* Cowing, *Dear Folks at Home;* Carl Andrew Brannen, *Over There: A Marine in the Great War,* ed. Rolfe L. Hillman Jr., and Peter F. Owen (College Station: Texas A&M University Press, 1996); Hatcher, "Memoir of Service"; Herbert H. Akers, *History of the 3d Battalion, 6th Marines* (Hillsdale, Mich.: Akers, MacRitchie, and Hurlburt, 1919); Thomason, *Fix Bayonets.*

2. As a brigade commander at Belleau Wood, Harbord had bypassed his veteran regimental commanders, Wendell Neville and Albertus Catlin, to issue tactical orders directly to the infantry battalions. He followed the same practice as a division commander at Soissons, frequently ignoring Colonel Neville to issue commands

directly to the regiments. As a result Neville wielded little command initiative in either battle.

3. Lieutenant Cates, whose 96th Company initially followed in trace behind the 80th Company, believed Lieutenant Overton had been killed in the shelling that preceded the attack, stating in his 1967 oral history interview, "By the way, this artillery had killed the noted Yale runner, Johnny Overton, at that time while we were waiting."

4. Lieutenant Cates' battlefield report from Soissons became an inspirational message to succeeding generations of Marines: "I have only two men left out of my company and 20 out of other companies. . . . I have no one on my left, and only a few on my right. I will hold."

5. For more details on Yale classmates John Overton and Sam Meek, see Overton's biographic file in the Reference Section, HD, MCU, and "Meek, Samuel Williams," in *Who's Who in America*, 41st ed., 1980–1981, vol. 2. Later the bodies were collected from their temporary graves and buried in the Aisne-Ourcq cemetery. In 1923 Overton was reinterred in the family cemetery at Overton Hall, near Nashville, Tennessee. Meek reached the rank of captain, was wounded, and was well decorated. Subsequent to the war he had a highly successful career as a publisher. Many sports fans mourned Overton's loss. The noted sports writer Grantland Rice, then a reporter in France for *Stars and Stripes*, penned a forty-line poem as a eulogy to Overton, "A Marine Comes Home." Billy Queal, Yale's track coach, mused, "Johnny Overton was fully capable of becoming the world's first four-minute miler." In 2005 Overton was inducted posthumously into the Tennessee Sports Hall of Fame.

6. "Slum gullion" was a slurry of leftovers, typically a little ground beef mixed with a can of soup, poured over bread or rice.

7. Marine battle deaths for Soissons as compiled in 1921 were:

	KIA	DOW	Total
5th Regiment	43	36	79
6th Regiment	143	162	305
6th Machine Gun Battalion	10	10	20
Total	196	208	404

Data on total wounds and gassing were never satisfactorily completed.

Chapter 11: Marbache and St. Mihiel

1. Unless otherwise noted, the material in this chapter is derived from: Harbord, *Leaves from a War Diary*; Lejeune, *Reminiscences*; Metcalf, *History*; Brown, *A Few Good Men*; Barker biographic file; Bartlett, "Johnny the Hard"; 1st Lt. [*sic*] Ernest C. Williams, biographic files, Reference Section, HD, MCU [hereafter Maj. Williams biographic file]; Spaulding and Wright, *Second Division*; Ward, *First-Class Temperament*; Davis, *FDR*; Wise and Frost, *A Marine Tells It to You*; Erskine oral history; Paradis oral history; Simmons, "Appreciation of General Shepherd" and "Remembering General Shepherd"; U.S. Army, *2d Division Summary of Operations in the World War* (Washington, D.C.: American Battle Monuments Commission, 1944); U.S. Army, *Atlas: A Short Military History of World War I* (West

Point, N.Y.: U.S. Military Academy, 1950), plate 68; Waller, "Machine Guns"; Maj. Robert E. Messersmith, biographic files, Reference Section, HD, MCU; Gallivan biographic file; Hatcher, "Memoir of Service"; Cates letters.

2. John Hughes was promoted to lieutenant colonel, and he received the Navy Cross and two Silver Stars for his combat leadership at Belleau Wood and Soissons, but he would be transferred to the disability-retired list by midsummer of 1919.

3. Lejeune, in his reminiscences, says that Passaga offered a prize of 1,500 francs for the first prisoner taken; Wise says that the prize was two hundred francs for each prisoner taken.

Chapter 12: Blanc Mont

1. Unless otherwise noted, the material in this chapter is derived from: Lejeune, *Reminiscences;* Spaulding and Wright, *Second Division;* Maj. Edwin N. McClellan, USMC, "The Battle of Blanc Mont Ridge," *Marine Corps Gazette,* March 1922; Metcalf, *History;* Thomason, *Fix Bayonets;* Cates letters; Paradis oral history; Capt. [*sic*] George Kent Shuler, , biographic files, Reference Section, HD, MCU [hereafter Shuler biographic file]; Waller, "Machine Guns"; Simmons, "Appreciation of General Shepherd" and "Remembering General Shepherd"; Col. Robert H. Rankin, USMC (Ret.), *Small Arms of the Sea Services* (New Milford, Conn.: N. Flayderman, 1972); Col. W. Hays Parks, USMC (Ret.), "Joint Service Combat Shotgun Program," *Army Lawyer,* October 1997 (derived from Col. Parks' legal review of military shotguns, dated January 24, 1997, which he wrote for the Judge Advocate General, U.S. Army, while serving as Special Assistant for Law of War Matters); Gulberg, *War Diary;* Hatcher, "Memoir of Service"; Brown, *A Few Good Men;* Merrill L. Bartlett, *Lejeune: A Marine's Life, 1867–1942* (Columbia: University of South Carolina Press, 1991); Camp, *Leatherneck Legends.*

2. Blanc Mont was not particularly high—210 meters at best—but it dominated the flat approaches and bulged outward ("like the grip of a pistol") at its western end. A later generation of Marines would face a similar challenge in attacking Kunishi Ridge, Okinawa, in 1945. In its dominance of flat, exposed approaches, honeycombed enemy bunkers, and overall capability of decimating Marine battalions over a week's time, Kunishi Ridge approximated Mont Blanc.

3. Depending on the source, the number of prisoners taken on October 5 varies from 205 to 300 and the number of machine guns from sixty-five to eighty.

4. James Hatcher was hospitalized for three months in France and ultimately returned to the United States in May 1919. He later earned a commission in the army and, as a colonel in 1945, commanded the 255th Infantry Regiment in the Battle of Waldenburg, in Germany.

5. John W. Thomason quotes Marshal Petain as saying, "The taking of Blanc Mont is the greatest single achievement of the 1918 campaign." Unfortunately, this quotation is not corroborated elsewhere.

6. Marines, with wartime service in these units, could continue to wear their *fourrageres* regardless of their future assignments. As late as the Korean War, senior officers like Generals Shepherd and Thomas could be seen wearing their "pogey ropes," as other envious Marines called them, with their service and dress uniforms. Present-day members of the 5th and 6th Marines wear the cords but must doff them when they leave the regiments.

Chapter 13: The Meuse-Argonne Campaign

1. Unless otherwise noted, the material in this chapter is derived from: Metcalf, *History;* McClellan, "Blanc Mont"; Spaulding and Wright, *Second Division;* Lejeune, *Reminiscences;* Waller, "Machine Guns"; Fletcher Pratt, "Charles P. Summerall: Sitting Bull II," in *Eleven Generals: Studies in American Command* (New York: William Sloan Associates, 1949); Larry A. Addington, "Summerall, Charles Pelot," *Dictionary of American Military Biography,* vol. 3; Brig. Gen. Edwin H. Simmons, USMC (Ret.), "Through the Wheat," *Fortitudine,* Spring 1980, "Marines in the Meuse-Argonne, Part I: Reaching the Meuse," *Fortitudine,* Winter 1993–94, and "Marines in the Meuse-Argonne, Part II: Crossing the Meuse," *Fortitudine,* Spring 1994; Bruce N. Canfield, *U.S. Infantry Weapons of World War II* (Lincoln, R.I.: Andrew Mowbray, 1994); Millett, *In Many a Strife;* Biographic files for Capt. Macon C. Overton, USMC; Capt. [*sic*] George Andrew Stowell, USMC; Capt. [*sic*] Charles E. Dunbeck, USMC; Maj. Gen. [*sic*] Henry L. Larsen, USMC (Ret.); and Maj. [*sic*] Frederick Barker, USMC (Ret.); all in Reference Section, HD, MCU; Cates oral history interview; Gallivan biographic file; Brown, *A Few Good Men;* Brannen, *Over There;* Mackin, *Suddenly We Didn't Want to Die;* Col. R. D. Cail, USMC (Ret.), letter to editor, *Fortitudine,* Fall 1978; Capt. John Thomason Jr., USMC, "The Marine Brigade," U.S. Naval Institute *Proceedings,* November 1928; Maj. Gen. Samuel C. Cumming, "The Last Night of the War," *Fortitudine,* Spring 1980.

2. General von Gallwitz's recollection appeared in G. S. Viereck, ed., *As They Saw Us* (New York: Doubleday, Doran, 1929), as quoted in Spaulding and Wright, *Second Division,* 203.

3. For his exploits from Belleau Wood to the Meuse-Argonne, Capt. Macon Overton received the Distinguished Service Cross with oak leaf cluster, the Navy Cross, and the Croix de Guerre with two gilt stars and two palms. His mother, Mrs. Margrett C. Overton, received his posthumous awards. The destroyer USS *Overton* (DD 239) was christened in his honor in 1919.

4. Although he insisted that he was "Charley" Dunbeck, his official records show him as Charles E. Dunbeck. Medically retired in 1921 with a poison gas–induced heart ailment, Dunbeck returned to active duty at the outbreak of World War II, serving until 1946. When he died at ninety-three in 1978, Colonel Dunbeck was one of the oldest and most decorated officers on the retired list. As Gen. John Lejeune lay dying in 1942 he selected Charley Dunbeck as one of his pallbearers.

5. In May 1919, Col. Fritz Wise favorably endorsed the fifty-three-year-old Gallivan's application for a permanent commission as a second lieutenant but could not resist inserting one last barb about his friend's age: "Although a man well advanced in years, he proved under very trying circumstances that he could stand hardships as well as the youngsters."

6. On February 7, 1944, Maj. Sydney Thayer, USMCR, wrote Colonel Dunbeck, then retired, a note on the back of the field order that had sent the 55th Company across the Meuse. It read: "This mission was accomplished on 11 November 1918. I apologize for having waited for more than 25 years to report the capture of Belle-Font Farm."

Chapter 14: The Watch on the Rhine

1. Unless otherwise noted the material in this chapter is derived from: Spaulding and Wright, *Second Division;* Metcalf, *History;* Edward M. Coffman, *The War to End All Wars: The American Experience in World War I* (New York: Oxford University Press, 1968); Wise and Frost, *A Marine Tells It to You; Who Was Who in American History: The Military* (Chicago: Marquis Who's Who, 1975); Roger E. Spiller, ed., *Dictionary of American Military Biography* (Westport, Conn.: Greenwood, 1984); Lt. Gen. Robert Lee Bullard, USA, *Fighting Generals* (Ann Arbor, Mich.: J. W. Edwards, 1944); Maude Radford Warren, "The March into Germany," *Saturday Evening Post,* March 8, 1919; Waller, "Machine Guns"; Lejeune, *Reminiscences;* Cates letters; Thomason, *Fix Bayonets;* Brig. Gen. Edwin H. Simmons, USMC (Ret.), "Lejeune's Bad Fitness Report," *Fortitudine,* Summer 1989, "Appreciation of General Shepherd," and "Remembering General Shepherd"; Gallivan biographic file; Ward, *First-Class Temperament;* Davis, *FDR;* Vandoren papers; Thomason biographic file; Simmons, "Thomason's *Fix Bayonets*"; Paradis oral history; McClellan, *World War;* Major General Commandant, *Annual Report to the Secretary of the Navy,* 1918; Col. Albert Sidney McLemore, USMC, letter to Major General Commandant, January 14, 1919, "Recruiting," contained in McLemore biographical file; Simmons, *United States Marines;* Lt. Col. Laurence Stallings, biographic files; Brittain, *Lawrence* [sic] *Stallings;* Maxwell Anderson and Laurence Stallings, "What Price Glory?" in *Three American Plays* (New York: Harcourt, Brace, 1926).

2. As long as they lived, veterans of the 1st and 2d divisions would argue their respective laurels in terms of days in the line, yards advanced, casualties sustained and inflicted, prisoners taken, and guns captured.

3. Subsequently, Brig. Gen. James Roosevelt, USMCR (Ret.), the president's oldest son and a former Marine Raider, donated the German machine gun to the Corps for display in the Marine Corps Museum.

4. Thomason received a Navy Cross for a certain action on July 18, 1918, at Soissons wherein he and his gunnery sergeant took out a machine-gun nest holding two heavy Maxims and killing the crew of thirteen Germans. There were other decorations, including later a Silver Star.

5. Colonel McLemore continued as officer in charge of Marine Corps Recruiting until May 1919, when he was transferred to the Department of the Pacific in San Francisco. The long-felt pain in his gut turned out to be a carcinoma. He died in July 1921. An official biography put it delicately that he had "been largely responsible for developing the science of interesting the public in the Corps. . . . Under his supervision the real facts about the Marine Corps, its functions and its nature, and the life and duties of the Marine, have been and are constantly being placed before the public. "

6. James Gallivan on retirement returned to Holyoke and took a job in the circulation department of the *Springfield Daily News.* The owner-publisher was Sherman Bowles, who as a Marine sergeant and lieutenant had been under the gentle tutelage of Gunner Gallivan in France. Gallivan wore on the chain of his pocket watch the machine-gun bullet the surgeons had taken out of his leg at Belleau Wood. He died in 1938.

7. Laurence Stallings' *The First World War: A Pictorial History,* published in 1932, became a classic. One-legged Stallings, much in demand as a Hollywood screenwriter, came back to active duty in the Marine Corps in 1942 and was retired from the reserves in the rank of lieutenant colonel a year later. His second leg was amputated in 1963. His book *The Doughboys: The Story of the AEF, 1917–1918,* was published that same year. He died of a heart attack in 1968.

8. As an infantry colonel, Thomason did not get a command in World War II—he had a large problem that centered around the bottle he kept in the drawer of his desk. He served briefly on the staff of a fellow Texan, Adm. Chester Nimitz, Commander in Chief, U.S. Pacific Fleet. In August 1943 he returned to the San Diego area and was assigned to the Amphibious Training Command. He died in March 1944 in the U.S. Naval Hospital in San Diego. He was just fifty-one.

9. In 1920, when Major General Lejeune became Commandant, he named Shepherd as his aide-de-camp. In World War II, Shepherd commanded the 1st Provisional Marine Brigade at Guam and the 6th Marine Division on Okinawa. He served as Commandant of the Marine Corps from 1952 to 1956 and died in 1990 at age ninety-four.

Epilogue

1. Unless otherwise noted the material in the epilogue is derived from: Willmott, *World War I;* Catlin, *A Few Marines;* McClellan, *World War;* J. Robert Moskin, *The U.S. Marine Corps Story,* 3d rev. ed. (New York: McGraw-Hill, 1992); Thomason, "The Marine Brigade"; Col. Joseph H. Alexander, USMC (Ret.), "Marine Aviation Comes of Age," *MHQ,* Summer 2005; biographic files on Lt. Gen. Pedro A. del Valle, USMC (Ret.), and Lt. Gen. Keller E. Rockey, USMC (Ret.), Reference Section, HD, MCU.

Bibliography

Addington, Larry A. "Summerall, Charles Pelot." *Dictionary of American Military Biography,* vol. 3.

Akers, Herbert H. *History of the 3d Battalion, 6th Marines.* Hillsdale, Mich.: Akers, MacRitchie, and Hurlburt, 1919.

Alexander, Col. Joseph H., USMC (Ret.). "Marine Aviation Comes of Age." *MHQ,* Summer 2005.

Anderson, Maxwell, and Laurence Stallings, "What Price Glory?" In *Three American Plays.* New York: Harcourt, Brace, 1926.

The Annals of America, vol. 14, *1916–1928, World War and Prosperity.* Chicago: Encyclopedia Britannica, 1976.

Asprey, Robert B. *At Belleau Wood.* New York: G. P. Putnam's Sons, 1965.

Ballendorf, Dirk Anthony. "A Shot Not Heard Round the World: The U.S. Marines and the Start of World War I on Guam." Paper presented at the annual meeting of the Society for Military History, April 9–12, 1992, copy held in Reference Section, History Division [hereafter HD], Marine Corps University, Quantico [hereafter MCU].

Barker, Maj. Frederick A., USMC (Ret.). Biographic files, Reference Section, HD, MCU.

Barnett, Maj. Gen. George. Barnett biographic files, Reference Section, HD, MCO.

———. "Soldier and Sailor, Too." Unpublished memoir, bound copy, Reference Section, HD, MCU.

Bartlett, Lt. Col. Merrill L., USMC (Ret.). *Lejeune: A Marine's Life, 1867–1942.* Columbia: University of South Carolina Press, 1991.

———. "The Spirited Saga of 'Johnny the Hard,'" *Naval History,* June 2007.

Blake, Maj. Gen. Robert, USMC (Ret.). Oral history interview, 1968, Oral History Collection, HD, MCU.

Boyd, Thomas. *Through the Wheat: A Novel of the World War I Marines.* Originally published 1923; Bison Books edition, Lincoln: University of Nebraska Press, 2000.

Brannen, Carl Andrew. *Over There: A Marine in the Great War,* edited by Rolfe L. Hillman Jr. and Peter F. Owen. College Station: Texas A&M University Press, 1996.

Brittain, Joan T. *Lawrence* [sic] *Stallings.* Boston: Twayne, 1975.

Brown, Lt. Col. Ronald J., USMCR (Ret.). *A Few Good Men: The Fighting Fifth Marines.* Novato, Calif.: Presidio, 2001.

Bullard, Lt. Gen. Robert Lee, USA. *Fighting Generals.* Ann Arbor, Mich.: J. W. Edwards, 1944.

Cail, Col. R. D., USMC (Ret.). Letter to editor, *Fortitudine,* Fall 1978.

Camp, Col. Dick, USMC (Ret.). *Leatherneck Legends: Conversations with the Marine Corps' Old Breed.* St. Paul, Minn.: Zenith, 2006.

Canfield, Bruce N. *U.S. Infantry Weapons of World War II.* Lincoln, R.I.: Andrew Mowbray, 1994.

Cates, Gen. Clifton B. Biographic files, Reference Section, HD, MCU.

———. *History of the 96th Company, 2d Battalion, 6th Regiment, United States Marines.* Washington, D.C.: Headquarters, Marine Corps [hereafter HQMC], 1935.

———. Interview, March 28, 1967, Oral History Collection, HD, MCU.

———. Letters to his family from the war in France, 1918, Personal Papers Collection, MCU.

Catlin, Brig. Gen. Albertus W. *With the Help of God and a Few Marines.* Garden City, N.Y.: Doubleday, Page, 1919.

Chinn, Lt. Col. George M. *The Machine Gun: History, Evolution, and Development of Manual, Automatic, and Airborne Repeating Weapons.* Washington, D.C.: Bureau of Ordnance, Department of the Navy, 1951.

Clark, George B. *Devil Dogs: Fighting Marines of World War I.* Novato, Calif.: Presidio, 2000.

Coffman, Edward M. *The War to End All Wars: The American Experience in World War I.* New York: Oxford University Press, 1968.

Cole, Maj. Edward B., USMC. Biographic files, Reference Section, HD, MCU.

Cooper, Norman V. *A Fighting General: The Biography of Gen. Holland M. Smith.* Quantico, Va.: Marine Corps Association, 1987.

Cowing, Kemper F., comp. *Dear Folks at Home (Letters from the Battlefield).* Boston: Houghton Mifflin, 1919.

Cumming, Maj. Gen. Samuel C. "The Last Night of the War." *Fortitudine,* Spring 1980.

Cunningham, Maj. Alfred A. Alfred A. Cunningham papers, Personal Papers Collection, Marine Corps Archives, Gray Research Center, Quantico.

———. "Value of Aviation to the Marine Corps." *Marine Corps Gazette,* September 1920.

Cureton, Lt. Col. Charles H., USMC. "Parade Blue, Battle Green." In *The Marines,* edited by Brig. Gen. Edwin H. Simmons, USMC (Ret.), and J. Robert Moskin. Quantico, Va.: Marine Corps Heritage Foundation, 1998.

Cushing, 2d Lt. Charles P., USMCR. "When the Marines Shoved Off." *Recruiters' Bulletin,* July 1917.

Daniels, Josephus. *The Cabinet Diaries of Josephus Daniels,* edited by E. David Cronon. Lincoln: University of Nebraska, 1963.

———. *The Wilson Era: Years of Peace, 1910–1917.* Chapel Hill: University of North Carolina Press, 1944.

———. *The Wilson Era: Years of War and After, 1917–1923.* Chapel Hill: University of North Carolina Press, 1946.

Darden, Colgate W., Jr. Biographic files, Reference Section, HD, MCU.

Davis, Kenneth S. *FDR: The Beckoning of Destiny, 1882–1928.* New York: G. P. Putnam's Sons, 1971.

Day, Lt. Gen. Karl S., USMCR (Ret.). Oral history interview, 15 August 1969, Oral History Collection, HD, MCU.

DeChant, John A. *Devilbirds.* New York: Harper and Brothers, 1947.

del Valle, Lt. Gen. Pedro A., USMC (Ret.). Biographic files, Reference Section, HD, MCU.

Dunbeck, Col. Charles E., USMC (Ret.). Biographic files, Reference Section, HD, MCU.

Emmons, Roger M. *The First Aviation Force, 1917–18: Development and Deployment.* Manuscript file copy, n.d., Reference Section, HD, MCU.

Erskine, Gen. Graves B., USMC (Ret.). Biographic files and oral history interview, 1975, HD, MCU.

Feland, Brig. Gen. Logan, USMC. Biographic files, Reference Section, HD, MCU.

———. "Retreat Hell!" *Marine Corps Gazette,* September 1921.

Fleming, Lt. Col. Charles A., et al. *Quantico: Crossroads of the Marine Corps.* Washington, D.C.: History and Museums Division, HQMC, 1978.

Frank, Benis M. *A Brief History of the 3d Marines.* Washington, D.C.: Historical Branch, G-3 Division, HQMC, 1968.

Gallivan, Lt. James, USMC (Ret.). Biographic files, Reference Section, HD, MCU. [File includes Steve Donoghue, "A Salty Second Lieutenant." Unpublished manuscript, n.d., brief biography of James Gallivan.]

Gibbons, Floyd. *"And They Thought We Wouldn't Fight."* New York: George H. Doran, 1918.

Grun, Bernard. *The Timetables of History: A Horizontal Linkage of People and Events.* New York: Simon and Schuster, 1975.

Gulberg, Sgt. Martin "Gus," USMC. *A War Diary.* Chicago: Drake, 1927.

Haber, I. F. *The Poisonous Cloud: Chemical Warfare in the First World War.* Oxford, U.K.: Clarendon, 1986.

Handbook of the German Army in War, April 1918. London: Imperial War Museum, 1996; Nashville, Tenn.: Battery, 1996.

Harbord, Maj. Gen. James G., USA. *The American Army in France, 1917–1919.* Boston: Little, Brown, 1936.

———. "History of the Second Division." *U.S. Army Recruiting News,* November 20, 1929.

———. *Leaves from a War Diary.* New York: Dodd, Meade, 1925.

Hatcher, Col. James E., AUS (Ret.). "A Memoir of Service in World War I as a Private, USMC." Unpublished manuscript, n.d., Marine Corps Archives, Gray Research Center, Quantico.

Heinl, Col. Robert D., Jr. *Soldiers of the Sea: The United States Marine Corps, 1775–1962.* Annapolis, Md.: Naval Institute Press, 1962.

Hoffman, Col. Jon T., USMCR. *USMC: A Complete History.* Quantico, Va.: Hugh Lauter Levin Associates for the Marine Corps Association, 2002.

Holcomb, Lt. Gen. Thomas. Biographic files, Reference Section, HD, MCU.

Hughes, Lt. Col. John A., USMC (Ret.). Biographic files, Reference Section, HD, MCU.

Joffre, Marshall Joseph J. C. *The Personal Memoirs of Joffre,* trans. Col. T. Bentley Mott, 2 vols. New York: Harper and Brothers, 1932.

Johnson, Lt. Col. Edward C., USMC. *Marine Corps Aviation: The Early Years, 1912–1940,* edited by Graham A. Cosmas. Washington, D.C.: History and Museums Division, HQMC, 1977.

Johnstone, Maj. John H. *A Brief History of the 1st Marines.* Washington, D.C.: Historical Branch, G-3 Division, HQMC, 1968.

Kane, Capt. Robert J. *A Brief History of the 2d Marines.* Washington, D.C.: Historical and Museums Division, HQMC, 1970.

Larsen, Lt. Gen. Henry L., USMC (Ret.). Biographic files, Reference Section, HD, MCU.

Lee, Maj. Gen. Harry, USMC (Ret.). Biographic files, Reference Section, HD, MCU.

Lejeune, Gen. John A., USMC (Ret.). *The Reminiscences of a Marine.* Philadelphia: Dorrance, 1930.

Lemly, Col. William B., USMC (Ret.). Biographic files, Reference Section, HD, MCU. [File includes Lt. Col. Lemly memo to the Quartermaster, HQMC, January 14, 1918.]

Mackin, Elton E. *Suddenly We Didn't Want to Die.* Novato, Calif.: Presidio, 1993.

Marshall, Brig. Gen. S. L. A., USAR (Ret.). *The American Heritage History of World War I.* New York: American Heritage, 1964.

McClellan, Maj. Edwin N., USMC. "American Marines in the British Grand Fleet." *Marine Corps Gazette,* June 1922.

———. "American Marines in Siberia during the World War." *Marine Corps Gazette,* June 1920.

———. "The Aisne-Marne Offensive." *Marine Corps Gazette,* March–June 1921.

———. "The Battle of Blanc Mont Ridge." *Marine Corps Gazette,* March 1922.

———. "Operations of the Fourth Brigade of Marines in the Aisne Defensive." *Marine Corps Gazette,* June 1921.

———. *The United States Marine Corps in the World War.* Washington, D.C.: Historical Branch, G-3 Division, HQMC, 1968 [reprint of 1920 edition].

McLemore, Col. Albert Sidney, USMC. Biographic files, Reference Section, HD, MCU.

Metcalf, Lt. Col. Clyde H., USMC. *A History of the United States Marine Corps.* New York: G. P. Putnam's Sons, 1939.

Messersmith, Maj. Robert E., USMC. Biographic files, Reference Section, HD, MCU.

Miller, J. Michael. "A Single Day of Combat for a Marine Corps Rifle Company." *Leatherneck,* November 2005.

Millett, Col. Allan R., USMCR (Ret.). *In Many a Strife: General Gerald C. Thomas and the U.S. Marine Corps, 1917–1956.* Annapolis, Md.: Naval Institute Press, 1993.

———. *Semper Fidelis: The History of the United States Marine Corps.* New York: Macmillan, 1980.

Morris, Donald R. "Thomason U.S.M.C." *American Heritage,* November 1993.

Moskin, J. Robert. *The U.S. Marine Corps Story.* 3d rev. ed. New York: Little, Brown, 1992.

Nalty, Bernard C., et al. *United States Marine Corps Ranks and Grades, 1775–1969.* Washington, D.C.: Historical and Museums Division, HQMC, 1970.

Nihart, Col. F. Brooke, USMC (Ret.). "Muskets to Missiles." In *The Marines,* edited by Brig. Gen. Edwin H. Simmons, USMC (Ret.), and J. Robert Moskin. Quantico, Va.: Marine Corps Heritage Foundation, 1998.

Noble, Gen. Alfred H., USMC (Ret.). Biographic files, Reference Section, HD, MCU.

Otto, Ernst. "The Battles for the Possession of Belleau Wood, June, 1918." U.S. Naval Institute *Proceedings,* November 1928.

Overton, Lt. John W., USMC. Biographic files, Reference Section, HD, MCU.

Overton, Capt. Macon C., USMC. Biographic files, Reference Section, HD, MCU.

Paradis, GySgt. Donald V., USMC. Oral history interview, 1973, Oral History Collection, HD, MCU.

Parks, Col. W. Hays, USMC (Ret.). "Joint Service Combat Shotgun Program." *Army Lawyer,* October 1997.

Pershing, Gen. John J., USA. *My Experiences in the World War.* New York: Frederick A. Stokes, 1931, vol. 1.

Poague, Lt. Walter S., USMC. *Diary and Letters of a Marine Aviator.* Chicago: privately published, c. 1919, copy in Rare Books Collection, HD, MCU.

Pratt, Fletcher. "Charles P. Summerall: Sitting Bull II." *Eleven Generals: Studies in American Command.* New York: William Sloan Associates, 1949.

Rankin, Col. Robert H., USMC (Ret.). *Small Arms of the Sea Services.* New Milford, Conn.: N. Flayderman, 1972.

Rockey, Lt. Gen. Keller E., USMC (Ret.). Biographic files, Reference Section, HD, MCU.

Rogers, Maj. Gen. Ford O., USMC (Ret.). Oral history interview, December 3, 1970, Oral History Collection, HD, MCU.

Roosevelt, Franklin D. "Trip to Haiti and Santo Domingo, 1917," FDR Group 10, FDR Library, Hyde Park, New York.

Salladay, Lt. Col. Jay M., USMC. "The Occupation of the Virgin Islands of the United States of America." *Marine Corps Gazette,* September 1918.

Sanderson, Maj. Gen. Lawson M. H., USMC (Ret.). Oral history interview, July 14, 1969, Oral History Collection, HD, MCU.

Santelli, James S. *A Brief History of the 4th Marines.* Washington, D.C.: Historical Division, HQMC, 1970.

Schilt, Gen. Christian F., USMC (Ret.). Oral history interviews, November 17 and 21, 1969, Oral History Collection, HD, MCU.

Shuler, Maj. George Kent, USMC. Biographic files, Reference Section, HD, MCU.

Shulimson, Jack. "The First to Fight: Marine Corps Expansion, 1914–18." *Prologue* 8 (Spring 1976).

Sibley, Capt. [*sic*] Bertron William, USMC. Biographic files, Reference Section, HD, MCU.

Silverthorn, Lt. Gen. Merwin H., USMC (Ret.). Oral history interview, 1969, Oral History Collection, HD, MCU.

Simmons, Brig. Gen. Edwin H., USMC (Ret.). "An Appreciation of Gen. Lemuel C. Shepherd, Jr., VMI '17." Distinguished

———. "The First Day at Soissons." *Fortitudine,* Summer 1993.

———. "The Great War Crucible." *Naval History*, December 2005.

———. "Leathernecks at Soissons." *Naval History,* December 2005.

———. "Lejeune's Bad Fitness Report." *Fortitudine,* Summer 1989.

———. "Marines in the Meuse-Argonne, Part II: Crossing the Meuse." *Fortitudine,* Spring 1994.

———. "Marines in the Meuse-Argonne, Part I: Reaching the Meuse." *Fortitudine,* Winter 1993–94.

———. "Marines over the Western Front." *Naval History,* June 2006.

———. "Remembering General Shepherd." *Fortitudine,* Fall 1990.

———. "The Second Day at Soissons." *Fortitudine,* Fall 1993.

———. "Thomason's *Fix Bayonets.*" Military Classics Seminar, June 21, 1994, Personal Papers, HD, MCU.

———. "Through the Wheat." *Fortitudine,* Spring 1980.

———. *The United States Marines: A History.* 3d ed. Annapolis, Md.: Naval Institute Press, 1998.

———. "With the Marines at Blanc Mont." *Marine Corps Gazette,* November 1993.

Lecture, Virginia Military Institute, Lexington, Virginia, October 22, 1986.

Sims, Rear Adm. William S., USN. *The Victory at Sea.* Garden City, N.Y.: Doubleday, Page, 1920.

Smith, Maj. Edna Loftus, USMCR. *Marine Corps Reserve Aviation, 1916–1957.* Washington, D.C.: HQMC, 1959.

Smith, Gen. Holland M., and Percy Finch. *Coral and Brass.* New York: Charles Scribner's Sons, 1948.

Snyder, Maj. Harold C., USMC. "The Marine Officers' School." *Recruiters' Bulletin,* July 1917.

Spaulding, Col. Oliver L., USA, and Col. John W. Wright, USA. *The Second Division, American Expeditionary Force, in France.* New York: Hillman, 1937.

Spiller, Roger E., ed. *Dictionary of American Military Biography.* Westport, Conn.: Greenwood, 1984.

Stallings, Lt. Col. Laurence. Biographic files, Brittain, *Lawrence* [sic] *Stallings.*

Stallings, Laurence. *The Doughboys: The Story of the AEF, 1917–1918.* New York: Harper and Row, 1963.

Stowell, Maj. George Andrew, USMC. Biographic files, Reference Section, HD, MCU.

Strott, Lt. George G., HC, USN (Ret.). *The Medical Department of the United States Navy with the Army and Marine Corps in France in World War I: Its Functions and Employment.* Washington, D.C.: Bureau of Medicine and Surgery, U.S. Navy Department, 1947.

Talbot, Lt. Ralph, family. "Military History of Ralph Talbot, Late Second Lieutenant, Marine Corps, October 10, 1922." Talbot Collection PC 410, HD, MCU.

Thomas, Gen. Gerald C. Oral history interview, 6 September 1967, Oral History Collection, HD, MCU.

Thomas, Lowell. *Old Gimlet Eye: Adventures of Smedley D. Butler.* New York: Farrar and Rinehart, 1933.

Thomason, Col. John W., USMC (Ret.). Biographic files, Reference Section, HD, MCU.

———. *Fix Bayonets and Other Stories.* New York: Charles Scribner's Sons, 1925.

———. "The Marine Brigade." U.S. Naval Institute *Proceedings,* November 1928.

Tuchman, Barbara W. *The Zimmermann Telegram.* New York: Viking, 1958.

U.S. Army. *Atlas: A Short Military History of World War I.* West Point, N.Y.: U.S. Military Academy, 1950.

———. *Infantry Drill Regulations, United States Army, 1911, Corrected to April 15, 1917.* Washington, D.C.: Government Printing Office, 1917.

———. *2d Division Summary of Operations in the World War.* Washington, D.C.: American Battle Monuments Commission, 1944.

———. *United States Army in the World War, 1917–1919,* vol. 3, *Training and Use of American Units with British and French.* Washington, D.C.: Historical Division, Department of the Army, 1948.

———. *United States Army in the World War, 1917–1919,* vol. 4, *Military Operations of the American Expeditionary Forces.* Washington, D.C.: Historical Division, Department of the Army, 1948.

U.S. Marine Corps. *Annual Report of the Major General Commandant to the Secretary of the Navy,* for Fiscal Years 1915, 1916, 1917, and 1918.

———. *Marine Corps Recruiters' Bulletin* for November 1916 and April, May, June, and July 1917.

———. *Marine Flyer in France: The Diary of Captain Alfred A. Cunningham, November 1917–January 1918.* Washington, D.C.: History and Museums Division, HQMC, 1974.

———. Muster Roll, 82d Company, 6th Regiment, August 1918, Reference Section, HD, MCU.

———. Reserve Officers of Public Affairs Unit 4-1. *The Marine Corps Reserve: A History.* Washington, D.C.: Division of Reserve, HQMC, 1966.

U.S. Navy. *The American Naval Planning Section, London.* Washington, D.C.: Government Printing Office, 1923.

Vandoren, Lt. Lucian H. Letter to his father, May 19, 1918, Vandoren Letters, Personal Papers Collection, HD, MCU.

Waller, Maj. L. W. T., Jr., USMC. "Machine Guns of the Fourth Brigade." *Marine Corps Gazette,* March 1920.

Ward, Geoffrey C. *A First-Class Temperament: The Emergence of Franklin Roosevelt* New York: Harper and Row, 1989.

Warren, Maude Radford. "The March into Germany." *Saturday Evening Post,* March 8, 1919.

Wells, Maj. Edward F., USMC (Ret.). "FDR and the Marines." *Fortitudine,* Fall 1981–Winter 1982.

Who Was Who in American History: The Military. Chicago: Marquis Who's Who, 1975.

Williams, Lt. Col. Ernest C. Biographic files, Reference Section, HD, MCU.

Willmott, H. P. *World War I.* New York: Dorling Kindersley, 2006.

Willock, Col. Roger, USMCR (Ret.). *Lone Star Marine.* Princeton, N.J.: Roger Willock, 1961.

———. *Unaccustomed to Fear: A Biography of the Late General Roy S. Geiger.* Princeton, N.J.: privately published, 1968; reprinted by the Marine Corps Association, 1983.

Wise, Col. Frederic M., and Meigs O. Frost. *A Marine Tells It to You.* New York: J. H. Sears, 1929.

Yingling, Maj. James M., USMC. *A Brief History of the Fifth Marines.* Washington, D.C.: Historical Branch, G-3 Division, HQMC, 1963.

Index

About the Authors

Brig. Gen. Edwin H. Simmons, the late director emeritus of Marine Corps History, served in the Marines for fifty-three years: thirty-six in uniform and seventeen as a civil servant. A veteran of three wars, he commanded infantry outfits ranging in size from a platoon to a division. He fought on Guam in World War II, landed on D-day at Inchon, Republic of Korea, and battled the Chinese Communists in the "Frozen Chosin" campaign in North Korea. He later served two tours in Vietnam. During his twenty-five years as senior historian, General Simmons advised eight commandants, chaired the Marine Corps Uniform Board, and helped establish the Marine Corps Heritage Foundation. His combat awards include the Silver Star, two Bronze Stars, and the Purple Heart. Most notable of his many publications are *The United States Marines: A History, Dog Company Six, The Marines,* and *Frozen Chosin: U.S. Marines in the Changjin Reservoir Campaign.* General Simmons passed away in 2007 at the age of eighty-five.

Col. Joseph H. Alexander served twenty-eight years in the Corps as an assault amphibian officer, including two tours in Vietnam and five years at sea. As a colonel he was chief of staff of the 3d Marine Division and military secretary to the twenty-eighth commandant. He commanded a company in Vietnam and a battalion in Okinawa. His books include *Edson's Raiders: The 1st Marine Raider Battalion in WW II, A Fellowship of Valor: The Battle History of the U.S. Marines, Storm Landings: Epic Amphibious Battles in the Central Pacific,* and *Utmost Savagery: The Three Days of Tarawa.*

The **Naval Institute Press** is the book-publishing arm of the U.S. Naval Institute, a private, nonprofit, membership society for sea service professionals and others who share an interest in naval and maritime affairs. Established in 1873 at the U.S. Naval Academy in Annapolis, Maryland, where its offices remain today, the Naval Institute has members worldwide.

Members of the Naval Institute support the education programs of the society and receive the influential monthly magazine *Proceedings* or the colorful bimonthly magazine *Naval History* and discounts on fine nautical prints and on ship and aircraft photos. They also have access to the transcripts of the Institute's Oral History Program and get discounted admission to any of the Institute-sponsored seminars offered around the country.

The Naval Institute's book-publishing program, begun in 1898 with basic guides to naval practices, has broadened its scope to include books of more general interest. Now the Naval Institute Press publishes about seventy titles each year, ranging from how-to books on boating and navigation to battle histories, biographies, ship and aircraft guides, and novels. Institute members receive significant discounts on the more than eight hundred Press books in print.

Full-time students are eligible for special half-price membership rates. Life memberships are also available.

For a free catalog describing Naval Institute Press books currently available, and for further information about joining the U.S. Naval Institute, please write to:

Member Services
U.S. NAVAL INSTITUTE
291 Wood Road
Annapolis, MD 21402-5034
Telephone: (800) 233-8764
Fax: (410) 571-1703
Web address: www.usni.org